SAGE was founded in 1965 by Sara Miller McCune to support the dissemination of usable knowledge by publishing innovative and high-quality research and teaching content. Today, we publish over 900 journals, including those of more than 400 learned societies, more than 800 new books per year, and a growing range of library products including archives, data, case studies, reports, and video. SAGE remains majority-owned by our founder, and after Sara's lifetime will become owned by a charitable trust that secures our continued independence.

Los Angeles | London | New Delhi | Singapore | Washington DC | Melbourne

EDUCATION IN INDIA

Thank you for choosing a SAGE product!
If you have any comment, observation or feedback,
I would like to personally hear from you.

Please write to me at **contactceo@sagepub.in**

Vivek Mehra, Managing Director and CEO, SAGE India.

Bulk Sales

SAGE India offers special discounts
for purchase of books in bulk.
We also make available special imprints
and excerpts from our books on demand.

For orders and enquiries, write to us at

Marketing Department
SAGE Publications India Pvt Ltd
B1/I-1, Mohan Cooperative Industrial Area
Mathura Road, Post Bag 7
New Delhi 110044, India

E-mail us at **marketing@sagepub.in**

Subscribe to our mailing list
Write to **marketing@sagepub.in**

This book is also available as an e-book.

EDUCATION IN INDIA

Policy and Practice

Social Change in Contemporary India

Series Editor: Manoranjan Mohanty

Volume III

Edited by

JANDHYALA B. G. TILAK

Los Angeles | London | New Delhi
Singapore | Washington DC | Melbourne

First published in 2021 by

SAGE Publications India Pvt Ltd
B1/I-1 Mohan Cooperative Industrial Area
Mathura Road, New Delhi 110 044, India
www.sagepub.in

SAGE Publications Inc
2455 Teller Road
Thousand Oaks, California 91320, USA

SAGE Publications Ltd
1 Oliver's Yard, 55 City Road
London EC1Y 1SP, United Kingdom

SAGE Publications Asia-Pacific Pte Ltd
18 Cross Street #10-10/11/12
China Square Central
Singapore 048423

Published by Vivek Mehra for SAGE Publications India Pvt. Ltd. Typeset in 10.5/13pt Bembo by Fidus Design Pvt Ltd, Chandigarh.

Library of Congress Control Number: 2020952793

ISBN: 978-93-5388-742-1 (HB)

SAGE Team: Amrita Dutta, Syed Husain Naqvi, Parul Prasad and Rajinder Kaur

Contents

Section I: Education Challenges
Sectional Introduction

Section II: Education of Women and Social Change
Sectional Introduction

Section III: Higher Education and Research
Sectional Introduction

Section IV: Reforming Education
Sectional Introduction

About the Series

Social Change in Contemporary India is a series of thematic volumes carrying selected articles from the journal *Social Change* which is celebrating its Golden Jubilee. They are offered as important contributions capturing the momentous experience of people of India and their institutions since Independence.

Social change in Independent India has gone through three distinct phases. The first two decades saw the impact of the freedom struggle in most arenas where policymakers and common people shared some perspectives to initiate concrete steps to reduce poverty, hunger and scarcities with the objective of making progress towards the goals enshrined in the Constitution of India. Planned development with a focus on industrialization, the Green Revolution in agriculture, building educational institutions of high quality and above all promoting democratic institutions and procedures to meet the aspirations of all sections of society, characterized most of this era. The pluralistic character of Indian society, culture and polity was acknowledged and some important policy initiatives emerged.

But by the late 1960s, the crisis of this model had already surfaced. The food riots in 1966, the Naxalbari uprising in 1967 and the beginning of non-Congress governments in many states were symptoms of the emerging environment that heralded the second phase, 1970–1990, which witnessed the unfolding of most major contradictions in the Indian Republic. Assertion of rights by ethnic groups in different parts of the country was responded to by a certain centralization of power by the Union government which in turn was challenged by the emergence of strong regional parties and movements. Poverty eradication was prominent on the agenda, but progress was tardy. Education and health facilities expanded but not to the extent needed. An Indian middle class did emerge but was increasingly alienated from the masses. Challenges accumulated leading to mass movements and the Republic saw the declaration of Emergency followed by rule of alternative forces and return of the Congress to power. In the process, civil society organizations pursuing citizens' rights emerged and the struggle for democratic rights continued to expand. Internal disturbances, communal riots and atrocities on Dalits, minorities and women occurred from time to time. But the democratic structure continued to get consolidated and people's consciousness to defend constitutional values continued to grow.

In 1991, the neoliberal economic reforms were launched in the wake of a serious economic crisis. At that time, India was also experiencing a social upsurge over the rights of Dalits, backward classes, religious minorities and women. By this time, environmental issues had also acquired much attention. Thus, began the third phase. The Indian elite cutting across the dominant political parties accepted the agenda of globalization, liberalization and privatization. Mobilization on caste and religious issues took a new turn with Hindu nationalist forces becoming stronger by the day. Initially, the Congress, through its alliance of parties, was able to stem this trend. They handled contradictions for a decade by a strategy that promoted rapid economic growth, tried to provide rural employment and food security to the poor and addressed the grievances of minorities. But corruption and inefficiency made them unpopular and a BJP-led government came to power. This third phase of neoliberal growth, steered by Hindu nationalism, is in full swing though alternative forces continue to occupy a significant space.

This story of Independent India is captured by scholars and commentators as it unfolded during the past 50 years as contributions to the Council for Social Development's social science quarterly, *Social Change*. They narrate the multidimensional dynamics of social change experienced by various sections of people at local, regional and national levels and also in the global context. We decided to share these contributions on specific themes in several volumes with a wider readership for good reasons.

First, *Social Change* is a unique, inter-disciplinary journal that covers not only research papers in social sciences but also policy analyses and reports from the field in areas of social development. Right from the start, Durgabai Deshmukh, the founder of the Council of Social Development, wanted theory, policy and ground-level experience to be integrated, each benefitting from the other. So, each volume in this series has papers by authors defining concepts, explaining theoretical frameworks, analysing policies and presenting survey results and other evidence from rural, urban and tribal areas.

Second, the journal carried contributions from not only senior scholars such as Nirmal Kumar Bose, B. N. Ganguly, T. N. Madan and B. K. Roy Burman, policymakers like C. D. Deshmukh and social activists such as Devaki Jain, but also from a large number of young academics from all over the country who used the forum to present their findings from their most important research projects. Some of them later became eminent academics and important policymakers. The contributions by these writers over a 50-year period can help us identify key points in the history of policymaking as well as discourses during the three major phases of contemporary India. Some contributions clearly impacted public discourses and the policy–making process. Thus, we are able to capture shifts in policy in the early 1970s when the state took many active initiatives, and also the big change in 1991 when a new role of the state was visible in the economy giving a substantial role to the private sector. That trend continued in the first two decades of the 21st century. We may note the changing perspectives and the linkage with the global processes not only on theoretical issues of social development but also on policy debates concerning questions such as the privatization of health, education, rural development, forest and environment. Their implications for people's welfare and human rights were also dealt with by many authors in the recent years.

Third, an equally important consideration underlying these volumes is the fact that the Council for Social Development has a mission to serve the interests of marginalized groups through its research, publications and advocacy, and indeed this journal reflects that commitment. Therefore, the volumes carry articles on selected themes such as health, education, poverty, and agriculture with special focus on the marginalized groups including the Adivasis, Dalits, minorities, women, and urban and rural poor. Each of these volumes reflects what has been done in respect of the specific marginalized groups and analyses the nature of the development experience from the vantage point of the marginalized.

Each volume is edited by an expert who has done considerable work on the subject. A major and substantive introduction by the Editor of the volume not only puts the papers in perspective but also identifies the strengths as well as the gaps in the treatment of the subject. The Editor's Introduction also addresses current concerns in theory and policy, discourse and practice and presents suggestions for further thinking and action. These volumes are designed as studies on a theme for ready reference and use by students, researchers and general readers.

Manoranjan Mohanty
Series Editor

Foreword

This book is a timely contribution to the educational discourse in India at a time when the National Education Policy (NEP) 2020 has come into force and the country is debating how far did it respond to the challenges India is faced with today.

Edited by one of India's foremost experts on educational policy, planning and development, this volume is important for many reasons. First, the selected articles highlight the critical issues in the history of policy and practice in education in India at all levels, from elementary and secondary to higher education and research. Second, the editor has imaginatively organized the selected articles to sharply focus on the thrust of policy in specific periods to point out where the roots of success or failures lie. For example, expanding literacy, which was the goal in the 1950s was revived in the 1970s. But the problem persisted until universalization of elementary education became the focus with the passing of the Right to Education Act in 2009. Higher education attracted special attention in the 1980s, but did not get adequate resource support. In the recent years, a clear choice was made to selectively promote a few higher education institutions, public and private. Third, another significant aspect of the selection is the discussion on the philosophy and perspective on education proposed and deliberated at different points of history of Independent India from the Radhakrishnan Commission (1948) and Kothari Commission (1966) to the Kasturirangan Committee (2019) which was the basis for NEP 2020, among others. Above all, a reader of this work can know what different sections of society have achieved in the sphere of education and why education remains a neglected sector even today.

This is an especially valuable collection because it embodies a key commitment of the Council for Social Development and one of its flagship publications, the journal *Social Change,* to emphasize the role of education as an instrument of social development and democratic transformation. The half-century-long mission initiated by Durgabai Deshmukh and C. D. Deshmukh, together with stalwarts such as V.

K. R. V. Rao, Malcolm Adiseshiah, B. N. Ganguly and S. N. Ranade continues today with equal vigour under the leadership of CSD President Muchkund Dubey who has been on the forefront of the campaign to universalize education and to effectively implement the right to education in particular. As Chairperson of the Bihar Education Commission on Common School System, Dubey had initiated a process that triggered many campaigns to realize the constitutional mandate for free and compulsory education. Under his leadership, the Right to Education Forum (RTI Forum) located at CSD has been active in a sustained campaign to implement and monitor the RTE Act of 2009. The vision of CSD's founders and the continuous initiatives of CSD's research and advocacy have been reflected in the pages of *Social Change* throughout the 50 years since the inception of the journal in 1971. Many special issues of the journal were published and special articles appeared on topics such as literacy, women's education, secondary education and higher education carrying policy analysis, theoretical discourses and empirical studies from the field from different parts of India covering various marginalized sections. This volume is a testimony to CSD's firm commitment to promote equitable quality education for all to achieve the vision of the Indian Constitution.

Today, we face a serious crisis in social development in India when the state is cutting down its investment in education and health and the trend of privatization is on the rise. The neoliberal approach to education that puts stress on skill-building for meeting the specific requirements of economic growth and market demands has increasingly distanced itself from the vision set out by the Constitution, the Kothari Commission and many other commissions of Independent India earlier, including the Radhakrishnan Commission and the Mudaliar Commission. The logic that a well-educated citizenry is a solid foundation for socioeconomic development and substantive democracy does not seem to persuade our rulers. But the debate and the struggle for a different vision—a democratic vision—go on as was evident in the recent publication of the CSD, *Educational Visions of India* edited by Professor Dubey. Professor Jandhyala Tilak's concluding essay in the volume captures the dimensions of the ongoing debate and gives us reasons to believe that the battle for education as a fundamental right is not lost after all. It is noteworthy that NEP 2020 reiterates the five-decade-old commitment to spending 6 per cent of India's GDP on education and also talks about a wholistic vision of education. Whether it will actually open up opportunities for the marginalized to realize their constitutional right will be tested on the ground in the coming years. These essays will be a valuable tool to assess and guide the working of the NEP 2020.

We are grateful to Professor Tilak for his insightful Introduction and editing this volume as a Golden Jubilee offering of *Social Change*.

Manoranjan Mohanty
Council for Social Development

Preface and Acknowledgements

This book, prepared on the occasion of the golden jubilee year of the publication of *Social Change* of the Council for Social Development, is a collection of 20 articles on education in India selected from articles published in near about 200 issues of the quarterly journal, *Social Change*, published during the last fifty years (1971–2020). The criteria adopted in selecting these articles from a large bunch of articles and other details are described in my introductory chapter of the book. Editing of these articles has been kept to the minimum, confining largely to correcting typographic slips, spelling mistakes, grammatical errors, missing references and minor errors, if any. The intention is to retain the original flavour of the articles and the writing style of the scholars undisturbed.

The editing of this volume has been an extremely rewarding exercise for me, as it gave me an opportunity to reading and enjoying again some of the best articles on the theme of my serious interest. I am grateful to Professor Manoranjan Mohanty, the Editor, *Social Change* and the Editor of the present *Series on Social Change in Contemporary India*, and Professor Muchkund Dubey, President, Council for Social Development for the trust they posed in me in making this volume. Both have shown keen interest and extended all support to me in accomplishing this task.

In the preparation of the volume I have also received valuable support and assistance from the colleagues and staff at the Council for Social Development, particularly Ms. Mannika Chopra, Ms. Jaya Lakshmi Nair, Ms Gurmeet Kaur, Ms P.M. Arathi and Mr Dev Dutt.

Thanks are also due to the authors of various articles who have kindly given permission to reproduce their articles in this volume.

The special efforts of the members of the team at SAGE publications, New Delhi, in bringing out this collection in a short time and in such an attractive form are appreciated.

Last but not the least, my wife Punya and my children have been a source of great support in all my work.

Jandhyala B. G. Tilak

Education Policy and Practice in India
An Introduction

Jandhyala B. G. Tilak

A nation is advanced in proportion to education and intelligence spread among the masses.

—Swami Vivekananda

Recognising the transformative power of education to shape India's destiny soon after gaining independence in 1947, the Government of India considered making education available to all a priority, and it laid special emphasis on the development of education. Immediately after Independence, the government appointed the University Education Commission, popularly known as the Radhakrishnan Commission in 1948 (Government of India, 1951) to look into the needed measures for the development of a national higher education system in the country. In 1952, the Government of India appointed the Secondary Education Commission under the Chairmanship of Dr A. L. Swami Mudaliar (Government of India, 1952) to study the various problems of secondary education and to suggest measures for reforms on aims, teaching arrangements, organisation, the relationship of secondary education with primary and university education, and to suggest a required pattern of secondary education for the entire country.

The Government of India recognised clearly in the very first Five Year Plan that "education is of basic importance in the planned development of a nation". It further stated,

> The success of a democracy depends on the growth of a spirit of co-operation, disciplined citizenship and the capacity of the ordinary citizen to participate intelligently in public affairs. It is essential

therefore, that education should train the individual to place duties above rights and should develop in him the power of critical appreciation and the habit of logical thought (Planning Commission, 1952, p. 221).

Five year plans were launched as an instrument of development planning. The role of education in development is more clearly elucidated in the Third Five-Year Plan.

> Education is the most important single factor in achieving rapid economic development and technological progress and in creating a social order founded on the values of freedom, social justice and equal opportunity. Programmes of education lie at the bases of the effort to forge the bonds of common citizenship, to harness the energies of the people and to develop the natural and human resources of every part of the country ... in all branches of national life education becomes the focal point of planned development (Planning Commission, 1961, p. 573).

India started almost from scratch, and made significant progress during the post-Independence period. When the Plan era commenced in the country in 1950–1951, 19.2 million children were enrolled in primary schools, 4.4 million in secondary schools and 360,000 in universities and colleges of higher education. By the end of the Third Five-Year Plan (1965–1966), considerable progress was made. Enrolment at the school level increased from 24 million in 1950–1951 to 76 million in 1965–1966, and that in the universities and colleges increased from 130,000 to 1.2 million. The number of universities increased from a mere 27 to 79 and colleges from 816 to 5,362 during the same period. A few high-quality institutions like the Indian Institutes of Technology and Indian Institutes of Management, and research centres and central universities were established. These achievements made during this period were by no means small for a newly independent developing country. They have to be seen against the background of the magnitude of the total problem. The goal of universalisation of elementary education which was to be accomplished by 1960 as per a constitutional directive looked a distant dream with just 70 per cent gross enrolment ratio in primary education and 30 per cent in upper primary education in 1966. 'Economic development naturally makes growing demands on human resources and in a democratic set-up it calls for values and attitudes in the building up of which the quality of education is an important element' (Planning Commission, 1956, p. 500). The education sector has not progressed enough to match these growing demands.

Recognising the need to closely match education with national development, the Education Commission was appointed in 1964 under the chairmanship of Dr D. S. Kothari, which submitted a very comprehensive report in 1966, along with a large set of reforms that were needed (Government of India, 1966). Following this, the first National Policy on Education 1968 (Government of India, 1968) was formulated which promised a variety of reforms in education, including a uniform national system of education (10+2+3), universalisation of elementary education, vocationalization of secondary education, consolidation of higher education and quite importantly, the allocation of six per cent of the national income to education. Unfortunately, the formulation of the 1968 policy was followed by a series of serious economic problems caused by drought, a high rate of inflation, resource scarcity, apart from the post-1965 Indo-Pak war developments.

In the area of education, the Planning Commission realised that the substantial expansion in enrolments at all levels of education in India during the first 15 years of planning plus three years of a Plan holiday was regrettably accompanied by a certain measure of deterioration in quality; it could also grasp that the Indian educational system had not been sufficiently geared to economic development, especially at the primary and secondary levels, and insufficient attention was being paid to vocational and agricultural education. Girls' education had still a long way to go before it could catch up with boys' education, while certain parts of the country were significantly lagging behind others in respect of both boys' and girls' education; stagnation and drop-outs at the primary levels were very high, resulting in wastage of scarce educational resources. Public expenditure on education became meagre and planning under austerity had been the slogan everywhere. For the first time, Independent India gave a holiday to planning under the Five-Year Plans for three years.

In short, by the end of the 1960s, paradoxically along with the remarkable educational expansion, one finds a pathetic educational scene. A general feeling was that 'education in India is in perils'. At the very beginning of the 1970s, when the predictions of Philip Coombs (1968) regarding the world educational crisis were yet to be taken seriously, Amartya Sen (1970) had warned about the 'crisis in Indian education'. At the global level, the 1960s were described as a golden decade for education, and the 1970s were a decade of educational recession (Tilak, 2006b). In India, the 1970s proved to be the beginning of troubled decades for education. The 1970s began with another Indo-Pak war (in 1971), spiralling inflation and educational inflation, graduate unemployment, and losing of faith in the role of education in development, with serious questions raised on the theory and empirical validity of human capital theory of Schultz (1961) that originally boosted the image of education and public investments in it in the 1960s. These trends in education were not unique to India; most developing and even some economically advanced countries faced the same situation of disenchantment with education. Realising the need to relook at the very basic nature of education that we should develop and the relative priorities for the future of the nation, the Government of India (under the Janata Party) made an attempt to make a new National Policy on Education (Government of India, 1979) but it failed as the government changed in the mid-term elections that followed (Tilak, 1982).

The 1980s marked the revival of confidence in education. Economists and educational planners realised some of the erroneous assumptions and found that the basic tenants of human capital theory were valid. 'Human resource development' had become a favourite slogan by the mid-1980s, and education was regarded as an important component of human resource development. There were some systematic efforts to accord high priority to education. The second National Policy on Education was formulated in 1986 (Government of India 1986) in India and a series of reforms were introduced to improve the quality, quantity, equity and efficiency in education. While the Union government began to take interest in elementary education, which was de facto a State subject, decentralised planning was also adopted in education; among the many measures, the State Institutes of Educational Management and Training, District Institutes of Education and Training, district and block resource centres and so on were established in school education, Academic staff colleges were set up in higher education and many other reforms were introduced.

But by the beginning of the 1990s, these efforts were confronted by economic reform policies then familiarly known as stabilisation and structural adjustment policies associated with the World Bank and the International Monetary Fund, that had caused drastic adverse effects on all sectors, including specifically the education sector everywhere (Tilak, 1992, 1996). An attempt to review the National Policy on Education 1986, initiated in 1990 by the National Front Government (Government of India, 1990), was virtually aborted with the fall of the government again. After all, policy making is always intricately related to political structures (Ayyar, 2017). In the early 1990s, India was also to go for the first time to the World Bank for external aid for primary education (Tilak, 2008; Ayyar, 2016), and the more than a decade-long District Primary Education Project that was launched with the World Bank aid had its own effects on the education scene in the country. Many national and international aid agencies followed the World Bank and entered into primary education in India. While resource constraints for primary education eased to some extent, school infrastructure improved, a nation-wide midday meal programme was launched, and some management reforms got strengthened, all this was at the cost of many long cherished basic features of education; primary education which is considered not a candidate for foreign aid became almost aid-dependent; private education stabilised its legitimate position and expanded in the following period at an alarming rate of growth, at the cost of public education; para teachers entered under different garbs and replaced formal trained and qualified teachers in large numbers; not only barefoot teachers but also 'barefoot' schools were introduced as a mechanism of 'education guarantee'; cost recovery measures were resorted to in a big way; decentralised planning was centralised; public good character was gradually made to go into oblivion; and so on (Tilak, 2006a, 2008). It is ironic that along with a new thinking advanced by human development specialists in the early 1990s, when a new fillip was expected to be placed on education (and health) that considered education not just as a means for development but also as an end in itself and as a human right, many distortions took place in education policy design with the entry of international agencies and markets in this area.

While the last decade of the last century was a decade of 'adjustment', some important initiatives were made during the first decade of the next millennium. Drawing from the experience of the District Primary Education Project, in its place a national programme of

Sarva Shiksha Abhiyan—a time-bound programme of universalisation of elementary education—was launched in 2002, and towards the end of the decade, the Right to Education Act was enacted in 2009. The latter was hailed as a historic path-breaking measure in the education history of modern India. Also launched were the *Rashtriya Madhyamik Shiksha Abhiyan* for secondary education in 2009, and the *Rashtriya Ucchatara Shiksha Abhiyan* for higher education in 2013—both aiming at fast development of education on a mission mode. Attempts were initiated in more recent years to develop an integrated approach to the development of the entire school education, including teacher education, under the name of *Samagra Shiksha Abhiyan* (in 2018). A ranking framework was introduced to promote healthy competition among the institutions within India. ICT systems were strengthened, academic and curricular reforms attempted. Quite a few measures were introduced to improve the quality of teaching and also leadership in higher education, networking of institutions and so on. But by this time, the forces of liberalisation, privatisation and globalisation became strong, and in a sense the State weakened. The private sector took away the space available for the expansion of public education; in fact, the latter was fast getting replaced by the private sector. The current situation can be described as a weak State, strong market and underdeveloped civil society.

By the middle of the present decade, it was widely recognised that secondary education needed to be universalised, the gross enrolment ratio in higher education was too low to meet the nation's economic and other demands, inequalities between the rich and the poor in participation in education were widening, and the quality of education at every level of education was distressingly poor: learning levels of children in schools were alarmingly low (ASER, 2015); and no higher education institution in India figured in the top 100 global rankings. It was also recognised that the system required drastic reforms on all fronts—the architecture of the system, the governance, administration, teaching-learning processes, research, finances and so on.

Accordingly, a committee was constituted to formulate the third national policy on education first under the chairmanship of T. S. R. Subramanian (Government of India, 2016) and later another under the chairmanship of Dr K. Kasturirangan (2019). The latter (Government of India, 2019) suggested a large package of path-breaking reforms, including some controversial ones, in every level of education, which formed the basis for the National Education Policy 2020 (Government of India, 2020). Though one expected the Right to Education Act to be extended to cover secondary education, the Policy 2020 promises simply universal school education that includes secondary education. The Policy, however, proclaims a wide spectrum of curricular and pedagogic reforms, including avoidance of distinction between academic and vocational subjects, and between curricular and extra-curricular activities, three language formula, offering of Sanskrit and other Indian languages as third language in school education, and inculcation of Indian ancient, ethical, human and constitutional values. It is not simply a national policy on education in India, but also an approach towards a policy on national education.

But the effects of the global health crisis caused by the corona virus towards the close of the decade might produce unimaginable effects on the entire society in the years to come. While it may be too early to make exact predictions, it is likely that the effects on the education sector may be devastating and may be felt at least for few years, if not for a long term. First, because of adverse economic conditions, public funds for education might come down significantly, forcing sacrifice of several resource-intensive education programmes. After all, education is the last priority whenever there is an economic crisis. Second, the worsening economic conditions and levels of living of people may also cause a big decline in demand for education, particularly from the lower socioeconomic strata. Third, the new social conditions necessitated by COVID-19 might require innovative methods of imparting education, including effective online/distance education programmes, without compromising on quality of education and without widening the digital divide further. Fourth, many of the parameters of educational planning may have to undergo drastic changes. On the whole, the education scenario is not likely to be rosy at least in the near future, or certain.

***

It is at a time characterised by the beginning of a crisis in education in India when *Social Change* was launched in 1971, as a '…forum for the dissemination of systematically ascertained facts and the expressions of thoughtful views, [to] help in dissipating ignorance, inertias and inequity and restoring the primacy of the spirit in promoting the great national adventure of transformation and melioration of the lot of its vast millions' (Deshmukh, 1971, p. 5). The fifty years of *Social Change* coincides with the five decades of turmoil in education. Focussing on the area of education, on the occasion of the golden jubilee of the journal, this book attempts at giving a brief idea of how the journal traversed during this period and served its purpose.

During the half century of its existence, *Social Change* attracted contributions on education from a very large community of scholars, educational practitioners, policymakers, field workers, activists and a variety of representatives of the society, including a few foreign scholars, though it is not a journal exclusively devoted to education. As education is of course one of the most important concerns of *Social Change,* almost in every issue, or every alternative issue of the journal, at least one important article on education was published. There were also quite a few special issues or special sections in an issue devoted to education. It proved to be a daunting task to make a short selection of this kind from a large pool of articles on education published in the journal over the last five decades. Together the articles covered every level of education from pre-primary to higher education, including literacy, adult education, secondary education, vocational and technical education, general higher education, higher professional and technical education and research, formal and non-formal education, and indigenous and modern education. The range of issues covered includes a wide array of aspects of education from social, economic, political, psychological, cultural and administrative points of view: the slow, high and unsteady growth in education—rising enrolments, along with rising dropouts, failures, wastage, out of school children, widening inequalities—gender, social (by caste, religion and ethnicity), spatial/regional (rural-urban, inter-regional and intra-regional), and economic (poor and rich)—deteriorating quality, mismatches between education and labour market, high degree of deprivation and marginalisation, relationship between education and health, economy, political system, and aspects including capitalism, imperialism, colonialism, globalisation, privatisation and their relationship with education. Many were based on rich field level surveys conducted in various small and big areas of the country—rural and urban, in eastern, north-eastern, western, northern, southern and central regions. Some are based on village-level data, and some on district, and some on state-level and national-level secondary data. A few have provided international perspectives on educational issues in India. Some are short articles, comments, opinions, reflections on contemporary issues and some lengthy research articles and commentaries. The contributors included young minds as well as stalwarts and experts, experienced in research, administration and policymaking, scholars of eminence, serious academics, and social activists. Together, they provide valuable insights into complex issues at the grassroots as well as macro levels, from social, political and economic outlooks. All scholars share a firm faith in education as a major instrument of social change and development.

Now from such a wide variety of rich and perceptive articles numbering about 150, it has been an unenviable challenge to select only about 20 articles for this collection, a collection that shows what the *Social Change* has been during the last 50 years, but also a cohesive collection that will be valuable to a versatile community of readers interested in education issues in contemporary India, which is so dynamically changing. However, relevance to the present alone has not been an overriding consideration; but many issues raised in the 1970s and 1980s continue to be of relevance today. Given the constraints on size, we are highly selective and in the process have excluded many valuable articles. The interest of scholars in education has increased over the years. Accordingly, we find a larger number of full-length research articles published in the last decade-and-a-half than in the earlier decades. But we tried not to include a disproportionately high number of articles from the recent years in the present selection.

We have tried to cover in the initial screening all the articles on education published over a period spanning over five decades, starting from 1971 till 2020. The considerations in the final selection are: articles based on micro-level field level surveys which are rich in data but might lack universality of their results are omitted; articles with too many tables on national-level data are also not considered, as these data are now easily available in the public domain. As one expects, a good number of articles did highlight inequalities in education between Scheduled Castes/Tribes and others, but most of them are based on databases which are limited in size and horizon. A few excellent articles, which are somewhat technical in statistical methodology, are also not included here. Thought-provoking pieces, even when they are short, are considered for inclusion. We have tried to include those that provide new perspectives from theoretical, conceptual and empirical viewpoints. Not all important themes in education could be covered in this short selection. The final selection represents a compression of time and space. I must admit that in the entire process there are lots of errors of omissions and commissions.

The selection highlights a trend line in the thinking of the contributors of *Social Change* and how they reacted to the changing priorities of the period. There have been major shifts in education policy during the last five decades. For example, the constitutional directive of universal primary education by 1960 seemed to have been a consideration of the 1950s, and literacy and adult education were hot topics in the 1960s and the 1970s. Education for rural development was also a priority area. Reforming higher education was a major issue on public policy agenda in the 1970s and early 1980s and now it again re-emerged as important after neglecting it in between. In the 1980s, in addition to rural–urban inequalities, inequalities, particularly gender inequalities in education, became a critical issue for development, as gender issues turned out to be dominant in the global public policy discourses after the United Nations declared 1975 as the International Women's Year. After the 1986 National Policy on Education, universalisation of elementary education again began receiving serious attention with global movements of Education for All (initiated by the UNESCO), followed by the United Nations' Millennium Development Goals and later the Sustainable Development Goals.

Elementary education continues to be a haunting issue, as still a lot is to be done to make it truly universal in all its major dimensions—enrolment, completion and achievements in levels of learning. Secondary education was long ignored. Every National Policy on Education attempts to address the core dimensions of education—quality, inequality and quantity and how to reach a balance between the three, described as an 'elusive triangle' (Naik, 1978). These have been persistent themes in education in policy discourses in India during the post-Independence period. The invasion of markets and private sector in education which started slowly more than two decades ago has resulted into such a threating level that any policy discourse cannot ignore this anymore. The volume is an attempt to outline a trajectory of serious deliberations and lively discourses among the Indian social scientists on educational developments, policy and performance.

Finally this golden jubilee offering of *Social Change* to the knowledge on educational research and policy in India includes 20 articles that cover a range of related themes, which are arranged here under four major sections, namely, Education Challenges, Education of Women and Social Change, Higher Education and Research, and Reforming Education.

Though the literacy rate has improved to above 70 per cent, according to the latest available statistics, India still continues to home more than 300 million illiterates. In other words, about a third of the world's illiterates live in India! The first section opens with a perspective on literacy as a major challenge India faces by V. K. R. V. Rao and Malcolm Adiseshiah, and how the adult education policy addresses this major problem by Rajiv Balakrishnan. After literacy, universal elementary education and development of secondary education have been the major education challenges. While many initiatives have been taken with regard to universalisation of elementary education, the enactment of the Right to Education Act by the Government of India in 2009 is considered by many as a landmark development. Muchkund Dubey critically examines the Act and highlights how it misses a few critical aspects necessary for effective universalisation of elementary education. While many argue for universal secondary education, it is still not a major item on policy agenda. Rounaq Jahan raises a few important issues for discussion on secondary education. Vidhya Das goes inside the classrooms and argues that the focus on examination scores leads to different kinds of problems—juvenile stress and high suicide rates, and hence there is a need for mainstreaming children from different, lower socioeconomic backgrounds. Educational planning was highly favoured in the 1960s and 1970s. Though the glamour it had in the past slowly disappeared, it is still considered important. Educational planning helps in developing education in a cohesive way avoiding internal contradictions between different levels of education on the one hand and in linking education with other sectors and broader economic planning on the other. D. P. Nayar highlights the same, affirming that educational planning helps in developing education not only for economic development but also for social transformation.

Women lagging behind men in education has become an important concern of educational planners all around the world. There have been persistent inequalities in the education levels between men and women in India. As M. C. Paul describes, the neglect of women's education in India dates back to the colonial period, when it received only lip service. If there were some actors during this period who promoted women's education, they were philanthropic private bodies and missionaries. Even after Independence, women's education did not receive as much attention as it deserves from the State. For women to play an important role in social change, they need to be educated and towards this, Muriel Wasi argues, women need to be made aware that they are an integral and necessary part of social change. Karuna Chanana goes further and finds problems in the very conceptualisation of Indian educational policies. She finds little meaningful space in the final policy documents for gender concerns. Analysing the process of policy development, she unravels the rhetoric of inclusion–exclusion and the myopic decisions which hardly touch the structures of exclusivity by gender.

The third section focusses on higher education and research. As early as in 1970, K. N. Raj (1970) warned about the crisis in higher education. The crisis in terms of exploding numbers, falling quality and standards, and limited funds was recognised. But no adequate attention has been paid to the crisis, as a result of which, it swelled in size over the years. Moonis Raza referred to the uneven growth of higher education, the growth of unviable colleges which are too small in size (in terms of students) to impart any meaningful education, and poor quality education. Raza concludes, 'The tragedy of our time is that the Third World is already getting fragmented into the Third and the Fourth worlds, and the developing countries into the less and the least developed. Education is unfortunately playing a key role in this process of inequalization.' Despite a lot of criticism of the typologies of the kind— Third World and Fourth World, less developed and least developed among the developing nations, the paradigms of thinking have not changed. Focussing on India, Adiseshiah refers to inequalities in income, locale (rural–urban), gender, inter-generational, levels of education and international typology of how developing countries like India were helping the rich countries to grow richer through contributing to their science and technology. Subramaian Swamy in an interesting short piece describes how the process of brain drain, a major problem of the 1970s, takes place which helps rich countries to grow richer even at the cost of developing countries. Brain drain seems to have been a forgotten issue, but of late, planners have begun thinking of how to have reverse the brain drain, that is, getting people back to their own countries. Swamy refers to some of these aspects. One of the important problems in Indian higher education is separation of teaching and research. Both need to be directed to serve national development, as Ujagar Singh argues. In fact, most of higher education consists of undergraduate education in colleges where there is no research at all, and even universities are relegating research to backside. But research is an important function of the universities, and universities can play an important role in building a knowledge society only if they extensively promote high quality research. As Pravin Patel argues, there is need to guarantee substantial financial support for research in universities, to regenerate a research culture, and to ceaselessly transit it among the coming generations of students. While some policies and plans guided planning of elementary education, and to a lesser extent secondary education, higher education experienced a big policy vacuum for a long period and it has been managed through executive orders and quick fix solutions.

The final section is devoted education reforms. Several committees and commissions have given valuable suggestions on reforming education in India. Many of the recommendations made earlier are still relevant today, as many recommendations, including those of the Kothari Commission were not implemented (Naik, 1982). As a result, even today many will agree with many of the suggestions of several committees summed up by V. Eswara Reddy in 1985 for reforming higher education. The additional problem that arose during the subsequent period refers to the emergence of markets in education. Given growing markets, one would wonder, as Manish Kumar Shrivastava and Chandan Chowdhary did in their article, 'Where Are We Heading To?' Will the public education system collapse? One of the fundamental features of education that is long cherished and well understood is that education is a public good, a fact that is not being cared much nowadays. Kishore Singh strongly argues for strong measures to protect the public good character of education, by effectively regulating the private sector. In recent years, many a committee desired the closure of commercially motivated, profit-seeking private educational institutions in the country, stating that 'education is not for profit'. The Dr Kasturirangan Committee (Government of India, 2019) also emphatically states the same. But as Tilak observed in the last article of the book while making a critical commentary on the report of the Dr Kasturirangan Committee, all commercially motivated, profit-pursuing educational institutions were set up and are functioning under the garb of philanthropy only and it is just impossible to officially identify which is a profit-seeking institution and which is based exclusively on the principle of philanthropy to take any action. Some of these practical challenges necessitated marginal amendments in the final National Education Policy 2020 (Tilak, 2020).

Thus, the volume of 20 articles authored over a span of half a century by a galaxy of eminent scholars, not only presents a historical view of how some of the issues were perceived, examined, deliberated and discussed at different points of time, it is also a very valuable volume in the present context, as many issues raised are still relevant, and many recommendations and suggestions made 50 years ago are still valid. After all, many issues raised here are still being debated in various academic and other fora.

It is hoped that the selection will be valued by all those interested in education issues in Independent India and that it will contribute to informed policy discourses on education. The selection may be seen as a modest contribution of the Council for Social Development, and *Social Change* in particular, to discourses on education and social change in India.

REFERENCES

ASER Centre. (2015). *Annual status of education report: Trends over time, 2006–2014.* New Delhi, Pratham. http://img.asercentre.org/docs/Publications/ASER%20Reports/ASER%20TOT/fullasertrendsovertimereport.pdf

Ayyar, R. V. V. (2016). *The holy grail: India's quest for universal elementary education*. Oxford University Press.

Ayyar, R. V. V. (2017). *History of education policymaking in India, 1947–2016*. Oxford University Press.

Coombs, P. H. (1968). *The world education crisis*. Oxford.

Deshmukh, C. D. (1971). Social Change—Guest editorial. *Social Change*, *1*(1), 4–5.

Government of India. (1949). *The Report of the University Education Commission (December 1948–August 1949)*. https://www.educationforallinindia.com/1949%20Report%20of%20the%20University%20Education%20Commission.pdf

Government of India. (1952). *Report of the Secondary Education Commission: Mudaliar Commission Report 1952–53*. https://www.educationforallinindia.com/1953%20Secondary_Education_Commission_Report.pdf

Government of India. (1966) 1971. *Education and National Development: Report of the Education Commission 1964–66* (Chairman: Dr D. S. Kothari). NCERT.

Government of India. (1968). *National Policy on Education 1968*. Ministry of Education.

Government of India. (1979). *Draft National Policy on Education*. Ministry of Education.

Government of India. (1986). *National Policy on Education 1986*. Ministry of Education.

Government of India. (1990). *Report of the Committee for Review of National Policy on Education 1986*. (Acharya Ramamurthy Committee Report). https://www.educationforallinindia.com/1990%20Acharya%20Ramamurti%20Report.pdf

Government of India. (2016). *National Policy on Education 2016—Report of the Committee for Evolution of the New Education Policy* (T. S. R. Subramanian Committee). Government of India. http://www.niepa.ac.in/download/NEP2016/ReportNEP.pdf

Government of India. (2019). *Draft National Education Policy 2019* (Dr Kasturirangan Committee Report). Ministry of Human Resource Development, Government of India. https://mhrd.gov.in/sites/upload_files/mhrd/files/Draft_NEP_2019_EN_Revised.pdf

Government of India. (2020). *National Education Policy 2020*. https://www.mhrd.gov.in/sites/upload_files/mhrd/files/NEP_Final_English_0.pdf

Naik, J. P. (1979). Equality, quality and quantity: The elusive triangle in Indian education. *International Review of Education*, *25*(2/3) (Jubilee Number), 167–185.

Naik, J. P. (1982). *The Education Commission and after*. APH Publishers.

Planning Commission. (1952). *First Five-Year Plan*. Government of India.

Planning Commission. (1956). *Second Five-Year Plan*. Government of India

Planning Commission. (1961). *Third Five-Year Plan*. Government of India.

Raj, K. N. (1970) 1972. *Crisis in higher education in India* (Sardar Vallabhbhai Patel Memorial Lecture). Government of India.

Schultz, T. W. (1961). Investment in human capital. *American Economic Review*, *51*(1) (March), 1–17.

Sen, A. K. (1970). *Crisis in Indian education* (Lal Bahadur Shastri Memorial Lecture). Administrative Staff College of India.

Tilak, J. B G. (1982). Educational priorities in the Sixth Five-Year Plan. *Rajasthan Economic Journal*, *6*(2) (July), 1–12.

Tilak, J. B G. (1992). Education and structural adjustment. *Prospects*, *22*(4), 407–422.

Tilak, J. B. G. (1996). Higher education under structural adjustment, *Journal of Indian School of Political Economy* 8 (2) (April–June), 266–293.

Tilak, J. B.G. (2006a). Education: A Saga of Spectacular Achievements and Conspicuous Failures. In *India: Social Development Report*. New Delhi: Oxford University Press for Council for Social Development, pp. 33–49

Tilak, J. B G. (2006). Economics of human capital in India. *Indian Economic Journal* (89th Indian Economic Association Annual Conference Volume/Keynote address), 3–20.

Tilak, J. B G. (2008). Political economy of external aid for education in India. *Journal of Asian Public Policy*, *1*(1) (March), 1–20.

Tilak, J. B. G. (2020). A policy with many aright intention. *The Hindu* (3 August). https://www.thehindu.com/opinion/op-ed/a-policy-with-many-a-right-intention/article32254650.ece

Section I

Education Challenges

Sectional Introduction

Even before independence, India had identified some of the major education challenges and the needed reforms. However, measures proposed, for example, in the Government of India Resolution of 1913, Sadler Commission (Calcutta University Commission) report of 1917 and Hartog Committee report in 1929 have not been effective in the development of education in British India. So the independent India rightly recognized educating its children and youth as one of the most important challenges.

The Sargent Plan, the first plan of its kind covering all levels of education, also known as the Report of the Central Advisory Board of Education (CABE, 1944) has identified a series of tasks to be accomplished within a period of 40 years that include universal literacy, free and compulsory primary education for all children of the age-group 6–11, with mother tongue as the medium of instruction, secondary education—general (academic) and vocational—for the children of the group 11–16, with 50 per cent of the children to be provided free studentships, and improvement in standards in university education. The Sargent commission also recommended provision of adult education for the people above 10 years and up to the age of 40. The CABE desired achieving these targets within a period of 16 years. Independent India considered these as major education challenges and measures were initiated to address them.

By the middle of the 20th century, the youth formed a majority of the population in India, as in many developing countries. As V. K. R. V. Rao highlights in the opening chapter, 'youth is a human resource of utmost importance in any scheme of development. If its energy and enthusiasm could be harnessed to the tasks that lie before us the pace of development could take on a much faster rhythm.' How do you bring this about? Rao strongly argues, 'This staggering number of young people must be provided with the education, training and cultural opportunities....' The first part of the volume opens with Rao's essay discussing on some of these major challenges that India has been facing. Rao refers in 1972, to, what we are now discussing—the issues relating to growing youth population and the associated demographic dividend.

In 1951 as much as 82 per cent of the population (of the group 7+) was illiterate. Hardly 9 per cent of women were literate, while the corresponding figure was 27 per cent among men, which was also very low. Independent India took it as a major challenge. But during the first decade of development planning, the growth in literacy was rather sluggish; it rose to 28 per cent, and inequality between men and women widened to nearly 25 points. Thus, universal literacy posed a serious challenge to educational planners in not only Independent India but also in most counties that became independent around the middle of the 20th century, as Malcolm Adiseshiah describes in Chapter 2. Many used to rely exclusively on formal primary education to achieve adult literacy. But slowly it was realized that along with primary education, a vibrant adult education programme would yield quick results. Thus, as an important measure, adult education programmes have been launched in many countries, including in India, but they were also not as effective as expected. It was successful only in those very few cases where it was taken on war footing. Adiseshiah descibes some of the noveal experiments and needed action in India. The programme in India started as a token measure was considerably strengthened in the late-1980s, with the launch of the National Adult Education Programme, and literacy and post/neo-literacy programmes. While some dramatic improvements could be seen in the progress of literacy, still India is far away from the target of universal literacy. Rajiv Balakrishnan focuses in Chapter 3 on the strengths and weaknesses, and the performance of the adult education programme. Among its several components and variants, the total literacy campaign struck a responsive chord but only in regions with a history of social reform movements, peasant organizations and working-class struggles. Social mobilization on a large scale was, however, hindered in other parts of the country by barriers of caste, class, gender, and feudalistic fetters, apart from bureaucratic attitudes and reactions.

Recognizing the critical importance of universal primary education, it has been made a constitutional directive in 1950 and it was resolved to accomplish this goal within a 10-year period, that is, by 1960. But even after 70 years, the goal remains elusive. Realizing the ineffectiveness of the constitutional directive, and its inability to compel the government to fulfil this goal, and partly reacting to international and national pressures including the demands made by civil society, an amendment was made to the Constitution of India in 2002 making education a fundamental right. Accordingly, a comprehensive Act was made in 2009. Muchkund Dubey critically analyses the Right to Education Act in chapter 5 and observes that it failed to meet the vision of the nation behind the constitutional amendment. Though it has several plus points, as Dubey observes, it fails to check the perpetuation of multi-layer discriminatory education system. For example, it still allows the growth of private education directly, and allows its flourishing indirectly through provisions like quota for weaker sections in private schools and financial compensation for the same.

Both in the case of literacy and education, like in the case of most aspects of development, rural India lags far behind. In fact, the state of education in rural India is pathetic in terms of availability of schools, infrastructure, quality teachers and so on, all of which get reflected in poor levels of learning by the children, and the overall performance of the school system, which is pathetic and continues to be so. Hence, one notices big trends in the migration of population from rural to urban areas in the country. J. P. Singh describes in detail the challenge of rural education in India. Inadequate allocation of resources, poor school infrastructure along with rapid growth in population and poverty in rural areas often pose serious problems in achieving educational goals in rural India.

In the recent years, it is being increasingly realized that universal elementary education is not enough for the development of the nations in the 21st century. Accordingly, the need to provide good quality secondary education to vast majority of children is felt obvious. India, like a few other developing countries, began initiating plans for universal secondary education. But problems in universalizing secondary education are indeed daunting (see Tilak, 2020). In a stimulating address, Rounaq Jahan identifies in Chapter 6, partly drawing from her experience in Bangladesh where there has been an educational revolution, some of the important issues in universal secondary education that policy makers should necessarily take into serious consideration. She stresses the importance of strong political commitment and social pressures in any educational revolution.

Teaching and learning in schools became highly formal and heavily emphasized, ignoring an important dimension of learning—learning from outside the classrooms. Vidhya Das highlights how important it is in overall learning for life, and how it is completely neglected by formal education systems. Finding a solution for this is not easy. First, it needs to be acknowledged that there is a strong mechanism of production and dissemination of knowledge, which can be described as 'tacit knowledge' (Polyani, 1966), that cannot be brought into the formal school system. Then, as Das highlights,

> The real challenge is to conceive of an educational system, a process that takes into account the considerable knowledge and skills present amongst the uneducated and make a concerted effort to initiate all young people into these; that does not alienate but combines in a creative fashion the best in modern and traditional systems and sciences for control and use by one and all; that enables individuals to channelize their energies and potentials for creative and productive use, and does not reduce them to job seeking stooges in a bureaucratic megalith.

Immediately after Independence, India adopted development planning as the most important strategy for development, and launched development of Five-Year Plans, which were developed, executed, and monitored by the Planning Commission (1951–2014) and in a different structural model by the National Institution for Transforming India (NITI) Aayog (2015–2017). Goals, targets and schemes were set for development of every sector of the country. Education was also considered as an important sector that needs planned development, and accordingly educational planning was also taken up. It is important to note that India realized the importance of educational planning much before it became popular in other countries and in international organizations like the UNESCO-IIEP (International Institute for Educational Planning) where it happened only after the human capital revolution in economic thought was unveiled by Theodore Schultz (1960). Briefly reviewing the experience of educational planning in the first five Five-Year Plans, D. P. Nayar presents in the last chapter of the first section in this book, a wide perspective on a gamut of issues and challenges, along with a large set of recommendations. He also highlights, the need to effectively integrate it with social objectives and overall development planning. It is widely felt that such an integration of educational planning with overall development planning has unfortunately not taken place yet.

REFERENCES

CABE. (1944). *Report of the Sargent Commission on post-war education development in India*. Central Advisory Board of Education.

Government of India. (1913) 1915. *Indian Education Policy 1913: Being a Resolution Issued by the Governor General in Council on the 21st February 1913*. Superintendent Government Printing.

Hartog Committee. (1929). *Report of the Auxiliary Committee of the Indian Statutory Commission (Hartog Committee)*. Government of India.

Polanyi, M. (1966). *The tacit dimension*. University of Chicago Press.

Sadler Commission (Calcutta University Commission). (1919). *Report of the Calcutta University Commission 1919*. Government of Calcutta.

Schultz, T. W. (1960). Investment in human capital. *American Economic Review*, 51(1), 1–17.

Tilak, J. B. G. (Ed.). (2020). *Universal secondary education in India: Issues, challenges and prospects*. Springer.

Chapter 1

The Challenge*

V. K. R. V. RAO

The youth of the world today is not 'tomorrow's generation', not a
minority awaiting their turn as adults. The children and youth of this
world of the mid-20th century constitute a majority as a population
of the entire developing region. They are today's generation—a live
political force that refuses any longer to be frustrated. The impact of
affluent consumer society, technological advance, the nuclear scene
in which we are living, have all brought about a significant change in
the social climate of this country; it has also thrown the spotlight on
hunger, insecurity and despair and these are having a profound impact
on the youth of the mid-20th century.

Let me quote some figures:

By 1975, there would be about 460 million rural youth in the
developing countries. By 1985, the figure will have increased to about
550 million and India will claim a large proportion of such rural youth
as their nationals. This staggering number of young people must be
provided with the educational, training and cultural opportunities
which are directly applicable to their own economic and social
environments and which are adequate for the professions they would
be required to pursue.

Unchecked and with no motivating programme to involve the
young men in the national development, a vast number of unqualified,
unguided and frustrated rural youth will migrate to towns where few

* *Social Change:* June 1972: Vol. 2, No. 2, 42–45.

will find active employment and, therefore, social disorder and chaos will be the inevitable consequence.

Obviously, a massive involvement of young people can only be achieved through 'self-help' oriented youth groups organized at the local community level; youth programmes must be an integral part of national development programmes.

The question is, how do you bring this about? This brings me to the proposition that before we discuss the remedy, what orientation the older leaders must undergo in order that they are able to work not only for the youth but with the youth. We must, first of all, accept that it is natural that in a rapidly changing society, the gap between the generations would widen. The young in India today are not only proportionately more numerous than they were 20 years ago, they also play a far larger part in the economy of consumer society, as must be plain to anyone who looks at commercial advertisements. Second, it must also be recognized that in the attack launched by the young against adult society, whether in India or abroad, students, as somebody has aptly stated, 'form the general staff and the shock troops'. The rebellion of students is not an isolated phenomenon, it is an example and a particularly striking symptom of the anxiety felt by the youth of India in regard to a society which seems incapable of properly integrating them. I would venture to suggest that these small intellectual groups of the student community have set the style for a youth movement which tends to develop as an international youth culture in the fields of art, ideology and morals, in complete contrast to adult culture. They not only question academic culture which they regard as completely out-of-date but also the avant-garde culture of adults. Finally, we should note that for the young, culture no longer means a sort of literary and artistic embellishment of our lives; it is a way of life. It is here, perhaps, that the sharpest clashes occur, particularly over the ethics of work and success, rules of behaviour and pattern of human relationship. It is probably here that error of judgement occurs among the authorities, educators and adults in not recognizing the cause of the sharpest clashes. We admit that problems do exist but we are reluctant to allow the young themselves to pose the problems. Here, we claim to know better. We would like to pin-point youth problems and reduce them to what we would like them to be, to something which would be comprehensible and acceptable to us. I would quote an example.

When disturbances arise in universities, a handful of agitators or ring-leaders are singled out and carefully separated from the vast majority of students who are said to be reasonable; reasonable because we feel that this group has the same orchestration with our way of thinking. But this so-called 'reasonable' majority soon makes common cause with the ring-leaders and unrest grows. The adults in turn resort to forced and old-fashioned manoeuvring. It ends by creating mutual misunderstanding, increasing opposition, confusing the issue and therefore postponing a genuine solution. Perhaps the first step towards solution of the youth problem should be for us to stop and think about our own attitudes, our secret fears and our inhibitions in our dealings with the younger generation, and so come to see, if not to accept, the young as they really are, and not as we the adults, we the grown-ups and the older generation would like them to be.

Having stated this and having assumed that the change of attitude of the older generation would come about voluntarily because of the realization of the realities of the situation, I would like to state that youth is a human resource of the utmost importance in any scheme of development. If its energy and enthusiasm could be harnessed to the tasks that lie before us the pace of development could take on a much faster rhythm. How can youth, especially the rural youth of India, be encouraged and equipped to undertake the large-scale and constructive action which the situation demands?

In discussing youth programmes, we must accept the fact that the most significant characteristics of this key group of youth is the massiveness of its number, its problems and its potential for constructive or non-constructive involvement. Consequently, massive problems and opportunities require more comprehensive and broader programmes of action for constructive involvement; or, if available resources currently limit such action, planning and programme building must have a long-term massive orientation or, in other words, the programme must purposefully provide the foundations and the building blocks for expandable systems having wider potential for more extensive, comprehensive and integrated programmes.

The Ministry of Education have initiated pilot schemes for the student youth in our National Service Programme for involvement of students in the national development effort. The University Grants Commission is already giving consideration to the involvement of students in the university affairs. It is, however, the world of non-student youth for which we must do something—a body which presents special problems because of their much larger number, their large rural composition and the absence of institutional facilities for their get-together as is possible for students.

There is need for the establishment of volunteer-led youth clubs in selected rural areas in some of the states. These clubs should themselves develop programmes centring around supervised credit/production enterprises, cooperative activities in aid of agriculture, general continuing education and functional literacy programmes and for provision of recreational facilities. These pilot schemes have to be tried and tested in field conditions and should they succeed, urgent consideration will require to be given for their wider application.

In conclusion, I would assert that no plan of youth participation in development work is likely to succeed unless it answers their individual and collective urges. The supreme test of our leadership will be: are we able to give our youth a sense of mission and fulfilment in doing what we are asking them to do? I earnestly hope we can.

Chapter 2

Literacy in the Third World*

Malcolm S. Adiseshiah

Our country and our world are more illiterate in 1970 and 1971 than in 1960. India's illiterates have increased from 330 million in 1961 to 382 million in 1971. The number of illiterates in the world is over 800 million in 1971 compared to 740 million in 1961.

This increase in the number of our illiterate brothers and sisters in our country and in our world must be set against the pledge that we have taken in Article 45 of our constitution and Article 18-B in the International Development Strategy of the Second United Nations Development Decade. Article 45 of our constitution states that 'the State shall endeavour to provide within a period of 10 years from the commencement of this Constitution, for free and compulsory education for all children until they complete the age of fourteen years.' Article 18-B of the International Development Strategy states that:

> Particular attention should be paid to achieving enrolment of all children of primary school age, improvement in the quality of education at all levels, substantial reduction in illiteracy, the reorientation of educational programmes to serve development needs, and, as appropriate, the establishment and expansion of scientific and technological institutions.

In the 1970s, we must redeem these national and international pledges and to do that we face a serious uphill task.

I have just shown that the number of our illiterates is increasing nationally and internationally. The illiteracy percentage is however

* *Social Change:* August 1971: Vol. 1, No. 2, 7–12.

diminishing. World illiteracy has decreased from 39.3 per cent in 1961 to 34.8 per cent in 1971. The Indian percentage for the two periods has fallen from 79.97 to 70.65. The two reasons which explain this seeming contradiction are the rapid growth of population and the inefficacy of the school system. The population of the Third World has been increasing at the rate of about 2.5 per cent per annum during the 1960s, while the rate of literacy has been increasing at 0.5 per cent per annum. The gap between the two rates explains in part the decrease in the percentage of illiterates in the population and the increase in the number of illiterates during the 1960s. The second reason is related to the functioning of our school system. If literacy is equivalent to the education received in the first four classes of primary schooling, the dropping out of 55–65 per cent of pupils from the first four years of such schooling swells the illiteracy stream. It means that though the country continues expanding primary education, for every one person made literate through such education 1.5 to 1.6 persons are made illiterate.

Only one country in the 1960s took effective action to wipe out its illiteracy. Cuba devoted 1960 and 1961 to mobilizing all its students, teachers and government officials to teach its illiterates and thus made all its illiterate people literate. Since 1962, it has initiated the stage of post literacy which involves the further education of its literate men and women in both rural and urban areas. That plan, known as the Battle of the Sixth Grade, is being systematically carried out by its ministry of education, together with a special literacy programme which has dealt with its residual illiteracy of 3.9 per cent left by the 1960–1961 campaign.

Nine countries had launched mass literacy programmes in the late 1960s, with the aim of making all their people literate within a four- to five-year period. These countries are Guinea, Kenya, Burma, Jordan, Kuwait, Syria, Colombia, Guatemala and Iran. Guinea has opened 17,000 literacy centres, in which 15,000 secondary school students and 600 university teachers are used as instructors in order to eradicate the country's illiteracy by 28 September 1971. Kenya's plan for complete literacy is targeted for the end of this year. Dr Nyi Nyi, Burma's Deputy Minister of Education reported recently that 80 per cent of the people had been made literate and that the rest, living in inaccessible areas, are the subject of a special literacy effort. Jordan, Kuwait and Syria have launched a six-year literacy programme. Colombia initiated in 1969, which was the 150th anniversary of its liberation by Simon Bolivar, the Second Liberation Plan to make its people literate. Guatemala initiated in the same year a six-year plan to wipe out illiteracy in its territory. Iran has, through its Army of Knowledge, wherein recruits entering military service have a choice between soldiering and teaching, launched a programme to make all Iranians literate by the 1970s.

Such are the positive and encouraging literacy efforts in the 1960s. In other countries which form the vast majority of the Third World and notably in our country, the literacy effort has been limping along. Their political leaders, economic planners and educators have invariably concentrated their attention almost solely on school education. It is only the left-over crumbs that are handed out to the literacy programmes. Illiteracy has no organized constituency and no spokesman in any country. This is surprising because literacy is not only a human right, it is good business. I have earlier referred to our national and international pledges which are an expression of the right of every man and woman to education. Additionally, literacy has a high pay-off, which was first recognized by Adam Smith and has been highlighted more recently by the computations of S.G. Strumuelin, the Soviet economist and a host of other social scientists. But all this has made no difference to the neglect of our illiteracy situation by our leaders, political and intellectual, and so the mass of illiterates goes on increasing from year to year and from decade to decade.

It was to give fresh impetus to the urgencies of this stagnant and worsening world problem that UNESCO organized the World Congress of Ministers of Education in Teheran in 1965, at which the Experimental World Literacy Programme was launched. In four years, by 1969, 52 countries asked to participate in the programme and in 38 of them UNESCO helped to formulate literacy projects. As a result, three types of projects in the Experimental World Literacy Programme are now in operation and share two common characteristics. First, they explore and evaluate the relationship between functional literacy and development; and second, they apply and test new methods. These new methods aim at integrating literacy teaching with technical vocational training and adapting this to the needs of specific occupations. They determine the content for functional literacy, and train and build this into appropriate media and into the training of teachers and instructors. In short, they explore a variety of new approaches to the education and training of illiterate adults.

The three project types are as follows:

1. Large-scale experimental and pilot projects which are located in an agricultural or industrial area, in which literacy learning is part of improved agricultural practices or industrial skill instructions. These are now in operation in 15 countries, namely Afghanistan, Algeria, El Salvador, Ecuador, Ethiopia, Guinea, Iran, Libya, Madagascar, Mali, Niger, Sudan, Tanzania, Venezuela and Zambia.
2. Projects in which a functional literacy component is included in development schemes. This category so far includes two countries. There is a literacy programme included in the high-yielding variety programme in India and in a new agricultural development project in Syria.
3. Smaller and sometimes short-term projects (micro-experiments) in which the country's experts carry out research and experiments with teaching methods, the production of teaching aids and the use of audiovisual media which could be used in literacy programmes. These have been established in seven countries, namely Algeria, Brazil, Chile, Jamaica, Nigeria, Tunisia and Upper Volta.

The 1960s thus registered some advance in literacy together with a tremendous backlog which confronts us in the 1970s. We know the nature of the problem. It is our suffering, handicapped and discriminated men and women. We know through the Experimental World Literacy Programme what methods and techniques should be used to meet the needs of this deprived sector of our common humanity. It is a massive sustained effort to help people to learn reading and writing within the programme to combat rural and urban poverty. We know its costs in financial and human terms. It is less than 10 per cent of what we spend annually on arms and it is a few hours of daily intellectual effort. What is lacking and what is needed for the 1970s is the will to meet this need adequately.

For this, I have two suggestions.

First, every country in the world during the 1970s should set aside the necessary resources, human and financial, to make its illiterate people functionally literate. The resources exist within our countries. Our educated people and that part of our educational budget, which is now being wasted through the inefficiency of the school system, are adequate for this task. They can and must be mobilized for a time-bound literacy programme in each country.

Second, I turn nearer home to India. It is now necessary to turn from pilot demonstration and ad hoc efforts to mass programmes on the lines of the three-stage plan prepared by the report of the Education (Kothari) Commission. This literacy effort in India can be divided into a three-group effort. The first group would cover states which have a literacy percentage of 35 and above. They are the seven states of Kerala, Tamil Nadu, Maharashtra, Gujarat, Punjab, West Bengal and Mysore. The second group would be those who have a literacy percentage of 25 and above but below 35, which include the four states of Orissa, Andhra Pradesh, Madhya Pradesh and Uttar Pradesh. The third group would be those with the lowest percentage, the three states of Bihar, Rajasthan and Jammu and Kashmir. The first group of states should make their people functionally literate in five years and move on to a post-literacy programme, the second in seven years and the third in ten years. Eighteen months ago, at a State Literacy Conference in Madras, a five-year literacy programme for Tamil Nadu was established with my help from which I quote:

> The programme proposed will be aimed at making literate in the above sense, the one crore of illiterates of the age group 15–40 living in Tamil Nadu, within a period of five years. For this purpose, 40,000 literacy centres will need to be set up in the State, with each centre giving two courses a year, of about four months each.
>
> The staffing of these centres should be drawn from as wide and qualified a corps as possible. It should include volunteer teachers serving in the 8,500 higher and upper elementary schools of the State, retired teachers, women volunteers, high school and college students, particularly those enrolled on the National Service Corps, and the men and women in the villages, who have been educated up to the S.S.L.C course. Three conditions are suggested for recruitment to this teaching staff. First, only those who really volunteer for the services and

reside in the neighbourhood should be accepted. Second, every volunteer should pass through an orientation course which would include language teaching, adult psychology and techniques of adult teaching and learning, to be organised generally by the primary teacher training schools of Tamil Nadu. Third, each volunteer should undertake to teach at least one course at one of the centres. The voluntary teachers at a ceremony to be organised periodically should be awarded either an honorarium per course or an academic credit which will enable them to continue their further education.

The curriculum and study programmes for the centres should be developed by the teacher training schools and colleges and rural extension training centres of Tamil Nadu under the overall guidance of the State Board of Adult Education. Under the guidance of the Board, they should also be responsible for developing primers, reading materials and simple audio-visual aids, including suggestions for programmes for broadcasting by radio and television. The primers should be based on surveys of the vocabulary and the frequency of the words used by the appropriate group in its work and homes, their division into manageable stages and illustrative possibilities of the selected words. The learning process and materials are thus related to the age, sex, occupation and motivation of each group of learners. Lessons accompanied by art and music are found easy and acceptable. Similarly, the purpose of all education being the capacity to learn, that is the acquisition of learning skills, discussion groups, self-discovery and management workshops must intersperse all teaching.

The cost of this five-year programme for Tamil Nadu will be ₹9 crores for the entire five year period. This means that the annual cost of this programme will amount to ₹1.8 crores. It is recommended that the government of Tamil Nadu contribute ₹1.4 crores per year (₹7 crores for 5 years), and the local community contribute ₹40,00,000 per year (₹2 crores for 5 years). The government contribution will cover the teaching honorariums of ₹100 per course, orientation costs of ₹25, supervisory costs and follow up literature. The local community will be responsible for the primers, note-books, building and lighting charges.

It will be noted that this five-year literacy plan is sited in the daily preoccupation and living of the people of each locality. It is functional. Its cost contains two elements. It is practical. First, the mobilization of the educated people—the intellectuals—of the state for this priority task; second, an annual expenditure, for five years by the state, of ₹1.4

crores. The state is now spending ₹67 crores on school education. If a small part, 2.5 per cent, of the school wastage which I compute at over 10 per cent and which can be saved by reorienting and reforming school education, is diverted first to the five-year functional literacy programme and later for the post-literacy effort, a literate state can become a reality.

It is some such time-bound functional literacy programme that must now be launched in each state of the Indian Union, taking into account the level of development of each. Such a literacy effort can be undertaken. It must be undertaken.

Chapter 3

Adult Education in India*
Policy and Perspectives

Rajiv Balakrishnan

Adult education in India has diverse colours—the country's ancient and rich oral tradition for the transmission of scriptural knowledge; Emperor Ashoka's dissemination of the teachings of the Buddha through inscriptions on rocks and pillars; royal patronage in the medieval period to scholars, saints, teachers, artists and artisans for the spread of messages of peace and harmony; adult schools set up by British missionaries in an evangelical spirit, their efforts and those of 'enlightened Indians and socially committed British officials' to promote adult education; the adult education policy initiatives of the colonial government; the importance given to adult education by the leaders of the freedom movement and, post-Independence, the Total Literacy Campaign's (TLC) activist leanings, which galvanized women participants in the adult literacy classes in Nellore district, Andhra Pradesh, to mobilize against the evils of drunkenness, leading eventually to a state-wide ban on the manufacture and sale of liquor. Notwithstanding its promise, the TLC was plagued by serious deficiencies. It struck a responsive

---

* *Social Change:* September–December 2002: Vol. 32 Nos. 3&4, 181–194.

This paper is drawn from the report of a Planning Commission sponsored, Council for Social Development project on *Social Development in India—The Policy Canvas: An Overview of the Last Fifty Years & Emerging Issues for the Twenty-First Century.* Earlier it was presented in an in-house seminar at Council for Social Development. Comments offered by Prof. Partha N. Mukherji, helped crystallise the typology of 'capabilities', 'potentials', 'problems', 'needs', and 'opportunity needs linkages'.

chord in regions with a history of social reform movements, peasant organizations and working-class struggle, but mobilization was hindered by barriers of caste, class, gender and feudalistic fetters in parts of the country; there were limits to how radical a government-sponsored programme could be; bureaucratization had taken firm root, with development issues eclipsed by the total literacy declaration; and while the TLC was civil-servant driven, the civil servant's training was not geared to inculcate the qualities that were needed to tap the potential for social mobilization in a participatory mode.

As country after country emerged from colonial bondage, governments of the newly independent states began the process of nation building through 'centrally managed guided democracies'. Ironically, this led to critical thinking on the centralized model and provided an impetus to more genuine democratic leanings. With growing democratization, the spotlight began to play on sustainable development, environmental concerns and quality of life issues. Governments, for their part, began to realize that the skills and talents of their people were their greatest resource, and that the role of education needed to be thought through afresh. Development henceforth was to be 'of the people', 'by' the people and 'for' the people. In such a scheme of things, education was to play a critical role—on this, there is a global consensus, demonstrated perhaps most strikingly by the assessment of the progress of nations in terms of the human development index, a measure based on the premise that development should give people a decent standard of living, allow them to lead long and healthy lives and ensure that they are well educated. With the formal system catering only to the privileged few, 'continuing education' or 'lifelong learning' seeks to compensate by giving those who have missed the bus a second chance (APPEAL, 1997, pp. 2–5). This, then, is the overarching backdrop to 'adult education'.

ANTECEDENTS AND ROOTS

Adult education in India has ancient antecedents—the country's rich oral tradition for the transmission of scriptural knowledge dates back several millennia. With the advent of Buddhism, which did not recognize the caste divisions of Hindu society, education became less exclusive. Especially in the time of Emperor Asoka, the teachings of the Buddha, inscribed on rocks and pillars, were a medium of non-formal education for common people. In the medieval period, the tradition of oral transmission of knowledge, values and culture was sustained by royal patronage to scholars, saints, teachers, artists and artisans. Islam was egalitarian, it emphasized the acquisition of knowledge from the cradle to the grave, and education was open to all. In Akbar's time, handwritten books were read aloud and discussed in court, and Aurangzeb believed in free and compulsory education but could not enforce it throughout his kingdom (Shah, 1999, pp. 6, 8).

It was only later, in the 19th century, that new winds blew in from the West. The East India Company's main objective was commerce, but its Charter Act of 1698 acknowledged the role of missionaries in spreading education. The colonial policy was however not without ambivalence.

There was substantial opposition from the British parliament to the education of Indians; it was argued that the American colonies would not have risen in revolt if their leadership had not come from a determined educated class. A temporary ban on the activities of missionaries was followed by the Charter Act of 1813, which gave them the freedom to set up educational institutions (though the promised financial support could not be implemented for want of funds). Lord Grey, the Prime Minister of Britain, saw education as the cornerstone of progress in the colonies; and colonial administrators like Lord Elphinstone, Governor of Bombay (1819–1827), took an interest in the promotion of mass education—though that goal, by and large, was thought impracticable. Another important development came in the form of official criticism of the 'filtration theory', which envisaged the spread of education as a process by which it was to filter down from the upper classes, which had the leisure and the means to invest in education. It was in this context that, in 1854, the educational dispatch suggested measures for promoting mass education. The emphasis was on primary education, and the challenge of adult education was taken up by 'missionaries, enlightened Indians and socially committed British officials'. The leaders of the freedom movement, thinkers like Swami Vivekananda and social reform societies (Brahmo Samaj, Prarthana Samaj, Arya Samaj and the Indian Social Conference) were key actors, with universities such as Madras and Mysore organizing extension lectures for the masses along the extra mural lines of British universities (Shah, 1999, pp. 8–12).

In the policy sphere, recognition of the importance of adult education for socio-economic development came from the Royal Commission on Agriculture (1928) and the Auxiliary Committee of the Indian Statutory Commission (1929). 'Night schools' modelled after the British Adult Schools and established by Christian missionaries, the key adult education institution in the 19th century, had begun to receive grants in aid from 1921. The main objective was to promote basic literacy, but the course content varied. In Travancore, it covered history, health, hygiene and first aid. By the 1920s, adult education had come to be channelized also through libraries, community development projects and awareness programmes organized by social, cultural and political organizations. In addition to official initiatives, non-governmental organizations such as the YMCA and the Servants of India Society played an important role, and professional bodies like the Rural Reconstruction Association of Benares and the Bombay Sanitary Association helped educate the masses on issues of health, society, economy and politics. In the 1930s, adult educators worked to develop primers in local languages, and Dr Frank Laubach, American missionary and author of *India Shall Be Literate*, provided professional leadership to Indian adult educators (Shah, 1999, pp. 12–14).

By 1919, the nationalist movement and the prospects of *swaraj* had drawn attention to the dangers of an ignorant electorate. Nationalist leaders such as Lala Lajpat Rai and Lokmanya Bala Gangadhar Tilak organized night as well as summer schools for literate adults. Political parties organized schools to train young adults for the freedom movement. Following the transfer of power to elected representatives by the 1935 Act, mass literacy programmes were organized in different parts of India—in Bihar, United Provinces, Bengal, Bombay, Madras, Punjab and Assam. The colonial power provided support to adult education, even during the war; it was seen as a way to divert attention from the ongoing freedom struggle, whose leaders saw it as a means to mobilize and motivate the masses. With the resignation of Congress ministries, however, adult education lost steam and became an official activity of educational departments. In most of the princely states, especially Mewar, it was opposed for fear that it would stimulate subversive activities (Shah, 1999, pp. 12, 14).

The adult education of the 1920s—an activity in which non-officials were the moving force, was to become an official programme in the 1940s. The success of provincial mass literacy programmes, initiatives of non-officials and social reformers and the freedom struggle were factors shaping colonial policy in this regard. By 1944, the Sargent Commission, in its Report of Post War Educational Development in India, advocated a 25-year plan to eradicate illiteracy and make arrangements for adult education (Shah, 1999, pp. 12, 14–15).

VOCATIONAL AND 'SOCIAL' EDUCATION

In 1939, the Adult Education Committee of the Central Advisory Board of Education had conceived adult education not just as a process whereby literacy is imparted to adults; it emphasized the need to awaken the interest of the learner, and felt this could be best achieved through vocationalization, but to make adults literate and keep them from lapsing into illiteracy was envisaged as the primary aim. It was after independence, in 1963, that another committee on adult education stressed the need for a 'social education' which not only covered basic education, numeracy and opportunities for further learning through libraries, clubs and the like, but was also linked to such concerns as citizenship, democracy, cultural heritage, health, cooperation and moral values. In 1952, social education was integrated with the Community Development Programme. Most of the states however failed to fully utilize the sanctioned outlay, mainly due to deficiencies in planning and financial administration (Shah, 1999, pp. 16–17, 19, 20–21).

FUNCTIONAL LITERACY

In the 1950s, the adult education programme received financial support from UNESCO and the Ford Foundation, as also training for Indian adult educators from Dr Frank C. Laubach and Dr Wealthy Fisher. Dr Laubach's proposal to the Government of India for an All India adult literacy campaign in the 1950s was shelved due to a paucity of funds.

The official policy was one of universalization of elementary education by 1960, which was thought to be a more effective way to tackle the problem of illiteracy. That goal was not achieved. This, together with the limitations of the social education programme, was among the factors that paved the way for a policy shift in favour of 'functional literacy'. The functional approach was given a stamp of legitimacy in the Report of the Education Commission and in the fourth five-year plan. In 1968–1978, the Farmers Training and Functional Literacy Project was in place to educate farmers to participate in the 'green revolution'—but the beneficiaries were mostly well-off farmers. The Functional Literacy for Adult Women programme, introduced in 1975–1976 and meant to facilitate women's participation in development, covered 23 states and union territories by 1977. In the functional phase of adult education in India, two key adult education institutions were established—the National Board of Adult Education in 1969 and the Directorate of Adult Education in 1971. In 1974, the Central Advisory Board of Education advocated that functional literacy programmes be planned in relation to development schemes. Efforts were made to implement this in the fifth and sixth plans. Krishi Vigyan Kendras aimed at providing technical literacy in agriculture and allied fields, while the Shramik Vidyapeeth sought to improve the professional competence and enrich the lives of urban workers. Other programmes included the Nehru Yuvak Kendras, Rural Welfare Extension and the Family & Child Welfare Programme (Shah, 1999, pp. 22–26).

NATIONAL ADULT EDUCATION PROGRAMME

By the 1970s, Paulo Freire's writings became influential and education came to be seen more as a process of human liberation. The National Adult Education Programme was conceived with equal emphasis on literacy, functionality and social awareness, but the functionality and awareness components got neglected. Still, a high participation of scheduled castes, schedule tribes and women was a significant achievement of the NAEP. The NAEP had specified a time frame for the literacy component——300–500 hours over a 10-month period. Subsequently, in 1980, a review committee recommended a three-year programme of 300–350 hours of basic literacy in the first phase, followed by two reinforcement and vocationalization phases of 150 and 100 hours (Shah, 1999, pp. 27–28). The NAEP Review Committee's proposed three-year scheme was shelved and, in 1980, the NAEP itself was replaced by the newly constituted National Programme of Adult Education (NPAE). In 1982–1983, the government began to fund programmes to supplement the basic literacy component—post literacy (four months) and follow-up (one year). This eventually led to the Jan Shikshan Nilayams, established all over the country and conceived of as a permanent institution in rural areas to institutionalize post-literacy and continuing education (Daswani, 2002, pp. 36–37).

NATIONAL LITERACY MISSION

While the problem of adult illiteracy had been long recognized in official circles, it was formal schooling and its rapid expansion that was emphasized in the country's five-year plans, with such adult literacy initiatives as were undertaken ad hoc and limited in reach and scope. This was to change after 1988, with the establishment of the National Literacy Mission (NLM; Dighe, 2000, pp. 11–12). Although set up to provide technological and material inputs, the NLM was to soon acquire the colouring of a 'societal mission' in a 'campaign mode' designed to mobilize large numbers of participants (Daswani, 2002, p. 41). This followed a campaign for total literacy set in motion in the Ernakulum district of Kerala, one that was marked by a spirit of voluntarism, mobilization of people from all walks of life, an alliance between the bureaucracy, social activists and voluntary groups, and support of the government at the central, state, district and local levels. Spearheaded by the Kerala Sasthra Sahithya Parishad, an NGO working to popularize science, the movement set the stage for the concept of the TLC, which was then taken up for replication in other parts of the country (Dighe, 2000, pp. 12–14).

Post Literacy and Continuing Education

As many learners in the TLCs either did not acquire the recognized levels of proficiency or, having done so, lapsed into illiteracy, post-literacy programmes, it was envisaged by the NLM, would cater to those who had slipped through the net. Post-literacy was however seen to also have a broader agenda; according to a 1998 NLM document, it was expected to fulfil the goals of

> remediation (those not covered by the TLC to be made literate, those below the minimum level of learning to be enabled to achieve it); continuation (stabilisation, reinforcement and upgradation of learning); application (to living and working conditions); communications (group action for participation in the development process), and skill training (life skills, communication skills, vocational skills).

A 1999 policy document envisaged TLC and post-literacy as 'two operational stages in the learning continuum...now under the same scheme'. Meanwhile, in 1995, the JSNs were replaced by Continuing Education Centres, meant to cater to neo-literates. Its objectives extended to the provision of facilities for retention and reinforcement of literacy skills; application of functional literacy for quality of life improvement; dissemination of information on development programmes for participation; creation of awareness on national concerns; training in vocational skills; provision of a library and organization of cultural and recreational activities (Daswani, 2002, pp. 43, 45–47). In the post-literacy and continuing education stages, the emphasis is more on skill development and new learning. The principles that underlie it include lifelong learning to cater to the needs of all sections of society, and learning to be seen as capacity building in the broad sense (NLM, 2000, p. 23). The Zilla Saksharata Samiti, headed by the district collector with assistance from voluntary agencies, mahila mandals and PRIs, Nehru Yuva Kendras and so on, is responsible for implementing the continuing education programme and has the freedom to create new grassroots structures to facilitate effective implementation. It is guided by four broad programme areas of Asia-Pacific Programme of Education for All (APPEAL):

> Equivalency Programmes (EPs)—designed as alternative education programmes equivalent to existing formal, general or vocational education; Income Generating Programmes (IGPs)—designed for acquisition or upgradation of vocational skills for income generating activities; Quality of Life Improvement Programmes—designed to equip the

learners with essential knowledge, attitudes, values and skills, both as individuals and members of the community; and Individual Interest Promotion Programmes (IIPP)—designed to provide opportunities for individuals to participate in and learn about their own chosen social, cultural, spiritual, health, physical and artistic interests. (Daswani, 2002, pp. 47–48)

Changing the World

The NLMs ideological colouring, according to one of its official publications, draws upon Satyen Maitra's poem, whose words 'guide and direct all our endeavours at making our country fully literate'. The poem stresses the need to be literate so as to read simple books, keep accounts, write letters and read newspapers and asks whether literacy can help one live better, starve less, have a newly thatched roof above one's head, take care of one's health and be aware of the laws designed to protect and confer benefits (NLM, 2000, p. 3). The transformational ethos of the NLM is evident also in its track record. In Pudukkottai, literacy was linked up to issue of livelihoods, thus fuelling the motivation of learners, and bringing together activists and administrators. It helped women quarry workers petition the Assistant Director (Mines) for permits to sell stones from the quarries in defiance of the contractors. The women learnt to write bills and receipts, and manage accounts as well. The adult literacy programme also helped Pudukkottai women enter the gem cutting industry, for which numerical skills were needed to handle precise machine calibrations (Rao, 1993, p. 917). In Nellore, even in the pre-TLC phase itself, the adult literacy programme was embedded in a context of social mobilization strategies that stressed issues of low wages, untouchability, powerlessness and social evils such as dowry, drinking and wife beating, with literacy seen as a key to understand exploitation (Shatrugna, 1998, pp. 250–251). The TLCs were in fact a landmark in a new perception of literacy, as not just about 'reading the world' but about transforming it. Mobilization strategies drew upon the song, dance and street plays (*kalajathas*) to stress issues of poverty, oppression, caste discrimination, gender inequity and the absence of employment opportunities (Dighe, 2000, p. 22). In the post-literacy phase, Jana Chetna Kendras (Centres for People's Awareness) were established. These 'village parliaments' were not only venues to discuss the general problems of the village, they were also a place where women could get together and play a key activist role, as the experience of Nellore district has shown (Shatrugna, 1998, pp. 251–252).

The post-literacy primers contained lessons dealing with day-to-day problems of the people. One of them, 'Seetha Katha', which tells the tragic story of Seetha, the wife of a liquor addict, turned out to be incendiary. The story, read out in night school to the women of Doobagunta, a small village some 80 km from Nellore town in Andhra Pradesh, struck a chord in the village women, whose earnings from wage labour were spent by their menfolk on toddy and arrack; even their household provisions were sold for liquor, and drunken husbands made their wives miserable. Moved by Seetha's plight, the women mobilized to obstruct the liquor contractor and defy the police and the collector. The event was reported in a primer *Chaduvu Velugu (Light of Knowledge)* as a lesson titled *Advallu Ekamaithe (If Women Unite)*. Disseminated through the evening classes of the NLM, *If Women Unite* had an electrifying effect. Women advised their menfolk not to drink and saw to it that arrack shops were closed, and women squads kept vigil to prevent arrack from entering their villages. The demand for a ban on the manufacture and sale of arrack took root in this fertile soil, and eventually culminated in a ban on the manufacture and sale of all liquor in the state (Shatrugna, 1998, pp. 252–258). That the transformational aspect the TLCs injected had great potential is attested further by the people's initiatives that emerged in the wake of the TLC's mass mobilization campaigns; cooperative societies and the *Pani Bachao Andolan* (a 'save water campaign') in Maharashtra and the setting up of nursery schools in Assam are cases in point (Dighe, 2000, p. 22).

Adult Education in Urban Areas

Adult literacy initiatives have mostly been confined to rural areas and the adult literacy needs of the urban poor were relegated to the background. It was in this context that the Urban Literacy Project, a new initiative under the NLM, was conceived '...to explore, identify and suggest appropriate strategic interventions, based on documented experiences, authenticated data and research studies, for widening literacy and continuing education in urban areas' (ULP, n.d., p. 1). In a workshop meant to deliberate on urban literacy strategies, it was pointed out that literacy had more economic value in the urban setting, where there was no land to fall back upon, and that the urban cognitive world is large and complex; hence, urban adults have special literacy needs—slums, poor civic amenities, urban poverty, the growth of the informal sector, unemployment and underemployment, hopelessness, crime, violence against women, alcohol and drug abuse and AIDS are all part of the urban scene. At the same time, the poor are unaware of government schemes and continue to be exploited; hence, there is a need to educate these marginal sections (ULP, n.d., pp. 5–7, 17–19). The workshop also identified the need for networks to coordinate and mobilize activists, NGOs and government bodies to collaborate with the local people in such areas as slum improvement, urban basic services and poverty alleviation.

Critical Assessment

1. The literacy campaigns were marked by the spirit of voluntarism and decentralized community participation (Saldanha, 1995, pp. 1182, 1191). However, overall, the TLCs got bureaucratized and did not live up to their promise. Districts were classified into A, B, C and D categories, depending on how successful they were in relation to the norm of the total literacy, which led to falsification of data and eroded the credibility of the TLCs (Dighe, 2000, pp. 16–17, 23–24). The 'total literacy' declaration and standardized tests deflected attention away from social and development issues. Instead, the focus should be on social accountability to plan for the PL phase and facilitate individuals or organizations that have played a major role. In particular, uneven outcomes among learners should determine how the post-literacy phase is to be organized (Saldanha, 1995, pp. 1181, 1185).
2. The literacy campaigns have drawn in women, weaker sections and disadvantaged groups in a big way and have succeeded in penetrating the structures of deprivation, but they have failed to change these in a major way due to the 'lack of concurrent processes

of organisation of the oppressed'. At best, the ground has been prepared for this to happen (Saldanha, 1995, p. 1191).

3. The uneven success of the programme suggests an element of ad hocism. In Pudukkottai, the programme was marked by official enthusiasm, emergence of district, block- and village-level committees and the establishing of participatory structures at the grassroots (Athreya & Chunkath, 1996, pp. 145–146, 165–170). Likewise, in Pasumpon, the TLC 'concentrated on and developed a network of participatory grassroots village, panchayat and district level structures to ensure the continuity and sustainability of the movement'. A significant feature was the gram panchayat coordinator, the link between the village centres and the district, who is appointed by the village people (Rao, 1993, p. 916). These districts have been cited as 'success stories' (Dighe, 2000, pp. 19–20), which suggests that they stand apart, so that the developments here have not occurred uniformly. It appears that, at the policy level, there is a recognition that 'each district is unique', so that the NLM has permitted and encouraged great flexibility and innovation in designing and implementing post-literacy campaigns. The concerned Zilla Saksharata Samiti is free to create a model that suits the needs of the district and its learners (NLM, 2000, p. 21). However, there does not seem to be a policy thrust to facilitate an identification of potentials of each district so that they are tapped to the full.

4. The TLCs were also subject to structural constraints. Authors of one study note that one of their study districts—Birbhum, in the State of West Bengal, where adult education programmes had been in place for at least three years, was a 'politically aware' region. Here, 'Devolution of power of local self-government has helped bridge the chasm between the people and the administration' (Chatterjee & Khan, 1997, p. 14). Another analyst argues that regions that had a history of social reform movements, peasant organizations and working-class struggles were receptive to the campaign approach of the TLC. In the 'Hindi belt', class, caste, gender and semi-feudal relations in agriculture were stumbling blocks. Thus, there is a need to take cognizance of each region and devise a suitable

strategy; indiscriminate replication of the TLC model is not feasible (Saldanha, 1995, pp. 1189–1190).

5. When mobilization does take place, the question arises as to how much 'space' a government-sponsored radical programme can provide. In Nellore, the police cracked down on women's groups in places where the anti-arrack agitation was weak. Following this, the post-literacy textbook that sparked off the agitation was withdrawn, as were functionaries in the forefront of the agitation (Dighe, 2000, p. 26; Dighe, 1998, p. 261). On the heels of the anti-arrack movement in Nellore, and the 'new euphoria that was engulfing the district', women established about 7,000 of their own thrift and savings groups. Loans were taken out for traditional activities such as vegetable vending, dairying, and goat and cattle rearing, along with consumption loans to spend on health problems, marriages and the education of children (Dighe, 1998, p. 260). The savings movement, however, petered out after the government co-opted it into an impersonal banking system (Ramachandran, 1999, p. 879). In Pondicherry, a mass awareness campaign which sought to make the poor aware of their rights was seen by the government in power as dangerous. The government did not sanction the post-literacy budget; material for 530 post-literacy centres could not be procured and committed volunteers were disillusioned (Rao, 1993, p. 915). The chief minister objected to a post-literacy primer that asked, 'Freedom for the country, but why poverty for us?' Officials were transferred and a voluntary agency associated with the post-literacy phase delinked from it (Dighe, 2000, pp. 27–28).

6. Political will has wavered and was not uniform, which was one of the hazards of the 'ideological' model of the TLC (Dighe, 2000, p. 29).

7. The NLM's 200-hour basic literacy component spread over 6–8 months is questionable. The NAEP Review Committee had found even a 350-hour basic literacy segment over a 10-month period insufficient. The result is that the programme has only succeeded in creating 'fragile literates', who are at risk of lapsing into illiteracy. There is recognition of this by the NLM itself and has been commented upon by an expert group as well. The problem has been aggravated by long time lags between the literacy programme

and the 24-month phase of post-literacy programme. The coverage of post-literacy too, it seems, has been hamstrung. As per the data from districts covered by the TLC, out of the 448 TLC districts, in only 234 have PL programmes been sanctioned (Daswani, 2002, 43–44).

8. The campaign mode, to which the civil servant-driven TLCs were geared, required qualities in the civil servant that their administrative training had not sought to build upon or inculcate. The civil servant-driven model of the TLC needed exceptional individuals to operate it from the top and was beyond the reach of routineers, howsoever competent (Ramachandran, 1999, p. 878). This in fact can be one reason for the uneven success of the programme. Thus, the Bodhan subdivision of Nizamabad district, which did much better than the other subdivisions, was led by a dynamic sub-collector (Rao, 1993, p. 918). On the other hand, it has been argued that the literacy campaigns provided on-the-job training to government officials and brought them closer to the people. They also drew attention to the need for a different sort of administrative ethos in the field of development (Saldanha, 1995, p. 1191).

ADULT LITERACY—A ROAD MAP

To identify agencies that could participate in the adult literacy programme, there is a need to assess the *types* of capabilities such as administrative capacities, political will, the clout of PRIs and the role of personal factors like the temperament of the civil servant and whether their background equips them to function in a manner that encourages participatory initiatives. In addition to such official capabilities, the adult literacy programmes to be set in place need also to be shaped by the potentials in the society that lend or do not lend themselves to social mobilization and people's participation— whether self-help groups are operating in the area, how much voluntary effort can be expected, etc. In regions with a high potential for people's participation, the programme can be truly a 'people's programme'. Well-trained collectors with an aptitude for a participatory mode of functioning can be posted in such areas, and participatory potentials tapped to the full. In areas where the campaign mode is not likely to be effective, other strategies can be tried out. Last but not the least, identification of problems and needs should help shape the proposed programmes; to that end, needs assessment is to be carried out.

All these factors taken together should not only determine the character of the adult education programmes to be set up, but can be expected also to facilitate the identification of a nodal agency that is best equipped to coordinate the functions of the different actors (e.g., the more the programme depends on a participatory mode, the more will be the need for a nodal agency that has the expertise to manage it). Structured and unstructured survey instruments may be used, together with participatory methodologies like focus group discussions, depending on what is feasible, to assess potentials, capabilities, problems, needs and opportunity-needs linkages. An assessment of needs and the scope of the existing institutional arrangements to cater to them in the sampled locales can be a point of departure. This should facilitate identification of gaps, assessment of how and the extent to which governmental and non-governmental agencies can rise to the occasion, and how literacy and adult education can fit into this scheme of things.

REFERENCES

Asia Pacific Programme of Education for All (APPEAL). (1997). *Challenges of Education for All in Asia and the Pacific and the APPEAL Response*. Bangkok: UNESCO Principal Office for Asia and the Pacific.

Athreya, Venkatesh B. & Sheela Rani Chunkath.(1996). *Literacy & Empowerment*. New Delhi: Sage Publications.

Chatterjee, Bhaskar & Qutub Khan. (1997). *Impact of Non-Formal Adult Education in the Asia-Pacific Region: a Four Country Synthesised Study*. Bangkok: UNESCO Principal Regional Office for Asia & the Pacific.

Daswani, C. J. (2002). 'Education beyond literacy: 'Changing Concepts and Shifting Goals, in R. Govinda (ed.) *India: Education for All – A Report. A Profile of Basic Education*. Oxford University Press. Post Literacy and Continuing Education in India', in National Institute of Adult Education, *Education for All: Spotlight on Adult Education*. New Delhi: National Institute of Adult Education.

Dighe, Anita. (1998). 'Postscript' (to M. Shatrugna, 'Literacy as Liberation: The Nellore Experience'), in Sureshchandra Shukla & Kaul, Rekha. (1998). *Education, Development and Underdevelopment*. New Delhi: SAGE Publications.

Dighe, Anita. (2000). *Social Mobilization and Total Literacy Campaigns.*(Education for All Assessment 2000). National Institute of Educational Planning and Administration/Indian National Commission, UNESCO.

National Literacy Mission. (2000). *A People s Movement.* Directorate of Adult Education.

Rao, Nitya. (1993). 'Total Literacy Campaigns: a Field Report'. *Economic & Political Weekly.* 28 (19): 914–918.

Ramachandran, V. 1999. 'Adult Education: A Tale of Empowerment Denied', *Economic & Political Weekly.* 34 (15): 877–880.

Saldanha, Denzil. (1995). 'Literacy Campaigns in Maharashtra and Goa: Issues, Trends and Direction'. *Economic & Political Weekly.* 30 (20): 1172–1196.

Shah, S. Y. (1999). *An Encyclopedia of Indian Adult Education.* New Delhi: Adult Literacy Mission.

Shatrugna, M. (1998). 'Literacy as Liberation: The Nellore Experience', in Shukla, S. and Kaul, R. Eds. *Education, Development & Underdevelopment.* SAGE: New Delhi.

Urban Literacy Project. (n.d.) *Towards Urban Literacy Strategies.*

Chapter 4

The State of Education in Rural India*
Problems and Prospects

J. P. Singh

Education assumes special importance in the process of nation building and its relevance needs no emphasizing, particularly in the context of a developing country like India, which is characterized by massive illiteracy. Education is one of the well-known determinants of social mobility. It is also a catalytic agent of various kinds of social, economic and political processes. Perhaps realizing these facts about the importance of education in life, the makers of modem India made constitutional provisions for the compulsory and free education to all children in the 6–14 age group by 1960. A study of the constitutional provisions, various plan documents and policy statements of the government on education suggests in unequivocal terms that the Government of free India, ever since its inception, has been committed to the cause of universal education in the country. The country has made substantial progress in the field of education during this period. For instance, the level of literacy has gone up from mere 17 per cent in 1951 to 52 per cent in 1991. But this, on the contrary, also suggests that the country has failed miserably to achieve universal education in a period of 50 years of planned development. So far, the country is only halfway through its target of 'education for all'. The situation is still the worse in rural areas where the level of literacy is about 45 per cent as

* *Social Change:* September 2001: Vol. 31 No. 3, 1–19.

against 73 per cent in urban areas, according to the 1991 census. The prevailing state of affairs with low level of literacy in rural India puts a big question mark against the government's sincerity to the cause of universal education in the country.

OBJECTIVES AND DATA SOURCES

Considering the aforementioned facts, there is need to look back and do stocktaking of what we have accomplished or missed out so far. This is necessitated with a view to locating the pitfalls in our programmes and policies that have directly or indirectly held us back in achieving the set targets, despite redefining programmes and policies time and again. This chapter seeks to analyse the nature and level of infrastructure at hand for education in rural India with a view to explaining the reasons for differing levels of education across the states. The chapter offers a detailed discussion on the patterns of spatial distribution of educational facilities, namely primary, middle, high/higher secondary schools and so on, which have direct bearing on the spread of education in rural areas.

The study is essentially based on data from the Census of India, 1991. Data on the availability of different types of facilities of basic nature in villages have been collected by the census organization as a part of the census operations since 1951 and are presented under the village directories. These directories constitute an integral part of the district census handbooks. They furnish very useful information on some of the basic demographic and socio-economic characteristics as well as on the availability of certain important basic amenities in each village and town in the respective district. The study, however, uses information on the availability of infrastructural facilities relating to education only.

At the outset, it is worthwhile to add that the chapter is unable to cover the 2001 census because of the non-availability of relevant data. The village-level statistics for different states, which form the basis of this chapter, were compiled and released for the first time for the 1991 census only. Such data were never released for any other census ever since the census count was launched in India and furthermore, there is no guarantee that such data would be released on a continuous basis for the 2001 census also. In addition, the census authorities have not yet released literacy data cross-classified by rural and urban areas so far. Even if the relevant data set is released in near future that can never be enough for the present chapter because the chapter, as said before, is primarily based on the village-level infrastructure data which may or may not be released for the 2001 census.

As this study is concerned primarily with the village-level reality, it is important that the notion of village is defined at the outset. The definition of village is necessitated also because most people, including social scientists, generally differ among themselves with regard to the conceptualization of village. Since this study is based on the Indian censuses for the purpose of data, we follow the census definition of the village. Under the Indian census, a village means a revenue village or *mauza*, which may be a single village or it may comprise surrounding hamlets (or satellite settlements) that have sprung up in the periphery of the main village. In the case of the forest and hilly areas, where the scattered houses are a part of the village, a village includes all houses within the administrative boundary (Census of India, 1971, p. 336). Here, it is obvious that the concept of village operationalized in the census is different from what the lay people commonly mean by it. While to a social scientist, every independent settlement of contiguous houses usually constitutes a village.

Here, it is also important to point out that the actual number of villages is much larger than the census villages in the country. The Indian census has defined the village in such a way that the number of villages in the country is actually underreported. This can be readily obvious from the fact that of all the villages, 73 per cent of them had primary schools according to the 1991 census, but when all the villages, both main and satellite ones, were counted separately, as was done in the case of the Sixth All-India Educational Survey in 1990, only 50 per cent of the villages were recorded to have primary schools (here decline in percentage is the result of counting of smaller villages independent of revenue villages). Therefore, in the following discussion, it should be borne in mind that the availability of infrastructural facility in terms of facility for schooling has obviously got over-reported. The problem inherent with data cannot be rectified. Furthermore, with a view to studying the issue of infrastructure for education in rural areas, there is no source other than those of census reports. Since there is a consistency in operationalization of the definition of village and the compilation of village-level data across states in census reports, generalizations made on the basis of such data are undeniably tenable and reliable. Yet another strength of the data is that they are longitudinally comparable because of uniformity in the definition of village from one census to another. Since the study is primarily based on the 1991 census data, other data used here are of the similar period for the purpose of comparability. Hence, data from educational surveys subsequent to the 1991 census are not so much brought to bear on the discussion.

GOVERNMENT'S PROGRAMMES AND POLICIES

Before the problems of universal education in rural India are examined, it is important to briefly highlight the programmes and policies concerning universal education pursued so far in the country. Before 1976, education was exclusively the responsibility of states; the central government was concerned only with certain areas like coordination and determination of standards in technical and higher education and so on. In 1976, through a constitutional amendment, education became a joint responsibility. Decisions regarding the organization and structure of education are largely the concern of the states. However, the union government has a clear responsibility regarding the quality and character of education. At the central level, the Department of Education in the Ministry of Human Resource Development is primarily concerned with the overall administration of education, planning and implementation of programmes, determination of school syllabus and evaluation of curriculum and different educational boards, standard of higher education, scientific and technical policies and priority programmes. The Central Ministry is guided by numerous Central Advisory Councils such as CBSE, NCERT and NIEPA. In the management, administration and implementation of the educational programmes, a three-tier mechanism exists—central, state and district or local levels. All plans are examined, approved and finalized by the Planning Commission through the National Development Council.

In order to achieve universal education in India, several policies of education have been formulated and time to time revised in view of the possible constraints. The national educational policy statements of 1986 and the revised version of 1992 have laid special emphasis on the fulfilment of constitutional obligations of attaining universal education. The successive Five-Year Plans have repeatedly promised to take the nation towards this goal. However, the goal remains elusive even after the lapse of four decades of the deadline of providing universal education, as stipulated in the Constitution of India. The prevailing situation may inevitably compel some concerned people to conclude that India has not taken the objective of universalization of elementary education within 10 years of the constitution coming into effect so earnestly.

The National Policy of Education (1986) envisaged the provision of universal elementary education for children up to 14 years of age and eradication of illiteracy in the 15–35 age group through the programme of adult education. With a view to implementing the scheme, several programmes were chalked out. These included (a) a primary school for every habitation with a population of 200–300, (b) introduction of 'Operation Black Board' to ensure minimum facilities, equipment and at least two teachers for every school, (c) introduction of a system of non-formal education for school dropouts, un-enrolled and working children and (d) special incentives for girls and economically weaker sections. The National Literacy Mission launched in May 1988, planned a strategy for imparting functional literacy to million adults (illiterates in the 15–35 age group) by 1998–1999. According to the Common Minimum Programme of the United Front Government at the centre, it was planned to make India fully literate by 2005.

The governments at the centre have formulated and executed several programmes and policies to achieve universal education in the country during the last five decades of Independence. This is clearly obvious from Table 4.1 where a summary of information relating to different commissions and committees on education along with their thrust areas have been broadly specified. But the present low level of literacy signifies nothing but considerable failure of different governments on the front of universal education.

Despite the genuine efforts and intention of different governments to universalize education, the level of education, compared to that of most developing countries, is quite low in India. Amazingly, now the country has the largest number of illiterates in the world. India has 30 per cent of the world's illiterates and about 22 per cent of out-of-school

Table 4.1 *An Overview of Commissions/Committees on Education of Post-Independence India*

Year	Commissions/ Committees	Main Thrusts
1952	*L Mudaliar Commission*	To review the entire secondary education system and make detailed recommendations for its reconstruction. Continue to favour the institution of central authority.
1956	*Ramachandran Committee*	Evaluation of the progress of basic education in the country and to make suitable recommendations for future course of action.
	Basic Education Committee for Public Schools	To make a first-hand study of the public school system and to make suitable recommendations for the introduction of basic education in the elementary classes of these schools to steer away from the system of exclusively preparing for university entrance.
1958	*Smt Durgabai Deshmukh Committee*	Constitution of national committee on girls' education to suggest the special means necessary for women's education at primary and secondary levels.
1958	*Children's Literature Committee*	To establish Sahitya Rachanalyas to train authors in the technique of writing suitable books for children.
1962–1964	*Hansa Mehta Committee*	Adoption of co-education as the general pattern at the elementary stage with common curricula for boys and girls.
1963	*Bhaktavatsalam Committee*	To investigate the cause of lack of public support for girls' education.

(Continued)

(Continued)

Year	Commissions/ Committees	Main Thrusts
1964–1966	Kothari Commission	Emphasis on the development of academic staff as an important dimension for educational transformation and review of the Indian system of education in its totality.
1985	Chattopadhyaya Commission	Pay Commission.
1986	National Policy on Education	Emphasis on preschool education and education of girls, education for equality, decentralization of education and adoption of child-centred approach.
1990	Acharya Ramamurti Committee	Review of the National Policy on Education (1986) and its implementation to make recommendations regarding the revision of the policy.
1992	National Policy on Education and Programme of Action	Revision of National Policy on Education and Programme of Action, 1986.
1992	Janardan Reddy Committee	Emphasis on the development of academic staff as an important dimension for educational transformation.
1993	Yashpal Committee	To advise on the ways and means to reduce the load on school students at all levels, particularly on younger ones, while improving quality of learning including capability for lifelong self-learning and skill formation.
1993	Arun Ghose Committee	Adult education.
1993	Chaturvedi Committee	To examine the recommendations made by the Yashpal Committee.

children. Given an annual addition of 17–18 million people, the number of illiterates will keep on rising still further for some more time.

With respect to literacy, the rural–urban divide is very sharp and conspicuous. In rural areas, only 45 per cent of the total population is literate as against 73 per cent in urban areas (here literacy refers to number of literate at ages 7 and above) based on the 1991 census. This is not unusual since merely three-fourths of the villages are provided with primary or middle schools in India so far. There are great variations with respect to the availability of different kinds of formal organizations for schooling.

INFRASTRUCTURE FOR EDUCATION

According to the village directory data of the 1991 census, only three-fourths of villages in the country are provided with government-sponsored schools. At the state level, as is evident from Table 4.2,

Table 4.2 Percentage of Inhabited Villages with Different Kinds of Educational Facilities in India, 1991

Availability of Educational Facilities	Percentage
Any educational facility	74.8
Primary school	72.8
Middle school	19.3
Secondary school	7.7
Junior college/higher secondary/senior secondary school	1.3
Degree college	0.3
Adult literacy centre	7.1
Industrial training school	0.1
Other training school	0.2
Any other	3.8

Source: Census of India, 1997, Availability of infrastructural facilities in rural areas of India: An analysis of village directory data (Census of India, 1991), New Delhi: Office of the Registrar General, India, p. 17.
Note: Excluding Jammu & Kashmir, where Census is not held in 1991.

the extent of availability of educational institutions in villages varies quite widely, that is, from more than 90 per cent in Kerala, Gujarat and Maharashtra to less than three-fourths in Bihar (including the new state of Jharkhand), Orissa and Uttar Pradesh (including the new state of Uttaranchal). On the other hand, the majority of the villages of smaller states and most of the union territories have at least one school within their precincts. It is thus only in two states, namely Arunachal Pradesh and Himachal Pradesh, where an educational institution exists in less than 50 per cent of their villages. Such variations suggest a strong regional dimension of universalization of education in the country.

Primary and Middle Schools

'There are great variations with respect to the availability of government schools of different kinds in rural areas. Primary schools that are indisputably most essential for promoting education at the grass-root level are available in merely 73 per cent of the villages' (Singh, 2000, p. 13). But within the distance of 1 km, 94 per cent of the villages are provided with primary schools, as it appears from the annual report of the Ministry of Human Resource Development (1996–1997).

At the state level, there is considerable divergence in the distribution of primary schools. For instance, over 90 per cent of the villages of Goa, Gujarat, Haryana, Kerala, Maharashtra, Punjab and Tamil Nadu have got primary schools within the village itself. Next to these are the states of Andhra Pradesh, Assam, Karnataka, Madhya Pradesh, Mizoram, Nagaland, Sikkim, Tripura and West Bengal, which have recorded a higher percentage of villages with primary schools than the national average of about 13 per cent. On the other hand, the states of Arunachal Pradesh, Bihar, Himachal Pradesh, Manipur, Meghalaya, Orissa, Rajasthan and Uttar Pradesh are way behind in this regard, as they have recorded a much lower percentage of inhabited villages with primary schools (Census of India, 1997, p. 17). In such a situation, substantial variations in the level of literacy across the states are not really unusual.

Middle schools have been opened in only 19 per cent of the villages in the country. At the state level, the proportion of villages with this facility vary quite widely, that is, from more than 90 per cent in

Kerala to less than 10 per cent in West Bengal and Gujarat. Due to the amalgamation of middle schools with primary schools or at some places with secondary/matriculation schools, the number of villages with middle schools constitutes less than 1 per cent in certain states. The percentage of villages having middle schools in other states is less than 50 and in Bihar, Himachal Pradesh, Madhya Pradesh, Uttar Pradesh this distribution, however, varies from 10 per cent to 15 per cent. Among the smaller states, Goa has the maximum percentage, that is, almost 50 per cent villages enjoy the facility of middle schools followed by Mizoram (44%) and Sikkim (40%), whereas Arunachal Pradesh has recorded the lowest figure of 9 per cent. In the case of union territories, 71 per cent villages in Lakshadweep and more than 62 per cent villages in Daman & Diu are provided with primary and middle schools. In Andaman and Nicobar Islands, this facility was, however, available in 16 per cent of the villages only (Census of India, 1997, p. 17).

One of the most serious problems with primary and middle education is that a large number of such schools are being run either in dilapidated buildings or under the open sky. The Sixth All India Education Survey has revealed that of the total primary schools, only a little over 50 per cent of them are being run in brick-built structures and about one-tenth of them in the open areas. Innumerable are the government primary and middle schools in North India, particularly in Bihar, where the condition of schools is quite deplorable. They bear ample testimony to the gross apathy of the government towards education in general and educational institutions in particular (Singh, 2000, pp. 39–41). The teachers of the government schools often rue the lack of means and funds to run their schools. There is dearth not only of teaching materials and scientific instalments, but most of the schools have in fact no building of their own.

Moreover, those who possess it are no better either. The children take their lessons under the open sky or shades of the veranda of local people's houses. No less serious is the problem of general absence of teachers from their usual duty.

It has been reported through the print media many a times that the condition of some school buildings in Bihar is so bad that it is sheer luck that the pupils manage to get back home unscathed every day. The entire construction seems war-ravaged, with roof of some of the schools having caved in and others leaking from various places. The tilted walls threaten to give way any moment, while there is virtually nothing here that a school must possess. Situation in other parts of the rural areas of most Indian states may not be substantially different. The students have to sit on the floor which is often uneven and dusty. The teachers, too, do not get any better deal either. The furniture in the schools is virtually non-existent. Even the teachers have to arrange a chair for themselves. Fund is merely sanctioned for furniture and other necessary items. Therefore, the students and the teachers have to contribute whatever they can for the basic necessities such as registers and chalks. In addition, there are also schools without teachers. Some schools are being run on paper and the so-called teachers are regularly paid their salary for their sham work in sham schools. What has pushed the government schools into ruins is really hard to understand (Singh, 2000, pp. 39–41). Chauhan (1997, p. 3) has reported, 'In remote areas, half of the villages have no primary schools. As a result, one-fifth of the children in the 5–10 age group remain out of schools.'

Secondary and Higher/Senior Secondary Schools and Above

Higher level schools exist in approximately 8 per cent of the villages of the country. Thus, it is apparent that majority of the students are required to go to other villages or nearby towns to pursue education above the elementary level. At the state level also, except for Kerala (77%), not even one-fourth of the villages of any of the states are equipped with such schools. Among the smaller states and union territories such as Goa, Tripura, Delhi, Lakshadweep, Chandigarh and Daman & Diu, the proportion of villages having these schools are relatively better, as more than one-fourth of the villages are having these schools (Census of India, 1997, p. 17).

Only 1 per cent of the villages in India are having higher level educational institutions, namely junior college/higher secondary schools. The reason for meagre availability of higher level educational institutions in the village is quite obvious, these institutions are normally opened in urban areas and especially in medium or large towns. There cannot be one junior college or higher secondary school in every village because there cannot be enough students to run a secondary school or college at the level of one or two village(s).

Percentages of villages with senior secondary schools or junior colleges, degree colleges and also those with adult literacy centres and other training schools (including industrial training schools) are quite insignificant. Junior colleges (including higher/senior secondary schools) and degree colleges, as states before, are normally found in urban areas—especially in medium or large towns. However, in such states as Kerala, Gujarat, Madhya Pradesh, Punjab, Tamil Nadu and Uttar Pradesh, higher level institutions have been opened in rural areas as well, though in smaller proportions, that is, less than 1 per cent except in Kerala.

At the state level, Kerala tops the list among the states with little more than 5 per cent of its villages enjoying the facility of junior colleges including higher/senior secondary schools followed by Gujarat and Tamil Nadu with 3 per cent and Haryana, Karnataka, Madhya Pradesh, Punjab and Uttar Pradesh with about 2 per cent each. Among the smaller states, Tripura has the highest percentage, that is, 10 per cent followed by Goa and Sikkim. In the remaining states about 1 per cent of the village is having higher/senior secondary schools. Lakshadweep leads the list of union territories in respect of the availability of this facility.

Vocational Training Schools

A very small proportion of the villages in India have industrial training institutes and other training schools (that is, less than 1%), which include typing/shorthand and other vocational courses. At the state level, as regards industrial training schools, only in Kerala 5 per cent of its villages have this kind of institution. While in Assam, Orissa and other smaller states and union territories, not a single village has such an institution. As regards 'other' training schools, Dadra & Nagar Haveli is having somewhat better position as more than 73 per cent of the villages have such an institution. It is followed by Chandigarh (12%) and Kerala (7%).

Vocational training schools cannot be run at the level of individual village, as it may not get adequate number of students for running the institution properly. The rural people who are interested to receive vocational educational education tend to go to nearby towns for this purpose. And, therefore, all such training centres are located in towns and cities.

Adult Literacy Centres

In addition to primary education, the government has accorded special attention to adult education. With a view to promoting literacy among the adults, the Government of India in collaboration with the state governments started a programme of adult literacy throughout the country for all such people who could not be able to receive education in their childhood. But so far, only 7 per cent of the villages are covered under this programme. The success or the failure of the programme is not uniform across the states. Variations between the states are quite marked.

In such states as Andhra Pradesh, Gujarat, Rajasthan, Arunachal Pradesh and Tripura, about 20 per cent or more villages are covered under this programme, while the situation in Goa, Mizoram, West Bengal and Uttar Pradesh is more or less similar to the national-level situation. In all other states, including Kerala, adult literacy centres are not so prominent. Kerala is the only state where this scheme is hardly required in view of the already high level of literacy in the state. The programme of adult education is an important area where efforts are being made to make at least 75 per cent of the people literate in the 15–35 age group by 2005. Efforts are on, but the pace of attaining success is reported to be quite slow.

Only 4 per cent of the villages in India have access to other types of educational facilities, which are not covered under any of the aforementioned facilities, as noted in Table 4.1. These include non-formal or traditional kind of schooling such as Sanskrit Pathshala, Makhtab and senior basic schools. These institutions are found in most of the states, but their proportion, in comparison to the public educational institutions, is not very significant. For example, in Andhra Pradesh, Bihar, Kerala and Uttar Pradesh, the percentage of villages with other kinds of facilities for education vary between 5 and 9 per cent. Tripura is different from all the states in the country in the sense that non-formal kind of education is quite popular there. About 18 per cent of the villages in the state are served by such a system of education.

Physical Facilities

At the end of the discussion on infrastructure for schooling in rural areas, physical facilities of schools also need to be covered. Since the discussion at level of individual states, on the line of preceding discussion, would make the presentation cumbersome, available facts are touched upon briefly at the national level only. It is evident from one of the publications of the NCERT (1991) that the available physical facilities were quite inadequate in government-run schools. Quite often, schools had no facility to meet some of the basic needs such as drinking water, toilets and playground. Only 54 per cent of the rural schools could boast of having *pucca* buildings of their own. Of all such schools, 37 per cent could have only one room and only 45 per cent were provided with drinking water facility during 1986–1987. They often lacked the amenity of separate toilet facilities for girls. Of all the rural schools, merely 3 per cent could have separate urinals and 1 per cent separate lavatory for girls (see NCERT, 1991). In addition, about one-third of the primary schools could have only one teacher. Hardly is there any reason to imagine that this situation has undergone any drastic improvement by the turn of the 1990s.

VARIATIONS IN RURAL LITERACY BY STATES

As there are considerable variations concerning the availability of infrastructure, there also exist substantial variations with respect to the level of rural literacy in the state. The states of Andhra Pradesh, Arunachal Pradesh, Bihar, Orissa, Madhya Pradesh, Rajasthan, Meghalaya and Uttar Pradesh tend to show a lower level of rural literacy than the national average of about 45 per cent. On the other hand, the states of Goa, Gujarat, Himachal Pradesh, Kerala, Maharashtra, Manipur, Mizoram, Nagaland, Punjab, Sikkim, Tamil Nadu and Tripura have recorded a much higher level of rural literacy than the national average (see Table 4.3). The other states, which are not listed here, are those which are situated somewhere near the national average of literacy. Among the union territories, Dadra & Nagar Haveli have recorded a level of literacy lower than the national average and all other union territories have recorded more than 55 per cent of the level of

Table 4.3 *Level of Literacy in Rural India by Sex, 1991*

States/UT	Total	Male	Female	States/UT	Total	Male	Female
India[a]	44.7	57.9	30.6	Punjab	52.8	60.7	43.9
Andhra Pradesh	35.7	47.3	23.9	Rajasthan	30.4	47.6	11.6
Arunachal Pradesh	37.0	47.0	25.3	Sikkim	54.4	63.4	44.1
Assam	49.3	58.7	39.2	Tamil Nadu	54.6	67.2	41.8
Bihar	33.8	48.3	17.9	Tripura	56.1	67.1	44.3
Goa	72.3	81.7	62.9	Uttar Pradesh	36.7	52.1	19.0
Gujarat	53.1	66.8	38.6	West Bengal	50.5	62.1	38.1
Haryana	49.9	64.8	32.5	Union Territories			
Himachal Pradesh	61.9	73.9	49.8	Andaman & Nicobar			
Karnataka	47.7	60.3	34.8	Islands	69.7	76.0	62.0
Kerala	88.9	92.9	85.1	Chandigarh	59.1	65.7	47.8
Madhya Pradesh	35.9	51.0	19.7	Dadra & Nagar			
Maharashtra	55.5	69.8	41.0	Haveli	37.0	50.0	23.3
Manipur	55.8	67.6	43.3	Daman & Diu	61.6	75.2	46.7
Meghalaya	41.1	44.8	37.1	Delhi	66.9	78.5	52.2
Mizoram	72.5	77.4	67.0	Lakshadweep	78.9	88.7	68.7
Nagaland	57.2	63.4	50.4	Pondicherry	65.4	76.4	54.0
Orissa	45.5	60.0	30.8				

Source: Census of India, 1998, *Stale Profile, India* (Census of India, 1991), New Delhi: Office of the Registrar General, India, Ministry of Home Affairs, pp. 88–92.
Note: [a]Excluding Jammu and Kashmir where census was not held.

literacy. Here, it may be stated that the states and union territories, which have got predominantly tribal or Christian population, tend to record a higher level of literacy. Such states exhibit a lower amount of variations in the level of literacy by sex as well.

Here, it is not to be taken to mean that the availability of infrastructure alone can solve the problem of massive illiteracy in rural sector. Other factors too are accountable for a low level of literacy. There are numerous factors behind the low level of the slow-moving pace of literacy. Reasons obviously vary from region to region depending upon the local circumstances, but poverty and resource crunch at the disposal of states are certainly the most important reasons for such a state of affairs. Here, no effort is made to explain different socio-economic factors accountable for massive illiteracy in the country, as they have been discussed at a great length elsewhere by several social analysts such as Naik (1975), Tilak & Varghese (1990, pp. 24–59), Weiner (1991), Shariff & Ghosh (2000, pp. 1396–1404) and Singh (2000, pp. 39–41). While formulating different plans and policies for universalization of education, various social and economic factors hindering the process should be taken into account. Otherwise, it would be difficult for the government to achieve the goal of 'education for all', especially in rural areas.

BIHAR AND KERALA: A COMPARATIVE CONSPECTUS

By now, it has become quite obvious that there is a substantial divergence with respect to the availability of infrastructure and so also with respect to the level of literacy or the success of the programme of universal education across different states. With a view to explaining this reality, there is need to make a comparative analysis of two contrasting situations. Keeping this objective in view, a comparison is made between Kerala—a state characterized by the highest level of literacy (89%) on the one hand and Bihar (including the present state of Jharkhand)—a state characterized by the lowest level of literacy (34%) among all the states of the Indian Union, but for Rajasthan, on the other. The discussion is different factors accountable for divergence in the level of literacy. The discussion is brief also because a detailed comparison can form the theme of an independent research paper.

This comparison would show as to how the differing levels of bureaucratic efficiency, peoples' voluntary involvement, corruption in public life and historical circumstances account for differing levels of literacy between the states. Variations in these facts also account for differences in other areas of socio-economic development and various other demographic processes which are not discussed here. The relevant facts are placed thus.

In Bihar, there are about 53,000 primary (5,000 of them are closed for want of teachers and other reasons) and 15,000 middle schools, 25 per cent of them possess no buildings of their own and the rest of the schools are functioning in dilapidated structures (the government admitted this fact on the floor of the Bihar Assembly in July 2000 that 3,553 primary schools in the state have no building of their own). Under the New Education Policy, the government had once launched Operation Blackboard Scheme under which each primary school was to be provided material facilities and learning equipment besides two large rooms useful for all weathers and two teachers including a woman teacher selected from the local educated women, but the scheme was hardly implemented. The concerned officials of the state government have now conveniently forgotten that there was ever any operation blackboard scheme launched by the government to effect qualitative improvement in primary education in the state. At many places for want of school buildings, three or four schools are functioning in one school building.

What is strange is that over 80 per cent of the 53,000 primary schools in Bihar are functioning without headmasters. The state government is rarely worried to post headmasters in those primary schools despite repeated requests and protests from the Bihar State Primary Teachers Association. Similarly, 50 per cent of the middle schools in the state are functioning without headmasters and 35,000 posts of primary teachers have been lying vacant for a long time. Besides, over 6,000 primary schools are single-teacher schools. Under the situation, the schools have to remain closed when their teachers proceed on leave. The number of such single-teacher schools keeps moving up and down as a result of transfer of teachers from one school to another. The transfer of teacher from one school to another is reported to be a very lucrative business for the high government officials as well as politicians.

The state government once introduced mid-day meal to attract enrolment of children in the primary schools, but it soon became ineffective and defunct because of mismanagement. It is pity that the state government could lift only a little over 20 per cent of grains of its total allotment from the godown of the Food Corporation of India for distribution from 1995–1996 onwards. It was also stated on the floor of the State Assembly that the substantial amount of the grains went to the black market. Under the scheme, the students were not given cooked food; rather, raw wheat grain was given to them and that too after two–three months. At the same time, it was taken also by those who were not students in the school in connivance with the block officials. The teachers were not in a position to lodge complaint against such practice, for fear of unnecessary harassment by the block development officers. The sordid story of primary and middle-level schools does not end here. It should not be a matter of surprise that the teachers have to bribe the officials of the district education office for their promotion and other routine matters, including the payment of usual salary and retirement benefits. The officials discharge their duty only on some inducement. If any teacher tries to protest, they should be prepared to face the consequences in the form of their transfer, suspension, the loss of personal file, stoppage of payment of salary or pension on one pretext or the other.

The local people rarely protest against such a state of affairs in the field of education, because of the general lack of motivation for quality education. Those who are aware of this reality have taken it for granted that corruption is an accepted part of life now. Either people fighting against corruption are silenced by the corrupt elements or the highest officials are themselves so corrupt that they rarely take any cognizance of complaint against the corrupt officials. Hence, the local people are either indifferent or loath to give sincere support to the crusader, for they are either fearful of revenge or do not expect any worthwhile result. No doubt corruption is rampant throughout the country, but perhaps it is the most virulent and widespread in present-day Bihar. In addition to those stated before, other background factors have also been at work, adversely affecting the educational system in Bihar.

Now, we turn to the other side of the picture of elementary and middle-level education in the country. In this respect, the state of

Kerala, as noted before, is often cited as the best example. With respect to bureaucratic efficiency, per capita expenditure on education, infrastructural facilities at schools, work culture, people's awareness of their rights and corruption in public life, which together affect the quality of education, presents a totally different story—at least much in contrast with Bihar. In fact, Kerala is different from Bihar in so many ways (Singh, 1985). But there is no necessity of going into the details of those differences here.

When it is said that Kerala is a model of successful government policies in education, it is suggested that the government should try to raise its expenditure on education and consequently everything would naturally look after itself. Many experts, therefore, suggest to raise India's spending on education to 6 per cent of the GDP. When we delve deeper into Kerala's situation, it appears that Kerala's success story lay not in government policies alone but, to a large extent, in community action as well.

Historically, education in Kerala was provided to the masses using temples as centres of learning. At later stages, the rulers of Travancore and Cochin states gave considerable leadership in education (Zachariah, 1998, p. 78). However, the real spark for the spread of modern education commenced with the effort of Christian missionaries who set up the first modern, open-to-all schools in the old state of Travancore about a century ago. This spurred the Nairs led by Mannathu Padmanabhan on to set up a chain of community schools. Muslims and Ezhavas soon followed the example. Kerala's community initiatives also led to the popular reading room movement and consequently libraries were started even in the smallest villages. Official efforts were supplemented with private efforts.

After Independence, the Left parties unionized the teachers, brought all the private schools under the state control and forced the government to pay their regular salaries. However, even today, 65 per cent of Kerala's 12,400 schools are in private hands. The lesson from Kerala is that success in education comes through private and community intervention and not solely through the state intervention. Their best schools are in communities where parents are involved and parent–teachers associations are quite strong. Had the idea of community initiative been tried elsewhere through the gram shiksha samitis as in Madhya Pradesh and Andhra Pradesh or through NGOs in Bihar or other states, it would have made all the difference, despite hurdles from the inefficient bureaucracy.

Facts, as stated earlier, alone do not adequately explain the educational differential between Bihar and Kerala. Both the states differ quite significantly from each other in terms of their sociocultural heritage. The socio-economic system of Bihar has been such that it has always blunted the pace of social development in the state. In addition to differences in political systems, since long, the state of Bihar has been reeling under the semi-feudal system, while Kerala has been characterized by much greater social and economic equality and equity. A detailed discussion on this subject can be seen elsewhere (Nag, 1983; Singh, 1992, pp. 235–259).

SUGGESTIONS FOR UNIVERSALIZATION OF EDUCATION

Until now, our experience is that most state governments are highly inefficient in providing education to the people. The Indian state spends ₹2,000 per child per year for primary education, but a third of our children are still illiterate. The reform of Indian education has to begin with the conviction that schools have to become accountable to parents and neighbourhoods instead of to bureaucrats at the district headquarters or the state capital. The people have to fight for the autonomy of schools and make teachers accountable to parents.

Since the state has failed as a provider of education, its role should change to one of enablers. The state should completely get out of classroom teaching and NGOs, panchayats or private sector organizations should run schools and charge fees. The state should give parents, particularly to those belonging to the poorer or depressed sections of society, coupons worth ₹3,000 per child per year. Here, the central idea is to enhance competition among schools for quality education. If their neighbourhood school is bad, parents would be in a position to move their child to some other schools. Thus, schools would obviously compete for students and try to become innovative in providing better education. Parents will be economically empowered to choose right schools, teachers will be forced to become 'customer friendly' and the mission of providing education to all will be a great success. This may sound somewhat radical but the idea of putting parents in charge of the ₹3,000 per child per year is based on the fact that we spend that much money on education today. And, therefore, it is a sensible proposition.

Here, some might rightly argue that this system may not work well in those states, especially in some Hindi-speaking states, where corruption is well institutionalized in the bureaucratic system. In fact, this new system may help develop a vicious relationship between some teachers and guardians to grab the money coming through the government coupons at the cost of education of children. The unscrupulous government officials can readily create fake schools, teachers and guardians on papers to grab the coupon money. No system can be fully free from some loopholes for unscrupulous elements of society. Hence, no programme can have a success unless the government agencies are candidly committed to the cause of common people. A fairly reasonable amount of integrity and sincerity on the part of the state machinery is a sine qua non for the success of any programmes and policy.

CONCLUSION

It is a quite difficult, if not impossible, task for the government to provide necessary facilities for providing education to all in rural areas. The problem of universal education steadily looms larger with the passage of time, following addition of an increasingly greater number of illiterates to the existing vast size of population in the country as a consequence of rapidly rising population. There were about 628.7 million people living in over 634,000 villages according to the 1991 census. The population of rural India grew from 298.6 million in 1951 to 628.7 million in 1991, recording an average annual exponential growth rate of over 3 per cent. It means that the rural population was doubled in four decades, despite the fact that a large number of rural people migrated to urban areas in search of employment or a better living condition. They comprised about three-fourths of the total population of India in 1991. It is estimated that there would be around 721 million people in rural areas, constituting about 71 per cent of the total population in 2001. It is, therefore, very difficult task for a poor and slow developing country like India to mobilize enough resources to meet the educational needs of such a rapidly growing population. Rapid rise in population has been one of the important reasons why the government could not fulfil the constitutional obligations of providing compulsory and free education to all children in the 6–14 age group by 1960. For a similar reason, the country also failed in its programme of 'Education For All by 2000'.

The latest target of making 75 per cent of India's population literate by 2005, through the much-publicized ambitious programme of Sarva Shiksha Abhiyan launched in 2000, is yet another populist plan of the government. This too is going to end in fiasco for the aforesaid reasons. It is indeed a herculean task for any government to make a big stride towards the goal of 'education for all' within a period of five years from now. In view of the poor infrastructure for education in rural areas, as it is obvious from what has been discussed earlier, it would be still more difficult—perhaps insurmountable—in case of rural areas. This is in no way a pessimistic view; rather, it is a harsh reality that we all should be prepared to admit under the given circumstances.

REFERENCES

Census of India (1991), *Availability of Infrastructural Facilities in Rural areas of India: An Analysis of Village Directory Data* (Office of the Registrar General and Census Commissioner, India, New Delhi. 1997).

Census of India (1991), *State Profile 1991, India,* (Office of the Registrar General and Census Commissioner) India, New Delhi. 1999.

Freire, P. (1972), *Pedagogy of the Oppressed,* London: Penguin.

Government of India (1999), *Expert Group Report on Financial Requirements for Making Elementary Education a Fundamental Right,* Ministry of Human Resources Development, Department of Education, New Delhi.

King, E. M. & Hill, M. A. (eds.) (1993), *Women's Education in Developing Countries: Barriers, Benefits and Policies,* Baltimore: The Hopkins University Press for the World Bank.

McDougal, Lori (2000), "Gender Gap in Literacy in Uttar Pradesh (Questions for Decentralised Educational Planning)", *Economic and Political Weekly,* 35 (19), May, 6–12: 1640–1658.

Ramachandran, V. K., Rawal, Vikash & Swaminatban, Madhura (1997), "Investment Gaps Primary Education: A Statewise Study", *Economic and Political Weekly,* 32 (12) January: 4–11.

Saldanha, Denzil (1999), "Residual Illiteracy and Uneven Development-Ill: Performance of Literacy Campaigns and Prospects", *Economic and Political Weekly*, 34 (29) July, 17–23: 2019–2033.

Shariff, Abusaleh & Ghosh, P. K. (2000), Indian Education Scene and the Public Gap, *Economic and Political Weekly*, 35 (16) April, 15–21: 1396–1404.

Shariff, Abusaleh (1999), *Indian Human Development Report: A Profile of Indian States in the 1990s,* New Delhi: Oxford University Press.

Singh, J. P. (2000), "The Problem of Illiteracy in Bihar", *Yojana*. 44 (3): 39–41.

Singh, J. P. (2000), "The State of Development in Rural India: An Overview", *Kurukshetra,* June: 12–18.

Tilak, J. B. G. & Varghese, N. V. (1990), "Resources for Education for All", *Journal of Education and Social Change,* 4 (4) January-March: 24–59.

UNDP (1990), *Human Development Report 1990,* New York: Oxford University Press.

United Nations Development Project (UNDP) (1999), *Human Development Report 1999,* New York: Oxford University Press.

Visaria, Leela & Visaria, Pravin (1998), "India's Population in Transition" in *Studies in Social Demography (Ed.),* New Delhi: M D Publications.

Weiner, Myron (1991), The *Child and the State in India: Child Labour and Education Policy in Comparative Perspective,* Delhi: Oxford University Press.

World Bank (1990). "Primary Education: A World Bank Policy Paper", Washington, DC: World Bank.

World Bank (1997), *India: Achievements and Challenges in Reducing Poverty,* Washington, DC: World Bank.

Chapter 5

The Right of Children to Free and Compulsory Education Act, 2009*

The Story of a Missed Opportunity

Muchkund Dubey

The Right to Free and Compulsory Education Bill, 2009, was enacted into law after it was passed by both the Houses of the Indian Parliament and signed by the president of India. Its main purpose is to provide free and compulsory education for children in the age group of 6 to 14 years (GoI, 2009). There have been extensive debates on the extent to which this Act will help in implementing the right to education as provided in Article 21-A of the Indian Constitution (GoI, 2008a). What has been ignored in the discussions is that the Act misses the excellent opportunity provided to the nation for bringing about a radical transformation of the school education system in India.

While discussing the problems of school education in India, a few issues are repeatedly raised: absence of teachers from schools, lack of interest on the part of the parents or guardians, deficiencies in curriculum and syllabus, wrong methods of teaching and so on. But these problems cannot be viewed in isolation and in a fragmented fashion. For their roots are spread deep in the entire system. Therefore, if one wants to solve these problems, then it would be necessary to

---

* *Social Change:* March 2010: Vol. 40, No. 1, 1–13.

transform the entire education system. What are the systemic and fundamental problems of the Indian school education system?

ACCESS

First, there is the problem of access. School education is simply unavailable to the vast number of children in the country. During the last few decades, there has been significant progress in improving enrolment. Gross enrolment ratio (GER) from Class I to VIII was 94.9 per cent and from Class I to XII, 77 per cent (GoI, 2008b). The Government primarily relies on GER to bolster its claim for progress made in expanding school education in India. But enrolment is a very unreliable basis for assessing the degree of access to school education. First, enrolment figures are generally rigged and exaggerated for various administrative and political purposes. Moreover, in order to assess the progress in expanding school education, it is important to take into account the figures for attendance and also for dropouts from among those who are enrolled. The attendance has generally been found to be at least 25 per cent below enrolment. The dropout rates are exorbitantly high. For the country as a whole, the dropout rate from Class I to X was 61.6 per cent; and in a state like Bihar it was above 75 per cent. Among those who dropout, the percentage of children belonging to Scheduled Castes in the country as a whole was 70.6 and of the Scheduled Tribes was 78.5. In Bihar, the figure was close to 90 per cent for both the categories (Government of Bihar, 2007). The net result is that a sizeable percentage, as much as 30 per cent, of children in the school-going age in India are out of school; the percentage is as high as 50 in Bihar (15 million out of 30 million children in the school-going age group). Upto 13 per cent of habitations have no schools even at the primary level (NCERT, 2005).

Thus, a huge number of children are excluded from school education. This is a colossal waste of human resources. Besides, educational exclusion is the worst form of exclusion because it means exclusion from other walks of life and areas of activities such as livelihood, knowledge, status in society and human dignity. Moreover,educational exclusion becomes cumulative as it is carried over from generation to generation, for it is seen that educated parents are more inclined to educate theirchildren than those who are uneducated. Besides, exclusion from school education, particularly at the primary level, is a denial of human rights both in accordance with the provision in the Indian Constitution and the relevant provision of the Universal Declaration of Human Rights (UNO, 1948).

The Act sets no dateline for the universalization of education from Class I to VIII. Different datelines have been given for different purposes, which are not mutually consistent and, in the absence of any plan or resources required for achieving them, it is doubtful that they would be adhered to. The most important dateline is in Section 6 of the Act which states:

> For carrying out the provisions of this Act, appropriate government and local authority shall establish, within such area or limits of neighborhood as may be prescribed, a school, where it is not so established, within a period of three years from the commencement of this Act.

It is further stated that teachers will acquire the requisite qualification and prescribed training within a period of five years. At another place, it is laid down that pupil–teacher ratio of 40:1, prescribed in the Act, will be achieved within six months. Does this mean that all the teachers required, even though they are not qualified, will be recruited within six months? Is it feasible at all? Even if it is so, but if the schools are not there, where will they teach? This provision also implies that pupil–teacher ratio could be maintained at least until the next five years, by continuing the practice of appointing para-teachers or untrained teachers. The Act makes no estimate of the additional number of schools to be built, additional number of teachers to be recruited and trained, and training institutions to be created and restored. This has all been left to be determined by the appropriate government and local authority. The way the government machinery functions, it is doubtful if these tasks would be accomplished within the specified time limits. All this should have been done and additional financial requirement should have been calculated and provided for before moving the Bill in the Parliament. In the absence of the fulfillment of these requirements, the attainment of targets set in the Act and of the overall goal of universalization appears highly improbable.

The Common School System Commission, Bihar, in its report, estimated that in order to universalize free and compulsory education for children in the age group of 5 to 14 in five years, universalize education for children from Class IX to X in eight years and to facilitate transit to Class XI to XII of 70 per cent of those who will pass Class X, in nine years, 25,900 additional primary schools, 15,500 middle schools and 19,100 secondary schools will have to be built. The number of additional teachers to be recruited for achieving the aforementioned goals would be 255,000 at the primary level, 324,000 at the middle level and 429,000 at the secondary level (Government of Bihar, 2007). It stands to reason that the very first and the most essential requirement to be fulfilled for universalizing quality school education is to build these additional schools, recruit these additional teachers and provide training for them. As already stated, the Act does not make any attempt to quantify these requirements.

QUALITY

The second systemic problem of school education in India is its abysmally poor quality. This has been attributed to a variety of factors, including poor curriculum and syllabus, deficient pedagogy, negligent teachers and parents who are unconcerned. But the real reason is the gross under-funding of school education in India. If the required magnitude of funding is available, many of the factors allegedly accountable for the poor quality of school education would disappear. For example, it is unfair to blame teachers who are compelled to teach in a school which does not have blackboards, teaching aids, laboratories for experiment and adequate space, and which do not provide facilities or incentives for improving their skills and environment and for pedagogic innovation. Besides, as the required number of teachers is not in place, the norm of at least one teacher per class is not observed and the practice of multigrade teaching is continuing. Moreover, a large number of teachers have no training. They are also obliged to carry out non-educational activities. The members of the Common School System Commission, Bihar, during their visits to schools, did not find any school which had a properly functioning laboratory. Thus, we simply cannot get away from the fact that the quality of school education in India is decisively influenced by the quantity or the magnitude of funding.

The most effective and important means of ensuring quality is to establish minimum norms and standards relating to all relevant aspects of school education and ensure that they are applied uniformly to all schools. No doubt, some norms have been laid down in the Schedule attached to the Right to Free and Compulsory Education Act. But they are utterly inadequate. There is no mention in the Schedule of a number of some extremely important norms, such as distance of the school from the habitation of the child, sitting area in sq. meters per child, number of children per school, number of classes per school, furniture in the class and office rooms, teaching aides, computers, equipment in a laboratory, the qualification and training of teachers, scales of their pay and allowances, and other conditions of service, including scope for promotion. Some norms are mentioned in the Act only as items, and against them is written the phrase 'as the government may determine'. This means that these norms will not be justiciable and may never be established. It also implies that the present practice of recruitment of para-teachers and the multigrade teaching may continue. In the absence of adequate and legally enforceable norms, it is superfluous to talk about quality.

FINANCIAL IMPLICATION

The main reason for a large proportion of the children remaining out of school and the poor quality of education in schools is the under-funding of school education. Normally, the Act should have provided a financial memorandum which should have indicated the exact amount of resources required for giving effect to the Act. But this has not been done. The position of the government is that 'it is not possible to quantify the financial requirement on this account at this stage.' This statement is not correct. In the last 10 years or so, additional resources required for providing free and compulsory education to children in different age groups have been estimated several times in the country.

Two expert groups set up by the Government of India and the Common School System Commission, Bihar, laid down norms and standards for providing quality education, put price tags on these norms and standards and, on that basis, calculated the additional cost to be incurred for providing free and compulsory education and universalizing school education, within a time-bound framework. The two expert groups set up by the Government of India confined themselves to providing free and compulsory education to children in age group of 6 to 14 years. The Expert Group under the chairmanship of Professor Tapas Mazumdar, set up by the Government of India in 1999 (GoI, 1999), estimated an additional cost of ₹137,000 million per annum over the next 10 years for providing free and compulsory elementary education according to the norms prescribed by it. The Expert Group set up by a Committee of the Consultative Advisory Board on Education (CABE) estimated in 2005 a total additional cost of approximately ₹730,000 million per annum over the next six years for achieving the same goal. The Bihar Commission report which covered the entire school education from one year of pre-primary to Class XII, estimated an additional expenditure of ₹99,500 million for the first year of the nine-year implementation period. Although this amount is not the average for the nine years, it is a good broad indication of the additional estimated expenditure per annum. The non-implementation of the recommendation of the expert group led by Professor Tapas Mazumdar resulted in a cumulative gap reflected in a manifold increase in the additional expenditure calculated in 2004 to be incurred for achieving broadly the same purpose. If the recommendation of the second expert group also remains un-implemented, as has been the case until now, then the cumulative gap will grow further and, say, in 10 years from now, we would need an astronomically large sum of resources for universalizing elementary education. Perhaps at that time, the government in power will raise its hand in despair and drop the whole idea of universalization, and India will continue to stagnate for years to come at a low level of school education, both quantitatively and qualitatively, to the detriment of its unity and future development.

Perhaps the assumption in the Act regarding resources is that those available for the Sarva Shiksha Abhiyan (SSA) in the 11th Five Year Plan would suffice to meet the resources required. But the fact is that in spite of these resources having been nearly doubled in the 11th Plan as compared to the 10th Plan, they are at the level of about ₹300,000 million per annum, which is less than half of the ₹730,000 million per annum of additional resources required, according to the Expert Group of the CABE Committee (2005). Even under an assumption of higher pupil–teacher ratio, the additional resources required per annum, calculated by this Expert Group, is ₹535,000 million per annum, which is much higher than ₹300,000 million.

India's National Education Policy (GoI, 1992) lays down the goal of setting aside at least 6 per cent of GDP for expenditure on education. This target, originally recommended by the Kothari Commission (GoI, 1966), has also found place in the manifestos of almost all major political parties. But the maximum share of GDP devoted to education in India has been close to 4 per cent and, on most occasions, the ratio has been around 3 per cent. The Minister for Human Resource Development has recently conceded that the resources gap is huge, particularly when we consider the fact that in many advanced and several of the more developed among developing countries, expenditure on education is 10 per cent or above of the GDP. He has expressed the view that only the private sector can fill in the gap. He has, therefore, made a plea for public–private partnership in education.

Although public–private partnership in education has been talked about for the last few years, the progress in this direction has been negligible. Even otherwise, the record of the private sector in meeting the demand for school education is not all that impressive. About 89.1 per cent of the primary schools in India were in the public sector (government and local body) and only 10.9 per cent in the private sector; for upper primary schools, the percentage was 72 to 78, respectively (GoI, 2008b). The enrolment from Class I to VII/VIII was 72.23 per cent in government schools and only 27.61 per cent in private schools (NUEPA, 2009). In the case of Bihar, the contribution of the private sector to school education at the elementary level, in terms of number of schools as well as percentage of enrolment, is below 6 per cent (Government of Bihar, 2007).

If after 60 years of Independence, the private schools have filled in a gap of only a little over 10 per cent, so far as the total number of primary schools are concerned, there can be no assurance that they will be able to contribute significantly to providing free and compulsory education to children in the age group of 6–14 years and to universalizing secondary education. At the current rate of their contribution, and if the state does not step in to cover the gap, we may have to wait till the end of the century for universalizing school education in India and even then it may not come about. It may take even longer to universalize secondary education, because the number of additional schools to be constructed and additional teachers to be recruited at this level is many times higher than those required for universalizing elementary education. Besides, school education is a social good, the provision of which is the responsibility of the state. The provision of free and compulsory education is now a fundamental right available to children in the age group of 6–14 years. It is incumbent upon the state to ensure this right with immediate effect. It is legally and morally untenable for it to make the fulfillment of this right conditional upon the contribution of the private sector.

DISCRIMINATION

The third systemic problem of education in India is the rampant discrimination characterizing it. Children of the rich and the elite have access to good quality private and special types of public schools, whereas children of the vast majority of the poor, including the minorities and marginalized groups, go to government schools which are in shambles. Thus, the class division in the society is carried over to the school system. This has been a major contributory factor to the perpetuation and accentuation of social inequality. It also makes for bad education. Empirical studies have demonstrated that schools which bring in children from different communities and classes provide better education and even the children of the rich and the elite stand to benefit from such a school system.

The Right to Education Act perpetuates the multi-layer discriminating school system in India. It legalizes the currently operating four categories of schools in the country: (a) government schools, (b) aided private schools, (c) special category schools and (d) non-aided private schools. According to the Act, the government schools will provide compulsory and free education to all children in the age group of 6–14 years admitted therein, and the aided private schools will provide such education in such proportion of children admitted therein as its annual recurring aid or grant bears to its recurring annual expenses, subject to a minimum of 25 per cent. The special category schools and non-aided private schools shall admit in Class I, to the extent of at least 25 per cent of the strength of that class, children belonging to weaker section or disadvantaged group in the neighbourhood and provide free and compulsory elementary education till its completion. These last two categories of schools will be reimbursed expenditure so incurred by them to the extent of per-child expenditure incurred by the state, or the actual amount charged from the child, whichever is less.

These provisions, apart from perpetuating the present multi-layer system of schools, are in violation of Article 21A which calls for the provision of free and compulsory education to all children in the age group of 6 to 14 years. However, 75 per cent of the children in this age group in aided private schools will not be provided free and compulsory education. In the last two categories of schools, the children in this age group admitted therein, but not belonging to disadvantaged or weaker groups, will not be provided free and compulsory education and for these groups also, only 25 per cent of the children will be provided free and compulsory education in these schools. This also is a violation of Article 21A.

There were two ways in which the government could have significantly mitigated, if not eliminated, the discrimination characterizing the Indian school education system. The first was by establishing exhaustive and justifiable norms and standards, and applying them rigorously to all schools, both public and private, and second, by embracing and enforcing the concept of neighbourhood schools whereby the state would have delineated the neighbourhood for each school, which would have been required by law to admit and educate till completion, all the children residing in the neighbourhood. In India, we have advocates of freedom of choice and freedom of profession who argue that the concept of neighbourhood school militates against the exercise of these freedoms. They forget that this concept has been applied for decades, if not centuries, in countries where democracy has taken firmer roots and where freedom is valued much more than in our country. I shall illustrate this by a personal example. When I was posted in New York in the early 1970s, I had to send my two children to a public school there. Since I stayed on the 89th Street and 1st Avenue in New York, I was told that my children could go only to the nearest public school which was on the 96th Street and 2nd Avenue. This location is on the fringe of Harlem which was known for its high incidence of crime and drug addiction. But I had no choice but to send my children to this school. This was according to the law of the city and nobody complained that it was in violation of their fundamental rights. Apparently, individual rights cannot take precedence over the public purpose enshrined in the Constitution, of ensuring social equality. There is no reference to the concept of neighbourhood school in the Right to Education Act, except that there is a provision for making reservation of 25 per cent of the seats for children of weaker and disadvantaged groups coming from the neighbourhood. This is a far cry from the concept of neighbourhood schools as practised in most developed countries and a number of developing countries which have a common school system.

EDUCATION REPLACED BY LITERACY

Another systemic malady which has afflicted school education in India is the transformation of the very nature and meaning of education, brought about by the forces of globalization and liberalization in which international agencies have played no small role. In most developing countries, including India, education has to a large extent been replaced by literacy for which it is strictly not necessary to go to schools. According to the new paradigm, education is defined in functional terms, that is, making the recipient qualified for the marketplace. In this sense, educational system as a whole has been commodified. Today, the purpose of school education is merely imparting skills of literacy and numeracy. The basic philosophical purpose of education is to enhance the capacity of the children to comprehend, to discern, to contest what, according to them, is wrong, and to develop the urge to transform what is wrong and unjust. These philosophical goals have been set aside and replaced by the functional goal of meeting the demand of the market. Under the globalization/liberalization paradigm, schools have to a large extent been replaced by literacy and informal centres, trained teachers have been replaced by para-teachers and the system of at least one teacher for every class and for every important subject has been replaced by multigrade teaching. Training is no longer regarded as essential for teaching. The Government of Bihar officially notified in 1991 that training was no longer necessary as a qualification for appointment as a teacher. This whole process of the distortion of the meaning and purpose of education started systematically since the mid-1980s and has by now been completed.

This transformation of the nature of education has seriously affected its quality and has relegated to the background the concept of schooling as a means of socialization, nation building and formation of social capital, which has been practised for centuries by important developed countries. It has also been used to rationalize non-universalization of school education and its under-funding. The Right to Education Act does not make any provision for reversing the process of the distortion of the meaning and purpose of education.

A HOLISTIC VIEW OF SCHOOL EDUCATION

The Right to Education Act should have covered the entire school education system including one or two years of pre-primary education, elementary education (i.e., the age group of 6 to 14 years which is its present coverage) and secondary education. The distinction between pre-primary, elementary and secondary education may be valid from the peadagogic point of view, but this distinction becomes arbitrary when it comes to guaranteeing right of education, universalizing school education, ensuring its quality and removing discrimination. There are strong reasons for providing free and compulsory education, preferably for two years, and at least for one year at the pre-primary level, and also for universalizing secondary education. A Group of Experts which met at UNESCO Headquarters at the end of 2007, of which I happened to be a member, arrived at the consensus that 'basic education should consist of at least nine years after pre-primary and ideally it should extend to 12 years.' In most of the advanced developing countries such as China, Mexico, South Africa, Brazil, Thailand and Indonesia, the task of universalizing elementary education was accomplished a long time ago and the current pre-occupation of the educational planners and policymakers is for universalizing quality secondary education.

Depriving the children in the age group of, say, 4 to 6 years, of free and compulsory education as the Right to Education Act does is totally arbitrary and a flagrant denial of human rights. Article 45 of the Indian Constitution directed the state to provide free and compulsory education up to the age of 14 years, which included children at the preprimary level of education (GoI, 2008a). The famous Unnikrishnan judgement which regarded the right to education as a part of the right to life also covered children up to the age of 14 years.

However, when the 86th amendment to the Indian Constitution was enacted in the form of Article 21A, the government arbitrarily— almost by a sleight of hand— excluded children in the age group of 0 to 6 years from the ambit of the amendment. Thus, some 170 million children were disenfranchised of their right to free and compulsory education. However, this right still exists because the amended version of Article 45 states: 'The State shall endeavor to provide early childhood care and education for all children until they complete the age of 6 years.' If this is read with Article 21, as was done in the Unnikrishnan judgement, then the children in the age group of 0–6 years also enjoy the fundamental right to free and compulsory education.

The Integrated Child Development Services (ICDS) (GoI, 2009) is the only program me which provides for education to children in the age group of 0 to 6 years, but access to services under ICDS is neither a universal nor a legal right. ICDS covers only 42 per cent of the children in the relevant age group. Besides, it is not a right but a service voluntarily offered by the state. Evidence shows that a good percentage of the children covered by the ICDS are not enrolled under it. Besides, the delivery of prescribed services to those who are enrolled is irregular and inadequate. The education component of the ICDS is the most neglected service. It is either not delivered at all or only partially delivered. A social audit of the functioning of the ICDS in the district of Anantapur in Andhra Pradesh recently carried out by the Council for Social Development bears out these facts. The foundations of our educational system will remain weak until quality pre-primary education is provided to children in the age group of 4 to 6 years. Denial of the right to education at the pre-primary level will hamper our efforts to develop human resources in the country.

The Act should have provided for the universalization of secondary education also that is, for children in the age group of 15–18 years. The definition of a child according to the UN Convention on Child

Rights includes children up to the age of 18 years. India is a party to this Convention. Moreover, the universalization of education at this level is also a logical consequence of universalizing education up to Class VIII because, if secondary education is not universalized, then the children who complete Class VIII would have nowhere to go except dropping out. For, according to regulations in force in the country, a child has to pass Class XII for getting entry into any institution of higher or technical education which can qualify them for entering the job market.

It was in view of these considerations that in the Report of the Common School System Commission, Bihar (2007), a single legislation was recommended covering school education from one year at the pre-primary level to Class XII. The report also prescribed separate norms and standards for the three levels of school education, that is pre-primary, elementary and secondary. Although most of the norms are common to these three levels, there are also significant differences. The Right to Education Act, therefore, should have covered the entire school education system, universalizing education from pre-primary to higher secondary level, providing free education from pre-primary to at least Class VIII, if not Class IX and X, and applying norms for ensuring quality and equity to all schools at all the three levels of school education.

LANGUAGE POLICY

The Right to Education Act should have also included a language policy which would have provided the best opportunity for the flowering of the talents of the children and which, at the same time, would have been a major factor for uniting the country. Unfortunately, the government missed this opportunity. The legislation has no language policy. It only states in one of the clauses that 'medium of instruction shall, as far as practicable be in child's mother tongue.' The inclusion of the phrase 'as far as practicable' will give a *carte blanche* to private schools even at the elementary level to continue their present practice of giving instructions through the medium of English. Moreover, the term 'mother tongue' is not defined. For example, for a child coming from the Maithili-speaking region, will the mother tongue be Maithili or Hindi?

The enactment of the legislation also provided an excellent opportunity to make a beginning with the implementation of the three-language formula recommended by the Kothari Commission and included in the National Education Policy. But this opportunity has also been squandered. The language policy laid down in Annexure II to the legislation recommended by the Common School System Commission, Bihar, demonstrates that the implementation of the three-language formula is feasible, if there is a political will to do so.

STATUTORY COMMISSION FOR SCHOOL EDUCATION

Finally, the Act should have created a mechanism vested with the overall responsibility of overseeing progress in the restructuring of school education, bringing about improvements, through research and public discussion, in the norms and standards included in the Act, adjudicating disputes where called upon to do so and being the Court of Last Appeal so far as the implementation of the Act is concerned. This would have been possible only by establishing a fully empowered judicial or quasi-judicial Commission. The government seems to be very keen to set up such a commission for higher education, which is perhaps needed and for which there is considerable public support. However, such a commission is needed equally, if not more importantly, for school education. In lieu of this, the Act provides for the establishment of central as well as state advisory councils. This is hardly likely to serve the purpose. Such advisory councils are vested with very limited powers. Their membership is in the nature of patronage or favour bestowed by political leaders and, in most cases, their advice is seldom sought or sought only as a public relations and politically motivated exercise.

POLICY RECOMMENDATIONS

The implicit policy recommendations in the aforementioned paragraphs can be summarized as follows:

1. For the nation as a whole and for each state, a plan for achieving universalization of school education, within a time-bound framework, should be drawn up. The time limit should not exceed

five years for children up to the age of 14 years, because education in the age group 6 to 14 years has become a fundamental right.

2. Education has to be free and compulsory for the children in the age group of 6 to 14 years, according to Article 21A. There is a strong reason for its becoming so for at least one year at the pre-primary level and also for the children in the age group of 15 to 16 years.

3. Detailed, specific and legally enforceable norms and standards should be established to ensure both quality and equity in school education.

4. An annual plan should be prepared and implemented for building schools, recruiting teachers, providing teacher training, expanding and upgrading teacher training institutes and applying other norms and standards.

5. A price tag should be put on each norm, which should be the basis for calculating the additional expenditure to be incurred for revamping the school education system of India.

6. There should be a legal requirement both for applying the norms and standards, and for providing the resources for this purpose. These resources should be one of the first charges on the budget of the central and the state governments on par with expenditure for the implementation of other fundamental rights.

7. School education should be based on the concept of neighbourhood schools whereby the state should declare the neighbourhood for each school, which should be required by law to admit and educate till completion, all the children in the required age group residing in the neighbourhood.

8. A high-level mechanism in the form of a statutory commission should be set up which should be vested with the responsibility for overseeing progress in school education, for being the last court of appeal, for adjudicating where called upon to do so and for improving, through research and public discussion, the norms and standards.

A school system based on the aforementioned parameters is called the common school system. It has been practised by almost all developed nations around the globe. In India, there has been no interest in building such a school system, mainly because of the influence in policy-making of the elitist class which manages to send its children to high fee-charging private schools and special category schools.

A deliberate attempt is being made, mainly by the private school lobbies, to spread the canard that such a system does not permit the running of private schools and therefore imposes uniformity and prevents experimentation and innovation so far as curriculum, syllabus and pedagogy are concerned. This is far from the truth. The fact is that there is full scope for the existence and even expansion of private schools in a common school system, subject to the condition that they, like government schools, must also apply the norms and standards legally laid down and subject themselves to inspection by the agents of the high-level commission on school education. The private schools have to provide free and compulsory education at least to the children in the age group 6 to 14 years. It should be clear that their function essentially is to provide good education which does not leave scope for making profit and that, in the ultimate analysis, the responsibility for universalizing equitable and quality education rests squarely on the state.

Seen in the light of the what has been discussed earlier, several of the measures adopted or announced by the government recently for improving access to and quality of school education are redundant and designed to serve mainly political purposes. They are also devices to distract attention from the systemic problems. For example, if the norm to build a primary school at a distance of a kilometer from the habitation of children, a middle school at a distance of 3 km and a secondary school at a distance of 5 km is applied, there is no need to build hostels, including for children of the minority and the marginalized groups.

If school education is provided free of cost in the comprehensive sense of the term, there would be less need to provide scholarships. If the principle of neighbourhood is applied, reservation of a particular percentage of seats for the children of the poor households in private schools is not necessary because the private schools will have to admit all the children from the neighbourhood and provide free and compulsory education according to the legal provisions made by the state. It is for the state to work out in consultation with the private schools the basis of burden sharing. Similarly, if the norms and standards are strictly applied with the provision of adequate resources for this purpose, it will no longer be necessary to establish model schools on a selective basis, because all the nearly 12 lakh schools in the system would become model schools and not only 6,000, that is, one model school for each block, as proposed by the prime minister of India.

REFERENCES

CABE. (2005). *Report of the Central Advisory Board of Education (CABE) Committee on Free and Compulsory Education Bill and Other Issues Related to Elementary Education.* New Delhi. Retrieved from http://www.education.nic.in/cabe/Fcebill.pdf

Government of Bihar (2007). *Report of the Common School System Commission.* Patna: Government of Bihar.

Government of India (1966). *Report of the Education Commission 164–66.* New Delhi: Ministry of Education.

Government of India (1992). National Policy on Education, 1986 (As modified in 1992), Ministry Human Resource Development, New Delhi.

Government of India (1999). Expert group report on financial requirements for making elementary education a fundamental right, (Mimeo), New Delhi: Ministry of Human Resource Development.

Government of India (2008a). *The Constitution of India.* New Delhi: Ministry of Law and Justice.

Government of India (2008b). *Educational Statistics at a Glance 2005–06.* New Delhi: Ministry of Human Resource Development.

Government of India (2009). *The Right of Children to Free and Compulsory Education Act, 2009.* New Delhi: Ministry of Human Resource Development.

Government of India (2009). Integrated Child Development Services (ICDS) Scheme, New Delhi: Ministry of Women and Child Development, http://wcd.nic.in/icds.htm

NCERT. (2005). *Seventh All India Education Survey.* New Delhi: NCERT.

NUEPA. (2009). *DISE Flash Statistics 2007–08, Elementary Education in India, Progress towards UEE.* New Delhi: National University of Educational Planning and Administration.

UNO. (1948). *Universal Declaration of Human Rights, Adopted and Proclaimed by General Assembly resolution 217 A (III) of 10 December 1948.* Retrieved from http://www.un.org/events/humanrights/2007/hrphotos/declaration%20_eng.pdf

UNESCO. (2007). *Experts' Consultation on the Operational Definition of Basic Education,* Paris, 17–18 December.

Chapter 6
Universalization of Secondary Education*

Rounaq Jahan

My perspective is shaped by my own experiences in Bangladesh where we face many challenges similar to those of India. In some areas, we have undertaken innovative initiatives which have addressed specific obstacles and yielded positive results, such as the introduction of stipends for girls which resulted in the rapid expansion of girls' enrolment in secondary schools. The enrolment of girls increased from 442,000 in 1994 to over 1 million by 2001 (Bhatnagar, Dewan, Torres, & Kanungo, 2018). As a result, Bangladesh achieved gender parity in enrolment in secondary schools. In fact, there are now more girls than boys enrolled in secondary schools. The ratio of girls to boys changed from approximately 45:55 in 1994 to 55:45 in 2001 (Bhatnagar et al., 2018).

But expanding school enrolment with quality education remains a big challenge for us, as is the case in India. We too have seen the gradual development of disparity between public schools delivering poor quality education to children from low-income households and private schools providing better quality education to children from upper-income households. We also have the divide between vernacular-medium schools and English-medium schools which are now attracting

* *Social Change:* March 2019: Vol. 49, no. 1: 144–53.

This chapter was based on the inaugural address presented at the national seminar on the Universalisation of Secondary Education organized by the Council for Social Development in July 2018.

students not simply from upper-middle-income households but from middle and lower-income households. We have the added challenge of the rapid expansion of madrasa education where children from extremely poor households go because they can get free room and board. We face similar challenges of governance—lack of monitoring and accountability. Absenteeism of teachers, despite increase in salary, is a persistent problem. Professional bodies such as teachers' associations are preoccupied with demands for increasing teachers' salaries and do not pay much attention to issues concerning the improvement of quality of education.

However, despite our past experiences of being disappointed with the inadequacies of public policy responses, we still look forward to policies and actions from the state to address the myriad problems we face in the education sector. After all, in a democracy such as India and Bangladesh, citizens should be able to reasonably expect that public policies and actions will be geared towards improving the quality of education for the majority of the electorate. So some of the recent initiatives of the Government of India such as the Right to Education Act, Rashtriya Madhyamik Shiksha Abhiyan (RMSA), the integration of the Sarva Shiksha Abhiyan (SSA) with RMSA and teacher training, and the Integrated Scheme for School Education are very welcome news indeed.

POLITICAL WILL AND SOCIAL COMMITMENT

My first question is: how adequate is the level of political will and social commitment in India to universalize secondary education? In Bangladesh, I often feel frustrated when we end a seminar with a statement that policy X or action Y could not be implemented because of the lack of political will and social commitment. Political will often becomes a catch-all phrase to shift responsibility or explain away all deficits. If political will and social commitment are the critical ingredients for the success of any public policy or public action, then should we not first assess what is the level of our political will and social commitment before we embark on any public policy or programme initiative? If we think the level of political will and social commitment is inadequate, then can we not devise some strategies to create that additional level of political will and social commitment?

I raise this question of political will and social commitment because in an excellent paper, Professor J. B. G. Tilak has written on the experiences of East Asia, titled 'Building Human Capital in East Asia: What Others Can Learn' a key lesson he highlights is the importance of political will and social commitment. He states the following:

> ...political will and social commitment to education is one particular feature that explains the growth of the education system in East Asian economies ...In every country...education was an item of national obsession; it is regarded as the most important means of achieving social status, occupational mobility and economic advancement — individually and as a society. ...Investment in human capital has been regarded as the cornerstone of nation building and the key factor of economic development in East Asia. This realisation is critically important. (Tilak, 2002, p. 38)

One must ponder on this lesson drawn by Professor Tilak and ask: has education now finally become a 'national obsession' in India more than 70 years after Independence? Do the national and state governments regard investment in human capital as the 'cornerstone' of nation building and economic development? If the answers to both questions are 'yes', then of course this seminar does not need to spend much time deliberating on them. But if the answers are 'no' or 'not yet', then we need to think how can we make education a 'national obsession' and a 'cornerstone' of our development policies.

POLICY DESIGN AND IMPLEMENTATION

My second question is: how realistic and implementable are the designs of these recent initiatives announced by the government of India?

I often read policy and programme documents which are full of good intentions but their targets and time frame are unrealistic; they lack specific instruments to address specific constraints and insufficient resources are allocated to achieve the policy and programme objectives. Our persistent record of gaps between policy design and policy implementation creates serious credibility and trust gaps between government and citizens. But these credibility and trust deficits appear not to be taken seriously by our policymakers. Our policies and programmes are rarely scrutinized from the perspective of feasibility of their implementation. Often, policy implementers, mostly bureaucrats, go along with unrealistic and ambitious policies and programmes because they know that policymakers are more concerned with policy pronouncements rather than policy implementation.

In Bangladesh, we have often noticed wide gaps between policy and programme adoption and their implementation. Sometimes a much-heralded policy or initiative of one government gets neglected when there is a change in government. Sometimes ministries fail to spend allocated resources because of the slow rate of implementation. For example, a recent budget analysis found that 13 per cent of the allocated budget of the education sector and 40 per cent of budget of the health sector were not spent, though these sectors were allocated only a small portion of the annual budget (approximately 5 %) (CPD, 2018).

I note that the objectives of India's new Integrated Scheme for School Education are 'to improve school effectiveness measured in terms of equal opportunities for schooling and equitable learning outcomes' and raise 'allocative efficiency and optimal utilization of budgetary and human resources'. Providing equal opportunities and attaining equitable outcomes are challenging enough objectives! Combining them with 'allocative efficiency' and 'optimal utilization of resources' makes the achievement of all these goals even more challenging. The goals of achieving equality and efficiency may not always go together as efficiency is often interpreted as cost-cutting. When policy implementers are given the tasks of ensuring both equality and efficiency, they may not be able to deliver on either of them.

A report highlighting some challenges of universalization of secondary education in India notes that most states will not succeed in achieving the targetted secondary-level gross enrolment ratios by 2017 and they will find it difficult to do so even by 2020 (UNESCO, 2016 April 21). The report further notes that with the current level of financing and availability of trained teachers and facilities, expanding opportunities for groups and areas that are so far left behind to meet the stated targets will be a near-impossible task for many states (UNESCO, 2016, April 21). One may deliberate on the prospects of realizing some of the goals and targets of these initiatives.

We need to also discuss the problems associated with setting up quantitative targets. The Millennium Development Goals (MDGs) with their quantitative targets pushed countries to focus on increasing the number of student enrolment rather than the quality of their education. Increasing the number of students is important but we should not lose sight of what they are learning. The MDGs and the current Sustainable Development Goal (SDG)-4, which is quality education, have not succeeded in developing satisfactory indicators to measure improvements in quality and this remains a singular challenge for tracking the progress of SDG-4.

QUALITY

My third question is: are the planned measures to improve the quality of education adequate to produce the desired outcomes? The planned measures include many interventions, such as the provisioning of infrastructure, appointment of additional teachers, in-service training of teachers, review of curriculum, residential accommodation for teachers. But are there sufficient resources, financial and human, to implement these measures? For example, if we are to take the feasibility of one intervention, such as the appointment of teachers and training of teachers, will it be feasible to appoint adequately trained teachers to impart quality education within the time frame of 2020, particularly in underperforming states?

In their recent study, *An Uncertain Glory: India and Its Contradictions*, Jean Dreze & Amartya Sen highlight the huge burdens created by poor standards, particularly in government schools. They note that of the children aged 8–11 years enrolled in government schools, only 50 per cent can read, 43 per cent can subtract and 64 per cent can write (Dreze & Sen, 2013). The adverse teacher–student ratio, particularly in government schools, again, is a huge problem.

In Bangladesh, too, students demonstrate poor capability in reading, writing and mathematics. We are faced with not only a shortage of teachers but a shortage of teachers who will be able to improve the quality of education. A recent survey found that 78 per cent of heads of institutions were not aware of either the strength or the weakness of their curriculum; 35 per cent of teachers reported receiving no training to improve the quality of their teaching and 30 per cent of students felt that their teachers were not knowledgeable (Campaign for Popular Education [CAMPE], 2007, pp. xxix-xxx). About a half of the schools had no science laboratory; only 15 per cent had a library with a modest collection and 37 per cent of schools claimed to have computer education facilities but a fifth of these schools had only one computer (CAMPE, 2005, pp. xxxvi-xxxviii). In public sector schools, the teacher–student ratio in computer education is 4,207 as compared to 755 in private sector schools (CAMPE, 2015).

We need to come up with a few innovative ideas to add value to the measures already being planned to improve the quality of education. Moving forward, we need to change teaching methods and teaching materials to make our education competitive in the global market. The low scores of India in the PISA ranking, compared to the consistent top ranking of East and Southeast Asian countries, should be a matter of great concern for policymakers. We need to also pay attention to the contents of curriculum. Sometimes efforts are made to change school curriculum, as has happened recently in Bangladesh, to downgrade the importance of diversity in our cultural tradition. We need to be vigilant against such efforts, particularly at a time when globally and in our region a conscious political campaign is being mounted to portray the 'other' as the enemy.

INEQUALITY

My fourth question is: are the recommended interventions to reduce inequality likely to produce equitable outcomes by 2020? Do these measures adequately address some of the sources of inequality, such as the exclusion of marginalized groups and the growing divide between public and private sector and vernacular-medium and English-medium schools? In South Asia, we have produced and nurtured a dual system of education—one for the rich and another for the poor. Will inclusion of excluded groups be accommodated within the existing dual system with ever-increasing disparity between English-medium private sector schools on the one hand and public sector vernacular-medium schools on the other hand?

The recommended measures for inclusion appear to be geared towards increasing coverage of excluded groups such as students coming from rural areas and urban slums, Scheduled Tribes and Scheduled Castes and girls. Will the expansion of existing facilities, building of new schools, free boarding facilities, cash incentives and so on be adequate to address the myriad of economic and social obstacles that hold back the children from these groups from attending schools?

In Bangladesh, as I noted earlier, we introduced a special cash incentive of providing scholarships for girl students for secondary education. This not only contributed towards a fast increase in girls' school enrolment, but there were other collateral benefits such as the reduction in the number of young women marrying before 18 years of age. For example, the overall proportion of 13–15-year-old married girls declined from 20 per cent in 1992 to 14 per cent by 1995 (Bhatnagar et al., 2018). But we have also noticed that cash incentives often were not enough to counter the parents' concerns of safety and security for girls in an environment of fear of sexual harassment and violence against girls.

If we are to ensure equitable outcomes for girls' secondary education, then we need to think of multi-pronged measures to improve girls' and women's condition, and status and community and society's support for enhancing women's empowerment. I have annexed a table comparing gender-related indicators in India and Bangladesh which is taken from Dreze & Sen's (2013) book, *Uncertain Glory*. Table 6.1 shows Bangladesh doing better than India in all indicators including literacy, school enrolment and labour force participation. Female literacy rate is 78 per cent in Bangladesh as compared to 74 per cent in India, secondary school enrolment ratio for girls is 113 in Bangladesh compared to 92 in India and labour force participation rate is 57 per cent in Bangladesh compared to 29 per cent in India. These improvements in Bangladesh have been made possible by consistent and conscious policies and actions pursued by government as well as the non-government sector over the last four decades.

I believe if we are serious about addressing the issue of inequality and inequity, then we have no alternative but to improve the standards of government and vernacular-medium schools so that children from upper-income households do not flee from these schools and flock to private English-medium schools. The growth of the dual system of education has consolidated a widening social gap between a narrow privileged elite and the large excluded masses. This inequality has expanded over the last half a century. In Bangladesh, we have now reached a situation where many people have given up efforts to improve the quality of public sector and believe that the public sector is beyond repair!

But this divide between vernacular-and English-medium and public and private sector schools was not there when I went to school and university in the 1950s and early 1960s. Most of us studied in Bangla-medium government or private schools in *muffasil* towns (small towns). I did not have that many postgraduate teachers in my schools but I received sound basic training in reading, writing and mathematics from highly motivated teachers which enabled me to make the transition to an English-medium college and university after matriculation, and ultimately earn a PhD from Harvard University. I think it will be much more difficult and unusual for a student trained in Bangla-medium *mufassil* schools these days to make this kind of transition to an elite university in the USA. I believe many of my age groups in India also were able to go through a similar transition from vernacular-medium schools in small towns to top universities in India and even in the USA or the UK.

Even if we think that given the ground realities, inequality has to be bridged by provisioning of a public–private sector mix, we still have to improve the standards of the public sector where the majority of our students are enrolled. I hope we will come up with many different options involving both public and private sector. One recommendation of the Right to Education Act which drew our attention in Bangladesh was the reserved quota for underprivileged children in elite private schools. It will be interesting to know how far this measure has been implemented.

Another issue I would like to draw your attention to, which is not generally discussed in seminars, is the availability and quality of translation. When I was in school, I could read excellent Bangla translation of world literature including those of Shakespeare, Tolstoy, Dostoevsky, Chekov, Maxim Gorky, Erich Maria Remarque and so on. In fact, I enjoyed reading the Bangla translation of Arthur Conan Doyle's *Lost World* when I was in school much more than the original English edition which I read later when I was in college. I was exposed to books published in the West mainly through Bangla translations. These days, I do not find good quality Bangla translation of books published in other countries. This has narrowed the horizon of Bangla-medium students. The Internet, with all its limitations, is their only window on the world.

Professor Muchkund Dubey's recent translation of Fakir Lalon Shah's poems and songs from Bangla to Hindi has added a new dimension to translation. I feel translation from Bangla into Hindi, rather than just English, has widened the readership of Lalon and created an opportunity for a much larger Hindi reading public to understand and appreciate the rich syncretic cultural legacy of Bangladesh which had traditionally focused on mystical and devotional aspects of religion. I believe many more such translations from one vernacular language to another will help foster greater appreciation and understanding between different regions of South Asia.

GOVERNANCE

My fifth question, again, is: are the measures planned by the initiatives to improve governance sufficient and appropriate? In their book, Dreze & Sen (2013) highlight several governance challenges including those of management, accountability and the role of professional organizations. They highlight the problem of absenteeism of teachers as an example of governance failure. They have calculated that with 20 per cent absenteeism of teachers and 33 per cent absenteeism of students, in effect, the probability of any effective teaching in a school in any day is 50 per cent (Dreze & Sen, 2013, p. 120). They further note that despite improvement in salary, absenteeism of teachers has continued which underscore lack of monitoring and accountability. They point out the narrow focus of teachers' associations which mainly demand improving the conditions of teachers rather than the condition of the education sector as a whole.

In Bangladesh, too, we face similar problems of student and teacher absenteeism. Absenteeism of head teachers is 20 per cent in primary schools and 18 per cent in secondary schools. Over the years, teachers' salaries, though still inadequate, have improved, but this has not contributed towards a reduction in absenteeism. Again, I do not remember teachers being absent when I was in school, though those teachers were also poorly paid. Moreover, nearly 40 per cent of teachers are involved in private tutoring (Campaign for Popular Education, 2015, p. 17). Teachers' associations are politicized and political parties use them to expand their vote base. Before every national election, teachers' associations start agitations to increase their salaries. Members of Parliament have expanded their holds on school boards and use them as a patronage resource.

Governance reforms are critical to improving quality and reducing inequality. But these reforms are not feasible without a strong political will and social commitment, the very first question I started with this chapter. Academics, policymakers, political leaders, civil society activists and the media should be continuously engaged in pushing for governance reforms, improvement of standards and reduction of inequalities in the education sector.

APPENDIX

Table 6.1 *Gender-related Indicators in India and Bangladesh*

	India	Bangladesh
Female labour force participation rate, Age 15+, 2010 (%)	29	57
Female–male ratio in population, 2011 (females per 1,000 males)		
All ages	940	997
Age 0–6 years	914	972[a]
Ratio of female to male death rates, 2009[b]		
Age 0–1	1.01	0.89
Age 1–4	1.55	1.25
Ratio of Female to male school enrolment, 2010 (%)		
Primary	100[c]	104[d]
Secondary	92	113
Literacy rate (age 15–24 years), 2010 (%)		
Female	74[e]	78
Male	88[e]	75
Proportion of adults (age 25+) with secondary education, 2010 (%)		

(Continued)

(Continued)

	India	Bangladesh
Women	27	31
Men	50	39
Women's share of seats in national parliament 2011 (%)	11	20
Total fertility rate, 2011 (children per woman)	2.6	2.2

Source: Dreze & Sen (2013, p. 125).
Notes: [a] Age 0–4 years; [b] 2007 for Bangladesh; [c] 2008; [d] 2009; [e] 2006.

REFERENCES

Bhatnagar, D., Dewan, A., Torres, M. M., & Kanungo, P. (2018). *Empowerment case studies: Female secondary school assistance project, Bangladesh* (Project Brief). Washington DC: The World Bank. Retrieved from http://siteresources.worldbank.org/INTEMPOWERMENT/Resources/14828_Bangladesh-web.pdf

Campaign for Popular Education (CAMPE). (2005). *Education watch report 2005. The State of Secondary Education—Quality and Equity Challenges.* Retrieved from http://www.campebd.org/page/Generic/0/6/18

———. (2007). *Education watch report 2007.* The State of Secondary Education—Quality and Equity Challenges. Retrieved from http://www.campebd.org/page/Generic/0/6/18

———. (2015). *Fact sheet on status of teachers in primary and secondary schools in Bangladesh* (p. 15). Dhaka: Rasheda K Chowdhury.

CPD. (2018). *State of the Bangladesh economy in FY2017–18 second reading.* CPD's Budget Recommendations for FY2018–19. Retrieved from https://cpd.org.bd/wp- content/uploads/2017/10/Paper-on-IRBD-CPD per centE2 per cent80 per cent99s-Budget-Recommendations-for-FY2018–19.pdf

Dreze, J., & Sen, A. (2013). *An uncertain glory.* London, UK: Penguin Group.

Tilak, J. B. G. (2002). *Building human capital in East Asia: What others can learn.* The World Bank. Retrieved from https://siteresources.worldbank.org/WBI/Resources/wbi37166.pdf

UNESCO. (2016, April 21). *Universalizing secondary education in India.* International Institute for Educational Planning (IIEP). Retrieved from http://www.iiep.unesco.org/en/universalizing-secondary-education-india-3531

Chapter 7

Education Beyond Classrooms*

Vidhya Das

Children are eventually the victims in any society, and perhaps more so in a democracy in which the major players shrug their responsibility for running the accepted system as historically established and even much more so, when they are children of victim parents themselves, such as the Dalits and tribals. In the tribal regions, children are born in the lap of nature and grow up singing, playing and learning to her rhythms. As they are a part of the natural world, dangling from trees, tasting the best of fruits, playing in mud and water, unfettered and free, so also are they a part of their families' work culture and routine. The play things that the tribal communities provide for their children are down-sized implements that they would use as adults and in imitating their elders in fun, the children learn the work they will do at a later stage easily and naturally. They grow up much as their parents did, working, toiling, learning to make a living through hard labour and accepting much that goes on without questions.

A seemingly idyllic life. Yet it does not take much to discern that this near perfect situation can just as easily slide into one quite the reverse, as children suffer with their parents the ill-effects of poverty and extremes of injustice, not just exploitation. Here, if a child has survived hunger and its side effects (the lack of resistance to almost any infection), repeated and persistent attacks of malaria, almost a non-existent system of medical aid forcing dependence on local methods of first aid for any contingency major or minor, and becomes an adult, they are still in

---

* *Social Change:* December 2011: 41, No. 4, 599–609.

danger of forced hunger, as labour contractors, or even government departments forget to pay wages for several days of work—this after five years of the National Rural Employment Guarantee Act (NREGA)—of loosing entire crops of grain to landslides, despite the several watershed programmes taken up, of being cheated of Public Distribution Systems (PDS) rations and even old-age pensions, of being forced willy-nilly to leave their home due to large-scale development projects and having to pick up the threads of life in a new place with scarcely any support systems, save a paltry sum left of the compensation. When people face such insecurities, what education can they give to their children? For a girl growing into adolescence and eventually adulthood, these insecurities are a complex set of threats that deny her almost all opportunities and freedom. The several displaced in the Koraput and neighbouring tribal districts do not even become eligible for ration cards under the PDS for many years. Their children do not find a place in the lists for childcare supplies for ICDS and other programmes. Here, the concept of human rights has never been thought of, and the landlord as Maha Prabhu (Lord and Master, rather than God) and the government official as Aya, Bua (mother and father) rolled into one reign supreme and despotic. Tribal girls in such a situation are often forced into prostitution, as is evidenced in several studies, including those undertaken by Agragamee (Agragamee, 1991: 23). A member of the tribal community feels inferior, by the very fact of being born in the tribal community, and all talk and actions of the more dominant non-tribal community emphasize this feeling, beginning with the government school teacher who takes a token class now and then in the village to justify their salary.

What place do mainstream emphasis of reducing child labour, day care centres and so on have in a situation like this? We let Sumoni Jhodia of Siriguda in Rayagada District, Bado Muduli of Bagchema in Koraput District and other friends from the tribal community answer the questions of researchers: 'My parents forced me to go to school,' says Bado.

But I found it very difficult to study as I was hungry all the time. Then one day, I went to my uncle's house in a neighbouring village, and they asked me to look after their baby. They said I could stay with them and they would give me food if I looked after their child. My parents were very upset, they scolded me and tried to force me to go to school. But I was happy because I no longer felt hungry, and so I did not study any further,

concludes Bado matter-of-factly.

I went to school for a few months. Sometimes I was absent as I had to help my mother. The master would shout at me like anything, whenever I was absent. Then one day, he beat a boy so much for some mischief, that the eight of us from my village who were going to school stopped going, as we felt that we might also get beaten like that someday.

Children do work in poor households across the country, not just in tribal hinterlands. Some work for money, some like Bado, just for boarding and lodging, some along with their parents to help ease the burden that little bit, some because their parents think they would use their time better learning the family trade, and some just because all their friends are out there, and sitting in those dismal classrooms and studying is not attractive enough. Often, the situation suits one and all. The poor parent does find it a help when the little ones pull their weight and, of course, the teacher finds it a good excuse: these stupid tribals do not send their children to school, so what can I do. The children too; out of school, they learn many essential skills of survival, which unfortunately, our education system has never thought of addressing. So money is spent, salaries paid, school buildings constructed, or rather half-constructed, and things continue just the same.

Consider the contrast, which perhaps underlines the dilemma of education today. On the one hand, we have students committing suicide because of the overburden of studies, on the other, we have a system of education that barely touches the lives of children across the country. We have the highest suicides in the world, with an average of 95–100 people committing suicides every day, with 40 per cent of them being adolescents! (*Express India*, 10 Jan 2010).

The alarming rate of suicides is a serious indicator of the malaise that affects education in our country. Suicides after board exams, suicides because of teacher pressure, often physical abuse. These events most often occur in 'public' private schools, where exams' scores play a major role. These suicides scream out the inher-ent problems with these models. Such schools by their very scale create stress and strain within the administration and within the teachers. Quite apart from deny-ing all possibility of giving the child the respect and dignity due to a human being, the children are grouped together and treated like herd animals, and any child that cannot immediately conform to the rules of the herd is either violently forced to do so or rejected from the system, with terrible consequences to the mental well-being of the child, as well as the entire family. Schools persistently try to hush up and gloss over such events. But is it just the fault of the schools, or the entire sys-tem of school education?

Small sections of the society, enlightened beings, few and far between in number are actually beginning to realize the harm in treating children like ranch cattle and there is an increasing effort to get back to a much smaller scale for schooling, with the emphasis being on 'helping children learn' rather than on 'educating them'. Experiments on small schooling are coming up, growing up out of the mud as it were in different situations and different parts of the country with unexpected impact and long-standing implications.

G. Gautam in his article on schools emphasizes:

> The only option to the impersonal large school model is to find a system that values the relationship between the child and the teacher. If we set up large systems, control will have to be maintained by centrali-sation and authority. If we have large systems tolerance for aberration would have to be small…We need to shift in our thinking from the mechanical model to the intelligent living system models.

Let us now pause for a moment and juxtapose the other conundrum against all this: noble objectives: Strenuous effort for the … provision of free and compulsory education for all children up to the age of 14 years (National Policy on Education, 1968: 2) high-level committees, and endless flow of funds, programmes, yet a poorly educated population, with low retention rates, and even worse achievements. Much has been said about the 'mainstreaming of out of school children'. Magsaysay awardee Shanta Sinha's achievements in this regard are nothing short of super-human: her programme extends to 2,500 in four districts, as well as Hyderabad, 500,000 children put through bridge course camps, 30,000 activists mobilized to liberate children! These formidable achievements of her organization MV Foundation, on the basis of her initial experiments in Ranga Reddy district prove that children can be successfully brought into mainstream society through government schools and have engendered an overwhelming opinion of compelling poor children into government schools.

While one cannot have two opinions on this, there is a jarring contradiction; while one school of thought has come round full circle, and espouses the cause of small decentralized systems of schooling, in which the teacher themselves could be selected by the parents, with a corresponding flexibility in approach, curriculum and method, the other school stridently shouts 'no alternate schooling,' 'all children should be "mainstreamed" into government schools' with their completely centralized systems of recruitment, management, training and curriculum development. This contradiction becomes somewhat explicable, if one realiszes that the former is the voice of those concerned about education of children of those people who can afford it. Afford to buy quality, afford to buy a good teacher, afford to buy good performance by their children, afford almost anything, at almost any price, while the latter is being said in the context of the poorest of the poor, the children of landless and bonded labourers, who cannot even afford to buy two square meals for themselves and their children several days in a month. Explicable, but not resolved!

The former in this country have several choices, they may put their children in any school they want, they may not put their children in any school at all and engage the best teachers for their children, they may question quality, and compare and contrast different models, and make informed decisions for their offspring. If the quality of education is not good enough in this country, they may even send their children to better schools in any country across the Atlantic or the Pacific.

The latter, the children of daily wage earners and bonded slaves, the children of the majority in this country, do not have choices. They may not eat when they are hungry! Because they can eat only when they or their parents find some employment for wages, or when people generously throw leftover food from a feast in rubbish heaps! These people who by all estimates form nearly three-fourths of the population of this country may not even think about such things like education and a career for their children. A charitable organization like the MV Foundation offers them some hope, because their children can at least get some food and a place to study in. There are several efforts like the MV Foundation, some offer bridge courses to help the children join the government schools, some offer alternative schooling to provide literacy learning opportunities for the children in their spare time, some work with teachers to improve teaching performance in schools, others develop teaching learning material that can provide additional inputs. Each and every one of these efforts is necessary and essential in a pluralistic society like India where the government has been allowed to wash its hands off efficiency, delivery and accountability, and ministers are busy raising party money through employment and transfer of teachers and other government functionaries. Such efforts are essential alternatives where paid tuition is the solution by default to the indifference and apathy of the government, as underlined in Amartya Sen's 'Pratichi Report' (Rana, Rafique, and Sengupta, 2002: 123–125).

However, pedagogy takes a back seat here, as simplistic slogans like 'any child out of school is a child labourer' and 'all work is hazardous and harms the growth and development of the child' come to dictate our mindset. There is, however, no effort to even ask: are we ready to live by these slogans? If we are, then they might work. But, even as we repeat them like magical mantras for the universalization of education, we close our eyes to the apathetic performance of the government schools, which force children to go for tuition even in the first and second standards. We close our eyes to the situation of the myriads of children on the streets who would not be able to eat unless they begged. Education is the responsibility of the state. But in a country like India, where the state takes all the rights, but admits no responsibility, what does such a responsibility mean? Practically nothing, especially in the case of the underprivileged sections. Communities, parents do not produce children to exploit them. They would not allow their children into bondage if they themselves were not exploited to the verge of death. Yes, there would be some aberrations, where parents might be wilfully cruel to and exploit-ative of their children, but these would be the exceptions that can be treated by the existing laws. On the other hand, if parents wish to put their children through apprenticeships that enable them to become skilled in certain trades, this should not be prohibited or discourage, provided the child is also allowed to complete basic elementary education. From an early age, children of the middle class and upper class in the cities, against whom we could perhaps compare other learner situations are put through additional coaching for various skills whether it is the performing arts such as dance and music, or whether it is computer courses, arts or athletics and sports, and so on, to name just a few. Why cannot children in rural areas be encouraged to learn additional skills as part-time apprenticeships? Even after Kailash Satyarthi's huge campaign rescued thousands of children from carpet industries and raised an international stink about child labour in exported car-pets, the people in the villages of North Bihar still did not think it wrong that children worked in carpet industries. The children who were engaged were proud that they were earning at this young age. Yes, they were not able to have 'education'. But what kind of education? In the village schools, they would have sat in classrooms where teachers did not come. If one cannot change this situation, then what right does one have to stop children from working, and having an opportunity for some relevant education, but perhaps of a different kind.

'Mainstreaming'! What a word to use for efforts in education. What does it mean? How many people who are so keen for 'mainstreaming' children from poor families are actually mainstreaming their children? I can say with complete confidence almost none. For these people have already found alternate education streams for their children through the private schools which have mushroomed all over our country. These are the alternates to our more or less defunct government system of education that are being sought by all who can afford it in this country today. And since they are alternate efforts, they are not bound by rigid norms and budgets set by the government and come in several forms, as and how the parents who seek them can afford to pay. But, increasingly, there is a resistance to 'qualitative alternatives for the children of the poor, even though the government itself has established different forms of schooling for children of the same levels'.

The divisive nature of the present system is further heightened in the Right to Education Act. Anil Sadgopal points out:

> In conceiving the RTE Act, the state was guided by two key features of neoliberal economic order. First, children of different sections of society shall have access to varying quality of schooling in accordance

with their socio-economic and cultural status or purchasing capacity or both. This is evident from the very definition of 'school' in clause (n) of Section 2, which provides for four categories of schools of varying quality and provisions. The Act insists on compartmentalising RTE in these categories. For instance, Section 5 provides for the right of the child to seek transfer to another school under certain circumstances. However, in the very next breath, it restricts the right of the child to seek transfer to schools of 'specified category' (that is, Kendriya Vidyalayas, Navodaya Vidyalayas and other similar elite schools) and private, unaided schools. This implies that almost 80 per cent of the children in the 6–14 age group shall be denied education in schools which the state itself considers, rightly or wrongly, as providers of higher quality education. This deception destroys the very basis of education as a Fundamental Right read in conjunction with Article 14 (equality before law), Articles 15 (prohibiting the state from discriminating) and Article 16 (social justice) (Sadgopal, 2011: 8).

John Holt writes:

People, even children, are educated much more by the whole society around them and the general quality of life in it than they are by what happens in schools. The dream of many school people, that schools can be places where virtue is preserved and passed on in a world otherwise empty of it, now seems to me a sad and dangerous illusion. It might have worked in the Middle Ages; it cannot work in a world of cars, jets, TV, and the mass media.... (John Holt, 2002)

Even without TV and mass media, this is true in India, where children learn the class, caste and gender divide much before they even think of going to school. Schooling is more for rote memory, and learning to excel with maximum competitiveness, something that many in schools fail to do in fact! That there is a world of education outside of the schools is something that is sadly ignored by the system. This perhaps explains the high rates of dropouts after primary school, much higher among girls. A school that does not deliver is a colossal waste of time, something that poorer communities can ill afford. Just look at the poor achievements in the lower classes of our schools. Children in class V can't read class II textbooks, children in class VII unable to do class III maths! (Pratham, 2010: 2, asercentre.org).

Women bear the worst burden of poverty, and if girls education is to increase, then it is essential that educational systems factor this in, rather than getting girls, who essentially help their mothers, to come and waste time in understaffed schools, where the teachers are poorly qualified and ill-motivated anyway. The RTE does not even forbid teachers from doing other work. The Act specifies that no teacher shall be deployed for any non-educational purpose other than the decennial population census, disaster relief or duties relating to elections to the local authority or the state legislature or Parliament as the case maybe. Where in a private school would people tolerate teacher absenteeism for any purpose whatsoever? Where teachers are regular, and there is effective delivery, dropout rates come down significantly. In tribal schools for girls, run by Agragamee, in some of the most interior tribal pockets of Orissa, 75 per cent of the girls who join in class I continue to class V. Villages, where male literacy was 5 per cent and female literacy 0.5 per cent, have seven to eight girls studying in high school, as many children jump classes when they go for further studies after passing out from Agragamee schools.

Of equal or more importance is perhaps educational content. Emphasizing on learning levels, rather than the prescribed syllabus, the teaching in the Agragamee schools also helped children relate to their village situations, talking about their land and agriculture, and encouraging them to write about what they grew in their lands, and about their local festivals. Government programmes and schemes for the tribal communities as well as the relevant acts and provisions have also been introduced into the syllabus. Children are encouraged to go back to their villages and ask their parents, and who ever else they can about these schemes and write about these. This has helped children observe and take more interest in the situation within their villages and begin a newspaper *Dangar Katha*, where they describe their everyday experiences, including the functioning of the government school, the situation of wage employment, as also various events.

And this is where the beyond classrooms nature of education, the multiple learning, that is, education gets emphasized. Agragamee's efforts as a matter of fact began with illiterate tribal women. The initial effort was to teach them literacy, when we discovered that this in fact curtailed the considerable shared learning that would help this exploited and deprived community overcome its many problem. As we began work with the women, we learned that in the largely barter economy in the tribal regions, women were the most exploited in the markets and in their homes. Whatever the tribal community produce and sell is bought at the least value. And women who provide the major labour to produce these commodities, either labour in the fields and farms to cultivate the crops, or for collection, drying and storage of produce from the forest, bear most of the loss. We began a dialogue and discussion to understand the situation better, and work out alternatives. Even as we encouraged the women to form thrift and credit groups and invest their savings in buying their own minor forest products as collectives, so that they could sell it at a higher price in the market, they came up against the unfair policy of the government, which only allowed licensed contractors to trade in these products. Indignant and stymied, the women wrote petitions to meet the chief minister for a change of policy, the permission granted, the meeting led to the chief minister agreeing to their demands and allowing registered women's groups to have license for trade in the Market Facilitation Programme (MFP). The forest department however did not see eye to eye and the women were back to square one. They did not give up, however, and persevered, using the chief minister's orders, and going in for civil disobedience, where they collected the forest produce and refused to sell. Their stock was seized, and they had to face criminal cases. Agragamee helped with legal aid. The struggle lasted for seven years, and the government finally agreed to change the policy!

Learning began anew now, as this group, which had got together and challenged the might of the government had to learn the tricks of the trade, as they entered into trade. That, however, is another story, as they have established themselves as the most successful tribal entrepreneurs in Orissa. What we need to understand here is the importance of collective learning, and building on each others strengths. Agragamee recognized the inherent strengths of the tribal people and sought to help them capitalize on these, which eventually helped them fight against unfair monopolistic policies.

Chief Minister Biju Patnaik too, at that time, realized the strength in these tribal women and appointed them as his advisors for tribal development. A monthly dialogue with the tribal women and his secretaries was scheduled. As the secretaries sought to evade the questions and complaints of the tribal women, the chief minister came down heavily on them, saying 'they maybe illiterate, but they know more than you, so you have to listen!' Illiteracy and knowledge; are they mutually exclusive? In today's information-driven world, it would seem to be the case, but is it not this divide which in fact makes for the many problems that we face today? If these women had been educated within the four walls of regular classrooms, would they have had the courage and ability to challenge a government and change its policy? It is anybody's guess.

What are we trying to achieve through formal, classroom schooling? Surely not happiness? Look at the hundreds of children who are out of the school in the villages. These kids are surely learning their life skills in the best possible way! Paulo Freire talks about the static nature of education, and the banking concept, which only serves to increase the student–teacher divide (Freire, 1970). Mahatma Gandhiji held that education should be such that it should help one realize their full potential as a human being (Gandhi, 1937). Admittedly, much greater minds than mine have pondered deeply on this onerous question, and yet I struggle for answers, the bewilderment is more as I look at the numerous schools imparting education. The more serious ones seat their pupils in row upon rows, and subject them to inhuman feats of memorizing leaving them quite bored and stupid. However else they began, in the higher classes, huge quantities of syllabus are thrust down the throats/minds, as if one is acting to catch up with every bit of information that was ever produced in the history of mankind. Here, the tendency is that the more one studies (read: gets educated), the more one needs to study. Then when one does finally get out, it is in the midst of a mad rush for jobs, with the few who do get it, having achieved everything in life and the majority who do not get it, subject to a sense of defeat and failure for the rest of their lives.

The not-so-serious schools (mostly the municipal or the panchayat schools of the School and Mass Education Department) of course do not even bother with these tedious processes, they—the teachers, the children and the schooling system in general—all go their different happy ways, with not much visible impact of the schooling process on either the children or on the community in general. Here, finances are allocated, aims and ideals stated, targets defined and funds spent, few question the poor achievements. Perhaps, everyone, including the hapless community which is denied of its just benefits from the allocated funds and the programme feel it is best this way.

The question becomes even more bewildering as I look at the 'uneducated' people in the villages. The women, the men, who without a day spent in the portals of a school, know very well how to fend for themselves and also do a whole range of works for us the educated. If they do not get a job, they do not give in to despair and get classified as the unemployed, they seek out work, and silently, diligently carry it out. Without going into the intricacies of engineering courses, they have built beautiful houses, designed their canals, ponds and water management, they produce their own food as also food for a growing consumer population and have the knowledge to manage entire ecosystems in sustainable, self-sustaining ways. Textiles of the most intricate designs and patterns, pottery, cane—the list is endless, all are produced by the many 'uneducated' people in this country.

Much more we need to realize that it is their unpaid and underpaid work which has sustained this top-heavy economy of ours.

Much has been and continues to be said and written about education, I probably can claim the least qualification for adding to this verbiage, yet, I plod along, because in our rush towards qualifications, degrees and information, we are negating a vast system of knowledge that already exists, which has formed the basis of survival of our past generations and is in imminent fear of becoming extinct due to this neglect. The world sits up and takes fearful note when the sloth bear, or a duckbilled platypus is about to become extinct, why are we so complacent even as we sit on the threshold of blanking out our own history, culture and knowledge systems that have been built up over the past centuries, which have helped us live, produce and grow to become one of the most complex and skilled civilizations in the world? Why instead are we reaching out for alternatives which are increasingly proving to be destructive and violent? The education we have today, in our schools is indeed an education for change, but we should take a long pause and ask ourselves, is this the change we want? It is a change towards creating dependencies, a change towards denying the value of established skills and creating new ones for which there may not be a need.

No I am not crying for a return to our glorious traditions, there is much in these that need to be jettisoned, but appeal to one and all to look beyond this facade into what our people knew and even now know, at the techniques developed, at the sustainable patterns of resource use when there is so much talk of sustainable development today, and pause a while to ponder wether we should continue to go headlong with the present system of school education or dare think differently.

A difference that respects people and people's knowledge and experience that respects children's minds and tries to build on the good things from our past rather than starting with a blank slate of negation of all that is past. Today, we put our children through processes, we would not be able to tolerate. Hours and hours of sitting in one place, having to repeat patterns and symbols over and over again, in small spaces, then later on commit to memory a great deal of facts, most of which have very little connection to our everyday life.

The real challenge is to conceive of an educational system, a process that takes into account the considerable knowledge and skills present among the uneducated and make a concerted effort to initiate all young people into these; that does not alienate, but combines in a creative fashion, the best in modern and traditional systems and sciences for control and use by one and all; that enables individuals to channelize their energies and potentials for creative and productive use, and does not reduce them to job-seeking stooges in a bureaucratic megalith. Today, with growing disillusionment with the existing system, many creative alternatives are being tried out. There should be more government support for these in terms of subsidies, research supports, infrastructure and so on. There should also be a systematic effort to help these initiatives provide long-term sustainable alternatives, as many of them are forced to submit to the larger system in the long run, due to the mainstream pressure. A much greater effort needs to be made to encourage such initiatives in the rural areas, as many of the present efforts centre in and around cities. Supports for these efforts should consider ensuring adequate infrastructural facilities, long-term financial assistance for efforts targeting Harijan or tribal communities, and research, training and informational backup. An essential link up in all this should be with rural livelihood systems of production, resource use and management, social ordering and controls and traditional learning.

There should also be a systematic effort to look at other communities and countries efforts for educations and learn from them. In *How Children Learn*, John Holt speaks of children's innate urge to learn through various means, including imitation, institution, logic and other means. Sylvia Ashton Warner speaks of how quickly children learn, when one attempts to understand them and their cultural underpinnings first and then teach. These are the writings of extremely creative people, who have made breakthroughs because of their sincere wish to know and understand, and build on what is there within each person, within each culture, rather than to impose a system without any questions as to its relevance and contextuality. May be if we try and learn from such experiences and also attempt a continued learning even as we presume to plan and design educational policies, we can come up with a clearer picture of what kind of education and social change one should strive for and then perhaps we can have a system that is meaningful and actually works.

REFERENCES

Friere, Paulo. (1970). *Psychology of the Opperessed*. New York, Herder and Herder.

Gandhi, M.K. (1937). in: *Harijan* (July 31).

Gandhi M.K. (1937). *Basic Education*, Navajivan Publishing House, Ahmedabad.

Government of India. (1968). *National Policy on Education 1968*. New Delhi, Ministry of Education.

Holt, John C. (1967). *How Children Learn?* Pitman Publishing, New York.

Pratham. (2010). *Annual Status of Education Report*. Mumbai.

Rana, K., Abdur Rafique & Amrita Sengupta. (2002). *The Pratichi Education Report*, Number 1, TLM Books, Delhi.

Sadgopal, Anil. (2011). Neo-Liberal Act, *Frontline* (July 15). https://frontline. thehindu.com/cover-story/article30176063.ece

Chapter 8

Overall Educational Planning in India[*]
Retrospect and Prospect

D. P. Nayar

INTRODUCTION

Overall educational planning is the process of drawing up alternative strategies to meet overall societal objectives defined by the overall political authority to enable us to decide on the most appropriate strategy. Education is to be planned not as an isolated activity but as an integral part of overall development planning. That requires providing for the essential requirements of the other sectors depending on education and also ensuring that the necessary inputs for education from the other sectors are fully taken into account. The establishment of effective inter-sectoral linkages is at the heart of integrated development and is essential for optimizing results by fully exploiting the mutually reinforcing capabilities of the various sectors.

The overall objectives in the Indian context have been defined by the Constitution and spelt out in the various development plans, policy resolutions issued by the government, the election manifesto of the ruling party and so on. While there have been deviations—intended and unintended—in implementation, the statement of objectives of Indian development has always been clear. They may be summed up in the term 'democratic socialism' and spelt out as increased production,

* *Social Change:* June 1978: Vol. 8, No. 2, 3–13.

equitable distribution and maximum involvement of the people. A number of sub-objectives would ensue as a logical corollary, such as employment, equality of opportunity (including the educational), democratic decentralization, availability of basic essentials of life at reasonable prices and so on. These objectives and sub-objectives have implications for the education planning. The equality of opportunity would require universalization of elementary education, remedial learning opportunities and liberal scholarships for the weaker sections of society at the secondary and collegiate stages. The demand for increased productivity would call for the introduction of the teaching of basic skills as an essential part of the curriculum from the earliest class, the introduction of mathematics, science and technology prominently in the curriculum, emphasis on encouraging the innovative spirit and inculcating the habits of cooperation and teamwork through the use of appropriate methodologies of education and so on. The objectives of full employment would call for emphasis on inculcation of basic skills, emphasis on work experience and the vocationalization, cooperation and building up of the capacity of the pupils for self-employment, by developing in them qualities of initiative, resourcefulness and leadership on the one hand and giving an all-round training, beginning from the buying of raw materials to the sale of finished products in our vocational institutions.

The first Five-Year Plan succinctly sums up the role of education and the consequent objectives of educational planning in planned development:

Education is of basic importance in the planned development of a nation. The educational machinery will have to be geared for the specific tasks which the nation sets itself through the Plan so as to make available in the various fields personnel of suitable quality at the required rate. The educational system has also an intimate bearing on the attainment of the general objectives of the Plan in as much as it largely determines the quality of the manpower and the social climate of the community. In a democratic set up, the role of education becomes crucial, since it can function effectively only if there is an intelligent participation of the masses in the affairs of the country. The success of planning in a democracy depends also on the growth of the spirit of co-operation and the sense of disciplined citizenship among the people and on the degree to which it becomes possible to evoke public enthusiasm and to build up local leadership. It is essential for the successful implementation of the Plan that the educational programme helps to train the people to place responsibilities before rights and to keep the self-regarding outlook and the force of the acquisitive instinct within legitimate bounds. The educational system should also satisfy cultural needs, which is essential for the healthy growth of a nation. The system should stimulate the growth of the creative faculties, increase the capacity for enjoyment and develop a spirit of critical appreciation of arts, literature and other creative activities. The fulfilment of the objectives mentioned above, will lead to the development of an integrated personality in the individual, which should be the first and foremost aim of any system of education.[1]

IN RETROSPECT

Looking at more than a quarter of a century of educational development in India as a part of overall development, the following conclusions emerge.

Expansion

The most obvious achievement is the tremendous expansion of education that has taken place which will be clear from Table 8.1. It will be seen that in 1951–1979, the increase in enrolment is estimated to be more than fourfold at the primary stage, by seven times at the middle stage and nearly by 10 times at the secondary stage. At the university stage, the increase was still more phenomenal. The enrolment increased from 360 thousand (less than 1% of the corresponding age group 17–23) in 1950–1951 to 3 million (anticipated) (4.4% of relevant age group) in 1973–1974 and is expected to go up to 4.65 million[2] by the end of the Fifth Plan. This means that the increase in 1951–1979 would be thirteen-fold. Similar phenomenal increase took place in professional and vocational education. For example, in higher professional educational institutions,[3] the enrolment increased from about 5,000 in 1950–1951 to about 32,000 in 1970–1977 in agriculture, in engineering and technology from 13,000 to about 228,000 in medicine from about 15,000 to

Table 8.1 *Growth of Enrolment in Educational Institutions*

Classes	Age Group	Enrolment (Figures in Millions)			% of Corresponding Age-Group		
		1950–1951[a]	1973–1974	1978–1979[b]	1950–1951	1973–1974	1978–1979
I–V	6–11	19.2	63.8	77.1	42.1	84.0	96.0
VI–VIII	11–4	3.1	15.0	21.1	12.7	36.0	46.0
IX–XI–XII	14–17	1.3	8.5	11.5	5.3	22.0	25.0

Source: [a]*Selected Education and Related Statistics at a Glance* Planning Commission, Government of India, March 1976, p. 29.
[b] *Fifth Five Year Plan, 1974–1979,* p. 76, Planning Commission, Government of India.

about 98,000 and in teacher training from about 6,000 in 1950–1951 to about 184,000 during the same period. Similar increases took place in vocational education at lower levels.

This expansion has a threefold significance. First, education on such a massive scale creates a ferment and promotes social and occupational mobility. Second, when accompanied by increased scholarships, mid-day meals, free uniforms for girls, free textbooks and so on, it takes us a step further towards equality of opportunity and social justice. Third, and very importantly, the large-scale increase in our scientific and technical manpower has enabled us to develop a highly diversified industrial structure, including some of the most sophisticated industries. It is a matter of gratification that we are today the third or fourth largest country in the world from the point of view of scientific and technical manpower. Many of the developing countries look forward to us for technical help and our experts have fanned out into the world to do technical and scientific tasks of the developing world, both through the United Nations and through bilateral agreements. A rough idea of the total expansion that is taking place in education is that the annual expenditure on education has risen from ₹114.38 crores in 1950–1951 to ₹811.31[4] crores in 1968–1969 and is likely to rise to ₹2,500 crores by 1978–1979.

Fall in Standards

Looked at from another point of view, our very success has been the cause of our weakness, namely our poor educational standards. The breakneck speed at which the educational system has expanded without the corresponding increase in resources has resulted in bringing down the standard of the average institution in our country and this has happened in spite of the fact that we have spent generously on education.

During 1960–1961 to 1976–1977, while our national income increased only at the rate of 9.9 per cent[5] (compounded) per annum, at current prices, our educational expenditure during the same period increased at the rate of 12.5 per cent (compounded) per annum at current prices.[6]

Outdated Curriculum

The increase in numbers enrolled is also largely due to the enrolment of the poorer sections of the community. The heterogenous composition of the institutions, consisting of pupils with varying aptitudes and needs, requires variegation of the curricula provided. The single type curriculum which, to some extent, suited the middle classes has consequently got outdated. Our attempt to diversify the courses provided has so far not met with any success for various reasons and, therefore, the curriculum continues on old lines with its irrelevance to and unsuitability for large sections of the student population.

Weak Linkages with Overall Objectives—Social Justice

The linkages of the education system with the overall objectives of achieving social justice remain weak. Even in regard to the quantitative aspect of social justice, the Directive of the Constitution in regard to elementary education is still far from being realized. The heavy dropout from the system shows that neither the manner nor the content of education provided are related to the actualities of the socio-economic situation.

Government has not been able to provide adequate support services which are required to bring to school the children of the poorest classes. Nor have they been able to generate in any effective manner community self-help and support for the same purpose. There are vast regional disparities in the provision of facilities and within different areas of each region. The first Finance Commission gave grants to weaker states but this was made infructuous by smaller provisions in the plan so that these funds became substitutive instead of being additive to the plan funds. Similarly, the Sixth Finance Commission recommended transfer of resources to the weaker states on the non-plan side so that their non-plan funds would in course of time equal those of the more prosperous states. But ultimately these funds were taken over by the Planning Commission in their estimate of resources for the Plan. Second, the quality of the institutions available to the higher classes and those available for the weaker sections varies so much that there can only be an illusion of providing equality of opportunity. Higher education still remains, by and large, the preserve of the higher classes and its subsidy benefits these classes and limits the aid that can be made available to the weaker sections in the form of scholarships and so on.

Employment

The system does not make any effective contribution towards the employment of the educated. Education can assist its clientele by linking itself to manpower needs by giving skills germane to all occupations as an essential part of its general education, thereby increasing the general employability of the products of education and, finally, by preparing people for self-employment through the development in them of initiative, resourcefulness, the spirit of cooperation and teamwork and so on. In a country with large manpower and the limited capacity of the organized sector to provide employment, self-employment assumes utmost importance; properly trained, technical and educated manpower should provide the main thrust of development. Through their initiative, resourcefulness and technical knowledge, they should be able to exploit the natural resources, lying in abundance in developing countries, using techniques which do not require much capital.

While professional education has met out needs for trained manpower to some extent, the general system of education has not developed its potentiality to any marked degree. The number of registrants at the employment exchanges is very high and is ever increasing. There is widespread unemployment and underemployment in the rural areas. Education has made practically no contribution to the upgradation of the traditional sector, which is and will remain, for as long as one can see, the main source of employment in our country. Consequently, migration of rural talent to the towns takes place on a large scale with tragic consequences both for the country side, which gets denuded of talent, and the urban areas, where this large influx only worsens the existing unemployment position and adds to many social problems which have to be tackled at great social cost. Even among professional people, there is unemployment because their capacity for self-employment and adjustability to changing market conditions has not been developed.

Productivity

Closely linked to employment is the question of increasing the productivity of the people. Our productivity in agriculture is probably the lowest in world. Our general education system makes no contribution to inculcating habits of planned and systematic work to increasing the skills and knowledge required in increasing our productivity in agriculture, rural arts and crafts and so on; our workmanship except in certain specialized hereditary occupations is generally poor; and our educational system creates an aversion to manual work. The absence of training in marketing skills and management also adds to our incapacity to increase our profitability.

Inadequate Relationship with Environment and Developmental Needs

There is very little relationship between the school and its socio-economic environment. For example, the timings of the school are such that the majority of the students cannot attend it in keeping with their domestic duties and have to drop out. Again, the holidays do not take into account the time when the farming families need their children most to work with them. Consequently, a large number of students drop out during or at the end of the elementary stage which provides no preparation for life either in terms of skills or in terms of attitudes, or ability in carrying forward their own self-education. The majority of the people are concentrated in manual labour activities, but there is hardly any place for it in the curriculum. Work experience is discussed a great deal but has yet to take off the ground. As a matter of fact, the type of education prevalent in our schools creates a distaste for manual labour. While we need leadership, which would effectively handle the surrounding physical, social and economic problems, none of these problems are reflected in the school curriculum. For educating the new generation for initiative, resourcefulness, cooperative team spirit and so on requires dynamic methods of teaching, but our methods are still largely based on rote learning which does not encourage or stimulate the child's creativity and dynamism. The net effect of education in the rural areas is a distaste for their habitat and a large-scale migration of talent to the urban areas. The system prompts them only to escape from their fellowmen.

Even professional education is not effectively related to the needs of development. While our country is predominantly rural, our professional education is largely urban oriented. Although our institutions are beginning to realize this problem, so far, barring a few exceptions, their contribution to the evolution of appropriate technology, the training of the local population in skills and their involvement in the development of the local areas has been minimal. Their research projects also centre round international rather than national interests. Even in regard to urban industry, the linkage of education to manpower needs is not effective and no satisfactory solutions have been found to overcome the difficulties of manpower planning. Admissions are made in response to the students' subjective reactions to the employment market which can be quite misleading in regard to demands seven or eight years later, as they are not based on any carefully assessed manpower needs.

The students' lack of practical experience during the training period is well known. The result is that the minds of the students do not respond constructively to the problems of the people even when they are sent to the rural areas for their training. The majority of them feel that it is a waste of time. After passing out, they tend to congregate in the urban areas, though they are required much more in the rural areas. It has even been heard that our medical graduates are being trained for the hospitals of England and America rather than for those of their own country.

Poor Response to Challenge of Excellence and Change

India faces the challenge of the need for excellence in the modern competitive world and also for adaptability to change in an age of sweeping changes. Our system of education has responded to the challenge of excellence to some degree and some of our best institutions today are better than the best of yesterday. But these peaks are far too few and the rapid expansions have not enabled us to build peaks of excellence. If our top institutions such as the Indian Institutes for Technology and Centres for Advanced Studies are effectively linked to the overall educational system for improving the system progressively, these would be supplying critical input.

Our educational system is extremely rigid. We have yet to learn the technique of the management of change. Our post-Independence record has been a consistent failure to prepare for and implement reform—whether it is basic education, multipurpose schools, the three-year degree course or any other innovation. Even the new pattern is still on the anvil and one can only watch its future with hope and trepidation. There is not enough experimentation in the system, and not enough monitoring and evaluation of these experiments to draw from them ideas in a continuous flow to be pumped into the general system. We have picked up new and promising ideas with half understanding, made headlines out of them and when they failed because of faulty planning and implementation we dropped them like hot potatoes.

Ineffective Intersectoral Linkage

Another failure of the education system has been the absence or ineffectiveness of intersectoral linkages. After 27 years of planning in India, even when their necessity is accepted in principle, these linkages have been persistently denied in practice. Education continues to be regarded as an isolated activity, though it is being more and more rudely disturbed by protesting voices from all over the country. Without an earnest effort to understand the involvements of interdependence for mutual gain, the mechanism for converting the accepted principles into everyday practice cannot be developed.

A deeper analysis reveals that there are a variety of factors which stand in the way of a putting into effect the ideas which cannot be theoretically refuted. First, there is the false sense of building our empires. The education departments are as great culprits in this regard as any other department. Second, there is a lack of clear-cut policy of coordination at the top. Third, the intra-agency communication chain is weak, with the result that even where policy decisions have been taken at the top, they do not reach the bottom easily. Fourth, there is lack of decentralization of decision-making in most government departments, whereas inter-agency coordination and cooperation requires a fair amount of manoeuvrability at every level where new procedures and attitudes have to be evolved to make effective coordination a reality. Fifth, the needed coordination required for pooling of resources at many places has not been effective for everybody. This results in wastage of resources.

For example, it is recognized that promotion of literacy is not the sole responsibility of the Ministry of Education and the education departments of the states, attempts have been made to link literacy programmes with developmental activities and services. The Fifth Plan emphasized that the agencies concerned should be responsible for organizing adult education programmes for their clientele and they will be assisted by the education departments in producing literature suitable for neoliterates. A good beginning has been made in this direction in the districts in connection with the Intensive Agricultural Development Programme.

PROSPECTS

The next questions which naturally come up are as follows: what are our future needs? What are the tasks ahead? How can we plan to achieve these? Can we build future success on the foundations of the failures of the past?

The future can be based on our goals and the prognosis of the forces already emerged and which any future educational development must address itself are creating avenues of employment of the educated, improving productivity, new devices for educating the increasing population, social justice, excellence, urbanization, building up national character, national identity and national integration, adaptability to rapid change and lastly, arresting rising costs. Although the Indian education system largely continues on old pre-Independence lines, as a result of impact of these changes already some stirring have become visible and the new trends in Indian education are the result thereof. These have crystallized in varying degrees of definiteness.

Unemployment

The most serious challenge to the education system has come from the ever-increasing unemployment among the educated. While the unemployment problem concerns the whole economy and its strategy of development, education has and can perform certain definite roles in this regard. To play its part, the education system has to make the following contributions:

1. Education at all stages must develop basic skills, and attitudes relevant to the entire spectrum of vocations, such as finger skills, muscle coordination and an eye for detail, initiative, resourcefulness, habits of planned and systematic work, a sense of the dignity of manual labour, a cooperative spirit and last, but not the least, qualities of leadership. These are best developed in an activity-centred and problem-centred education, closely related to the environment. The methods of teaching should be such as to promote scientific thinking on work.

2. Education should lend intelligent and research support to the improvement of the traditional sector through making education problem centred at the primary and secondary levels and taking up its problems for research and investigation under appropriate courses at the university stage. It will have a double advantage of (a) identifying pupils and teachers who can suggest simple improvements in the training of traditional vocations for the mass of

the agriculturists and artisans who can imbibe these improvements, and (b) second, such an exercise will throw up potential inventive talent, which can then be deliberately built up. Thus, a steady improvement of the traditional sector, with the help of science and technology, can play an important role in easing the unemployment situation in developing countries, where the traditional sector today supports the largest number of workers, and the possibility of absorption of the labour force in the modern sector is limited by preventing the shrinkage of existing employment opportunities through the stagnation and consequent desertion of the traditional sector.

3. The educational and vocational guidance services need to be developed so that the students can be guided in regard to the available and developing employment pattern. A suitable guidance system has yet to be evolved.

   The cooperation and coordination of the employment system and the educational system will need to be strengthened.

4. Vocationalization of the higher secondary stage is another identified need and, to some extent, developed, in engineering and agricultural polytechnics, training of para-medical personnel and so on. The vocations already identified have, however, limited absorptive capacity; and designing new areas require close cooperation between the employing authorities and the educational institutions. It is, however, doubtful if the organized sector will be able to absorb the large output from secondary schools, who will, therefore, have to be prepared for self-employment through the development assisted by the provision of necessary training and state help—financial, organizational and infrastructural. If most of the students coming out from secondary schools can be settled, the problem of numbers in our universities will become manageable.

5. At the higher stage, while professional education has to be and can be—within limits—related to the requirements of the economy, general education cannot be related to specific requirements—except in the case of teachers—and has to be regarded as a general up-grader of the labour force and an agency for the promotion of

social and occupational mobility. Our youth need to be trained to acquire realistic expectations from general education. It can and ought improve their general capability of fitting into available jobs and improve their productivity. The introduction of work experience and practical projects should help in this orientation of the student mind. Introduction of specific vocational courses should, however, be done only after a careful assessment of the market needs. For a vocationally trained man, if unwanted by their vocation, is much more frustrated than one who has gone through general education and trying to explore the employment market and adapt themselves to available opportunities.

INCREASING PRODUCTIVITY

Closely allied to the problem of unemployment is that of the need for increasing productivity. Education must be production centred or at least related to production. A very interesting experiment in this regard was represented by basic education which has been hailed by educationists all the world over. We must build on that valuable experience. In that case, productivity depends upon the basic skills of the worker and their attitude to and habits of work. The challenge of increasing productivity, therefore, reinforces the need for the educational reforms to an entirely new pattern.

EXPLOSION OF NUMBERS

The Indian education has seen an explosion of numbers—second only perhaps to China—due to the increase in population and the rising expectations of the people after Independence to realize which education has been the main means. The consequent constraint of resources demand an increasing use of non-formal education—correspondence courses, use of radio and television, evening colleges and so on. The small beginnings that have already been made will need to be developed very considerably in the future. Changes are also required in the curriculum, methods of teaching and examination more appropriate for meeting employment needs.

DEMANDS OF SOCIAL JUSTICE

The new entrants need careful guidance as to what to expect from education and which courses to take. In view of the large support services that need to be organized to enable the weaker sections of society to take full advantage of the educational facilities provided education will become more and more costly. To meet the situation, a number of measures will be called for, such as: first, the capacity of the school and college communities to help themselves must be progressively developed, so should their capability to help the community around and the nation at large, and consequently the latter would, in turn, build up schools and colleges; second, parents must be drawn into partnership with teachers, through parent–teacher associations and projects of adult education not only to help the education of their wards but also to mobilize resources for the school and to enable the education system to respond to change more smoothly; third, the facilities for non-formal education should be increased not only to conform to the concept of lifelong education but also to reduce costs.

CHALLENGE OF EXCELLENCE

In this competitive world, no nation can survive without the pursuit of excellence. Owing to our limited resources, India has adopted a policy which requires concentration of resources, of finance and talent in a few institutions. Here, the policy comes into conflict with the democratic urge for equality. The two can, however, be reconciled, as already stated, if those who enter these institutions are really talented, irrespective of the means of their parents. In poor countries, the problem is one of identification of potential talent, in spite of environmental advantages and handicaps. No reliable tests for such identification of potential talent have yet been devised and the challenge to educational researchers still remains to be met. After identification, the state must take complete charge of such children so that they are nurtured as a national asset. They should be put into the best institutions that the state can devise, emphasizing that the standard of living of the students is as austere as possible so that a leadership is evolved which is not loo far removed from the life of the people whom they have to serve. It is even more important in the case of such schools that they should be linked to the local communities through programmes of community service.

We can get maximum return from our institutes of excellence if, as far as possible, we can keep their cost not so far removed from the average institutions as to make the experience of the former irrelevant to these institutions, to which they should be linked and from which they should receive their feedback. They should also be linked with research institutions, such as the NCERT and the State Institutes of Education. A very alert system of evaluation should also be devised.

An effective intercommunication among these institutes of excellence must also be firmly established as well as a system of mutual sharing of their facilities such as libraries and workshops. The communication of these institutions with similar institutions at the international level should also be improved, leading cross-fertilization of ideas.

URBANIZATION

The prevention of large sections of the rural population, especially the educated ones, moving into urban areas and thereby impoverishing the countryside, must be recognized as a top priority programme in a country where more than 50 per cent of the GNP comes from agriculture and where the possibilities for the creation of additional jobs in the modern sector are severely limited. Further, the disillusionment and frustration of the people moving into the urban areas becomes an important factor in maintaining (or otherwise) social and political stability. Besides, heavy cost of providing the minimum social amenities to these migrants and other complications arising out of this vast migration of people to urban areas, it is necessary, therefore, to create more adequate and better paying jobs in the countryside. Hence, the need for building up of growth centres, creation of a network of infrastructural facilities for development such as roads, power and water supply and transport facilities, more investment in agriculture and agro-industries, more research to make existing industries in the rural areas more paying, and building up a system of education that would enable those in the traditional sector to absorb the results of research and to draw into its fold millions of people who can develop the habit and capacity of thinking rationally on these traditional occupations, thereby leading to their progressive improvement. The system of education must prove that the rural environment is as challenging as any other by making education problem-centred. The dignity of labour must be inculcated by introducing in manual work, thereby demonstrating the division between manual and intellectual work is artificial. The importance of rural areas in the total picture of development must be clearly brought out to the rural people so that they do not get the idea that they are second-rate citizens.

BUILDING NATIONAL CHARACTER, NATIONAL IDENTITY AND NATIONAL INTEGRATION

Resources, both material and intellectual, are important but what really determines the success or failure of a nation is its character, the sense of responsibility and dedication of its citizens, habits of thinking on what they do, capacity for teamwork, initiative and integrity. All this points towards a system of education which is activity-centred and problem-centred. This has implications for changes in the curriculum and methods of teaching.

The citizens have not only to be developed individually and in groups but have to be integrated into a nation. Every nation has a personality of its own which must be carefully identified and nurtured. For this purpose, we must develop our roots and understand our cultural heritage. We must know what we have achieved in the past to what extent it is relevant today in every field of learning and culture. These are the qualities that have enabled us to continue to exist in spite of the onslaughts of history. These qualities of synthesis and tolerance must be taught to our youth with pride. Interpreting of history plays a vital role in this area. Our cultural variety requires very active intercommunication between the various parts of the country. Consequently, we need to develop the capacity for learning various languages. It is only through the languages of one another that we can understand our subcultures. Also, education has to be in the mother tongue to promote talent and creativity. Hence, increasing priority has been attached to language development even for making our development plans more real and effective. This priority needs to be further upgraded.

Not only is it necessary for us to develop our sense of common heritage but also to develop a sense of common destiny. For this, it is necessary that the study of our constitution, our development plans and of our current social, economic and political problems, becomes an essential part of our education system. Our present problems must be studied in our universities in the perspective of history and with academic detachment. Lastly, the gulf between the masses and the elite needs to be bridged. In this respect, programmes, like the national service scheme, assume very high priority.

Building of national cohesion need not and should not mean international animosity and exclusion. It should be built through the inculcation of a sense of progressively widening social responsibility and the culmination of a progressive taming of the ego. The individual must learn to live for the family, the family for the village, the village for the district, the district for the state and the state for the country and the country for the world. By these expanding circles alone can we realize our destiny. The policy of exclusiveness can lead to annihilation. This perspective has to be built among children and kept up throughout their period of education through courses, books and appropriate activities.

CHALLENGE OF CHANGE

In a world of sweeping changes, of exploding knowledge and of on-rushing obsolescence, the education system has to turn out people who will not be swept over by change but will be able to stimulate, direct and, at the same time, adapt themselves to the rapidly changing environment. This requires that, in our educational system, there should be emphasis on an understanding of principles underlying this change and on a capacity for analysis and synthesis of observed phenomena. While principles would generally remain the same, their application would undergo changes; and the knowledge of principles would enable the future workers to adapt themselves to change in technology with ease. Again, there is need for greater emphasis on developing the capacity for acquiring knowledge through self-study rather than formal imparting/learning of maximum possible quantum of knowledge.

Emphasis will also have to shift from pre-employment education to a lifelong system of education, which will increasingly bring in non-formal agencies of education and training. In this lifelong system of training and education, the employing authorities as well as the employees will have to participate increasingly for expanding their learning and also contributing their knowledge for others. Adaptability to change requires innovation. Institutions for this purpose should be carefully selected and there should be a system by which innovations, found to be sound, can be incorporated into the entire educational system with ease. The parents must be associated with it and the administration must also develop the capacity for absorbing the impact of change. They have so far not been equipped for the purpose, yet this is the biggest challenge the country faces, which is to convert the education system and its administration from a conservative force to an agent of change.

RISING COSTS

The cost of education has skyrocketed not primarily because of the rising prices but also because, as already pointed out, of the need to provide incentives on a large scale to the poorer sections of society. It is, moreover, essential continually to improve the standard of education, which also requires more financial investments. In order to contain the expenditure within the limits of available resources, a new system of financing would have to be considered.

Financial burden must be dispersed among the beneficiaries, especially at the higher stages of education, when the benefits become substantial in economic terms and the beneficiaries can be clearly identified. The state finances provided for elementary education must be substantially augmented by contributions from local communities to whom its benefits are confined. As regards secondary education, its burden should be borne by the districts. Vocational education at the secondary and higher stages should be financed by the students as well as institutions of commerce and industry. So far as general education at the higher levels is concerned, higher fees must be charged from the students themselves, unless the education given is for the preparation of teachers in which case the education departments must bear the major burden.

Higher fees have, however, to be counterbalanced by a generous provision of scholarships for hardship cases including the underprivileged sections of society. Every programme must be cost-conscious. Maximum self-help must be developed among school communities by making education more relevant to the local communities and the nation. The technical and physical resources of institutions, especially technical institutions and universities, need to be used for solving community and national problems, thereby reducing certain categories of educated expenditure. For example, schools must be used as community centres for purposes of adult education, preschool education, and part-time education and as feeding centres, recreation centres, village libraries and so on. The schools should be linked effectively with the extension machinery and thereby helped to develop as centres of socio-economic change.

CONCLUSION

Thus, overall educational planning in India, linking education effectively with the overall societal objectives and with other sectors of development, is still in its initial stages of development and its expansion is largely the result of drift rather than of planned effort. While this large-scale expansion has created a ferment and led to occupational and social mobility, met the manpower needs of our growing industry, and made a definite move towards social justice, the system has yet a long way to go to establish equality of opportunity even quantitatively. Qualitatively, the difference between the institutions for the poor and the institutions for the rich is so great that the equality of opportunity is more an illusion than a reality. The breakneck expansion has also resulted in falling standards, which again largely affects the average and below average institutions and thereby undermines our attempts at social justice. The curricula are outdated and do not reflect the variegated objectives of the new class of entrants into our schools. The system has made no effective contribution to employment of the education or in increasing the general productivity of the people. Its relationship with the environmental and developmental needs is minimal. Even professional education is not related to the total developmental needs of the country. It leaves out many areas and its priorities are distorted in many respects.

The system attempts only haltingly to meet the challenge of excellence. It is too rigid to meet the challenge of change. The intersectoral linkages are ineffective.

If, therefore, education is to be made an agency of social transformation and economic development, from which there is no escape, then radical alterations in the system are called for. The major challenges to be met are those of unemployment among the educated, low productivity, explosion of numbers, social justice, excellence, urbanization, building up national character, national identity and national integration, adaptability to rapid change and, lastly, rising costs. The curricula and methodology of education will have to undergo radical changes. We will have to decide on new modes of financing education and devise new structures for managing change and development. We cannot afford to think of education only as an isolated activity. It has to be at the heart of national development. To achieve our tasks, we will have to clarify our ideas, draw up concrete programmes of action and choose men for strategic positions who will have the vision and drive to convert aspirations into reality. Let us hope we will rise to the occasion and turn a new leaf in the history of educational development.

NOTES

1. *First Five Year Plan*, Planning Commission, Government of India, p. 525.
2. Figure pertains to Draft Fifth Plan, Planning Commission, Government of India, p. 198.
3. Selected Educational and Related Statistics at a Glance, Education Division, Planning Commission, Government of India, March 1976, p. 31.
4. Selected Educational and Related Statistics at a Glance, Education! Division, Planning Commission, Government of India, March 1976, p. 103.
5. Economic survey. 1976–1977 Ministry of Finance, Government of India, New Delhi, p. 5.
6. Expenditure on Education as shown in the Central and State Annual Budgets 1974–1975 to 1976–1977 (cyclostyled), compiled from the Budget Estimates of 1976–1977—Studies in Educational Statistics— No. 6—1976—Statistics and Planning Division, Department of Education, Ministry of Education. & Social Welfare, Government, of India, New Delhi, 1976.

Section II

Education of Women and Social Change

Sectional Introduction

In the contemporary history of development of nations, the role of women in development was recognized relatively only recently. Issues relating to development of women like women's education have not attracted the attention of development planners for a long time. Though in ancient Indian literature we find some great women scholars and women's education was encouraged even during the first millennium, women's education was not paid sufficient attention by the modern society. In his pioneering work, *Investing in Human Capital*, Theodore W. Schultz (1971, p. 196) observed,

> If one were to judge from the work that is being done, the conclusion would be that human capital is the unique property of the male population... Despite all of the schooling of females and other expenditures on them, they appear to be of no account in the accounting of human capital.

Few major public policies until a couple of decades ago clearly aimed at enhancing and expanding female participation in education. As Gail Kelly (1984) noted, most international agencies and national governments did not even collect data detailing the number of women, as opposed to men, that entered school or kept themselves in schools system at successive levels of education.

> The literature on educational problems also revealed a bias against women: from the beginning of the 1950s to the end of the 1960s, or even the 1970s, a time when the sciences of education took concrete shape, there was very little attention to women in general and education of women in particular. (Eliou, 1987, p. 59)

It is only during the last couple of decades of the last century, women's issues began figuring prominently in development agenda of the nations and international organizations, and education has become one of the very important issues in development planning and educational research (e.g., King & Hill 1993; Tilak 2007). Yet in the contemporary education research in developing countries like India, gender- and women-related issues have not received as much attention as they should have (Sudarshan & Tilak 2018).

In the first essay in this section, M. C. Paul describes how disdainfully the issue of education of women was treated by the British during the colonial period in India. Obviously colonial rulers did not have much interest in education in general or women's education in particular. Both received only lip service at the hands of the British. The meagre growth in women's education that had taken place during the colonial period can be attributed to the people who were leading the socio-political movements not only for reforming the Indian society but also against the colonial rule. That is true in the case of most colonies. After independence the approach towards women's education began to change rather slowly.

Underlying the fact that women are major instruments of social change, Muriel Wasi argues in her short essay that education of women should help in social change in a big way. She decries the general non-involvement of women of upper middle classes in the radical changes through which our society is passing; and the realization that a major social revolution is taking place in which they are inextricably involved seems not to strike them. Women should be made aware through proper education of the fact that they are an integral part of social change, and they have to take major initiatives for social change.

Compared to the situation in 1971, when Muriel Wasi wrote this article, many might feel that situation has changed considerably, and yet they might also acknowledge that there is still a long way to go.

While concerns of policy makers include women's education and gender-related aspects figure conspicuously in recent policy planning exercises in many countries, according to Karuna Chanana, who has critically examined here the policy documents relating to higher education in the Eleventh Five-Year Plan in India (2007–2012), they are conceptualized within a very narrow framework on the one hand and are fragmented by a fractured vision of both the system of higher education and of Indian society on the other. As a result, gender concerns receive very little meaningful space in the final policy documents. This is because the cultural concerns colour the vision and value frames of the policy makers on the very societal conception of the feminine role. Despite seemingly impressive progress in numbers, Chanana underlines that there is still a lot to do in the march towards empowerment of women to play a significant role in societal development.

REFERENCES

Eliou, M. (1987). Equality of sexes in education: And now what? *Comparative Education, 23*(1), 59–67.

Kelly, G. P. (1987). Setting state policy on women's education in the Third Word: Perspectives from comparative research. *Comparative Education, 23*(1), 95–102.

King, E., & Hill, M. A. (Eds.). (1993). *Women's education in the developing countries: Barriers, benefits, and policies.* Johns Hopkins University Press for the World Bank.

Schultz, T. W. (1971). *Investing in human capital.* Free Press.

Sudarshan, R. M., & Tilak, J. B. G. (Eds.). (2018). *Gender in contemporary education research.* Gyan Publishing.

Tilak, J. B G. (Ed.). (2007). *Women's education and development.* Gyan Books.

Chapter 9

Colonialism and Women's Education in India*

M. C. Paul

Although right from 1813, and even prior to that, women's education had increased, the progress during colonial rule was very nominal in comparison to the total population and population of females to that of males' education. The most astonishing fact which obviously comes out of our study is that in spite of so many efforts made by various agencies during the last 150 years, the percentage of educated women has not yet reached desirable figures. Women's education had been a sort of ritual without any meaning or purpose. We know that education is the most important factor in achieving a rapid socio-economic development and technological progress. But during the colonial rule, its potential role in nation building and development got only lip service. And it was articulated at a low key. The reasons are as follows: (a) the British colonialists after the sepoy mutiny of 1857 did not take much interest in women's education and socio-economic reform; (b) they did not take much initiative to recognize educational reform demanded by the society and (c) recommendations of the Wood's despatch, the Indian Education Commission of 1882 and other commissions appointed from time to time, in the wake of various sociopolitical movements, were not implemented in true spirit by the colonial government. Thus, education had become unresponsive to the social, political and economic aspirations of women in particular and the people in general.

* *Social Change:* June 1989: Vol. 19, No. 2, 3–17.

An attempt is made here to explore how women's education was gradually and haltingly developed during the colonial rule, how the various movements influenced it and to what extent was it instrumental in breaking ground for new values to bring about social change.

During the Vedic period, women enjoyed high social status and educational opportunities along with men. They had a fair deal of freedom and equality. They enjoyed the same social rights as their husbands. Widow remarriages were the rule and not the exception. Boys and girls had similar education, and both were to pass through the period of *Brahmacharya* (celibate life). The *Upanayana* ceremony which marked the introduction of a child into the study of the Vedas was performed by both girls and boys. They had access to all branches of knowledge and took part in religious and philosophical discourses irrespective of sex. Several of them, namely Vachaknavi Gargi, Sulabha Maitreyi, Romasha, Urvashi, Katyayani, Yami Apala, Ghosha Kakshivati, Shraddha, Lopamudra and others are still household names because of their great distinctions in theology and philosophy. Moreover, many sacred hymns composed by women had position in the Vedas, the sacred book of Hinduism (Report of NCWE, 1958–1959, p. 1; Thackersey, 1970, p. 1; Dube, 1976, pp. 7–8; Dave, 1971, p. 22; Mookerjee, pp. 1–2; Altekar, pp. 410–411).

Unfortunately, the equal opportunities and positions enjoyed by women in the Vedic period diminished with the subsequent social, economic and political changes. The marriage age of women fell from 16–17 years to 8–9 years. Widows progressively lost their right to remarry. The custom of 'sati' unknown in the society came to surface. Free movement of women in the society was curtailed. The women were forced to be in the four walls of the house and lost their right to education. By and large, women's education was considered as a source of moral danger. Of course, a very few women appeared in all parts of the country as stateswoman, rulers, soldiers or saints from time to time and were honoured by men and women as well. But their glorifications could not reduce or cover the degraded social and educational conditions of the women as a whole (Desai, 1957, Ch. 1; Report of NCWC, 1950–1959, p. 1; Thackersey, 1970, ch. 1; Devdas, 1976, p. 46; Dube, 1976, pp. 7–16; Altekar, 1938, p. 354; Dave, 1971, pp. 24–26).

Then came the colonialists. When the British colonialists established political suzerainty over India, the social status of women had fallen to a new low. Much has to be said and discussed about the colonial period because it has a great bearing on women's education. This period opens quite a new chapter in Indian educational history. It was the period when there came a gradual decline in women's social status. On the other hand, it was the period when various social and political movements started by the stalwarts such as Raja Ram Mohan Roy, Mahadev Govind Ranade, Ishswar Chanda Vidyasagar, Mehrotra and Kandukuri Veeresalingam. They encouraged women's education and assiduously mobilized them to fight the injustice heaped on women both by the traditional system and the colonial rulers and preached restoration of the former high status of women in society. In the face of this onslaught, the colonial rulers took a ritualistic attempt in women's education. Their interest was political and economic. Thus, it was the missionaries and the private voluntary bodies, both Christians and Indians, as votaries of education, that took increasing interest in the promotion of women's education in the country. They took greater effort to set up schools and colleges in various parts of the country and bore the financial burden of women's education.

PERIOD FROM 1757 TO 1812

The colonialists introduced formal primary education in big cities. In Calcutta, half a dozen primary schools for women were established during this period. The curriculum of these schools consisted of learning three R's, needle work, lace-making and so on. Some schools taught French and dancing. Most of the girls admitted were from the Anglo-Indian and Indian Christian communities (Mukherjee, 1966, p. 24).

In this period, the British colonialists did not show any active interest in women's education. When the missionaries, such as the Portuguese, Danish, Protestants, Baptists and Germans intruded into India at the end of the 16th century, they established several educational institutions in different parts of India. Their aim, however, was to proselytize and infuse Christian religion. The colonialists did encourage these missionaries until the absolute consolidation of British colonial power in Indian soil. After 1757, it adopted a policy of religious neutrality so that it might not lose the political and commercial foothold. In the beginning, the missionaries were dissuaded not to engage in missionary activities in areas under colonial rule up to 1813. Thus, the effort of starting formal education by them came to a halt during this period. A few English people became interested to propagate English education. A few educated Indians in contact with English people also became interested in it with the sole aim to be absorbed in the job market. Thus, both groups opened English schools in Calcutta and showed interest in women's formal education (Mukherjee, 1966, Ch. 2). In Madras, Lady Campbell (the Governor's wife) founded the Female Orphan Asylum in 1757 exclusively for the children of European officers and soldiers (Nurullah & Naik, 1961, p. 55).

PERIOD FROM 1813 TO 1853

It was during this period of colonial consolidation with the renewal of the Company's Charter Act of 1813 that the colonialists were directly concerned with the expansion of English education in India. The missionaries were given an upper hand and ample opportunities to promote English education with religious fervour. Huge funds were set aside for this purpose. The Baptist Missionary Society of the United States, the Church Missionary Society of England, the Vestleyam Mission, the Scottish Missionary Society and so on were forced to spread their activities by opening women's institutions (Nurullah & Naik, 1961, pp. 80–82; Dave, 1091, p. 76; Asthana, 1974, pp. 13–15).

At the beginning of this period, women's education was almost non-existent, as it was in Britain, due to the age-old prejudice of the Britishers against women. It was in response to various movements by women in India and all over the world that the colonialists were forced to encourage the missionaries to spread women's education. They started girls' day schools and orphans' domestic establishments. The Calcutta Juvenile Society and the Serampore Female Society made notable contributions in this field, mainly in large cities. The Ladies Society for Native Female Education was formed in 1824 under the Patronage of Lady Amherst which managed more than 30 women schools. Both indigenous and missionaries efforts were welcomed by the women. The curriculum of women's schools consisted of three R's, geography, needlework and so on. In addition, religion was taught predominantly in missionary schools. The majority of women hailed from the Anglo-Indian, Indian Christian and Parsee Communities (Report of the NCWE, 1958–1959, p. 16; Dave, 1971, p. 250).

At the same time, the colonialists started collecting information on the existing socio-economic conditions of the people of India for the purpose of formulation of a sound educational policy to serve their purpose. Most of the schools were strictly confined to the education of boys. Of course, the women from the affluent families came out to get education wherever the school system reached them (Nurullah & Naik, 1951, p. 14 and p. 28; Mukherjee, 1950, p. 8). One of the most important factors why the women in this period could not see the light of education is the non-existence of women's educational institutions in most parts of India, even if the consciousness of the necessity of women's education started with the activities of social reformers, both Indian and Western (Report of NCWE, 1958–1959, p. 14). In fact, the colonialists did not pay any attention to promoting women's formal education. So they restricted the education to men and did not spend a single pie out of the educational grant of 1813 for women's education. Moreover, they refused to grant any financial assistance to private schools established for girls (Mukherjee, 1966, p. 108; Asthana, 1974, p. 131). It was the policy of excuse that the colonialists implemented. They believed that 'any attempt to educate women would create a very great commotion.' This fake belief boomeranged in course of time with the demand of women's education. Thus, it was proved that the conservative tendency among the colonial rulers discouraged them to promote women's education. The colonial rulers did not pay heed even if social reformers like John Elliot Drinkwater Bethune urged the government to take over a women's school established by him in Calcutta in 1849 (Nurullah & Naik, 1951, p. 154). J. E. D. Bethune, the law member of the Executive Council of the Governor General and the President of the Council of Education (1848–1851), donated his entire pay (about ₹10,000) to the school as the company did not give any financial aid. He was encouraged and assisted by the enlightened Indians. Land for the school was donated by the zamindar Dakshinaranjan Mukherjee. Thus, it is stated that 'the establishment of the Bethune School introduced a new era in the history of women's education in this country' (Mukherjee, 1966, p. 111). It was supported and financed by a private education body for 20 years (De, 1959, p. 51). The social reform movements started by people like Raja Ram Mohan Roy with the cooperation of saner and progressive educationists compelled the colonialists to show some interest in women's education.

In 1854, it was for the first time that the colonial government was forced to pass the Woods Education Despatch, thereby officially announcing their 'frank and cordial support' for women's education in India (Bhatt & Aggarwal, 1969, p. 10). The overall progress was slow, and the 1881 Census showed that there was just one woman under instruction for a population of 403 women in Madras. The ratio was 1:431 in Bombay, 1:976 in Bengal and 1:2226 in Assam. Every now and then, Indians too donated for the promotion of women's education. For example, ₹20,000 was donated by Raja Baidyanath of Calcutta (Dave, 1971, p. 78). The missionaries were also very active in promoting English education. They opened schools in North India such as in Mirzapur, Howrah, Khulna, Banaras, Allahabad and Bareilly. Boarding houses for orphans and destitute in some important cities were also set up. They were very particular to send Christian governesses to educate the upper class families (Mukherjee, 1966, p. 110). The Indian reformers did not like the way the Christian missionaries were infusing English education with religious overtones among the women in India. They started their own women's schools at different places such as in Uttarpara, Jessore, Nebudhia, Barasat and Sukhsagar (Bengal), Poona, Ahmedabad, Bombay and Madras Presidency during the 19th century. Various private societies were managing women's schools on their own. To counter the Christian missionary schools, the Indians sent their daughters to these schools. For example, by 1854, non-official efforts had led to the opening of 256 schools for women in Madras state, 288 in Bengal and 65 in Bombay (CIRTPC, 1975, p. 1.22). The government was apathetic in the promotion of women's education.

PERIOD FROM 1854 TO 1892

As mentioned, it was during this period that various social and political movements forced the colonial government to adopt a policy on women's education in India. Of course, the Woods Despatch of 1854 urged the British government to expand women's education, but it was greatly undermined by the latter. The uprising of 1857 which gave a blow to colonial government made them cautious and a policy of social and religious neutrality was declared by the Queen. The participation of large number of women including Laxmi Bai, Tara Bai, Sunder, and Moti Bai in the mutiny made the government a little more careful in the promotion of education. Consequently, not much was achieved with regard to women's education till about 1870 (Asthana, 1974, p. 133). However, a considerable private and collective effort made by the Indians and Europeans had helped in shaping women's education. For example, the Brahma Samaj started publishing journals to promote education and culture among the Indian women. The Arya Samaj Mahakanya Vidyalaya, the Arya Kanya Schools, beyond the primary school level, were set up. The number of primary schools for women increased from 626 in 1854 to 2,600 in 1882. The enrolment of women students in primary schools substantially rose from 21,755 in 1854 to 82,420 in 1882. Enrolment of women students in the co-education schools also showed an increase, but there was no universal education among women (Thackersey, 1970, p. 9; De, 1959, p. 6). Thus, the gap between the education of men and women was very wide. For every 1,000 boys in school, the number of girls was only 46 and while one adult boy out of 16 could read and write, only one adult girl in 434 could do so. The government policy mainly concentrated on primary education.

A department of education was created in 1882 to look into the problems of women's education and expand primary schools for women. Municipalities, local fund committee or boards were set up in rural areas for expansion of primary education. But progress was too feeble. However, most of the women's schools, including mixed primary schools, were not supported financially by the colonial government. The non-official private societies and local bodies came forward and bore most of the financial burden to run these schools. The stepmotherly treatment had upset the spread of women's education. In fact, the reason was due to the policy and traditional attitudes, of some officials in the Department of Education (Thackersey, 1970, pp. 9–12). A large number of progressive Indians who came in contact with Western college education at home and abroad had broadened their outlook and they took up the task of promoting women's education. For example, the Brahmos of Brahma Samaj in Bengal were championing the cause of women's education so that the other half of the society could be uplifted for the overdevelopment of Indian society (Kopf, 1979, p. 15). They firmly believed that with the betterment of the women's lot, the general progress and development of society would be possible. The individual initiatives by the Indians under the influence of various social reform movements encouraged many to establish a number of women's schools. For example, Pandit Ishwar Chandra Vidyasagar set up more than 40 schools for women between 1855 and 1858. In 1857, a large number of women's schools were opened in the districts of Agra, Mathura and Manipuri of Uttar Pradesh. Other parts of India were not lagging behind. In Poona, Mahatma Liba Govindrao Phuley started private schools for women where he himself taught. It was during the time when the official trend was in the downward direction that Mahatma Phuley raised the slogan of compulsory education. He was the first person who started a private school for Harijans in 1852 (Mukherjee, 1966, p. 136; Dave 1971, p. 80).

It was during this period that the secondary education for women made a humble beginning in different parts of the country due to the sociopolitical awakening. For example, 81 secondary schools for women were opened with a total enrolment of 2,054 women students in 1982. Of these, Madras had 46 schools with 389 women students; Bengal had 22 schools with 1,051 women students; Bombay had a school with 538 pupils; Uttar Pradesh had 3 schools with 68 women students. Most of these women's schools were concentrated in the urban areas only. Thus, the women folk of rural areas were deprived of their right to education. However, the schools in the cities were drawing women students mainly from Anglo-Indian, European, Indian Christian, Parsee and a few enlightened and well-to-do Hindu and Muslim families. Moreover, out of the total 81 secondary schools, the colonial government financed fully only six secondary schools. Only 50 women schools out of 81 were run by their grants-in-aids. The missionaries were still preoccupied with primary education only. All this hindered the growth of secondary education of women and the little efforts made by local bodies in promoting secondary education among the women could not make much headway. Furthermore, the women students in the secondary schools were prescribed the same syllabus and subjects as boys instead of reorganizing the syllabus and subjects to suit the former. Although domestic science was introduced as an optional subject, necessary equipment to teach this subject was not provided. Thus, it did not help the women students (Dave, 1971. pp. 277–278).

As mentioned, the Brahmos of Brahma Samaj pioneers in spreading women's education in various pockets of the country started college education with the help of Indian Christians after 1878. Of course, very few women joined the college and most of them belonged to the enlightened elite among advanced communities such as Indian Christians and the Brahmos of Bengal. For example, the Bethune College of Calcutta, the first institution of higher education for women, enrolled only six women students. Of course, the Sarah Tucker College at Palamcottah, started in 1879 (Mukherjee, 1966, p. 186; De, 1959, p. 5, Mukherjee, 1956, p. 7). In the beginning, the colonialists refused to do anything regarding the promotion of higher education among women. In 1879, after 30 years of its coming into being, the Bethune School got the status of Bethune College obtained financial support from the government and was finally affiliated to Calcutta University (Kopf, 1979, pp. 34–41). In fact, the establishment of the Calcutta, Bombay and Madras universities in January 1857 marked beginning of modern higher education in India. But women were not allowed to take admission in these universities. For example, the Calcutta University Syndicate in June 1875 took a decision not to give admission to women students. After much protest, only in 1877 the university allowed the women students to take the examinations (Mukherjee, 1966, p. 138). The University of London opened its gates to women for higher education only in 1878.

With the spread of secondary and college education among the women in India, the need for women teachers' training institutions arose. The need for professional training was recognized for the first time in 1860. But the colonial government took very little care to train lady teachers, even though the need for the training of teachers was proposed in the Woods Despatch in 1854. They did not open a single training institute for women teachers. The dearth of women teachers was a setback in the promotion of higher education for women (De, 1959, p. 6; Mukherjee, 1966, p. 137). However, after a long time, it took up the full financial responsibility to run 4 out of the 15 training institutions, namely 1 in Madras, 2 in Bombay and 1 in the Central Provinces, whereas the remaining 11 training institutions (3 in Madras, 2 in Bengal, 3 in Uttar Pradesh and 3 in Punjab) were given partial grant-in-aid. Of course, the efforts made by Christian missionaries and private individuals were notable with regard to training the women teachers. The objectives of the missionaries were twofold: 'To train women teachers to serve in their own girls' schools and to train the converted girls for useful careers' (Nurulla & Naik, 1961, p. 389). That is why the missionary training institutions for women teachers never attracted the Hindu and Muslim women teachers as they feared evangelization. The private effort in this regard was attempted first by pioneers like Miss Mary Carpenter of Britain. She planned to organize training colleges for women teachers in India with the cooperation of government officials. She received help from the Brahmo leaders like Keshab Chandra Sen who started a normal school to train women teachers. In Poona too, a women's college was established in 1870 to train the women candidates (Nurulla & Naik, 1961, p. 390; De, 1959, p. 6; Mukherjee, 1966, p. 137).

It was at the time when the popular movements in favour of development of education, particularly women's education, started gathering momentum that the colonial government in India had appointed the Indian Education Commission popularly known as Hunter Commission in 1882. The Commission tried to study the problems of women's education in India in detail and proposed many reforms. They found that women's education was in a very deplorable condition: 98 per cent of female children of the school-going age were outside schools, and that out of the total female population of 99.7 million covered by its enquiries, 99.5 million were unable to read and write. Therefore, it suggested to introduce the system of scholarship; establish women's hostels; extend the education to secondary level and prescribe different curriculum for women. The Commission in its report pointed out the serious need to promote women's education on equitable footing as it was in the case of boys' education (Bhatt & Aggarwall, 1969, p. 18; Nurullala & Naik, 1961, p. 393; Asthana, 1974, p. 135).

The Commission also supported private efforts to promote women's education; larger and easier grants-in-aid from the government were

Table 9.1 *Education of girls and women in India (1901–1902)*

	No. of Special Institutions for Girls	No. of Girls Enrolled in All Educational Institutions at This Level
1. Arts & science colleges	12	169
2. Professional colleges		87
3. Secondary schools	422	9,075
4. Primary schools	5,305	344,712
5. Training schools	45	1,253
6. All other special schools	17	1,117
Total	5,801	356,413

Source: Report of NCWE: 1958–1959, p. 22.

prescribed. Fee concession, awards of prizes and scholarships for women over 12 years for the purpose of attracting them to education were also recommended. But the colonial government did not take all the recommendations of Hunter Commission in true spirit. Two decades following the Commission's report were periods of financial stringency. The colonialists did tighten the allotment of funds and adequate grants, thereby strangling women's education. Thus, the progress on this front was slow and halting. Practically speaking, there was no women school in rural India (Thackersey, 1970, p. 24; Mazumdar, 1973; Mukherjee, 1956, p. 8; Asthana, 1974, 136). Table 9.1 shows the progress of women's education at different levels.

Social reformers such as Pandit Ishwar Chandra Vidyasagar, G. G. Agarkar, Justice M. G. Ranade and others played a major role in the promotion of secondary education among women in this period.

One of the most significant achievements during this period was the entry of women in the universities. For example, two Indian women (Kadambini Ganguly and E. C. Bose) graduated from Bethune College, under Calcutta University in 1883; one woman each from Bombay and Madras universities (in 1891) became graduates (Report of NCWE, 1958–1959; Nurulla & Naik, 1961, p. 396; Thackersay, 1970, p. 10; De, 1959, p. 7; Desai, 1957, p. 207).

PERIOD FROM 1892 TO 1947

Various reports show that college education for women was restricted mainly to the affluent and advanced well-to-do communities. Women on the whole were still almost totally illiterate. Not even one in one hundred women was able to read and write, the percentage of female literacy being 0.69 in 1901. For example, 264 students in arts and science colleges in 1901–1902 consisted of 148 Anglo-Indians, 49 were Indian Christians and 38 Parsees, 28 were Hindus and one belonged to 'other' group.

The important breakthrough in women's education during this period was the starting of separate colleges for women by private organizations. The number of separate colleges for women increased to 12 in 1881–1882. The number of women students in colleges rose from 6 in 1881–1882 to 264 in 1901–1902. Only the Bethune College was financed by the colonial government. The others were financed and managed by private bodies and missionaries (De, 1959, p. 7). There was popular demand for women's education, particularly professional education, in this period especially among the women of India. Table 9.2 shows the number of women students in professional education in India in 1901–1902.

In 1902, there were 76 women in medical colleges and 166 in medical schools. Besides, there were a fairly large number of women undergoing training as nurses, midwives and so on.

Table 9.2 Number of Women Students in Professional Education in 1901–1902

1. Teachers training schools	1,412
2. Schools of art	40
3. Medical schools	166
4. Technical or industrial schools	468
5. Commercial schools	26
6. Others	695
Total	2,807

Source: Report of the National Committee on Women's Education, 1958–1959.

The total number of students studying in the training colleges increased from 515 in 1881–1882 to 1,412 in 1901–1902. However, the Christian women students were having preponderance in these professional colleges. They formed 69 per cent of the total female teachers (Nurullah & Naik, 1961, p. 401).

As most educated women preferred to study medicine, the Countess of Dufferin Fund was created in 1885 to promote medical education among women. A large amount collected through the Countess of Dufferin Fund was utilized to give scholarships to women medical students (Smith, 1967, p. 725; De, 1959, p. 9). Many women started entering into this profession to become physicians and surgeons. This was mainly owing to the awakening created by the freedom movement and the First World War. However, most of the women students in the medical colleges were drawn from the Anglo-Indian, Indian Christian and Parsee communities. The Hindu and Muslim women in the higher professional education were almost non-exigent. They were not encouraged by the colonial government as the latter did not accept the recommendations of the Hunter Commission in true spirit. In 1911, Gokhale introduced a Bill for Universal Compulsory Primary education in India and it was defeated by the British and government-appointed members. In 1916, Patel introduced similar Bill that was also defeated by the colonialists and their stooges (Durant, 1930, 42). Thus, most of the educational facilities for the Indian women in several parts of India were maintained and financed by private bodies and associations such as the Indian National Congress, Arya Samaj, Brahmo Samaj and the Ramakrishna Mission. They worked untiringly to educate women in many parts of India (Desai, 1957, p. 208). When Curzon came to India as colonial ruler, the situation of women's education was astoundingly in low profile. Only 2.5 per cent of the female population of school-going age was in school and the total expenditure was 11 lakhs, as compared to 80 lakhs on boys' education (Nurullah & Naik, 1961, pp. 493.4).

In 1913, the colonial government of India was forced to prepare a new educational policy for women. It recommended special curriculum of practical utility for women such as needle work and music, and maintained that 'too much importance should not be attached to examination in the education of girls' (Bhatt & Aggarwal, 1969. p. 3; Dave 1971, p. 255).

Between 1907 and 1912, the universities of Allahabad, Calcutta, Madras and Punjab admitted external female candidates in their examinations.

In 1917, the Calcutta University Commission known as Sadler Commission was appointed. It authorized the Calcutta University to set up a 'Special Board of Women Education' and formulated a 'special curriculum according to the needs of women'. The commission also recommended the segregation of universal education, that is, two distinct types of education for Hindus and Muslims in accordance with their religious sentiments were recommended. This encouraged the religious value systems to mingle with women's education. For example, it recommended organizing Purdah schools for Hindu and Muslim women on the basis of Hinduism and Islam (Nurullah & Naik, 1961, p. 503). Instead of changing the attitudes and conservative value systems through the universal secular women's education, the colonial rulers encouraged and fostered the communal education system. In other words, when the women were ready to change the old values and attitudes in response to the various social reform movements and when they realized more and more the need for modern secular education on the basis of rationality and scientific temper, the said recommendation had given a setback to the promotion of secular universal education. Rather it helped in 'educational balkanization' with its emphasis on both modern and communal systems for men and women, respectively (Mukherjee, 1966, p. 195; Chaube, 1965, p. 2).

Table 9.3 shows the progress of women's education in India in 1921. In 1919, Abala Bose, wife of Jagdish Chandra Bose, a renowned scientist of India, launched the Nari Siksha Samiti with the aim of spreading education among adult women in their own mother tongue so as to enable them to play a constructive role in uplifting their own society and earn their own livelihood with self-respect in case of necessity. She also opened free primary schools for women students in the rural areas of Hooghly, Howrah, 24 Paraganas, Birbhum, Midnapur and Burdwan in West Bengal, Patna in Bihar, as well as Dacca, Faridpur, and other areas of the then East Bengal (now Bangladesh). They managed and financed their work totally out of their own resources.

As already mentioned, the secondary and college education were mainly concentrated in towns and cities only. For example, in Bengal,

Table 9.3 *Education of Women in India in 1921*

	No. of Special Institutions for Girls	No. of Girls Enrolled in All Educational Institutions at This Level
1. Colleges	19	95
2. Secondary schools	675	26,163
3. Primary schools	21,956	1,186,224
4. All other special institutions	1128	10,836
Total	23,778	1,224,128

Source: Report of NCWE: 1958–1959, p. 23.

out of nine, eight were in Calcutta and most of the enrolled women students were from affluent European and Indian families (Gray, 1930, pp. 30–35). It was also during this period that suitable changes in the curriculum for women students was made. Subjects such as physiology, hygiene and domestic science were included as optional in school leaving certificate examination. In some schools, subjects such as embroidery, drawing, needle work and music were introduced. But the changes in the curriculum for women were not effective as the allocation of finance was negligible. Shortage of trained women teachers was also one of the factors of unsuccessful implementation of this new curriculum (Nurullah & Naik, 1961, p. 575).

The important development in this period in college education was the establishment of SNDT (first Indian Women's University) in Poona in 1901 by Maharshi Annasaheb Karve on the model of the Women's University of Japan. Women realized that they should strive for the promotion of a standard system of education in order to elevate their position in the society. Initially, it was not recognized by the government and was managed by a private body. It was raised to the university status afterwards (Dave, 1971, p. 250). The expansion of educational institutions during this period made an impact on the women in India. They had shown (Table 9.4) increasing interest in joining various institutions in the fields of arts, commerce, law, agriculture, science, technology and medicine. This exploded the age-old myth of intellectual inferiority of women. They proved that

Table 9.4 *Education of Women in India (1921–1922)*

No. of Women under Instruction	
Colleges for	
1. Medicine	197
2. Teaching	67
3. Commerce	2
Schools for	
1. Teaching	3,903
2. Art	32
3. Medicine	334
4. Technical and industrial careers	2,744
5. Commercial careers	308
6. Agriculture	79
7. Other careers	3,170
Total	10,836

Source: Report of the National Committee on Women's Education.

women could successfully compete with men in fields which were earlier exclusively monopolized by men. There were no separate institutions for the various subjects enumerated earlier for the women students. However, separate women's colleges for education and medicine did exist. During this period, many women schools were taken over by the government and were given only grants-in-aid (Mukherjee, 1966, p. 115; Nurullah & Naik, 1961, p. 574).

Although direct control of government on women's educational institutions had increased considerably, the burden to running and financing these women institutions lay on missionaries and other private bodies. Only 4 out of 19 colleges in this period (1921–1922) were completely financed and controlled by the government. Out of 675 secondary schools (both high and middle), only 115 were under direct government control and 70 were controlled by local bodies. Of the 21,956 primary schools, 16,810 were aided and the remaining 5,146 were only partially aided by the government. It was in this period that the control of education was transferred from state to the Central Indian

Minister under the system of Dyarchy in 1921. Provincial Autonomy was introduced in 1937 and the states began taking increasing interest in the promotion of women's education. It was a deviation from the earlier 'hesitant and over-cautious policies of the colonial government' towards women's education in India (Report of NCWE, 1958–1959, pp. 23–25).

The mass sociopolitical movements forced the colonial government to enact various legislations and Acts during this period. This created, as a coincidence, general interest in women's education. The Sharada Act in 1929 fixed the age of marriage of women in India at 14 years. This Act was not enforced much among the women in rural areas. The women obtained the right to vote in the Indian Legislative Assembly in 1923 and the right to contest in election for Legislative Assembly was granted in 1931. These rights made them aware of their roles in the upliftment of our society.

The contemporary women's movements in Europe and America influenced women in India to fight for their emancipation from the shackles of colonial rules and the socio-religious orthodoxy. A spirit of nationalism penetrated deep into the women's mind. Leadership, from the women, both urban and rural, started emerging and various organizations for women's cause surfaced to agitate for the improvement of their education and socio-economic position. In other words, it was realized that freedom for women was an integral part of the national freedom. The earliest women organization born in the lap of the British rule was the women's Indian association founded in 1917 by Dr Annie Besant and Mrs Margaret Cousins. It was under the leadership of Dr (Mrs) Annie Besant that the Home Rule Movement gave shape to the people's urge for freedom. In 1925, the National Council of Women (now affiliated to the International Council of Women) was established. The All India Women's Conference (AIWC) came into being in 1926 and the first All India Women's Educational and Social Conference was held in 1927. Of course, these organizations of women remained middle-class organizations and were led only by the women of affluent and middle-class families. Simple peasant women like Matangini Hazra who boldly stood before the British bullets before she was shot down in Midnapore (West Bengal) did not find any place in AIWC. The women from the working class and peasantry did not find forum with the leaders of AIWC (Renu Chakraborty, 1972, p. 177).

Increasing participation of women in various sociopolitical movements widened their interest and opened new vistas before them. For example, the Non-Cooperation Movement in 1921, the Civil Disobedience Movement in 1931, the Quit India Movement in 1942 and so on to oust the colonialists were some of them. The women were enthusiastically involved in various social reform movements against prejudices and ignorance. This had ultimately served as a background for a demand for free, universal and compulsory women's education because the women's demand for the latter became the symbol of women's improved position and status (Mukherjee, 1957, p. 5).

The Hartog Committee (1937) recommended the equality of educational opportunities and the career of women. During this period, the Indian women increasingly participated in various professions to cope up with the hard economic situation (during the Second World War). More and more women felt it necessary to join women's educational institutions. But the absence of requisite number of women teachers, during this period, made the promotion of women's education slow.

Table 9.5 shows the progress of women's education in 1946–1947. The table evinces that the total number of women under instruction increased from 1,224,198 in 1921–1922 to 4,297,785 in 1947 including those in unrecognized institutions. At the primary stage, the enrolment increased enormously from 1,186,124 in 1921–1922 to 3,475,165 in 1946–1947. However, the number of separate primary women schools decreased from 21,956 in 1921–1922 to 21,479 in 1946–1947. The table alone shows that the number of women in the mixed schools were now larger than the separate schools. At the beginning of this period, primary education in the rural areas was very unsatisfactory due to obvious reasons already mentioned. At the secondary stage, the total enrolment rose from 26,163 in 1921–1922 to 602,280 in 1946–1947. There were 2,370 separate secondary schools for women in 1946–1947. The enrolment of women in mixed (co-educational) schools increased. In 1921–1922, only 35 per cent of total number of women were studying in mixed schools while in 1946–1947 the percentage increased to a little more than 50 per cent. But the

Table 9.5 Education of Women in India (1946–1947)

	No. of Girls under Instruction in the Institution of Boys	No. of Girls under Instruction in the Institution for Girls	Total No. of Girls under Instruction
Universities and arts colleges	11,262	9,042	20,304
Colleges for professional education			
1. Law	59	–	59
2. Medicine	1,190	539	1,729
3. Education	289	735	1,024
4. Agriculture	8	–	8
5. Commerce	77	–	77
6. Engineering & technology	6	–	6
Total	1,629	1,274	2,903
Secondary schools			
7. High	58,198	222,574	3,475,165
8. Middle English	43,016	111,400	154,416
9. Middle vernacular	17,014	150,078	167,092
Total	118,228	484,052	602,280
Primary schools	1,980,393	1,494,772	3,475,165
Special schools			
10. Arts	151	–	151
11. Medicine	419	15	434
12. Education	305	10,820	11,125
13. Technical & industrial	657	10,347	11,004
14. Commerce	791	142	933

(Continued)

(Continued)

		No. of Girls under Instruction in the Institution of Boys	No. of Girls under Instruction in the Institution for Girls	Total No. of Girls under Instruction
15. Adults		2,090	7,624	9,714
16. Others		11,313	11,416	22,729
	Total	15,726	40,364	56,090
	Grand total	2,127,238	2,029,504	4,156,742

Source: Report of the National Committee on Women's Education, 1958–1959, p. 26.

enrolment was much larger in the separate schools. Parents preferred to send their daughters to separate schools rather than to mixed schools at this stage. Higher education among women in the universities and arts colleges, too, increased considerably. The total enrolment at the universities and arts colleges rose from 905 in 1921–1922 to 20,304 in 1946–1947. There were 59 arts and science colleges exclusively for women. However, the enrolment of female students was higher in mixed colleges than the separate colleges. The latter were suffering from inadequate female teachers.

New professions such as law, medicine, commerce, agriculture, engineering and technology became popular among women which were formerly closed to them. No separate women's colleges existed for law, engineering and education. The total enrolment in the professional colleges increased from 266 in 1921–1922 to 2,903 in 1946–1947. The enrolment of women in special schools increased five times more than in the previous period. In 1921–1922, the enrolment was 10,836, while it was 56,090 in 1946–1947. This figure indicates that more women started entering professional careers. The movement for adult education for women was consolidated in this period. Women institutions for professional, technical and special education increased to 4,288 in 1946–1947 (Report of NCWE, 1958–1959, pp. 26–28).

CONCLUSION

The overall picture of women's education in India shows that enrolment as well as the number of women's institutions increased haltingly at all levels. When the colonial rulers left India in 1947, modern education for women was almost 125 years old.

During this period, it was the private bodies and missionaries rather than the colonial government who took more initiative for the quantitative and qualitative development of women's education. We have seen that the colonial government was more or less uninvolved in women's education in general and did not provide adequate financial assistance for the development of education. It did not even recognize the SNDT Women's University till Independence. Participation of women in various reform movements and the movements for Independence awakened them. The efforts made by private bodies and missionaries towards women's education showed great achievements qualitatively and quantitatively as well. But when we compare the development of women's education in India with that of other advanced countries during the same period, we feel that the women's education in India was not much developed. It was absolutely due to the negligence of the colonial rulers. In fact, the demand for women's education had been a part of the movement for raising the overall status of women in society. This, in turn, helped them to fight the discrimination against women by the colonial rulers in India. The percentage of literacy for women was only 6 per cent as against 22.6 per cent for men (Census of India, 1941). Moreover, women's education was concentrated mainly in urban areas and students were drawn from affluent Anglo-Indian, European, Indian Christians, Parsee, Hindu and Muslim families only. The rural women were denied the opportunity of education as there was hardly any school system for women in rural areas. This was the result of urban–centred development of women's education. Even if women schools were started in urban areas, the absence of female teachers made their growth slow.

The colonial governments' policy of non-interference with the so-called orthodox beliefs and traditions of society did greater harm to the growth of universal education in the beginning. Moreover, the inadequate and discriminatory allocation of funds for women's education hindered the expansion and promotion of women's education in India. Of course, the missionaries contributed much to the development of women's education but their religious overtones retarded the development of secular scientific temper among the women and could not attract women from every section. The private bodies who managed and financed some educational institutions were also not devoid of an ideology. The system of education which the colonialists aimed at can be clearly understood from Macaulay's statement: 'We must at present do our best to form a class who may be interpreters between us and the millions whom we govern. A class of persons, Indian in blood and colour but English in tastes, in opinions, in morals and in intellect' (Dave, 1971, p. 286). They attempted to spread and promote such education which would create a new caste of educated and uneducated to serve their own colonial interests and not on the basis on national needs and aspirations. That is why women's education as a whole was starved from adequate funds on some pretext or the other during the colonial rule.

REFERENCES

Altekar, A.S. (1938). *The Position of Women in Hindu Civilization*. The Culture Publishing House, Benaras.

Asthana, Pratima. (1974). *Women's Movement in India,* Vikas Publishing House, Delhi.

Bhatt, B.D. & Aggarwal, J.C. (1969). *Educational Documents in India (1813–1968),* Arya Book Depot, New Delhi.

Chakraborty, Renu (1972). *"New perspective for Women's movement"*, in *LINK*, Aug. 15.

Chaube, S.P. (1965). *A Survey of Educational Problems and Experiments in India,* *Ki*tab Mahal Private Ltd.

Das Gupta, Jyoti Prabha (1938). *Girls Education in India,* Calcutta, University of Calcutta.

Dave, J.K. (1971). *A Study of Evolution of Female Education In Gujarat till Independence,* unpublished thesis, Sardar Patel University, (Indian Council of Social Science Research, New Delhi).

De, S.K. (1959). "Progress of Women's Education in India", *Education* 38 (7) July.

Devadas, I. (1976). "Indian Women Through the Ages", in *Encyclopedia of Women in India,* Editor, B.K. Vashista, Praween Encyclopedia Publication, New Delhi.

Desai, Neera (1957). *Women in Modern India,* Vera & Co., Bombay.

Dube, S.C. (1976). Glimpses Through the Corridors of History," in *Encyclopedia of Women in India.* B.K. Vashista, Praveen Encyclopedia Publication, New Delhi.

Durant, Will. (1930). *The Case for India,* Simon and Schuster, N Y.

Gray, H., "Education" in *The Key of Progress*, A.R. Carton (Ed.), Oxford University Press, London.

Gupta, Sen. (1962). *Women's* education *of India*, Asia Pub. House.

Jain, Devaki (ed) (1975). *Indian Women*, Ministry of Information and Broadcasting, Delhi.

Kopf, David (1969). *British Orientation and Bengal Renaissance*, University of California Press, Berkeley.

Mathur. Y.P. (1978). *Women's Education in India*, Vikas, Delhi.

Mazumdar, Bhagaban Prasad. (1973). *First Fruits of English Education (1817–1857)*, Bookland, Calcutta.

McGully, Bruce. (1940). *English Education and the Origins of Indian Nationalism*, Columbia University Press, New York.

Misra, Lakshmi. (1966). *Education of Women in India*, 1921–66, Macmillan, Bombay.

Mukherjee, L. (1956). "Education of Women in India", *Education*, 3 (1).

Mukherjee, L. (1956). "Education of Women in India: Past and Present", *Education*, 35 (12).

Mukherjee, S.N. (1966). *History of Education of India*, Acharya Book Depot, Baroda.

Naik, J.P. (1966), *Equality, Quality & Quantity*, Allied Publishers, Bombay.

Nurullah, Sayed & J.P. Naik. (1961). *History of Education in India*, Macmillan & Co., Calcutta.

Sen Gupta, Padmini. (1960). *Women's Education in India*, Ministry of Education, New Delhi.

Smith, Vincent A. (1970). *The Oxford History of India*, Oxford University Press, 1967.

Thackersey, Pramila (1970). *Education of Women*, Ministry of Education and Youth Sciences, Government of India.

REPORTS AND THESIS

Post War Educational Development in India, Report by Central Advisory Board of Education, Jan. 1944, Published by the Manager of Publication, Delhi, 1944.

Report of the Women's Education Committee on Primary Education of Girls in India, Government of India Press, New Delhi, 1937.

Reports of the National Committee on Women's Education, May 1953 to Jan. 1959, Ministry of Education, Government of India, 1959.

Dave, J.M. *Study of Education of Female Education in Gujarat till Independence*, 1971 (Thesis: Sardar Patel University, Gujarat).

Mazumdar, Veena, *Women and educational development in India: 1947–79* (Report).

Chapter 10

Educating India's Women for Social Change*

Muriel Wasi

Most Indian women have been told *ad nauseam* that their country occupies a unique place in the society of nations. True, it is not a developed country. However, it cannot be lumped, without provisos, with other developing countries. It stands somewhere between these two antithetical groups that are now part of the accepted idiom of economico-social classification. As yet too poor and under-industrialized to be described as a 'developed' country, it has already set its feet firmly on the road to industrialization and its concomitant social changes, and so is nearer development than—shall we say?—the developing countries of Africa and some countries of Asia.

What most women do not know, because they are not constantly reminded of it, is that social change is not something external to us that takes place through the immutable abstract forces of national and international economics. It is something that is brought about through people. In the social situation, forces are not quite like those physical phenomena of nature—deluges, volcanoes, tidal waves, tornadoes, cyclones—that affect man calamitously, but are not of their making. A social revolution, even a social change, are the handiwork, conscious or unconscious, of large bodies of men and women. Women, indeed, are major instruments of social change.

* *Social Change:* August 1971: Vol. 1, No. 2, 24–30.

The speed with which a society such as ours can transform itself from backwardness, even primitiveness in large areas, wide disparities between its sophisticated urban areas and the stark barrenness and dirt of its villages, is largely determined by the concern of men and women that it shall be changed at a quicker pace today than yesterday. As an example of a subject of social interest, there has been discussion among women's associations and many women professionals recently about the need to make rural areas habitable for women doctors and nurses, if they are to go there as a matter of course for work. A recent study undertaken to see how we can maximize the national productivity of qualified women has revealed that 11.7 per cent of qualified women doctors (including surgeons) are voluntarily unemployed and that, despite the shortage of nurses, many nurses are also unemployed. The reasons are partly that such women marry, are privately happy and then forget the amount that has been invested in their professional education, reserving their professional skills for their families. Another reason—so qualified women urge—is that the rural areas do not yet offer them the physical security that they need to live and work there, and that they are not there guaranteed the most elementary conditions of sanitation and civic life.

PART-TIME WORK FOR PROFESSIONALS

The first argument is patently weak; a woman doctor could always take time off to marry, have children and run her home without opting out of the mainstream of professional medical service. The suggestion has been made—and it is entirely feasible—that registration for part-time work should be introduced and that advertised conditions of service, rules of encadrement, salary scales and benefits should be standardized so that women, who are unable to take on full-time work, may register for part-time work.

The second argument would appear to be valid. Authority, in the shape of central and state governments, must ensure that minimum conditions of physical security are made possible where women are required to work in rural areas. There are few rural areas in the country in which the need for women doctors, nurses and social workers is not deeply and widely felt. Conditions of sanitation, water, electricity must be made tolerable. One does not ask for them to be improved at par with the amenities of the town. But by and large, there are limits to self-sacrifice, dedication and a sense of mission and qualified women in general who do not get the postings that they want will not automatically take what they get if the area is left unequipped for modern professional living.

The merits of the case apart, a discussion that was run in columns of the daily press, has highlighted the general un-involvement of Indian women of the upper middle classes in the radical changes through which our society is at present passing. Most of them are not given to reading professional sociological studies. They tend to speak out of their own restricted experience in urban or semi-urban areas. Most women do not travel as a matter of course or interest in the far-flung regions of India; they tend to stay put, going out where family obligations take them temporarily from home, or more permanently, on their husbands' transfers. The realization that a major social revolution is taking place in which they are inextricably involved seems not to strike them.

ELEMENTS OF SOCIAL REVOLUTION

The elements of the social revolution that is now overtaking India could not easily have been foreseen 50 years ago. Today, they are plain for anyone who thinks about them at all to see. For one thing, the concept of egalitarianism is here to stay. Never again can social privilege hope to rear its head or to be taken seriously. This calls, secondly, for a de-stratification of society in which conventional strongholds are bound to fall. Third, unless this de-stratification is accepted wholeheartedly as necessary, it will be brought about violently and with greater pain to those who have wielded power in the last century. Fourth, the more willingly it is conceded, the more smoothly and imperceptibly the revolution will work itself out. Fifth, the need to assume responsibility at every level for service to the community as a token of the investment made in one's education, should now be a matter of course. Education, particularly professional education, constitutes for the individual and the group a debt to society that must be repaid. The notion that it is the business of government to find employment for its educated is antiquated. Education implies self-reliance. Educated people must be willing to create remunerative work of 'jobs' for themselves and not depend upon governments to provide for them.

Increased initiative on the part of individuals and social groups for their own maintenance is the concomitant of our economico-social revolution. For despite our socialistic pattern, we remain a liberal democratic society with personal and social responsibilities of our own.

Our concern in the present chapter is how women should be educated to promote desirable social change and how they should make themselves part of the change that is already afoot in India.

The first step in this process is to help them to be aware of a sub-continental situation. There is as yet in the middle classes, an amazing unawareness of what is happening. There was a time about 30 years ago when the best organs of the British press published regularly a 'Condition of Britain' double issue, which epitomized the total national situation in economico-sociological terms for that country and gave the common reader a chance to take stock of where they stood. The press in India has rarely attempted anything of this kind. For the most part, the daily editorial is not read by many hundreds of women with a first degree and is probably not read at all by those who have a higher secondary or equivalent certificate and have not gone up to a university. This makes the business of informing women of social change a necessary first chronological step in their education for social action. Whose responsibility is this? The responsibility of all of us, but to say this, really takes us nowhere. It is a job that is probably best done by voluntary organizations that are coming slowly to see themselves as having a predominantly educational function.

LEADERSHIP TRAINING

The old view of such organizations as the YWCA (that has a membership of about 20,000 in various parts of India) was strongly directed towards the development of the individual. The recognition that the individual is a drop in our tumultuous Indian situation, and that much of the work done with them does not percolate to the wide base of society, has come only very recently. National projects that cater for large numbers of potential leaders are now undertaken in the hope that they will reach large numbers. The multiplier can work only through social work-educators, teacher-educators in methods of literacy, lecturer-tutors in nursing education, professors of medicine and so on. The first step for social action is, therefore, the education and training of a woman leadership in these professional fields.

To have brought this home to women is a big step in the right direction. If one does not attach much importance to the work of such a body as the All-India Women's Conference, which has always focused attention on the group in preference to the individual, it is because there is little evidence that its ambitious paper programmes ever materialize. Meetings are held; perhaps discussions are lively; resolutions are passed; but the general competence is not of a high standard and follow-up would appear to leave much to be desired. It is important that such a body should continue to exist because it operates on a national platform and provides a structure within which competence, if and when it appears, can work collectively. However, the organization seems to lack self-criticism, does not demonstrate its effective determination to grow and to take responsibility for the education of its membership for social change.

ROLE OF VOLUNTARY AGENCIES

There are today 85 all-India voluntary organizations, many of which would appear to be effective in educating women for such change. It is to these organizations, that are primarily concerned with the education of a leadership (for no voluntary organization can really embark upon more, in a country with 270 million women and girls) that we must look for the preparation of a national programme of education for social change. The managements of these organizations have first to be taught to recognize the signs of change; they have to be given the instruments whereby, in constant touch with large movements, they learn to interpret them to themselves and to their associates and through them, to their membership.

The *modus operandi* are not difficult to understand or work. They consist of standing study groups, library seminars led by leaders in the region in which the seminars are held, the continuing development of literature that is lucid and readable in the languages of the region; the use of mass media of communication, indeed, any effective means to make the content of a total situation clear. With the character, the dedication, system and clarity in organization of which our women have shown themselves to be capable, it should not be difficult to develop, first, the knowledge and then, the social consciousness that this knowledge automatically confers on large numbers.

For centuries, we have been accustomed in India to let this initiative be taken at a national centre, whence it percolates to the regions, the local branches of all-India organizations. This has tended to be our way of planning too. Only very recently have we woken up to the need to plan from district level upwards, and not *vice versa*. After all, the smaller the initial unit of planning, the more knowledgeable the planners will be of real needs, and the more effectively will they take charge of action to implement their plans. Provided planners meet at regional and national level often enough to keep others similarly situated in touch with a total plan, planning this way will work. The same truth applies to the business of educating organizations, whether official or non-governmental, for social change. The signs of change are clearer in small than they are in amorphously large units. Action for social change begins at base and should drive upwards with local momentum. It should not be presumed always to seep slowly through from a remote centre, through layers of deep stratification, to a local spot where they eventually become a reality for action. *We have therefore constantly to remind local groups that the initiative lies with them* for making blueprints of action and improvement, and that only through the local awareness of social change, documented, studied and assimilated into the being of workers, will true education for national social change become a reality.

POINT OF DEPARTURE

We often speak of the need to involve people in such change and to obtain from them evidence of their commitment. These phrases have been explained again and again, misunderstood and re-explained, but they more often mislead than lead. An attitude is obviously important. Desirable social change can come more easily if people and, in particular, women whose influence within the home and through children is far-reaching, support rather than resist it. But an attitude takes a very long time to shape among the illiterate or uneducated, unless it is demonstrated to have results in the short term. This is where the need to capture the educated becomes crucial and must necessarily precede the education of the large mass of uneducated women. It is essential in this plan to seize upon a focal person. For instance, in promoting effective action to fulfil the Constitutional Directive that all children between the ages of 6 and 14 years shall have free compulsory education, the focal person is the mother of the family in rural areas. The lag between the schooling of girls and boys in this age group is what chiefly explains our failure to fulfil the directive. The girls, who are still not in school, are mainly in rural areas. Moral: seize the mother, educationally speaking; convince her of the benefits of putting her girls into school and keeping them there (whatever the inconvenience to her during that period) and she will act as a multiplier. There is no other way seemingly to meet the requirements of the directive. And this is a matter of the topmost national priority. Schemes of literacy that are not specifically geared to the purpose of making children in age group of 6 to 14 literate are of subsidiary importance. They are expensive, ineffective and evidently uneconomic. But take children of age 6 to 14 years captive in literacy and you will keep them literate. Through them, in time, their children become literate. Perhaps by a process of upward momentum, this is a way even to make parents literate. Influence the mother to make her daughters of age 6–14 years literate. The rest will follow with planned action.

In sum, the literate women of India and chiefly the educated and professional women of India have to be made to understand that they are an integral and necessary part of social change. If they are aware of this and if they allow themselves to be constructively used, social change will be of the desired kind. To be usable, they have to be made aware of the conditions of their region and, by inference, of India, in specific terms. To this end, they have to be persuaded to take the initiative at every level, and chiefly at the local level to *document their areas*, finding out how their community lives and what it needs in order to live better.

The methods that they should use to document this situation are routine, continuing study groups led by knowledgeable people, library seminars and continuing library improvement. The mass media of communication should also be used to the extent possible. The programme of education in each local organization should be periodically evaluated to see how it can be improved. Local leaders should meet at regional level once a quarter and at national level once a year. It will then be possible to have a total portrait of where we are going.

In helping themselves to know where they stand in each area of India, women are incidentally educating themselves and their political masters on the detail and the trend in regions that are at present haphazardly documented and commented on in the daily press only when something startling occurs. However, social change, like most natural things, often works imperceptibly. It is 'toil unsevered from tranquillity'. This is why it is so necessary to bring the searchlight of constant education, perception and experience to bear on it, converting society into a laboratory for constructive continuous experiment.

Chapter 11

Policy Discourse and Exclusion-Inclusion of Women in Higher Education in India[*]

Karuna Chanana

OVERVIEW

Restructuring of the system of higher education is a worldwide phenomenon. There is also a shift to a corporate profit culture in higher education which is in sharp contrast to the traditional image of the university as an agent of social change and of mobility. Indian higher education system is also undergoing changes in this direction, though, due to political, economic and social compulsions, the focus also remains on equality and social access. This concern is generally reflected in the different instruments of educational policy which identify several parameters which deserve attention in the changing scenario. Gender is one of them. Therefore, looking at educational policy and whether it promotes gender equality in higher education will tell a lot about the equality commitments of the system towards women. Further, women still do not enjoy parity with men in *participation and outcomes,* though *access* has improved. On the whole, their entry into higher education is not unproblematic. Therefore, higher education as an instrument to

---

[*] *Social Change:* December 2011: Vol. 41, No. 4, 535–52.

Presented at the South Asian Conference on Enhancing Social Inclusion in Higher Education Institutions, 26–27 April 2010, organized by Martin Chautari, Kathmandu, Nepal.

achieve high status as well as equality is an appropriate site to examine attempts to promote gender equality in society.

The central premise of this chapter is that the Indian educational policies designed to promote the education of girls and women are conceptualized within a very narrow framework, on the one hand, and are fragmented by a fractured vision of both the system of higher education and of Indian society on the other. As a result, gender concerns receive very little meaningful space in the final policy documents. This is because the cultural concerns colour the vision and value frames of the policymakers. Further, inclusion requires an understanding of sociocultural contexts and processes that produce the values and biases which go into the making of policy.

While the first part of the chapter focuses on access, participation and outcomes, the second part analyses some of the policy documents from a gendered perspective. It unravels the process of policymaking and formulation and exclusion–inclusion of women and their differentiation, within the framework of equality, in higher education in the eleventh five year Plan (2007–2012).[1] It interrogates the process of policy formulation by looking at texts of selected reports as primary data sources. These texts reflect the multi-stage and multi-tier character of policy framing. The aim is not merely to discuss the policy but also to analyse the process of policy development, unravel the rhetoric of inclusion and why very myopic decisions are taken which hardly touch the structures of exclusivity. Moreover, the implications of this process for the democratic nature of policymaking in the system of higher education can also be understood. The exercise for the twelfth Plan is underway and one hopes it will move away from mere rhetoric and be an improvement over the earlier ones both in terms of conceptualization and delivery.

Finally, the persistent gender gap in education reflects poorly on the Indian policies which have failed to incorporate the requirements of Indian women at the level of conceptualization and implementation. Further, in this day and age, when global trends and the market are impacting all aspects of the educational system and higher education is in a flux, when the provision of free and highly subsidized public higher education is a receding possibility, it is time to review the contemporary policy documents from a gendered perspective to see if they are more likely to increase the advantage or disadvantage for potential and actual women students and faculty in higher education.

WOMEN IN HIGHER EDUCATION: ACCESS, PARTICIPATION AND OUTCOMES

Indian women, like women elsewhere, are heterogeneous and the societal system of stratification is reflected in differential access to women from different socio-economic groups but the gender gap affects all of them. This is in spite of young women achieving better than men at the school board examinations.

Numerically, the Indian higher education system is one of the largest in the world, with 376 universities and 20,677 colleges (out of these 2,166 are women's colleges) and 504,812 teachers in 2006–2007. However, the gross enrolment ratio is very low at 12.4 per cent for all students: 14.5 for men and 10.0 for women.[2] Women comprise 40.55 per cent of total enrolment of 11,612,505.[3] In addition, 1,540,460 students were enrolled in distance education of which 39.9 per cent (614,659) are women (GoI, 2007: 26). Women comprise 38.6 per cent at undergraduate, 45.9 per cent at graduate and 41.7 per cent of enrolment at research level [GoI, 2007].[4]

Higher education was mostly publicly funded till the early 1990s (exceptions were some professional colleges set up in two states in the 1980s). It was also subsidized to a great extent so that its individual cost was very low. Even then, the gender gap was high and it was worse for the women from disadvantaged groups whose access was supported by the Constitutional provisions. For example, in 2006–2007, the proportion of Scheduled Caste[5] students was 11.8 per cent (4.2 % women, 7.6 % men) and Scheduled Tribe[6] students were 4.5 per cent (1.7 % women, 3.8 % men).[7] They generally join general education courses and are denied access to elite/courses and institutions. Proportionately and numerically, access is very limited to them as a whole but more so to the women from these groups. For instance, Scheduled Caste and Scheduled Tribe women comprised 10.1 per cent and 4.4 per cent, respectively, of all women enrolled in 2006–2007 in higher education (GoI, 2007: 26).

As the demands of the liberalized economy changed vis-à-vis higher education in the 1990s, the state or provincial governments allowed the setting up of new private unaided[8] (and for-profit institutions called self-financing colleges or universities) which offered the new market-driven subjects. But they were offered at a high individual cost. These are called self-financing courses,[9] colleges and institutions. On the other hand, very few government-aided[10] higher educational institutions have been established in this period. The existing public institutions, besides suffering from poor quality, are also offering the market-driven courses at a cost (also called self-financing courses) leading to the privatization of public universities.[11]

According to the eleventh Plan document, as it was circulated to the National Development Council (NDC), the share of private unaided institutions in the tenth five year Plan increased from 42.6 per cent in 2001 to 63.21 per cent in 2006. The enrolment increased from 32.89– per cent to 51.53 per cent in the same period. The projected educational expansion is from 10 per cent of gross enrolment ratio to 15 per cent by 2012. Half of this 5 per cent is expected to be in the private sector. This is especially going to be in the area of professional higher education (including teacher education) and in the so-called masculine disciplines.

Women are entering higher education in ever larger numbers and gaps in the enrolment of women and men have decreased as per the latest statistics available for 2006–2007 (UGC, 2007). However, while the maximum number and proportion of women enrol for education (48.7 %) and arts, humanities and the social sciences (45.8 %), their enrolment in sciences (38.0 %) has also been increasing due to the devaluation of pure sciences because men do not enrol in them.[12] Their proportion in education has decreased since 2000–2001 when it was 51 per cent and in 1980–1981 it was 51.7 per cent. This deserves attention when the number of private self-financing colleges of education has increased. On the other hand, there has been a gradual increase in women's enrolment in commerce (35.2 %). Similarly, the enrolments in engineering, law and veterinary science have also increased substantially, though they are not more than men in any of these fields.[13] They still remain predominantly male domains with women occupying only about 20 per cent seats. Thus, *access*, on the whole, has certainly improved. They are also choosing the traditional masculine subjects as is reflected in higher education enrolments in the first professional degree or undergraduate professional programmes.

Medical education has been a gender-balanced subject wherein the proportion of women is 44.3 per cent. It has not been a masculine subject in India (or South Asia or even in the Philippines) unlike in the Western, developed world because in a society where women are physically secluded, especially in North India,[14] women patients could not be treated by male doctors this could be explored in the other countries practising female seclusion for comparison).

However, *gender inequality in participation* has declined very little, for example, in the choice of subfields or specializations, as for example, men are over-represented in physical, mathematical and computer sciences and women in biological sciences both in the educational and occupational spheres. This is being referred to as *horizontal* segregation vis-à-vis *vertical* segregation. Even in medicine, specializations are differentiated in terms of status. This can be substantiated by the number of doctorates awarded in different subjects to women and men. In 2003–2004, when the author looked at the annual report of the Jawaharlal Nehru University (JNU), out of 567 doctorates awarded (a majority in the social sciences), 36 per cent were women and 64 per cent were men. The proportion of doctorates by Schools was: school of Social Sciences—47.2 per cent; Life Sciences—75 per cent (8/12); and Centre for Biotechnology—68.5 per cent (8/11). Again, women in science deserve special attention viz-a-viz access, retention and re-entry especially when men are exiting pure sciences and women are finding space in it.

According to Bamji,

According to the INSA report (2004: 1), over 37 per cent of PhDs in science are women but the number of women working in faculty positions in research institutions and prestigious universities is less than 15 per cent except in DBT and ICMR. Also very few women are fellows of science academies or recipients of prestigious awards like the Bhatnagar award even in biology—a field where there are more female than male students. *Thus the glass ceiling is more apparent at the level of practicing science and recognition than at the entry level.* (2008: 1) [emphasis in the original]

This takes us to an analysis of *outcomes* which requires looking at the benefits of education, one of which is the job prospects in the market or labour force participation of women. Here, the focus is on their participation in the academic and administrative positions in the system. For example, women academics have very low representation in senior academic and research positions as well as in senior administrative and managerial positions. Gender desegregated data on faculty are not available in India. In 1993–1994, the women teachers in colleges and universities were 18 per cent when the author collected unpublished statistics from the University Grants Commission (UGC). The break-up shows that 21 per cent were in the colleges (note that there are many women's colleges) and 11.6 per cent in the universities. Further, in 2004, in JNU, the proportion of women faculty was 25 per cent. Their distribution among different levels was as follows: 15.7 per cent professors, 34.5 per cent associate professors and 35.5 per cent assistant professors.[15] Faculty-wise too, they have less representation in the same subjects in which they are very low as students.

The *second dimension impacting outcomes* relates to the subject choices and their links with occupations. As mentioned earlier, in spite of gender equality in access, women are more likely to graduate from education, arts, humanities and social sciences and men from engineering, natural sciences and mathematics. These educational choices do not necessarily lead to high status and high-paying occupations or outcomes, especially with respect to the kind of jobs they get or take up. It is because the cultural discourse encourages women to make educational choices leading to caretaking occupations. Thus, so long as women and men choose different subjects or there is disparity in participation, gender parity in access is not going to lead to parity in labour force participation and in outcomes.

Given this situation of women in higher education, wherein the twin processes of exclusion and inclusion are working simultaneously, scholars and activists working with women have drawn the attention of the government, the planners, and policymakers to make it more inclusive. Therefore, whenever the process of planning of the country's development is undertaken, the issue of women and their development is also taken up. Extensive countrywide and intensive consultations are held with experts and activists and their suggestions and recommendations are also invited. They are critical to being included in the five-year plans of the UGC which is the implementing agency. The latest exercise took place in the preceding last few years (they start before the plan period but continue well into the plan period), before the government finalized the eleventh Plan (2007–2012). The reports are being critically analysed further from an inclusive perspective because the final document sets the tone for what women get or do not get in the next five years.

EXCLUSION OF WOMEN IN EDUCATIONAL POLICY: XI PLAN REPORTS AND DOCUMENTS

In preparation of the eleventh Plan, several committees were constituted by the government, relevant ministries and bodies associated with higher education. These comprise policy-focused groups which advocate gender equity in higher education. Further is a critical analysis of the documents that have provided the framework of what is to be done for women in higher education in the XI Plan. Only a few examples are cited as illustrations from the plan documents but one could do a gender audit of these documents. It provides a critique of these documents as aspects of discourse and representation. There are six documents which are reviewed here in order of their importance in the administrative and power hierarchy of policy formulation but conversely in decreasing visibility and increasing exclusion of women in the final outcomes or recommendations about them. In other words, the first two documents are inclusive in their approach, framework and recommendations. In the next three documents, women are almost excluded in the final recommendations and it is these which are critical in the power and decision-making hierarchy and in the ascending order.

1. The Sub-Group on Access for Women and Schemes for Women for the XI Plan (2006), appointed by UGC, submitted a very comprehensive report.[16]

2. The Committee on Women in Science (WIS—year not mentioned) also submitted its recommendations to the planning commission based on the *INSA* (Indian National Science Academy) *Report on Science Career For Women*.[17] The INSA Report and its recommendations[18] were also incorporated into those sent by the Committee on Women in Sciences to the planning commission.[19]

Both reports provide an overall perspective, suggest strategies and make recommendations for the inclusion and retention of women in higher education. Both mention support to girls from the school stage, which is a conduit to higher education. The Report of the UGC subgroup (henceforth referred to as UGC subgroup) is extensive and in-depth as is the INSA report. Both provide a social context. The UGC subgroup looks at women within the overall and general population but also within the different social groups, namely Scheduled Castes, Scheduled Tribes, Other Backward Classes and minorities. It has a twin focus: the institutions and the backward areas with special focus on women in the backward groups.

It goes on to recommend that women should mandatorily get a percentage in all schemes meant for identified social groups in correspondence with their proportion in the population. In addition to special schemes for women, the subgroup recommends that they should also get a proportion in all schemes of UGC.

In addition, rural–urban and regional imbalances in the context of gender receive a lot of attention in the two documents. For instance, it is mentioned that there are smaller numbers of women from small towns, rural areas, poor families and vernacular language schools. WIS report also observes that women scientists are generally from urban areas, high castes and classes.

Both the reports are comprehensive because they are written by scholars who are familiar with the situation on the ground and are committed to improving the situation of women faculty and students in higher education. Therefore, they are exhaustive and there are common issues, concerns and recommendations. However, government agencies who initiate these committees make no effort to integrate the recommendations of the two committees and to sift points of convergence and divergence and then compile a comprehensive report. Therefore, women in general education and universities, on the one hand, and women in science, on the other, are treated as separate categories.

3. While carrying forward the regional and sociocultural context, the eleventh five year plan report of the UGC selects a few sugges-tions and ongoing schemes from the UGC subgroup report. Under *gender equity*, it incorporates provision of hostels and other infrastruc-ture facilities for women in colleges and universities; day care centres, capacity building programme for women managers in higher education

and scholarships. All these are ongoing schemes and, thus, there is no addition to the tenth Plan schemes.

There is a separate paragraph on *social group equity*, which includes Scheduled Castes/Scheduled Tribes/Other Backward Classes/minorities and the poor. The first two groups were provided reservation in education in the Indian Constitution and now the third group is also included through a constitutional amendment taking the reserved seats to a maximum of 50 per cent. In this context, it is also recommended that the Equal Opportunity Cells be established in every university. However, gender is missing in the discussion on social groups.

In the UGC Plan proposals, with the exception of the chapter on access, equity and inclusiveness, exclusion of women is reflected in all chapters such as quality and excellence, relevance and value based education, ICT integration and governance, financing of higher education, emerging issues and challenges, strategies, policies and programmes of action. As if issues of quality, values, ICT integration and so on do not have a gender or an equity dimension. This exclusion is then carried over into suggestions, recommendations and financial implications.

4. The Draft Report of the Working Group on Higher Education of the Planning Commission sets out a broad agenda for the XI Plan. In the section on expansion of access in the chapter on policy perspective, it mentions women only in the context of hostels and scholarships. The same recommendation is repeated for increasing the enrolment of women in professional education. The sections on research, distance education, quality, faculty development, infrastructure development, curriculum development, use of technologies, database management, special schemes for persons with different abilities, do not mention women or gender as a parameter.

Later on, women are again mentioned along with the poor (urban, rural and tribal) only for the purpose of gainful employment with reference to community colleges. Again, the chapter on financial requirements reiterates its position of promoting inclusiveness and equity through grants for women's hostels in colleges and universities. The next section on social group equity misses out women.

The Draft Report comes back to issues relating to access in the chapter on equity and inclusive education. Using the NSS data in the discussion on enrolment at a disaggregate level—the focus is on interstate, inter-caste, interreligious, rural–urban, occupational, male–female disparities. It reiterates the well-known fact that gender overlaps with the rest of the parameters of disadvantage—something similar to the report of the UGC subgroup on women as well. Yet all this is ignored in the rest of the document.

Documents (3.) and (4.) converge on two points, namely excluding women from all aspects of higher education and from social groups for all practical purposes and limiting to recommendations regarding hostels and scholarships for women.

5. The Approach Paper to the XI Plan of the Planning Commission (2006) states that 'the plan must focus on ways of improving women's socio-economic status by mainstreaming gender equity concerns in all sectoral policies and programmes. Special efforts should be made to ensure that the benefits of government schemes accrue in appropriate proportions to women and girls' (p. 105). Here, too, the social context marked by region, caste, tribe and social disadvantage is highlighted. The focus is on general expansion in higher education as well as of the scientific pool and also on quality. Providing access to high quality institutions for the poor and the socially disadvantaged is also given priority. Gender is missing altogether.

6. The Plan Document as it was circulated to the NDC[20] also focuses on social groups and women, and clubs the two together only for fellowships. So much so that even when it is proposed that an Equal Opportunity Office for social groups will be established in every university, issues of gender are left out. As an exception, gender along with the other parameters of disadvantage is mentioned in the context of hostels for girls at the district level.

Again, it is mentioned in the same document that 6,000 colleges and 150 universities in underserved areas will be strengthened—it is not stated that the areas will be those where the proportion of women (along with Scheduled Castes, Scheduled Tribes, Other Backward Classes and minority students) who do not access higher education, is high. Again, in order to strengthen state technical institutions, it is envisaged that one-time assistance for project-based support and funds will be given to 200 state engineering institutions. The question is: while giving the grant, what will be the parameters on the basis of which colleges will become entitled for the special grants: will they be colleges in underserved areas, in which a substantial proportion of students are women and those from the disadvantaged sections? For science and technology, it is proposed that bright young students will be identified who can take up scientific research as a career. Here too women are missing from the proposed strategy, even though the Women in Science committee had made specific recommendations.

To sum up, except the UGC subgroup and the INSA report on women in science documents (1 & 2), *gender equity is separated from social group equity* as if women in these groups are not handicapped or are at par with men in access and utilization of education. Alternatively, women in general are homogenous and so there is no need to talk about them across caste, class and so on.

Thus, they adopt a very fragmented approach—as if they are bereft of any understanding of the social context without which it is difficult to understand women's participation or lack of participation in higher education. Or even when the social context is mentioned it remains as a backdrop. The understanding of multiple and overlapping disadvantage is not applied to the recommendations. This in spite of a very long understanding that women have multiple handicaps and deserve special attention within the marginal groups. As mentioned earlier, the recommendation to set up Equal Opportunity Office for social groups in every higher education institute overlooks women's inclusion even from these groups.

The framework and the understanding in which the first two are embedded are not utilized for improving the existing strategies and programmes and to move forward. Nevertheless, the last four reports are critical because their recommendations go into the final policy document and what support women get from the government (in fact, hostels and scholarships are the most agreed upon measures in all the documents). Most of them, however, provide patchwork solutions handed down for quite sometime as if they are stuck in a time warp.

The gender concerns are also not integrated or mainstreamed into other chapters on higher education as if financing, quality and so on do not have gender implications and deserve attention.

Women in science find no mention in most of the documents except the need to push women into professional and technical courses.

EXCLUSION-INCLUSION OF WOMEN: POLICY PROCESS AND DEVELOPMENT

Allan (2008) suggests four ways to improve the policy discourses. These are promoting awareness of policy as discourse; analysing frameworks and assumptions of policy reports; examining implications of policy recommendations and looking at how policy discourses construct images of women.

Experts also refer to policy development process as passing through several stages and levels, and is not linear or self-contained. Rather it is likely to occur at several levels simultaneously. Moreover, formulation and implementation are not distinct phases of the process of policy development but are seamlessly integrated and therefore it is better to talk of policy development or policy process instead of policy. In addition, 'policy is not merely represented by texts or statements.... It is a complex process by which the resources of power are mobilised in order to operationalise value' (Bell & Stevenson, 2006: 142). Nonetheless, it is possible to view them as discrete stages for purposes of policy analysis.

Conceptualization and Formulation

Educational policies adopt a compartmentalized approach by assigning a chapter to women in addition to separate chapters to others from the disadvantaged sections of society, for instance, gender and social groups are two of them. The two are neither integrated in a common frame nor does gender make an entry into the discussion on social groups. Again, there is no integration of gender within issues of finance (e.g., gender budget and audit), or of professional education (gender and subject choice). As a result, gender stands apart and gets very little attention. Thus, the fractured vision of the education players at the national level ensures that strategies and programmes for women remain distanced from social reality and thereby do not move forward.

Moreover, there is lack of correspondence between policy discourse and what is finally recommended. There is, for example, disjuncture between the two sets of documents, namely the reports of the first-level committees (numbered 1–2), consisting generally of experts in the field, and their suggestions and recommendations, on the one hand, and the reports of the higher level committees such as the UGC and the Planning Commission (numbered 3–6) on the other.

On the whole, there is no inclusive broad and comprehensive conceptual framework reflected in the documents. Lacking a common frame and vision, the formulation of policy is limited to the existing provision of special schemes, hostels, fellowships, more colleges and so on. The critical documents are not informed of a perspective consisting of incremental understanding from the last five-year plans and experience thereof.

The existing situation has led to another anomaly, that is, separate strategies are suggested for improving the enrolment and retention of women and the students from social groups and categories. Their specific needs and suggested strategies are neither integrated nor an overall comprehensive framework provided for the education of all the disadvantaged groups (Chanana, 1993: 86). This happens even when the problem is of a general nature.[21]

Implementation and Monitoring

It is also not enough to formulate policies and programmes or to introduce schemes and set aside funds because even the best ones may not be implemented. In addition, there is need to learn more about the outcomes of earlier initiatives, schemes, policies and strategies to promote gender equity in education. For instance, what is the utilization rate of general schemes by the women and also those meant for women.

For instance, in response to a UGC circular, very few universities constituted committees against sexual harassment on the campuses and there are no inbuilt mechanisms to monitor the implementation. Another example is of childcare centres, a gender-neutral facility, many universities have not established them. Why? What can be done to promote this scheme? UGC has given grants for building hostels for women to several universities. There is no feedback on its utilization and its impact on women's enrolment and retention. Again, the information about state-level initiatives, such as reservation of seats in higher education by Maharashtra and Andhra Pradesh, or the impact of free school education or scholarships to girls in schools on their transition to college will also deserve attention.

Moreover, how have women in general and women among the socially disadvantaged groups benefited from the existing schemes and programmes? Neither is there any recommendation made nor strategy suggested to include women from the under-represented categories. If women are to get equitable access, then the proportion of women in each social group has to be targeted for which the UGC subgroup has also worked out the percentage growth for the plan period for each group.

TO REITERATE

Researchers and activists have provided enough data to substantiate the fact that disadvantage for women is multi-layered. And that there is need to identify women in all the groups, namely among the minorities, the disabled, the urban deprived, those living in isolated areas, among certain castes and tribes (GoI, 2001: 6). Therefore, the educational policies and programmes are expected to overcome the constraints imposed by social reality (Chanana, 1993). Further, policies and programme should be formulated keeping in focus the links between social disadvantage and gender. Sadly, there is a lot of rhetoric about it in the documents under discussion which remains in the background or remains a preamble but becomes marginal in the final outcome.

While inclusive approach will require stress on increasing access, retention and re-entry of women and their participation within an enabling environment the final recommendations for the eleventh Plan have come down to two, namely hostels[22] and scholarships[23] and do not go beyond the existing schemes for women. Even these are not comprehensive enough. This is in spite of the fact that the UGC subgroup provides a feedback on the tenth Plan schemes and recommendations for their continuance. Yet the final outcome is bereft of any such understanding. How good is such a half-baked public policy which lacks perspective and is not contextualized?

As mentioned earlier, the first two committees or subgroups consisting of professional women in higher education made comprehensive recommendations which were contextually embedded but they were not high on the power hierarchy in comparison to the agencies such as UGC, Planning Commission and the National Development Council. *The receding importance of the gender perspective in the policy process is inversely related to the power enjoyed by the last three agencies.* According to Bell & Stevenson,

> The texts of educational policy frequently reflect a variety of discourses that compete within the socio-political environment, an arena within which, by definition, a range of ideologies are struggling for supremacy. Such discourses will not only reflect differing value perspectives, but also the differential access to power since those with the power resources to mobilize can more readily shape policy debates. These discourses are therefore contested.... (2006: 160)

The consequence is that gender equity is pushed to the background. As examples of fine tuning the needs of women students and the social context, the recommendations of the UGC subgroup and the WIS report about hostels and fellowships are worth looking at.

> The UGC subgroup recommends that the eligibility condition of at least 30 per cent of enrolment of women in an institution for hostel grants be reviewed. Even after the review it may not be viable to have hostels for one college for women or one coeducational college. Therefore, the model of a hostel for a cluster of institutions at the district headquarter is suggested as the alternative. It also recommends that financial support and hostels should begin from the colleges and schools which are the catchment areas for the universities (UGC, 2006: 36–37).

The UGC subgroup also recommends scholarships and fellowships to women in self-financing courses both in the public and private higher education institutions and in distance education in order to promote access to professional and technical courses in addition to support for coaching and private tuition across the spectrum of higher education system (UGC, 2006: 35). WIS recommends the expansion of the special scholarships and fellowships depending on the life stage of women so that those who want to come back can do either after marriage or after relocation due to husband's transfer (Bamji, 2008: 3).

Lacking a contextual perspective for the provision of two schemes, the effect is likely to be marginal. In fact, one is forced to ask the questions: how far is this public policy really for public good? What kind of democratic processes end up in such a narrow vision and end product? Are we serious about the role of education in promoting change and gender equality in the age of globalization and privatization? This is especially so when global changes are viewed as gendered, racialized and classed. Again, when profit is the central parameter defining educational priorities and choices, considerations of gender, marginality, race, caste, class and ethnicity are lost (Brine, 1999).

Thus, the agencies involved in planning and in providing a vision and direction to growth and development of higher education have to adopt an overall approach or model which will encompass the general population as well as the social groups including women in all types of educational institutions. Sadly, this is not happening with the higher level agencies which call the shots and whose recommendations go into the final policy documents. Higher education cannot be a change agent without a holistic view and without engaging with all the complexities of gender equality as it is expressed both within the educational system and in the wider society in which the system operates. It is a challenge to address these issues and to incorporate them in the policy.

Finally, the foregoing discussion demonstrates that policy analysis from a gendered perspective is missing (Chanana, 2006). Further, no effort is made to integrate equality into all policies and programmes from the stage of formulation to implementation. Needless to say that it is critical to incorporate gender concerns in the overall policy relating to the educational institutions and affecting students, faculty and staff. For this to happen, a comprehensive conceptual framework has to evolve for the inclusion of women in higher education and to bring an end to the process of exclusion. In its absence, one has to understand why are the policy recommendations stuck in a time warp. Will the XII Plan come out of it which is currently in the process of formulation?

Why Stuck in a Time Warp?

The paradox lies in the fact that while, on the one hand, the state policy and public discourse on education put a premium on the need to promote education among girls and women to generate positive forces at the macro-level, the macro policy, on the other hand, is coloured by the cultural contours surrounding the societal conception of the feminine role. Lesley & Watson (1999: 6) refer to the embeddedness of women's exclusion in some of the critical concepts in social policy discourse. Therefore, according to them, the discourse of inclusion and exclusion has to be replaced with an inclusive discourse of difference (Gale & Densmore, 2000: 123). Rees (1999) contends that a paradigm shift is required to integrate equality into all policies and programmes from the stage of formulation to implementation.

The history of women's education reveals a dialectic between the demand for women's education and the opposition encountered in the process; how to live up to the promise of education and also perform the feminine role. The state policy can neutralize the adverse impact of sociocultural practices by providing for the kind of education that is socially desirable. However, educational policies have to be informed by social sensibilities but be forward-looking. The differentiation between social access (Acker, 1984) and access to education is used by scholars to bring home to the policymakers and those who implement the programmes that making facilities available is not a sufficient condition to attract girls and women to formal educational institutions (Chanana, 2001: 3). What is needed is socially responsive infrastructure and facilities, such as socially acceptable location of schools (and hostels).

It seems that the dominant discourses of femininity and cultural reproduction impact on the recommendations in the final analysis. Thus, Bell & Stevenson (2006: 29) argue that while policies are decisively shaped by powerful structural forces of an economic, ideological and cultural nature, it is critical to understand how societal culture shapes state policy.

When we pay close attention to the frameworks of cultural meaning people use to interpret their experience and general social behaviour, we see not only the recipients of educational policy but also its authorized formulators and purveyors as fully cultural animals as well (Sutton & Levinson, 2001: 3).

According to Lesley & Watson, 'There are many ways in which the…state both constructed and was underpinned by, delineated roles for women, mainstream social policy analysis remains sadly uninformed by questions of gender' (1999: 1). Sadgopal (2004: 59) argues that exclusion and discrimination are inherent in the present operating education policy. Sutton & Levinson (2001: 1) contend that policy is a complex social practice and is also a process of normative cultural production.

Going through the various documents, it is evident how the educational policies are subverted in the process of its formulation by the gendered visions of custodians of formal education, namely educational administrators, planners and policymakers. Thus, the process of subversion, conscious and explicit or indirect and implicit, continues unhindered (Chanana, 2001: 57).[24] It has a negative impact on the inclusion of women in higher education. Therefore, it is essential to ensure that policies remain informed and underpinned by questions of gender throughout the stages of conceptualization and formulation to make them meaningfully operational.

NOTES

1. Since its Independence, India has been planning its development on a five-yearly basis and these are known as plans. As mentioned earlier, currently the eleventh Five Year Plan is underway. Before finalization of the Plan document, countrywide extensive and intensive consultations and deliberations are undertaken and reports prepared at different levels by experts. These go into the making of the final document.
2. It is much lower in the rest of the South Asian region, for example, as per the data for 2007, Bangladesh 7 per cent [9 % male, 5 % female]; Bhutan 5 per cent [7 % men, 3 % women]; Nepal 11 per cent [breakup not given]; Pakistan 5 per cent [6 % men, 5 % women]. The other countries of the South Asian region such as Afghanistan, Maldives and Sri Lanka have not provided any information, though Sri Lanka would be much better on all the parameters [UNESCO 2009, Table 8, p. 134].
3. This figure excludes students enrolled in polytechnics and Industrial Training Institutes, which are post secondary, but run diploma and certificate courses and do not grant degrees.
4. The percentages are worked out from Table B-1, pp. 9–13, India 2007. It includes the category 'others' that is, of unspecified subjects such as law, agriculture, veterinary science, music and fine arts.
5. The untouchable castes which were provided constitutional protection through reservation of seats in all public educational and occupational

organizations were labelled Schedules Castes. Now they are also referred to as Dalits or the exploited.

6. Some of the tribes were also provided the same protection as the scheduled castes. They are also now referred to as Scheduled Tribes or Adivasis or the original inhabitants.

7. The reservation for scheduled castes is 15 per cent, for scheduled tribes 7.5 per cent. From the current year, 27 per cent seats have been reserved for the other backward castes.

8. Unaided institutions do not receive any financial aid from the government to run the institutions. They are expected to make no profit since the land is given to them at almost no cost. They are also set up as charitable trusts and organizations, etc. This is how the private educational institutions under the colonial period were established. Now, however, they flout all the provisions and make profit and so I prefer to call them for-profit ones.

9. The high cost of professional and market-driven higher education mainly in the private but also in the public or state universities and colleges sector is likely to have gendered impact. In a country (in other countries of the Asian region with the culture of son preference as well), the reluctance of parents to educate daughters is well known. For instance, high cost of marriage in the form of dowry is likely to be a barrier to women's education and subsequent utilization in the market. Parents choose between the expenses on a daughter's dowry and her education, especially if they have a son or sons. So dowry and son preference complicate the situation. There is a flip side to it too. The value of a daughter in the marriage market increases as the chances of a groom with equivalent or higher qualifications and a high status job increases.

10. They receive 90–95 per cent funds from the UGC or state governments.

11. The public higher education institutions have also introduced the same academic courses and programmes which are fee paying. Although the amount of tuition fees is much lower in the public institutions in comparison to the private ones, it is difficult for those from the disadvantaged groups to bear the costs.

12. I have explained the increase in women's enrolment in the sciences elsewhere (Chanana 2007).

13. What is noteworthy is that there is a decline in the women's enrolment proportionately (not numerically though) in most of the subjects such as science, commerce, education, engineering, medicine, law, agriculture and even veterinary science between 2005–2006 and 2006–2007.

14. In North India, women from across religions, Hinduism, Islam, Sikhism and Jainism were generally secluded. While female seclusion is a social practice widely associated with Islam, it would be interesting to get statistical data to substantiate the point that the traditional social practice of female seclusion pushed women into modern education of medicine and profession of medical doctor—something which has come rather late to the USA (after the 1960s–1970s women's movement).

15. This was culled out from the telephone directory.

16. I am very grateful to Professor Armaity Desai, former chairperson UGC, and chair of the subgroup to send me the report.

17. I am very grateful to Professor Mahtab Bamji, member of both the committees, who sent me the INSA report and the recommendations of the women in science for the planning commission. She is located in Hyderabad. She retired from the National Institute of Nutrition and is now associated with an NGO, Dangoria Charitable Trust, working in the villages of Medak district, with its headquarters in Narsapur district. In addition, I have been in communication with Professor Vineeta Bal, MD, (National Institute of Immunology, Aruna Asaf Ali Road, New Delhi 110 067) and Professor Rohini Godbole, Centre for High Energy Physics, Indian Institute of Science, Bangalore 560012, India. Both of them were members of the committee to draft recommendations for inclusion of women in Science. I am grateful to them for a quick response to my SOS.

18. The study on which this report is based was undertaken by SNDT University, Mumbai.

19. Personal communication from Professor Rohini Godbole. Professor Godbole was a member of S &T advisory committee to cabinet SAC(C).

20. The document circulated to the National Development Council was sent by Professor Bhushan, NUEPA, for the consultation meet.

21. No doubt the recommended schemes can be effective in bringing in more women into higher education and also in retaining them there but the impact will remain marginal unless an inclusive framework is conceptualized and impact is monitored.

22. Married students hostel, a gender-neutral facility, on the basis of my experience in JNU, is also very supportive of women students to complete PhD. This will be very important for science students. Additionally, childcare centres, a gender-neutral facility, be mandatory in all higher education institutions which may be used by both women and men students and faculty.

23. In this context, the example of DST fellowships was recommended for all women scientists across the country. In response to an advertisement, 2,000 women responded, out of which 1,100 were from life sciences. In each subject, 9–10 per cent got selected except life sciences where 6 per cent got in, the numbers are evidence that women scientists want to come back (SNDT report). WIS also recommends modification of recruitment rules, especially in the case of women scientists, namely husbands and wives cannot be appointed in the same institution.

24. For instance, when the feminists raised the issue of 'home science' being labelled as a feminine discipline, they were arguing for a broader framework and for making it gender neutral. But several elite private co-educational schools in Delhi discontinued this subject thereby closing the option of a career (as home science school teachers) to women. Perhaps, considerations

of cost went into this myopic decision because home science entails setting up laboratories. It also meant saving on teacher salary.

REFERENCES

Acker, Sandra. (1984). Women in higher education: what is the problem? In S. Acker & P.D. Piper (Eds), *Is higher education fair to women?* (pp. 25–48). Surrey: Society for Research into Higher Education and NIER.

Allan, Elizabeth J. (2008). *Policy discourse, gender and education: constructing women's status.* New York and London: Routledge, Taylor and Francis Group.

Bamji, Mahtab. (2008). Suggestions for improving indian women's participation in study and practice of science. Unpublished.

Bell, Les, & Stevenson, Howard. (2006). *Education policy: process, themes and impact, leadership for learning series,* London and New York: Routledge Taylor and Francis Group.

Brine, Jacky. (1999). *Under educating women: globalizing inequality.* Buckingham: Open University Press.

Chanana, Karuna. (1993). Accessing higher education: The dilemma of schooling women, minorities and scheduled castes and tribes in contemporary india. In Suma Chitnis & P.G. Altbach (eds.) *Higher Education Reform in India: Experience and Perspectives* (pp. 115–154). Sage: New Delhi.

———. (2001). Introduction. In *Interrogating women's education: Bounded visions, expanding horizons.* Jaipur: Rawat Publications.

———. (2006). Educate girls, prepare them for life? In Ravi Kumar (Ed.), *The crisis of elementary education in India,* Sage, New Delhi, pp. 200–223.

Gale, Trevor, & Densmore, Kathleen (2000). *Just schooling: explorations in the cultural politics of teaching,* Buckingham: Open University Press.

Government of India (GoI) (2001). Working group report on elementary and adult education: Tenth five year plan 2002–2007, Departmentt of Elementary Education and Literacy, New Delhi: Ministry of Human Resource and Development.

———. (2007). *Selected educational statistics India abstract—2006–07.* New Delhi: Ministry of Human Resource Development.

Indian National Science Academy (INSA) (2004). *Science career for Indian women: An examination of Indian women's access to and retention in scientific careers.* New Delhi: Indian National Science Academy.

Lesley, Doyal, & Sophie Watson (Eds.) (1999). *Engendering social policy.* Buckingham: Open University Press.

Planning Commission (2006). *Towards faster and more inclusive growth: An approach to the 11th five year plan.* New Delhi: Planning Commission, November. Mimeographed.

———. (undated). *Draft report of the working group on higher education of the Planning Commission: 11th Five Year Plan.* New Delhi: Planning Commission.

Rees, Teresa (1999). Mainstreaming equality. In Doyal Lesley & Sophie Watson (Eds.) (1999). *Engendering social policy* (pp. 165–183). Buckingham: Open University Press.

Sadgopal, Anil (2004). Globalisation and education: Defining the Indian crisis. *XVI Zakir Husain Memorial Lecture*, New Delhi: Zakir Husain College, University of Delhi.

Sutton, Margaret, & Levinson, Bradley A.U. (Eds.) (2001). *Policy as practice: Toward a comparative sociocultural analysis of educational policy*. Connecticut and London: Ablex Publishing.

UNESCO (2009). *Global Education Digest*. Paris: UNESCO.

University Grants Commission (2006). *The Sub-Group on XI Plan Schemes for Women*, unpublished.

University Grants Commission (2007). *Annual Report 2006–07*. New Delhi: University Grants Commission.

Section III

Higher Education and Research

Sectional Introduction

With rapid growth in higher education during the first three Five-Year Plan periods, quite a few serious problems began to come to surface. Prominent among them were educational inflation, graduate unemployment, fall in standards in higher education and devaluation of degrees. The trade-offs between quality, quantity and equity became visible. The trajectory of higher education was pulled by populist pressures in the direction of quantity at the cost of quality. Paradoxically, the growth in student numbers in higher education was explained in terms of attractive rates of return to education in labour market (Blaug et al., 1969). But by the end of the 1970s, the rate of growth in enrolments in undergraduate higher education has declined to a very low level of about 2 per cent, compared to about 15 per cent in the early 1960s. The absence of manpower planning was found to have caused serious mismatches between higher education and labour market (Burgess et al., 1968). The Education Commission (1966) that examined in depth the problems of higher education, apart from those associated with the entire education sector, made a series of recommendations for reforming the education sector, including consolidation of higher education. The inability of the University Grants Commission in ensuring proper 'promotion and co-ordination of University education and [...] the determination and maintenance of standards of teaching, examination and research in Universities'–the main tasks assigned to the UGC as per the UGC Act 1956 (UGC 1956), has given scope to widespread criticism of functioning of the UGC and to demands for its overhaul.

According to Moonis Raza, the growth in higher education was artificially induced, with educational inflation. He also notes several dimensions of crisis in higher education: concentration of quality in a limited number of elite institutions; extensive spread of poor quality mass institutions; the unsustainable structure of the higher education system consisting of a large number of affiliating colleges grown out of political compulsions; a growing but limited number of examining universities; the absence of meaningful academic relationships; imbalanced growth of different disciplines in the higher education system—dominance of arts and commerce faculty over faculties of science, engineering, technology, agriculture, veterinary, education, health, etc.; rural–urban and regional inequalities; skewed distribution of enrolments by gender; rising costs and so on.

Higher education in India is characterized by a high degree of inequalities for a long time in relation to economic levels of population (income), regional (locational)—rural and urban and inter-state and intra-state, gender and inter-generational. In the recent years, we note a decline in inequalities in participation in higher education by gender and social groups (caste); but inequalities between rural and urban regions are still high; and highest are the inequalities between the rich and the poor in their participation in education. In fact, the last category of inequalities, for example, economic inequalities in higher education seem to be increasing, while in the case of all other types of inequalities one finds modest to significant improvements (Tilak 2015). Apart from analysing the growth of some of these inequalities in higher education and the exogenous and endogenous factors responsible for the same, Malcolm Adiseshiah raises a very important question relating to global or international inequalities, happening through brain drain from India and other developing countries to industrialized ones which reinforces the science and technology competence of the advanced countries leaving behind the other group of (drained) countries with lower educational and scientific levels. Under international inequity typology,

The poor countries help the rich countries to grow richer through contributing to science and technology ... a kind of reverse foreign aid from developing countries to the industrialized ones, adding further to the net flow of resources now taking place every year from the poor to the rich countries.

Adiseshiah wonders whether this pattern is inbuilt into the world system of higher education itself. Though the global order is changing, this is still an important question, and hence countries like India and China are contemplating on measures to attract the migrated brain back home. On this issue of brain drain, Subramanian Swamy raises a pertinent question: Why do scores of talented Indians permanently migrate every year to developed countries. He finds the problem lying in the partisan, inefficient and hierarchical Indian system that is not able to use efficiently the foreign educated Indians or for that matter, Indian educated Indians, offering academic freedom and attractive research environment. He offers a few important tips to the government when it attempts to get the brains back to home.

Teaching and research are the two important functions of universities, apart from the social function of community engagement and service. But with respect to all the three, there is a huge deficit in higher education institutions in India. The deficit in the first two aspects is increasingly noticed. It is not only necessary to develop orientation of our higher education institutions to high-quality teaching and research, but also as Ujagar Singh, highlighted about 40 years ago, we need to develop "an integrated approach which means equal importance to technical as well as liberal education" and to religious education and science and technology education, and an integrated approach towards research and teaching in all higher education institutions. How interesting it is to note that some of these are still being raised in the current policy discourses! The National Policy on Education (Government of India, 2020) makes a promise in this direction.

In the 21st century, every country desires to become a knowledge society, but only a few recognize that a knowledge society can be built only on strong foundations of robust structures of universities with a vibrant and dynamic research culture. In the concluding chapter of this section, Pravin Patel underlines this aspect. 'Modern research-oriented university is the mother of knowledge society.' As he argues, countries became economically and socially rich, and technologically strong, only by promoting, generating and regenerating scientific research culture and transmitting it among generations of students; and in this case, we can learn from and emulate quite a few advanced countries.

REFERENCES

Blaug, M., Layard, R., & Woodhall. M. (1969). *The causes of graduate unemployment in India.* Allen Lane.

Burgess, T., Layard, R., & Pant, P. (1968). *Manpower and educational development in India, 1961–1986.* Oliver & Boyd.

Education Commission. (1966). *Education and national development: Report of the Education Commission* [Kothari Commission]. National Council of Educational Research and Training. [Reprint 1972].

Government of India (2020). *National education policy 2020.* New Delhi.

Tilak, J. B. G. (2015). How inclusive is higher education in India? *Social Change, 45*(2; June), 185–223.

UGC. (1956) 2002. *The University Grants Commission Act, 1956 (as modified up to the 20th December 1985) and Rules & Regulations under the Act.* University Grants Commission.

Chapter 12

Crisis in Higher Education in India*

Moonis Raza

In ancient times, around 5th century BC, Indian institutions of higher learning attracted students from distant lands such as China and Greece. But the pattern of higher education as we know it today is only a little more than a hundred years old—having been ushered in by the Education Despatch of 1854. Under British rule, Indian universities grew up in isolation from the historically evolved system. An unnatural mixture of moribund tradition and spurious modernity was concocted in the crucible of colonial India.

SYSTEM

Since many of the attributes of the system of higher education introduced during the colonial period still persist and since some of the crucial infirmities and inadequacies of the contemporary system are the function of this persistence, it may be worthwhile to identify the characteristics of the colonial system of higher education.

First, it was quantitatively small in size. At the end of the 'civilizing mission' of British rule, enrolment in research per 1 lakh of the population was an appalling 0.14, in postgraduate courses 2.31, undergraduate stream 14.87 and in engineering and technology a mere

* *Social Change:* September 1985: Vol. 15, No. 3: 28–32.
This chapter has earlier appeared in *The Statesman*, New Delhi.

1.84. Only 0.88 persons per lakh were enrolled in teachers' training courses and 1.07 in agriculture. Law and commerce attracted 2.16 and 4.19 students per lakh, respectively, and medicine drew in 2.83. Out of every 1 lakh persons, only 30.31 were enrolled for higher education.

Second, higher education in colonial India responded to the needs of the alien administration, rather than to those of socio-economic development. Higher education was not required to provide the scientific technological base and trained manpower for economic development. It was instead expected to produce graduate cogs and wheels for the administrative machinery. Figures for faculty-wise enrolment in higher education in 1947–1948 reveal this clearly. Of those enrolled in higher education that year, 13.82 per cent had opted for commerce, 8.35 per cent for medicine, 7.14 per cent for law, 6.07 per cent for engineering, 2.91 per cent for teaching, 9.76 per cent for veterinary courses, 0.24 per cent for forestry studies and the remaining 57.16 per cent of the students had gone in for general subjects.

It is clear from the above that while only 4.54 per cent of enrolment was linked with the primary and 6.7 per cent with the secondary sector, the rest was geared to the bloated and essentially dysfunctional tertiary sector.

Further, the educational structure was highly pyramidical, with very acute angles at the base. Postgraduate and research work constituted a disproportionately small share in the total enrolment, that is, 11.5 per cent for the former, and 0.83 per cent for the latter. Most of higher education was concentrated at the undergraduate level.

This undergraduate base was structurally delinked from the rest of higher education by the existence of affiliated 'degree' colleges. The continuum of higher education was thus fractured. Undergraduate teaching, which nourishes in symbiosis with post-graduate teaching and research got separated from these.

Higher education in colonial India was concentrated in and around its gateway port cities; this enclavization being in conformity with the nature of colonial underdevelopment. Taking eastern India, for example, it is noteworthy that 57 per cent of higher education enrolment in 1974–1975 and 45 per cent in 1899–1900 were concentrated within the Calcutta conurbation—Presidency College of Calcutta alone accounting for 41 per cent and 32 per cent in the respective years. The degree or spatial concentration was even higher in the case of medicine, wherein 97 per cent of students were based in Calcutta in 1974–1975; in engineering, all the students were enrolled in a Calcutta college during the same year.

Higher education in colonial India had an extremely narrow socio-economic base. Its gates were closed to the vast majority, particularly members of the Scheduled Castes or Scheduled Tribes. This was true of women too, whose share in total enrolment was as low as 1.24 per cent in 1916–1917 and reached the high water mark at 9.35 per cent on the eve of Independence.

Progress towards transforming the inherited pattern into an instrument of development after Independence, however, seems to have been regulated through a system of contradictory forces exerted by bipolar objectives; for example, the pulls of quantity and quality or of concentration and dispersal. The model since Independence has not been articulated by clear options between the good and the bad or the progressive and the retrogressive. It has essentially been based on decisions relating to trade-offs between, so to say, two 'goods'.

The magnitude of quantitative expansion since Independence may be assessed from the fact that enrolment in 1982–1983 was nearly 18 times that of 1950–1951; the system of higher education in India is, perhaps, the largest in the world. Every eighth student enrolled in higher education on the globe is an Indian. The absolute size of the enrolment in Indian higher education may be gauged from the fact that it accounts for about 43 per cent of the total enrolment in the developing countries.

The rate of growth of enrolment has not, however, been uniform since Independence. Enrolment in higher education grew at an annual rate of 12.4 per cent between 1950–1951 and 1960–1961. During the following decade, it increased further to 13.4 per cent. But there was a sharp drop to 3.8 per cent between 1970–1971 and 1981–1982. The average annual growth rate for the three decades has, however, been impressive at 9.7 per cent.

It is quite possible that the trajectory of Indian higher education may have been pulled in the direction of quantity by populist pressures during the first phase. The dangers of artificially induced expansion, however, became obvious within a few years of the college explosion. Corrective measures were thereafter introduced, and remedial steps taken to check the malignancy. The search for 'excellence' led to the establishment of 'Advanced Centres' as well us 'Departments of Special Assistance' within the university system and to an increasing diversion of research funding from the blighted universities towards institutes and government departments.

This policy resulted in the emergence of a few enclaves of excellence and the widening of the gap between such centres and the rest of the system. This has led to a situation where the higher education system currently produces, on the other hand, a limited quantity of high quality products from a small number of centres and, on the other, a large quantity of poor quality products from a massive number of marginal institutions.

Since the growth of higher education in Independent India has attracted severe criticism, particularly from some international agencies, it may be worthwhile to probe this phenomenon a little further. The percentage of students in higher education to the total population in the age group 17–23 increased from 0.8 in 1950–1951 to 4.8 in 1980–1981. Let us examine whether the level or the growth rate is too high.

International comparisons are hazardous because of the problems of comparability of data. The indicator constructed in a World Bank Report relates to share of enrolment in the population aged 20–24. The choice of the age group distorts the enrolment data in the case of India. Notwithstanding this limitation, the report has shown that higher education enrolment has trebled in India during the period 1960–1979. This is similar to the cases of Nepal, Sri Lanka, Senegal and Egypt. It has, however, increased 20 times in Kenya, 12 times in Ecuador, 10 times in the Dominican Republic, 9 times in Nicaragua, 8 times in Honduras as well as El Salvador, 6 times in Thailand, 5 times in Congo and 4.5 times in Liberia. Indian growth rates do not appear to be exceptionally high by international comparison.

With a view to achieving better comparability, we have analysed the number of students enrolled in higher education per 10,000 inhabitants in terms of UNESCO data for the 1960s, the period of highest expansion in India. India's growth rate of 12 per cent compares with those of Burma and Pakistan but pales in the context of corresponding figures for Algeria (27%), Kenya (25%), Libya (22%), Saudi Arabia (21%), Nigeria (19%) Ethiopia (18%) and Indonesia as well as Vietnam (16%). It is clear from the above that the picture of an over-expanded higher education sector in India does not present the post-Independence trend correctly. The crisis of Indian higher education does not lie either in its size or in its rate of expansion. Higher education in India has in fact to expand further to meet the requirements of socio-economic transformation on the basis of scientific and technological self-reliance. The crisis of Indian higher education is rooted in certain inherited structural deformities and inadequacies. India does not need less of the same kind but more of a d liferent kind of higher education. The situation calls for strengthening of its vital segments, spreading out to uncovered areas and improvement in quality.

Expansion has taken place mainly at the undergraduate level: the bloated belly of higher education appears to have become more bloated since Independence. The share of undergraduate to total enrolment has gone up from 83.7 per cent in 1981–1982. The high watermark, however, was recorded at 89.5 per cent in 1969–1970. A slow but gradual decrease may be noticed since that year. The proportion of postgraduate enrolment has shown a corresponding fall from 11.5 per cent in 1950–1951 to 9.7 per cent in 1981–1982—the low water mark of 8.2 per cent having been touched in 1970–1971. The share of research has, however, shown an upward trend—from 0.83 per cent in 1950–1951 to 1.2 per cent in 1981–1982. It may be noted that additional undergraduate enrolment accounted for 85 per cent of the increase in total enrolment during the 1950s. This share touched the high watermark of 91 per cent during the 1960s. It was only during the 1970s that a downward trend became discernible when this proportion reached 82 per cent.

LOWER

It was only during the 1970s that the growth rate of undergraduate enrolment fell at a substantial rate: from 14.89 per cent during 1961–1966 to 2.27 per cent during 1976–1981, and became relatively lower than those of postgraduate and research enrolment rates. It may be noted that the figure of 2.27 per cent for 1976–1981 is an underestimate. As a result of the 10+2 system, a substantial number of students were pushed back for purposes of calculation into the higher secondary segment. It would, therefore, be more appropriate if the decline were taken to be from 14.89 per cent during 1961–1966 to approximately 6 or 7 per cent during 1976–1981.

What makes undergraduate education particularly anaemic is the fact that approximately 9 out of every 10 undergraduate students are enrolled in the affiliated 'degree' colleges which are delinked from postgraduate teaching and research and have very little say in curriculum development or evaluation of its students.

The number of 'degree' colleges has increased at a rapid rate since Independence and touched the figure of 5,246 by 1983–1984. The share of enrolment in degree colleges to total enrolment in higher education was 86 per cent in 1975–1976 but has been declining slowly since then and has fluctuated around 83 per cent in the last few years.

UNVIABLE

Quite a few of these colleges are unviable: they are, in some cases, set up under 'political' pressure and constitute a source of income for 'academic' entrepreneurs. A college is considered to be viable by the University Grants Commission, if it has an enrolment of 400 or more after excluding PUC/inter/PP enrolment. It has been observed that nearly half the colleges were non-viable in 1973–1974 and that their share came down only marginally by 1977–1978. At the same time, it needs to be noted the other end of the spectrum are some prestigious colleges, which enjoy academic reputation of a high order vying with good university departments. More than half of the postgraduate and 13 per cent of research students are enrolled in these colleges.

While there are multiple reasons for the crisis in Indian higher education, there would be general agreement on the assessment that most reforms and innovations have broken down because of the persistence of the anaemic nature of the affiliated 'degree' college and the parasitic character of the 'examining' university.

This may be illustrated by the fate of the examination reforms. There is general agreement that the persistence of the end of term, external essay type examination is strangulating higher education in the country and may be considered to be at the root of the weakness of the learning ethos; the flourishing of the knowledge-made-easy industry, note dictation in the classroom, corrupt practices in the examination hall and student indiscipline. Attempts were made to move towards a meaningful evaluation system. But a higher education system consisting of the affiliated 'degree' college and the 'examining' university are congenitally incapable of such innovations.

The future of higher education in India largely depends on its ability to transform the liability of the affiliated 'degree' college into an asset. Some of the measures which may assist in the achievement of this objective include raising those postgraduate colleges with a dynamic record to the status of universities or autonomous colleges; pooling together of the academic resources of the affiliated 'degree' colleges into an academically viable centre of higher learning: trying out model multi-campus universities in metropolitan centres with clusters of 'degree' colleges assimilated within it in a meaningful manner and developing some degree colleges particularly in the less developed regions as resource centres for regional development as well as centres of general education combined with vocational courses linked with the regional job market.

Let us now scrutinize the response of higher education to the needs of socio-economic development. First, enrolment in the amorphous 'Arts' faculty continues to have a dominant share in total enrolment. The trend of its changing share shows a bimodal distribution curve— the two maxima being recorded at 43.4 in 1956–1957 and at 44.9 in 1973–1974. Since that year, the share has been consistently falling, being 40.3 per cent in 1980–1981. It is interesting to note that this share is very high in some of the economically less developed regions of the country—Arunachal (86%), Jammu & Kashmir outer hills (70%), Meghalaya (68.9%), Nagaland (68.5%), Manipur plains (68.3%) and Manipur hills (61.9%).

Second, the curve of the share of science faculty enrolment takes the shape of an inverted U. Hovering around 20 per cent during the 1950s, it gradually went up to 28.45 per cent in the mid-1960, but slid down gradually to 18.2 per cent in the mid-1970. A gradual upward trend is discernible since then. The growth rate was consistently high till 1970–1971, the highest rate of 18 per cent being recorded for the period 1960–1961. The rate for the period 1971–1976 was negative at −2 per cent. It has, however, picked up in the latter half of the

1970s—being 2.9 per cent in that period. This trend is disturbing and calls for suitable remedial action.

Third, the share of commerce faculty enrolment marked time—fluctuating around 10.5 per cent—till the end of the 1960s, when it picked up and increased consistently, reaching 21.3 per cent in 1981–1982. It currently ranks second, having pushed the science faculty out of this position in 1979–1980. In some parts of the country, commerce has acquired the first place, having more enrolment than even the Arts faculty.

Fourth, the trends of enrolment in faculties related directly with the production sectors are highly disturbing. The share of engineering and technology in enrolment had reached 8 per cent in 1963–1964. But deceleration set in during the later years of that decade and continued during the first half of the 1970s, the lowest point of 3.8 being recorded in 1974–1975. It is picking up slowly and now fluctuates around 4.5 per cent.

Fifth, the most surprising feature of higher education in Independent India appears to be the low growth rate of enrolment in agricultural and veterinary sciences. The share of the agriculture-linked segment of higher education has actually gone from 1.8 per cent in 1950–1951 to 1.3 per cent in 1981–1982. The share of the veterinary sciences shows a similar trend, marginally changing from 0.6 per cent in 1950–1951 to 0.7 per cent in 1981–1982. However, the rate of growth of agriculture faculty enrolment appears to be picking up lately.

Sixth, while the share of both the segments of higher education linked with social services—education and health—have gone down since 1950–1951, the fall has been considerably sharper in the case of medicine, where it has been consistently coming down from 8.78 per cent in 1950–1951 to 3.9 per cent in 1981–1982. The growth rate of education enrolment has also been coming down at an alarming rate from 2.4 per cent during 1951–1952 to 1.46 per cent in 1976–1981. However, the growth rate of enrolment has kept an even tempo—7 per cent, 9.9 per cent and 9.5 per cent during the, 1950s, 1960s and 1970s, respectively.

Although special efforts have been made since Independence to extend the benefits of higher education to weaker sections of society and particularly to the Scheduled Castes and Scheduled Tribes, the situation is still far from satisfactory. As against their comprising

15 per cent in the total population, the share of the Scheduled Castes in higher education enrolment barely touches 7 per cent. It is, however, encouraging to note that their enrolment has increased at a faster rate as compared to that of the non-Scheduled Caste population. The gap has narrowed no doubt, but it is still quite wide.

As regards the spread of higher education among Scheduled Tribes, the position is even more unsatisfactory. The share of Scheduled Tribe enrolment to total enrolment was only 1.6 per cent in 1977–1978. The position with regard to their enrolment in postgraduate and research is even more depressing. In the case of professional postgraduate courses, for example, the Scheduled Tribes account for a meagre 0.23 per cent.

Sustained efforts have been made since 1947 to extend education among women. The share of women in total enrolment increased from 21.5 per cent in 1966–1967 to 27.7 per cent in 1981–1982; in spite of such a substantial increase, the ratio of male to female students in higher education is as disparate as 3:1.

Female enrolment is concentrated in the Arts faculty though its share has gone down from 64.5 per cent in 1971–1972 to 55.7 per cent in 1981–1982. There has been a substantial increase in the share of Commerce faculty—from 2.2 per cent in 1971–1972 to 12.85 per cent in 1981–1982. The share in engineering (0.72%) and that of medicine (3.65%) continue to be very low and the latter has in fact fallen from 4.25 per cent in 1971–1972.

The relative deprivation of women in the field of education is particularly significant because it underlines all other attributes of deprivation. The Scheduled Castes are deprived no doubt, but Scheduled Caste women are more deprived than their men. The rural population is deprived, but rural women are even more so.

The regional variations in enrolment per lakh of population are very large. It varies from 61 in Arunachal Pradesh to 1,266 in South Kerala. It is no doubt true that the enclavized character of higher education in India has changed to some extent during the last three decades of planned development, but the position is still far from satisfactory.

In recent years, it has been argued that it is necessary to reduce allocation of resources to higher education and make more funds available to other levels, particularly elementary, secondary and adult education. It is true that per pupil expenditure is highest for universities and institutions of higher education. Even within the institution of higher learning, the per student expenditure in professional colleges is nearly three times that of the per student expenditure for general higher education. This is as it should be in view of the high level of infrastructure required for professional colleges.

The per student cost at current prices shows increasing trends over the last three decades. The cost per student has increased 4.8 times for primary education, 3.8 for middle, 3.5 for secondary and only 2.47 for higher education. In the context of inflationary trends, the cost per student in higher education has actually gone down. In fact, for college education, the expenditure per pupil has shown a significant decline. The situation is even more serious in the case of professional colleges where the real expenditure per student has dropped to nearly half in 1975–1976 as compared to 1950–1951.

A tentative analysis of the item-wise expenditure of a large central university has shown that the share of expenditure associated with non-academic work approximated to nearly 41 per cent in 1971 and constituted about 47 per cent of the total revenue budget of the university for 1980–1981. Similarly, an analysis of the budget of another university showed that the ratio of salaries between the academic and non-academic staff changed from 52:48 in 1976 to 44:56 in 1980. It may not be proper to generalize on the basis of a single observation. However, it points to the need for a deeper probe into the relative weights of academic and non-academic expenditure in higher education.

TRAGEDY

The tragedy of our times is that the Third World is already getting fragmented into the Third and the Fourth worlds; and the developing countries into the less and the least developed. Education is unfortunately playing a key role in this process of inequalization. Where do we wish India to be in this scheme of things? The exercise of the option (and there is an option) should determine our educational policies, particularly with reference to higher education.

Chapter 13

The Foreign Educated Indian*
His Dilemma

Subramanian Swamy

I

Much has been written about the problem of the 'brain drain'. It is not my purpose here to repeat this discussion. I propose here to discuss at a micro-level the kinds of problems that an able scientist with a good research degree from abroad faces on their return to this country, and the types of forces that interact on them. There is of course no need for special sympathy for a scientist with a foreign degree. In most senses, the foreign educated Indian has unfair advantages over his 'swadeshi' colleague. However, the foreign educated Indian represents an investment. Not to utilize them would be a folly. In many cases, the foreign educated is a person with a brilliant academic record and with special skills. The nation is in need of such persons, especially in programmes such as atomic energy and space development. But we find that instead of this utilization, scores of such Indians are permanently migrating abroad every year in search of opportunities to employ their skills.

Why do these scientists go abroad? Is it because our nation is not sufficiently developed to absorb them? I think not. Is it that these people get used to a high standard of living abroad and cannot adjust here? Certainly not. The causes are much deeper than that. In actual fact, the great majority of the foreign educated come back with a

---

* *Social Change:* June 1972: Vol. 2, No. 2, 20–24.

sense of commitment and a resolve to bear with hardships. But what they ultimately face here upon arrival is not the lack of comforts or a lack of adequate salary, but an entirely new system of hierarchy, work and recognition, something which they had no conception of or appreciation of during their teenage.

To be sure, there are some among the foreign educated who upon spending a few years abroad become completely alienated from India. They find it extremely difficult to readjust to the ways of their native brothers. During the 1920s, 1930s, 1940s and 1950s, such people were of a sizeable number. But now they are few and ever declining in strength.

In this chapter, I shall therefore confine myself to discussing the problems of the foreign educated Indian who is sober, balanced and went abroad primarily to learn the advanced skills in his field.

II

Most Indians who go abroad for higher studies arrive in the foreign country, notably the USA, with the bare essentials of life; some clothes, a few books and a minimum amount of money. The life such a student begins is, from the very first day, a struggle. They soon realize that they will have to buy expensive winter clothing, lots of books and rent an apartment. The money they have with them invariably turns out and is not enough. So on the very first or the second day, they approach the University authorities for waiving their tuition fees or postponing the payment. This represents their first encounter with a foreign system. The encounter is almost always pleasant. The authorities usually accede to the request and the matter is quickly resolved by a telephone call to the Accounts department. To my knowledge, all Indian students are profoundly impressed by this. And it is this that begins to condition the Indian mind—a refreshingly new system that seems to work impartially and with speed, especially in trivial personal matters.

Gradually, such types of encounters with the system multiply. The mind becomes conditioned to this, and soon one begins to expect this to happen automatically. Later, upon returning home, this conditioning proves to be a stumbling block to adjustment, a source of 'pinpricks' and frustration.

If you ask any migrating scientist the reasons for their decision to leave the country, they will almost certainly mention, among other reasons, the inability of the Indian system to deal with trivial personal problems impartially and with speed. If, for example, they are proceeding on a tour and would like their salary cheque a few days earlier, they will have to conduct a major bureaucratic operation at the end of which they will not be able to know the result. Those who do not go abroad have the advantage that they have been conditioned to a partial and inefficient system. They are apathetic to it since they have no expectations. But the foreign educated mind is conditioned to the smooth and automatic functioning of the system in such matters. The frustration is multiplied manifold when they find that the inefficiency is not impartial. If one has 'influence' or if the head of the institution where they are working likes them, then the system functions instantaneously. If not, then they literally run up *against* the system.

There is thus a big difference between living in a country such as the USA and living in India for a scientist. In the USA, for example, though the Indian there is a foreigner, in matters of day-to-day problems, they can expect the system to function as smoothly as it would for the president.

The second phase of conditioning begins when the Indian student begins to work for their doctorate. Their relationship with their thesis supervisor is an informal one in which disagreements over academic matters are frequent. The discussion is lively and fruitful. The thesis supervisor is helpful and 'promotes' their students as a salesman would promote their products. This relationship blossoms further when the student obtains their doctorate and either joins a research group or (more rarely) a university faculty. Thereafter, the person enjoys nearly full freedom in their teaching, research and conference activities. Rank consciousness in research matters is non-existent. It should be remembered that most of our students who go abroad are in their early 20s. At this age, they would not have tested the knowledge of Indian conditions. Therefore, at that young age, they get conditioned to the easy informality of the research atmosphere.

Upon return to India, the rigid hierarchy, the stiff formalities and the inflexible educational curriculum descend on the unsuspecting scientist. The head of the department acts in a dictatorial manner. All requests for research facilities have to be 'routed' through them. Even to write to a colleague in another department, it has to pass through the head of the department. Further, invitations and acceptances to attend conferences have to carry 'prior' approval of the head. Such nonsensical rules pile up and can, when the head chooses to, confront the researcher with the most degrading of situations. I have myself received letters from the director of the IIT asking as to why I had left my office at a specific moment without first obtaining their permission! Here again, there is no impartiality in all these rules. If you are liked by the authorities, everything is waived. If you are disliked, then, not only is nothing waived but a few more rules are dug up.

Thus, the second factor that is responsible for frustrating a foreign educated scientist is the rigid hierarchy, stiff formalities and inflexible educational curriculum.

The usually advanced reason of good salaries and comforts comes as a poor third for the dedicated scientist. Most of them have a social conscience and they know that a salary of ₹1,000 or more places them in a privileged position vis-a-vis most of their countrymen. Besides, the so-called good salaries or comforts of foreign countries are highly overrated since the costs are also quite high. Most scientists live abroad in a two- or three-room apartment in a crowded city, or in a small house in a suburb which is 20–30 miles away from the place of work. Rents are quite high and generally account for 25 per cent of one's salary. Domestic services are entirely out of the reach of the scientist. Hence, on weekends, the familiar sight is of this brilliant scientist going to shop for the household groceries, washing the household clothes, repairing the car, sweeping the house and cleaning the bathroom and commode. These services they can easily afford in India. Further, the cost of educating their children in the USA is enormous. A family with three children would have to save very consciously to put the children through school, college and university.

Jobs in the USA also carry a heavy risk element. There are very few permanent jobs. As Indian scientists are now learning, if the economy has a recession, they are very likely to be unemployed. The work is also exhausting and competitive. A scientist working for a research laboratory or a company frequently has to leave their home at 7 a.m., drive for an hour to their place of work and return at 6 p.m. Once home, they have to look into the family affairs. If they have young children, then they and their wife have to be confined to the home in the evenings since 'babysitters' are quite expensive on a long-term basis.

In my view, the usually advanced argument of high incomes abroad is not very persuasive. It is true that a car and electric household gadgets are within the easy reach of one's income abroad, but then the human mind is easily saturated. In any case, the Indian scientist can have the best of both worlds by living a few years abroad and then returning with these equipments to India.

Furthermore, the 'high' incomes have to be matched with the almost total cultural alienation. Indian scientists abroad are not very happy people. More than 90 per cent of them abroad would tell you that they plan to return to India someday, though in actual fact they have no such plan. This represents an escapism from the alienation. Indian scientists generally live together in the same neighbourhood. They cook Indian food, celebrate Deepavali and crowd to Subbalakshmi's recitals. They read the overseas *Statesman* and *Hindustan Times* more avidly than the local papers. To some extent, this behaviour is typical of any foreign settlers but, for Indians, this is in the extreme. Further, the local population is not receptive to Indian participation in local problems of the society. This renders the Indian a 'social cipher'. With the passage of time, every Indian scientist begins to feel alienated, as an unglorified cog in the foreigner's system. A deep urge develops to return to their motherland.

III

In the previous paragraphs, I have outlined, perhaps stylistically, the factors that operate on the foreign educated Indian scientists. Two of them press them to remain abroad, and another two pull them to return home. The impartial and speedy working of the foreigner's system, and the partisan and inefficient working of the Indian system is one factor why the scientist wishes to remain abroad. The other factor is the informality, personal freedom and equality in the educational system abroad. In India, the scientist faces rigid hierarchy, stiff formalities and an inflexible educational curriculum. As against this, the hard life and cultural alienation abroad drive them back to India.

In my view, therefore, if we want our scientists to come back and to remain here, then our policymakers should shift their attention from trying to 'bribe' these scientists with higher starts and better pay to changing the system that operates in the country. Nothing short of that can stop the brain drain. If we are able to change the system, then not only will our scientists return to the country but there will be fewer incentives to go abroad in the first place.

Chapter 14

Issues in Development of Higher Education*
The Indian Context

Malcolm S. Adiseshiah

FUNCTION OF HIGHER EDUCATION

While equity promotion or attainment is not one of the functions of higher education, should it be one of the fallout effects of higher education within the context of the new policy?

There is no doubt that is exactly what is expected by the public of all education, including higher education. We, in India, are in the process of formulating our Eighth Five Year Plan, for which we have established with the agreement of all our 22 states the basic approach to the Plan. On the education component of this approach, our leading news agency (UNI 1990, p. 8) states:

> a thorough revamping of the education system has been recommended in the approach paper to the Eighth Five Year Plan to make education less of a passport to privilege and access to white collar jobs and more as a means to enhance the capabilities of the people.

The traditional functions of higher education, and the university as its apex institution, have been the double one of safeguarding and

---

* *Social Change:* December 1990: Vol. 20, No. 4, 3–9.

The paper was written in 1990 and presented in the conference of Executive Heads of Commonwealth Universities, New Delhi. 14–18 January 1991.

ensuring the unity of knowledge and of conserving, transmitting and diffusing knowledge over the centuries from generation to generation, through the twin instrumentalities of teaching and research. The University Grants Commission of India issued in 1978 a Policy Frame for the Development of Higher Education in India in agreement with the Association of Indian Universities in which it states, inter alia, 'if the university system has to discharge adequately its responsibilities to the entire education system and to the society as a whole, it must assume extension as the third important responsibility and give it the same status as research and teaching' (UGC 198, p. 12). This addition of a third function to higher/university education involved the higher education system extending the services of the university and college teachers and students to the community to the poverty-stricken village or urban slum, as part of the undergraduate and postgraduate curriculum, for which the student receives credit in their assessment and the teacher is given the appropriate workload adjustment. These proposals for higher education to counter inequalities in society are reiterated in the latest approach to education adopted by the Parliament—the *National Policy on Education, 1986* (GoI 1986a, paras 2.3, 3.2, 3.6 & 3.8), and the *Programme of Action* (GoI 1986b, pp. 100 and 105–21) attached to it.

THE CHALLENGE OF EQUITY TO HIGHER EDUCATION

In a developing country like India, equity confronts the higher education system on both the exogenous and endogenous dimensions.

Exogenous Factors

Poverty

One exogenous factor is the mass poverty of the people of the country. On this, a rough and ready nutritional measure of poverty has been devised, which requires that an adult must consume daily 2,400 calories in the rural areas and 2,100 in urban areas to stay alive above the poverty level. On this basis, the official reckoning is that some 200 million people are living in poverty today as Table 14.1 shows.

Table 14.1 *Poverty in India*

Year	Percentage			No. of Poor in 000s		
	Rural	Urban	Total	Rural	Urban	Total
1972–1973	54.9	41.2	51.5	295.8	44.8	340.6
1977–1978	51.2	38.2	48.3	253.1	53.7	306.8
1984–1985	39.9	27.7	36.9	237.1	50.5	272.7
1989–1990	28.2	19.3	25.8	168.6	42.2	210.9

Source: 28th to 38th NSS Rounds: VII Plan document.

There is disagreement about the official trend shown in Table 14.1 of a decline and of the actual numbers living in poverty. My studies show that using the nutritional yardstick, some 300 million men, women and children are living in poverty, and while some have climbed out of the poverty morass, the increase in population, particularly among the poor families, has kept the members fairly stable. But there is general agreement that there is a large mass of people living in poverty and destitution, which confronts the enclaves of relative affluence that higher education represents.

It is to counter this that a call was made in 1978 and repeated in 1986 for higher education to transfer classroom and library learning and laboratory results to the poverty-ridden village or urban slum (which I did in my university requiring all undergraduate students and teachers to spend 2 hours a week and postgraduates 1 hour on it) which called on science students to apply their knowledge of physics to repair farm implements, their knowledge of chemistry to test and advise the farmer on the chemistry of the soil, their knowledge of botany and zoology to help improve the seed, land and water use and fish farming, even while safeguarding the environment, their knowledge of commerce in helping the village cooperative in keeping its accounts; their knowledge of political science in helping the village panchayats with its complex functions and in its periodic elections, their knowledge of health and medical science in improving the nutritional status of the preschool child and the pregnant mothers and promoting the small family norm, and their knowledge of agricultural and veterinary sciences in transferring to the farm their research results on countering crop and cattle pests and their knowledge of engineering sciences in training youth for entrepreneurial self-employment (Adiseshaiah 1986) (the equivalences were applied to slums). It was found that not only was this interface between higher education and the community helping in poverty alleviation, it also helped through a system of feedback to the boards of studies in reforming the curriculum, correcting its abstractness and keeping it more up to date and relevant and assisted the students 'to develop confidence and sufficient psychomotor skills to enter the world of work' (GoI 1986b p. 42; Devadoss 1977). Unfortunately, this essential programme of higher education to relieve poverty a little and so make a small contribution to equity has, after 15 years, yet to take off on a country-wide basis.

Inequality in Income and Asset Distribution

The other exogenous factor confronting equity in the country is the wide, growing and serious inequalities in income and assets ownership. The skewed distribution of incomes in both rural and urban societies under which the top 10 per cent of society has 20 times the income of the bottom 10 per cent is shown in Table 14.2.

Inequalities in the distribution of assets are even worse with the top 10 per cent in rural areas having 500 times more assets than the bottom 10 per cent as Table 14.3 on rural asset distribution shows.

Table 14.2 *Income Distribution in India, 1985–1986*

Decile Groups	% Share of Disposable Income in Percentage	
	Rural	Urban
Bottom 10%	1.83	1.97
Bottom 20%	4.88	5.17
Bottom 30%	8.65	9.43
Bottom 50%	18.88	20.43
Top 20%	53.33	59.54
Top 10%	36.04	36.52

Source: NCAER, All India Household Survey of Income, Saving and Consumer Expenditure., 1985–1986.

Table 14.3 *Inequality in the Distribution of Assets*

Decile Groups	Percentage Share in Assets		
	1961	1971	1981
Lowest 10%	0.1	0.1	0.1
Lowest 30%	2.5	2.0	4.0
Top 30%	79.0	81.9	80.0
Top 10%	51.4	51.0	50.0

Source: RBI All India Debt Investment Survey.

At this point, the exogenous and endogenous factors concerning equity merge in demonstrating rather sharply the effect of the inequalities of income and assets distribution on higher education. In 1965, the Indian Council of Social Science Research made a detailed survey, state by state, at the request of the Education (Kothari) Commission (1964–1966) of the parental incomes of those who were in high schools and colleges. Its finding was that 80 per cent of high schools and higher education (college and university) completers were from the top 20 per cent of society (recorded between the 3rd and 4th group in Table 14.3) (see ICSSR-NCERT 1971, p. 98). Twelve years later, in 1977, the University Grants Commission made a similar survey, and its finding was that '70 percent of seats in secondary schools and 80 per cent of seats in higher education are taken by the top 30 per cent of the income groups' (recorded in the last [fourth] group in the Table 14.3) (see UGC 1978, p. 2). This disparity becomes even more serious when account is taken of the fact that all education in India is subsidised by the state to the extent of over 80 per cent of its total cost, given the system of payment of teachers' salaries in all higher education institutions as well as the system of block grants to universities by the state government. Government revenues—both at the federal and state levels from which the state subsidies are paid out are to the extent of 90 per cent raised by indirect taxes, compared to 44% on the eve of the country's Independence (1945–1946) (MoF 1982, pt 2, p.2; Adiseshaiah 1990, p. 14), and unlike direct taxes which are paid by around 1.5 million well-to-do income tax, corporate tax and wealth taxpayers, indirect taxes are paid by all people, the majority of whom are poor or nearly so, so that they are to a major extent paid by the poor. This means that not only are the poor or those nearly so who are the majority in society a small minority among the higher education completers, as most of the beneficiaries of the subsidized higher education are the children of the affluent families (the top two-thirds deciles in Table 14.3), higher education has become an instrument for transferring such small resources as are earned or owned by the poor to the rich minority. There was a time when this kind of inequality amounting to inequity was accepted and justified in India as the price of development. Following the Kuznets' hypothesis, there was the gruesome conclusion in the middle of our planning exercises that 'some of inequality in income is an essential part of the structure of incentives (for savings and skills) in a growing economy' (Pant 1978, p. 14). This has now been shown to be without any theoretical or empirical basis. Per contra proposals have been made in the National Policy on Education to counter this regressive character of higher education, first by levying fees at the high school and higher educational levels on the students from well-to-do families (so that subsidized education is only for those from poor families) and second to organize special compensatory learning programmes for first-generation learners so that there would be some equivalence as between the outcomes of higher education and its access, which is the subject of a certain percentage of reservation (varying from 20 to 30) for students from poor families. Thus, it can be seen that higher education leaves alone the inequitable distribution of incomes and assets in the country doing nothing to correct it but tries to modify its (higher education's) tendency to contribute to the worsening of the inequities.

Endogenous Factors

In the realm of equity and higher education, there are some seven endogenous factors which need a brief comment, relating to the problems of location, gender, intergenerational class dualism, management, educational levels and international typology.

Location

On the location question, following the model of industrial countries, all higher education institutions, including those relating to agriculture and allied activities, in India and the other developing countries, are located in urban areas, whereas 80 per cent of the people live in rural areas, which in turn contribute 65–75 per cent of the national income. This also makes the relation between urban and rural sectors, as far as higher education is concerned, one of donor-beneficiary. India made an attempt just before and after Independence, under the leadership of Mahatma Gandhi, to break away from this spatial inequality model and develop a truly rural-based education policy and system. The history of that short-lived scheme of basic education and Rural Institute of Higher Education which the National Policy on Education has been trying unsuccessfully to revive today poses the question whether this inequality (of the urban industrial sector bias and the non-relation to the major social sector—the rural one) is in some way built into the system of higher education. This question is sharply posed with the formation and functioning of the present government in India which was brought into being in the 1989 general elections with the pledge to restore a balance, an equilibrium, as between the rural and urban sectors.

Gender

The gender inequality in higher education is amply documented in the annual reports of the Ministry of Education and University Grants Commission and recorded in UNESCO's Statistical Yearbooks. In 1975, of the 4.6 million students enrolled in higher education, 1 million were women while of its 2,35,822 teachers, women teachers were only 39,272; in 1978, of the 4.5 million total students enrolled, women students were 1.1 million, of 231,233 teachers, women teachers were 42,311; in 1979, of the 5.2 million total student enrolment, women students were 1.39 million and of 277,468 teachers, women teachers were 50,560; in 1980, of the 5.34 million students, 1.39 million were women and, in 1983, of the 5.47 million students, 1.55 million were women students (UGC 1970, 1977, 1984, 1989). There is a special drive underway today in all walks of life in India, and in education in particular to correct this imbalance. The National Policy on Education opens with a section on the means giving equal access to women students on which some progress has been made, and on the provision of better representation of women at the teaching and managerial level. On this, there is still a long way to go, as there are at present only 3 women vice chancellors of 150, and less than 10 per cent women heads of department of higher education/institutions. Here again, the question is posed, whether there is something in education, including higher education, where left to itself, there is the unequal treatment of girls and women as one ascends the educational ladder.

Intergenerational

On intergenerational inequality, the most vivid expression of this is seen in the financial provisions made for education of youth, of which public expenditure in higher education amounts to 18 per cent of the total educational expenditure, whereas 0.1 to 0.4 per cent has been and is set aside for adult literacy and adult education generally. This seems to be a general worldwide feature (UNESCO 1989, Table 2.1). So here again the question is posed, whether higher education is founded on the premise that it is the monopolistic right of the young, while education of the not-so-young is benevolent conceding of the second opportunity to the deprived and deficient, which is also a reflection of the structural relationship between schooling and work, between income earning opportunity and life chances for learning, which have given rise to the various open learning systems today.

Intragenerational

On class-based inequality, the earlier treatment of this intragenerational inequality showed that higher education policy has to be countered from reinforcing and directing a system in which children of the well-to-do minority who are the survivors of the primary and post-primary education stage tend towards exclusive access to higher education. In this connection, the UGC policy frame calls attention to the dualistic nature of the system of education including higher education. It refers to a small minority of educational institutions at all levels of good quality...but access to them is selective, is mostly availed of by the top social groups either because they can afford the costs involved or because they show merit which, on the basis of existing methods of selection shows a high correlation with social status. But this core of good institutions is surrounded by a penumbra of institutions, where although there is open door access, the standards are poor... and where the large majority of people including the weaker sections receive their education. (UGC 1978, p. 2).

The question arises as to whether this dualism is inherent in higher education in India, and whether the various measures being tried to bring about a certain degree of uniformity in standards are capable of realization in a basically inegalitarian society?

Management: On management causing inequalities, the question is raised of higher education being the most centralized system of teaching, learning and management, with the resultant waste of both teachers' time and students' capacity. The whole system is based on a top-down process—from the vice chancellor, the dean, the professor, on to the lecturer talking down to students, resulting in outdated content, repetitious teaching techniques and unmindful rote learning. This inequality between the teachers and the taught which is both historical in this country, going back to the *guru–shishya* tradition and hence built into all forms of higher education, is gradually breaking down, its vertical hierarchical dominance being questioned by horizontal egalitarian interaction. With the rate at which knowledge and information is exploding today, higher education is being forced gradually to lose its top-down nature and become a system of learning how to learn, in which there are no hierarchical superiors and mendicants, no teacher and taught, because all are learning all the time. I expect that we will begin the 21st century with replacing the platform on which the teacher stands, or even his standing in front of the class expounding their words of wisdom, as that form of inequality is a certain indicator that no learning is taking place there.

Educational levels: The equity issues as related to the levels of education raises difficult and somewhat emotional issues in this country. On the one hand, we have given ourselves a constitution in 1950 which provides for free and compulsory education to all up to the age of

14 years within 10 years, by 1960, a pledge which we keep repeating in every Plan. Forty years later, we have still over 40–50 million (depending on how the left outs, pushouts and dropouts are computed) without schooling and over 200 million illiterates. Even as we have mouthed the absolute priority for elementary education, during the seven Plans, the expenditure (Plan and non-Plan) on higher education was increased 10 times, while that on primary education increased five times (all at constant prices) (Tilak, 1990). And so I raised the question at the start of the VII Plan (in 1985) and do so again at the start of the VIII Plan (today in 1990) whether there should not be a pause for five years on the expansion of higher education, so that the released resources may (a) be diverted to realizing the priority of elementary education and (b) allow use of the residual to consolidate, improve and update the quality of higher education institutions.

International Typology

The international typology which the question of equity in higher education raises is whether our educational world will have to conform to the economic production stages into which we have divided our world, that is, will some countries as suppliers of raw materials be limited to extraction and subsistence labour and the education levels appropriate to it? Will a second group of countries be concerned mainly with the processing tasks and vocational education that they would require? And then, will there be a third group of countries where production is science and technology based, moving increasingly into what today is called the 'high-tech' areas, and where all industry including agriculture is research intensive, calling for a higher education system of science, technology and research to which scholars within the country and from outside are attracted (Sanyal 1982). This international inequity typology is not really as theoretical as it sounds, in the light of the brain drain from India and other developing countries to the industrialized ones, which reinforces their science and technology competence leaving the other group of (the drained) countries with lower educational and scientific levels (Altbach 1983). The question is whether this is built into the system of higher education under which the poor countries help the rich countries to grow richer through contributing to their science and technology, a kind of reverse foreign aid from the developing countries to the industrialized ones, adding further to the net flow of resources now taking place every year from poor to rich countries. This may also reinforce the case for a five-year pause in India in higher education.

REFERENCES

Adiseshiah, Malcolm S. (1986) Entrepreneurship *Development for Tamilnadu.* Affiliated East-West Press, Madras.

Adiseshiah, M.S. (1990). *Mid Year Review of the Economy* 1989–90. Lancer International, New Delhi.

Altbach, Philip G. (1983). *Perspectives on comparative higher education,* International Council for Educational Development, Occasional Paper, No. 16, Princeton, New Jersey.

Devadoss, Rjammal (1977). *Community and Social Service as curricular component in Higher Education,* Monograph 31. University of Madras, Madras.

GoI (1986a). *National Policy on Education: 1986,* Ministry of Human Resource Development, Government of India, New Delhi.

GoI (1986b). Programme of Action, *National Policy on Education:* 1986, Ministry of Human Resource Development, Government of India, New Delhi.

ICSSR-NCERT (1971). *Field Studies in the Sociology of Education,* New Delhi.

MHRD. (1986a). *National Policy on Education 1986.* New Delhi, Government of India, Ministry of Human Resource Development.

MHRD (1986b). *Programme of Action: National Policy on Education 1986.* New Delhi, Government of India, Ministry of Human Resource Development.

MoF (1982). *Taxation Policy:* Part II., (Roneoed) Ministry of Finance, Government of India, New Delhi.

Pant, Pitambar. (1978). Perspectives of Development 1961–1976, in *Poverty and Income distribution in India,* (Ed.) T.N. Srinivasan & P.K. Bardhan. Statistical Publishing Society, Calcutta.

Sanyal, Bikas C. (1982). *Higher Education and the New International Economic Order.* International Institute for Educational Planning, Frances Printer, UNESCO Paris.

Tilak, J. B. G. (1990). *The Political Economy of Education in India.* Special Studies No.24, Comparative Education Center, State University of New York at Buffalo (in collaboration with the University of Virginia).

UGC. (1977). *Third All-India Survey of Higher Education.* New Delhi.

UGC. (1977–1978). *Annual Report 1977–78.* New Delhi.

UGC (1978). *Development of Higher Education in India, A Policy Frame.* University Grants Commission, New Delhi.

UNESCO (1977, 1984, 1989). *Statistical Yearbook.* Paris.

UNI. (1990). United News of India press release: *Economic Times,* Bangalore, 3 June.

Chapter 15

Directing Teaching and Research in India for Development*

Ujagar Singh

INTRODUCTION

The destiny of India is now being shaped in her class rooms.
—Kothari Commission

The greatness of the nation depends upon education. It determines the level of prosperity and welfare and security of the people. The future citizens have to be so equipped as to take active part in all the schemes, tending to develop the national resources: material, social, intellectual and aesthetic life to a higher level. Until the Second World War, England and France were the leaders of the world in education (arts) and remained top powers in the world. After the war, America and Russia became leaders of education (science and technology), they became superior in power. The role of education in development is obvious. Education needs reorientation according to national requirement. In this chapter, the stress is given on higher education as 'research' is the attribute of higher education and it is expensive.

At present, the basic need of India is reconstruction and yet retain social stability at the same time: to reconstruct from close into open society, from ascribed roles into achievement roles, from caste system into secular social order. When India was a colony, the problem was of 'adaptation' or to maintain social status quo, to save the interest of

---

* *Social Change:* March–June 1979: Vol. 9, No. 1–2, 28–34.

the master in support of established system. The educational problem was to build the feeling or sentiment for habitual ways of life. The role of education was conservative, which could be performed through the process of 'socialization' (identification, introjection and projection). For this purpose, the role of informal agencies such as family and church are equally important.

But after Independence, the situation has been changed which raised the level of aspirations, hopes and values of people. These changes give rise to crises in 'evaluation'. It implies a critical awareness for evaluating and re-evaluating the old and new values, needed to select the proper value system to bring about not only change but desirable change, to meet the goals and aspirations of the people, it requires an educational problem to develop the capacity to think and rethink. Younger generation have to be prepared to 'perceive their proper role' in the society as expected by members of society. Education must be directed towards intellectual movement to meet the social requirement (change and social stability). For this end, the intellectual or academic responsibilities of the university cannot be minimized.

The educational problems to enable the younger generation to perceive their role in order to become the true servants of the nation and to participate for the uplift of the nation was stressed by Gandhiji.[1] He said that we should have an army of the chemists, engineers and experts who would be the real servants of the nation for the varied and growing requirements. For this purpose, we should have better laboratories and research institutes which aim at performance of social duty as basic obligation in addition to professional work and services. In this way, Gandhiji reconciled the pragmatic approach with idealistic concept of education with an equal stress on extrinsic and intrinsic values of life.

Effort towards 'intellectual movement', as the foremost requirement in education, was also stressed by Plato in his scheme of education. Plato laid stress on the 'wise use of knowledge', needed to find out universal solution to the basic social problem of an adjustment of individual with society. He believed that the function of education was to unfold the best element within the individual which, according to him, is 'reason'. Thus, the function of education is to sharpen and develop this intellectual potential so that each one may be able to make the best use of it by examining one's own needs and interests and values. He thought that imbalances for choice of values and roles are the basis of all social evils and conflicts.

But the problem before Plato was basically different from that of the contemporary India. India needs reconstruction, that is, desirable or qualitative change and, at the same time, social stability. For Plato, there was no such problem as of social change, but of social stability. Hence, in India, the main educational problem is to prepare the younger generation capable of thinking and rethinking, to examine and re-examine the values as basis for new social order. In this way, education needs 'reorientation' for achieving social development with an equal stress on immediate as well as long-term and permanent balance between the extrinsic and intrinsic values. It is necessary to clear the basic concepts of education and development in order to understand their dynamic role.

Education is an abstract idea, and it stands for an improvement in the form of understanding, skills, values, attitudes and social habits of an individual in relation to their social environment (i.e., sociocultural). It is required to do so, as the child at the time of birth in the technical sense is neither an individual capable for perception or to understand nor a person capable to examine the norms of social life to be influenced by them and in turn affect them. He is not capable for social 'interaction'. But they are 'an organism', a living entity with the bundle of living forces or impulses which are blind to interests of others. These natural forces are in need of 'regularity' or 'control' needed to make the excellent use of them and to enable them to adjust with the social environment for the purpose of development of both the individual and society.

Hence, personality development is the main function of education. It is a wider term and should not be identified with training, instruction and teaching. As a matter of stress, in case of training, the stress is on skilled part, in case of instruction, understanding is required which is partial, the instructor may or may not have regard for understanding as the part to whom they give instruction. In case of teaching, the process is bipolar, that is, between the teacher and taught, and both of them aim at improving understanding and sharing knowledge and beliefs. But education is neither a two-way nor tri-way process, but dynamic interaction between the person and their social environment and development in each case is reciprocal. Hence, education is the general and universal requirement for child and society from the time the child is born as an organism or instinctive creature.

DEFINITION OF DEVELOPMENT

Development refers to a process of achieving certain basic qualities for a society essential to ensure minimum standard of life for all, so that everybody may possess dignity and social status. It would require a standard of material possession which would ensure that no one was prevented from developing their personal potentialities.

Basic Qualities

1. Sufficiency and growth are basic to all development. Sufficiency stands primarily observance of want in terms of standards that would be considered 'adequate' for needs of growth in the society concerned.
2. National security is also essential. In the modern world of science and technology, there is certain interdependence between countries for which no adequate parallel in the past history of international relations is available. This added a new dimension to the concept of security.

   In case of developed nations such as the USA and the Soviet Union, security does not mean threat to their borders or sovereignty but also the system of functioning of their economy or their way of life. In case of developing nations, where political, economic and social entities are not yet stable for their security, it implies an environment in which development takes place without interference from 'without'. At social level where the individual is safeguarded from abuse by employers, landlords and all, the individuals have some part in the political process.
3. The emergence of new class because of their specific educational attainment comes to occupy key position in society because their technical skill enables them to contribute towards development; in this context, it stands for achievement and balanced social mobility. 'Development' has meant political independence and human fulfilment involving the building of new institutions, economic,

political and social grounded in the physical and cultural resources of the country. Hence, emergence of new class can also be an indication of development.

Basic Principles of Development

Equality and social justice are essential for development. Equality means that the gap between the pour and the rich must not be to the extent that the poor man or country are exploited by the rich. It does not mean 'uniformity' in matters of physical, intellectual, moral and aesthetic development of an individual as well as of a nation. The term 'social justice' assumes that everyone is properly rewarded for their services and contribution to development. The rewards gained by individuals should not vary so greatly that it leads to major inequalities of wealth and status. Social justice provides a system of security to all the members of the community from exploitation or victimization and thus provide incentive to work.

Development Model

Therefore, 'development' stands for certain qualities on the basis of certain principles. As such, it cannot he conceived only in terms of traditional economic model, that is, in terms of capital, increase in capital, land reform, technology and manpower. An economic model is not the correct way to look at development. Even rich nations are not always self-sufficient (i.e., Kuwait for wheat). The USA is not free from social prejudices and class conflicts on the basis of colour discrimination. We see that there are psychological factors as fear, insecurity, varying degree of acceptance, tolerance and clinging to status quo as well as social factors, such social structure and, with it, inequalities and stratification. These factors retard growth which cannot be eradicated simply by having right number of doctors, engineers or agronomists. It needs social reconstruction or creation of a new class which stands for a situation in which people are given positions of power on merit. Such a class of people should be given a positive role in society determined not by birth but by ability and training. In this sense, development is an integrated whole which stands for *economic efficiency, social and moral decency.*

NATURE OF PROBLEM

Nations are underdeveloped in terms of failure to make adequate use of resources. The people are not able to make the contributions they might have made to the life of community. It becomes difficult for a poor and developing country to absorb either unlimited capital for its development or the greatly increased number of persons through whose skilled activity the capital will become productive. Nations are underdeveloped because it is so frequently impossible to get the things done what would develop them. Sometimes it is because people are superstitious, and unskilled adopting crude forms of agriculture, who have never been brought into touch with national life and are completely uninterested in it. It needs a wide use of knowledge. It requires that educational attempts or practices be directed in such a way as to enable people to think and work along the most logical and appropriate lines.

Aims

The function of education is to develop the capacity to examine and think critically for (a) enhancing the efficiency and quality of work, (b) promoting personal well-being and social welfare, (c) eliminating any type of confusion with others and (d) bringing about emotional unity and integration among people.

At present, the main educational problem is to make it qualitative, to reshape social order on the basis of social values such as secularism, socialism and democracy, to establish egalitarian order in which everyone is ensured of a minimum standard of living, so that each person be given socially equal respect and may be able to live in a dignified manner. It is obvious that it requires transformation in existing caste-based socio-economic structure to meet the requirements of people. The main purpose is to end the social inequality and class privileges (which is the legacy of feudalism) by establishing modern state with the concept of social welfare and social justice. What is required is not change only, but qualitative change.

For this purpose, education needs orienting towards intellectual movement that is to enable each one to examine critically one's needs and interests, because at present it has become our foremost social need to lay stress on the quality of life rather than more scientific knowledge and advancement. The essence of it consists of values rather than wealth. In Indian context, the term 'equality' means a dimension of living beyond merely material needs but not excluding at the same time the essentialities of well-being without which the fullness of human life is difficult to attain. It requires equal stress on scientific and technical, moral and religious education to accelerate economic efficiency along with social and moral decency. It implies, therefore, meaningful pursuit between the material and the spiritual, the acquisition of knowledge and power on the one hand and of wisdom and happiness on the other hand.

The national necessity is to develop a design for development. The purpose of it is to free man from bonds, both physical and mental, a sense of balance between individual and society, regular constructive habits of work, experimental attitude and delight in imagination. This called for a collective approach under which everyone has to think and act in the larger national interest. We should seek more appropriate solutions in the field of education and training as the basis for all development and modernization. Hence, the motto of the university should imply social service.

TECHNICAL EDUCATION AND ECONOMIC DEVELOPMENT

The term 'economics' stands for vitality as to seek an impulse to live. The economic principle is universal, it means applicable to all irrespective of time and place. It is actual, immediate, real, rational and practical activity of man. It is independent of any moral and immoral direction. Impulse to live according to Dr Sigmund Freud is the instinctive or innate urge on the basis of pleasure principle which means comfortable and no restraint or postponement of its immediate satisfaction. In this sense, economic need is most significant and fundamental.

In a country like India, with huge population, economic problem becomes vital and of immediate concern and, as such, an essential condition for development. No doubt the main basis of Indian culture has been emphasized as religious and metaphysical, but it is not a country of saints but a country with common people with the requirements of their physical existence, common hopes and aspirations, and are, therefore, governed by the general laws of social development, with a stress on economic needs as a matter of immediate concern. According to the Reserve Bank of India,[2] 70 per cent people are living below the poverty line.

For this purpose, experience that teaches us how to earn our bread, save our lives and keep our health is an indispensable condition (may not be adequate) for rational freedom. It requires to improve production or economic efficiency to minimize poverty. For its efficacy, it needs trained manpower to make them alert and skilful. In this connection, the instrumental role of education, that is, to meet the economic needs, cannot be denied and, in turn, the role of technical education is an important key to minimize poverty and economic backwardness as noted in the following sections.

From 1950 up to the present, the increase in production of food grains approximately is by 2.8 per cent. It is higher than the population growth rate of about 2.1 per cent for the same period. In the colonial period when food grains production was 1.1 per cent per year the population growth rate was 1.5 per cent per year. Rice procurement this year has crossed 2.18 million tonnes as compared to 1.8 million tonnes, almost 15 per cent higher during the corresponding period last year. This has been achieved by adding more than 55 million acres to irrigation which resulted in production of food grains from 50 million tonnes to 118 million tonnes in 1950–1951 and 1975–1976, respectively.[3]

Economic efficiency is useful for production and country with threatening increase in population and poverty can ill-afford to neglect scientific and technical education in full measure. But with all this, it is not sufficient. It is not the indication of moral decency as crime is increasing in India as well as in the world. According to Indian Penal Code 1973, the rise in population between 1963 and 1973 was only 25.1 per cent, while there was an overall increase in crime (63.5%) during the decade ending, that is, in 1973. It is clear that economic efficiency based on technical education is essential, but to make the nation civilized and cultured, this is not adequate for men with stability of mind are needed. For this purpose, moral and religious education is essential and, therefore, technical and liberal education must be reconciled. Man desires that he should be treated equal in a dignified manner by the society. Social needs cannot be assumed to be identical with economic needs.

MORAL EDUCATION

Moral education gives mankind the will to do, what is right. It does not lay down rules either of conduct or analysis of the nature of actions, which are right—the quality which constitutes their rightness. This is the concern of moral philosophy. In this sense, moral education is needed to discriminate between right and wrong action; otherwise, impulse to live is common with animals. It requires mental stability by the control of reason over impulses which require self-training and self-discipline. This type of organized life is given the name of moral by following the order of rational-self over irrational-self. Thus, it is a matter of self-possession which is essential to make the best use of natural potentialities for the betterment of both the individual and society. In this sense, it is not contrary to vitality or impulses to live. Morality is surrounded to crown the vitality which man brings into play too for its own sake.

Mental stability by means of rational or instinctive control is needed to get victory over physical needs to attain rational freedom. It means the subjugation of the natural world to the purpose of intellect, conscience, deliverance from ignorance, passion, self-will and petty values. Only they are rationally free who appreciate the wisdom developed in the experiences of their race. In this way, rational freedom is an ever-enlarging ideal.

Rational freedom has its own quality and appreciated for its own sake and it cannot be conditioned by economic conditions. The nature of economic choice of buyer and seller cannot be qualitatively identified with moral choice between good and evil. John Stuart Mill is right when he remarks that it is better that Socrates should remain unsatisfied than have the satisfaction of a pig. It means man not only lives at the biological level but also lives according to certain standards of life. Restraint or repression of biological impulses is essential to attain the true level of culture. It is justified by Dr Freud, the founder of psychoanalysis, by his remarks that civilization evolves at the cost of repression. The quality of moral choice, which is an act of will, is sublime in man. In this respect, animals cannot produce culture, for restraint over impulses is not possible.

At present, in Indian context, while the nation is in the process of transition, moral education is most essential. Transition gives rise to crisis in 'evaluation' between the old and the new values. It necessitates to regenerate people capable for evaluation and re-evaluation to select desirable goals and values to reconstruct India on the basis of progressive national social values. Otherwise, imbalances between values are the basis of all social conflicts and social evils. India at this time needs men with stability of mind and character to make nation civilized and cultured in the real sense. Hence, moral education is most essential.

This ever-moving ideal is called liberal education. The condition of liberal education lies in the participation of each human being in advancing growth experience for all for understanding the unity of human history. Liberal education, in many of its details, may be much the same as those of technical education, but it always directs the learner to be in tune with the ultimate ideal of man, that is, the ideas of good, the truth and the beautiful the one absolute idea of the 'good'.

The secret of education lies in the personal influence of the teacher and in general moral atmosphere and the general spiritual values. The role of teacher is to provide inspiration, for learning should be measured by the effort of the learner than by imparting of information by the teacher to the learner.

RELIGIOUS EDUCATION

Religious education means spiritual development. Spirituality means expansion of our loyalties and services leading to universal brotherhood and interest in the welfare of mankind. In the contemporary world, spiritual unity is needed for human integration and world peace which is essential for national development. This type of religious education must not be identified with the theological discussion regarding the concept of God.

The 'modern man' has seen how beneficial our progress in science, technology and organization has been. At the same time, he also knows how catastrophic the consequences can be if these are misused. The world at present is going to be divided into narrow nationalism which adds fear and insecurity rather than peace, security and happiness. Adolph Hitler used to say that foreign policy is a means to an end and the sole end to be preserved is the advantages of his own nation. All other considerations, political, religious, and humanism, had to be completely disregarded in favour of this one. This kind of nationalism is an acquired artificial emotion. The nation-state came into being when man felt the necessity of a stable social order and only a strong central power would put down civil wars.

Human roots go deeper than nationality and our attachment cannot be limited to local, racial, national spheres only but can encompass the whole human race. Our preference for the present order need not be confused with an inescapable law of the universe. We need not confuse the familiar with the eternal. We can fight not for the country only but also for values of civilization and science, by cooperative organizational efforts to develop the world's resources—material and human—for the greatest benefit of mankind.

Under these circumstances, when the world is divided into power blocks, the necessity of these values of contemporary significance must be conveyed to the younger generation. The new generation requires to be trained in the ideals of sacredness and supremacy of spiritual life, the sense of brotherhood of mankind and love of peace. It is this idea of spirituality which must be practised in the universities and colleges and be equally applicable to authorities, teachers and students. In case of universities, undue promotions are made on the basis of caste and community rather than on the basis of achievement. This makes the teachers narrow-minded by showing undue favour in examination halls, whereas they should be working with zeal for the improvement of others. This trend deprives them of the awareness of their professional ethics.

The university must be a seat of *sath-sangat* which means to act according to the true spirit of reason and intelligence, in search of truth as well as to determine the merit. To act according to 'reason' was appreciated by Socrates and at the time of death he remarked that those who are against the true spirit of reason are his enemies. Plato also appreciated the supremacy of reason, in his scheme of education, needed to bring about social harmony. Gautama Buddha recognized the role of 'reason' to discriminate between 'desirable' and 'undesirable' to get rid of confusion, the cause of all misery.

Religious education stands for all-inclusiveness or universality or oneness which is the essence of Bhagavad Gita. It implies action with the spirit of 'sacrifice' without any selfishness or narrow consideration, but with the true spirit of duty and obligation for the sake of social justice and human dignity. It stands for true spirit of brotherhood as found in the Bible, 'love they neighbour as thy own self'. In this way, religious spirit will in no way stand on the way of secularism, socialism and democracy. It is the root of true civilization and culture. It leads to world harmony and happiness, emotional unity and integration which is the need of India at the national level as well as the need of humanity. Development orientation of teaching and research implies integrated approach which means equal importance to technical as well as liberal education to satisfy the immediate and permanent needs and interests. It is needed for general good. It is required to make education qualitative, useful and productive.

NOTES

1   *Harijan*, 9 July 1938.
2   *The Tribune*, Chandigarh, 22 January 1975.
3. *The Tribune*, Chandigarh (January 1, 1978).

Chapter 16

Research Culture in Indian Universities*

Pravin J. Patel

INTRODUCTION

Contemporary Indian policymakers, aspiring to make India a global power by calibrating a development trajectory with projects such as 'Make in India', 'Bullet Trains', 'Smart Cities' and 'Metros' need to recognize that economic progress in the emerging knowledge society depends largely upon a knowledge economy. Let me illustrate the point with a personal anecdote. In 1994, I was at a university in the UK as a Charles Wallace Fellow. During my stay there, once I had a chat with an economics professor. At some stage, I asked a simple question which had been bothering me as a non-economist for a long time: 'Professor, as an economist, how do you explain the huge difference between the value of British pound sterling and Indian rupee?'[1] He looked at me with a smile and said, 'Simple. We [in Britain] sell supersonic jets and you [in India] sell potatoes and onions!' I was flabbergasted. However, a moment's reflection made it all clear. What he meant was that a product like a supersonic jet involves much value addition, caused by extensive research in various areas. Such sophisticated products are in a high demand and fetch astronomical prices, contributing to the country's economic prosperity. On the other hand, raw materials

* *Social Change:* June 2016: 46, No. 2, 238–59.

I am grateful to A. M. Shah, N. R. Sheth and Bhikhu Parekh for their valuable comments on the earlier draft of the chapter.

such as potatoes and onions do not contribute much to a country's economic development. Thus, a country's capability to undertake path-breaking research enables it to become rich and powerful by globally marketing value-added products. Conversely, a country unable to do so remains economically underdeveloped. Thus, knowledge creation through scientific research is the key to economic development in a knowledge society.

This chapter argues that a knowledge society is the product of a modern, research-oriented university. Furthermore, taking America as a paradigm of knowledge society, it asserts that the country has become rich and powerful by promoting scientific research in its universities. Concurrently, while appraising India's progress towards a knowledge society, the chapter concludes that if India aspires to be a world power in the 21st century, it will have to become a knowledge society by promoting research not only by guaranteeing substantial financial support but also by regenerating research culture and ceaselessly transmitting it among the coming generations of students. The chapter is focused more on the natural sciences, since they play a crucial role in promoting a knowledge economy, the basis of knowledge society.

I
RESEARCH UNIVERSITY: THE MOTHER OF KNOWLEDGE SOCIETY

Human being's quest for knowledge is ancient. However, knowledge society originated in modern times due to the digital revolution of the mid-20th century caused by scientific research mostly done in universities.

The Knowledge Society

A knowledge society, heavily dependent on knowledge economy, creates, communicates and uses knowledge for the people's well-being (Bernheim & de Sauza, 2003, p. 1). It is a society characterized by transition from an economy based on material goods to the one based on knowledge (Drucker, 1969). The members of a knowledge society attain a higher average standard of education, and a growing proportion of its workers are employed as knowledge workers. Increasingly digitized knowledge provides enhanced access to information, data banks, communication technology and the Internet to its population. A knowledge society also invests heavily in education and research, and organizations become increasingly innovative.

Research University and the Origin of Knowledge Society

Although modern universities took root in Europe by the 15th century, research-oriented universities with the emphasis on science education emerged in the early 19th century with the establishment of the University of Berlin, now Humboldt University, in Germany in 1810 (Clark, 2006). The University of Berlin initiated a new trend in German higher education, making research an inseparable part of teaching; transforming traditional teacher–student relations into that of master apprentice; giving importance to the 'institutionalization of discovery' and publication of results based on original research; and sponsoring seminars, libraries and laboratories (Howard, 2009, pp. 130–211; Watson, 2010, pp. 225–26). By 1850, all these innovations became the German university's defining features (McClelland, [1980] 2008; Watson, 2010, pp. 225–37). Significantly, German society was largely underdeveloped and characterized by agricultural economy before 1800. However, after their disastrous defeat in 1806 by Napoleon, the Germans initiated wide-ranging reforms, including in university education, kicking off the processes of modernization and industrialization (Howard, 2009, p. 132; Watson, 2010, p. 227). Germany became the world leader in the chemical industry by the late 19th century due to chemical research taking place in German universities and industrial laboratories. And, by 1900, it became the largest economy and most powerful state in Europe.[2] Germany's dominance in scientific research is indicated by the fact that Germans won the highest number of Nobel Prizes in science subjects up till 1914.[3]

Impressed by the higher standards of German universities, many foreign students from Europe and the USA went to Germany for higher education. Consequently, between 1870 and 1905, the number of foreign students in German universities increased by nearly 70 per cent. The USA alone sent about 10,000 students to Germany in the 19th century for higher studies, many of whom were distinguished Americans who later became leaders in their fields (Howard, 2009, pp. 348, 363). Overwhelmed by the spectacular success of German universities in scientific research, many Western countries, including the UK, France and the USA, started following the German model, particularly after 1860 (Howard, 2009, pp. 363–78; Watson, 2010, p. 226). Gradually, many universities of these countries also emerged as knowledge producers.

The invention of the transistor by American researchers by the mid-20th century paved the way for the development of advanced digital computers, microchips and the Internet, heralding the digital revolution.[4] And gradually American economy became increasingly knowledge driven, giving rise to a modern knowledge society. Since the late 20th century, due to increasing globalization, the knowledge society has started spreading to other parts of the world, including India.

The Role of Research Universities in Sustaining a Knowledge Society

Research universities play a pivotal role in sustaining a knowledge society in two ways. First, by doing fundamental research, they create new knowledge indispensable for developing future products and processes. Second, they also produce future elites such as scientists, engineers, doctors, teachers, professionals, industrial entrepreneurs and political leaders, capable of original thinking through their training in research. Such elites enable their society to adapt to amazingly dynamic knowledge society, as discussed further.

Changing Economic Life

The changing economy in a knowledge society radically transforms the lives of the people, causing new challenges. After Robert M. Solow (1957), a Nobel laureate in economics, observed that technological innovations foster economic growth more than capital and labour augmentation, and that governments started investing more in technological research and higher education, making the economy more knowledge intensive. As a result, the employment opportunities for uneducated or less educated persons are steadily declining.

Moreover, the qualifications of educated persons also become obsolete rapidly due to the constant advent of new knowledge and advanced technology, requiring them to continuously update their knowledge and training and expecting them to be lifelong learners. However, today, the acquisition of knowledge is becoming more challenging due to the knowledge explosion.

Knowledge Explosion

Derek J. de Solla Price (1961, 1963), an eminent historian of science and a pioneer of scientometrics, observed that science grows exponentially as is indicated by the manifold increase in the number of scientific journals, papers, discoveries and scientists since the mid-17th century. According to him, 80–90 per cent of scientists who ever lived on planet earth were actually living in the 20th century. By following the growth of journals from 1650 onwards, Price formulated a 'fundamental law' that scientific journals double within a period 10 to 15 years. Price also observed that published scientific papers in many fields double every 5 to 10 years, and that the rate of important discoveries doubles every 20 years. Moreover, as Larsen & Ins (2010) note, publication in peer-reviewed journals still continue to increase, and if the publications using new channels such as conference proceedings, open access archives and the Internet are taken into account, the growth is astounding.

Additionally, the quantum of knowledge produced by academic disciplines also continually expands. For instance, as estimated by James B. Appleberry, the disciplinary knowledge doubled for the first time in 1750. In other words, it took 1750 years to double disciplinary knowledge for the first time. It then doubled after 150 years, that is, in 1900 and, subsequently, after another 50 years, that is, in 1950. Afterwards, it started doubling every five years, and it is projected that by 2020, it will double after every 73 days (Bernheim & de Sauza, 2003, p. 2; Gillani, n.d., pp. 3–4). This estimate may perhaps appear slightly overstated but it does indicate the geometrical nature of the knowledge explosion.

Besides, due to escalating disciplinary, interdisciplinary and trans-disciplinary research, several new disciplines, sub-disciplines and interdisciplines such as microbiology, biochemistry, biotechnology, socio-biology, nanotechnology and biomedical technology keep on emerging, indicating the qualitative aspect of the knowledge explosion. Clearly, we live in the age of 'information overload' (Toffler, 1970) and 'information anxiety' (Wurman, 1989), in which learning has become more demanding.

Explosion of Information

One more problem emerging in the dynamic knowledge society is the mind-boggling growth of information, due to the escalation in cheaper and faster computer chips. Gordon Moore, one of the founders of Intel, predicted in 1965, now known as 'Moore's Law', that the number of components of integrated circuit used in electronic equipment and the capacity of computer chips will tend to double roughly every two years. Consequently, increasingly smaller, faster and economical transistors have been produced, revolutionizing the electronic industry and drastically transforming the means of communications, transportation, educational pedagogy and office work.[5]

As a consequence, massive amount of data is generated, due to Instagram, Twitter, Tumbler, Facebook, Flickr, Blogs, instant messages, smartphones and so on. For instance, Eric Schmidt, the former CEO of Google, estimated in 2010 that every two days, we create data equivalent to the entire amount created from the dawn of human society up till 2003, equivalent to five exabytes of information. Besides, every minute we upload 300 hours of new content on YouTube. It is also estimated that digital data will grow by a factor of 10, to 44 trillion gigabytes or 44 zettabytes in the period of 2013–2020 (Seigler, 2010; Grossman, 2015). To handle this astonishing data explosion, to make the enormous amount of information comprehensible and to transform it into useful knowledge is yet another challenge faced by the contemporary knowledge society, necessitating the multitudes of well-trained and competent knowledge workers.

Shrinking Time and Space: Emergence of Global Village

In the emerging knowledge society, with the increasing speed of travel, time and space constrict constantly. For instance, in the early

Table 16.1 *Speed: Distance Comfortably Travelled in a Day*

Year	Miles Comfortably Travelled in a Day
1800	24
1900	120
2000	600
2100	3,000
2200	15,000

Source: Doren (1991, p. 406).

19th century, the animal-driven cart was the only mode of transport. However, as stated in Table 16.1, with the emergence of increasingly faster vehicles, travel speed has been increasing constantly every 100 years (Doren, 1991).

Consequently, the world has become smaller, accelerating the process of globalization and giving rise to the global village (McLuhan, 1962, 1964), causing new international trends, too complex and too fast to grasp instantly.

Need for Trained Elites

The rapid changes in the knowledge society, mentioned earlier in the chapter, often demand quick adaptations. However, society often finds it hard to adapt to these changes because the values, attitudes and behavioural patterns of human beings do not change as fast as the technology changes. As a result, strains develop in the society and several unprecedented social and individual problems emerge, requiring a huge army of enlightened elites who are capable of reflective and original thinking, have problem-solving skills and possess the necessary talent to handle information and the knowledge explosion. Research universities serve this function as they are the only places giving specialized training in research and awarding research degrees such as MPhil, PhD and the like.

Thus, the research university is the mother of the knowledge society since it plays a significant role both in the origin and sustenance of the knowledge society.

II

THE USA: A PARADIGM OF KNOWLEDGE SOCIETY

Recognizing the value of university research, the US government initiated a partnership with the nation's research universities during the Second World War, which made the USA a world power. Convinced by the importance of this partnership, the US government continued the collaboration with research universities even after the war ended. Today, the federal government supports about 60 per cent of the curiosity-driven and competitively awarded basic research in research universities (University Research: Understanding its Role, 2011). Clearly, as an instance of a contemporary knowledge society, the USA demonstrates that a nation acquires enormous power and wealth by promoting scientific research.

Scientific Knowledge: Source of Power

The 20th century is known as the American century due to its hegemony stemming from the extraordinary advances in the field of knowledge. The power of America, emerging from scientific research, was evident particularly during the Second World War. As the American Nobel laureate Isidor Isaac Rabi, who was personally instrumental in the development of the radar and atom bomb, proudly proclaimed: 'With the radar we won the war, and with the atom bomb we stopped the war; as unyielding Japan was compelled to surrender with the latter' (personal interview, August 1986 at Columbia University, New York). Moreover, as later history demonstrates, the USA is the world's sole superpower as no power in the world could stop America from devastating Vietnam, launching a war against Iraq, toppling Libya's Colonel Muammar Gaddafi, eliminating Osama bin Laden and disgracing the Taliban of Afghanistan.

Scientific Knowledge: Source of Wealth

The scientific progress has also enhanced America's material prosperity. Clearly, the US economy is now knowledge driven. Its leading industries are microelectronics, biotechnology, new materials science industries, telecommunications, computer technology (hardware and software), civilian aircraft and robotics. More than 700 products introduced in the market by 2006 had originated from the research done in US universities, and it is projected that, in the future, almost all industries will depend on the research done in American universities (Cole, 2012, pp. 4, 205).

American Universities: Scientific and Academic Achievements

Undoubtedly, most path-breaking research is done in the USA, particularly in its universities. It is the world's top-ranking country by winning 47 per cent Nobel Prizes in sciences up till 2014.[6]

Similarly, the USA tops in higher education also. According to the Academic Ranking of the World Universities (ARWU), 2014, 80 per cent of the top 10 universities, 68 per cent of top 50 universities and 52 per cent of the top 100 universities of the world are in the USA.[7] Naturally, millions of students of the world aspire to obtain a degrees from American universities, many of whom become elites later in their own countries. These US universities are mostly known as research universities due to their extensive research work. The USA has about 260 such research universities, of which about 125 are knowledge factories, contributing thousands of scientific discoveries, inventions, devices, concepts, techniques, tools, technological innovations and medical breakthroughs that have changed the lives of people all over the world (Cole, 2012, pp. 193–342, 519). Table 16.2 shows some most outstanding innovations made in the US universities.

Besides, most of the textbooks, reference books and research papers published in reputed journals, used by students and teachers the world over, are published by US scholars. Most elites of the USA working in different fields such as literature, academics, science, politics, military, business and industry are the products of the country's top universities. Many universities, their faculty members as well as their alumni have become multimillionaires by becoming entrepreneurs. Just one example of Stanford University illustrates this point. Since 1939, 2,235 members of Stanford University have established 2,450 companies, including giants such as Cisco Systems, Google, Hewlett-Packard, Sun

Table 16.2 *A Selective List of the Exceptional Contributions Made by American Universities in Different Areas of Knowledge*

Field of Knowledge	Exceptional Innovations Made in American Universities
Physical sciences	Radar, atom bomb, transistor, digital computer, FM radio, automatic teller machine (ATM), bar codes, global positioning system (GPS), Google search engine and so on.
Life sciences and medical sciences	Stem cell, organ transplant, DNA finger printing, fetal monitoring, scientific cattle breeding, laser, synthetic insulin, human growth hormone (HGH), magnetic resonance imaging (MRI), Viagra and so on.
Social sciences	Opinion poll, focused interviews, concept of self-fulfilling prophecy, theory of cognitive dissonance, impossibility theorem, game theory, concept of human capital and so on.

Source: Cole (2012, pp. 4, 207–342).

Micro System and Yahoo. Moreover, the university has earned more than US$250 billion from the three patents registered in 1980 and earns US$100 million every year from the patents registered in the 1990s. It also earned US$336 million by the technology transfer of the Google search engine developed by its two PhD students, Sergey Brin and Larry Page (Cole, 2012, pp. 193–99).

Besides Stanford, several other elite universities of the USA earn billions from their path-breaking research. For instance, eight universities located in the Boston area registered 264 patents, obtained 280 commercial licences and established 41 start-up companies, by which they contributed US$7.4 billion in the economy of the Boston area. If the 4,000 companies set up by the students and faculty members of the Massachusetts Institute of Technology (MIT) of Boston, employing 1.1 million workers and producing US$116 million, were counted as a separate nation, then it would have been 24th largest economy in the world, having a gross domestic product (GDP) more than that of Thailand and slightly less than that of South Africa (Cole, 2012, pp. 193–99).

Table 16.3 *Top 10 US Universities in Terms of Endowment Fund, 2014*

Sr. No.	Name the University	Total Endowment Fund (Billions USD)
1	Harvard	32.3
2	Yale	22.8
3	University of Texas system	22.5
4	Stanford University	18.7
5	Princeton University	18.2
6	Massachusetts Institute of Technology	11.0
7	Texas A&M University System and Foundations	8.7
8	University of Michigan	8.4
9	Columbia University	8.2
10	Northwestern University	7.9

Source: Vedder, Richard & Christopher Denhart (2014).

Not surprisingly, the unusual achievements and consequent reputation and wealth earned by the faculty and the alumni of these great universities make them proud of their alma mater, inspiring them to contribute generously to the latter's coffers. Some of the outstanding elite universities of the USA have amassed amazing amounts in endowment funds, as shown in Table 16.3.

III

KNOWLEDGE SOCIETY AND THE EMERGING KNOWLEDGE DIVIDE

On the one hand, as the instance of the USA shows, a knowledge society acquires enormous power and wealth by promoting scientific research. However, on the other hand, it also creates a hiatus between the developed and developing countries. Since scientific knowledge enables the former to enhance their wealth, as Table 16.4 reveals, they become richer, and the poor countries stagnate or, still worse, become poorer.

Table 16.4 *The Comparison of Developed and Developing Countries in Terms of GDP, Population, R&D Expenditure and the Number of Researchers, 1996–1997 and 2007*

Countries	GDP (%)		Population (%)		Expenditure on R&D (%)		Number of Researchers (%)	
	1996–1997	2007	1996–1997	2007	1996–1997	2007	1996–1997	2007
Developed	61.1	58.2	22.3	18.4	84.4	76.2	71.6	62.1
Developing	38.9	41.8	77.7	81.6	15.6	23.8	28.4	37.9

Source: UNESCO (2001, p. 7; 2010, pp. 2–8).

As Table 16.4 shows, the GDP of developed countries is much larger than that of developing countries, but their population is relatively much less. Obviously, they are able to plough back their enormous surplus in research and development and create a multitude of researchers. On the flip side, developing countries suffer from inadequate investment in knowledge-producing infrastructure. Table 16.4 also shows that not withstanding the recent progress of some developing countries to produce knowledge, a gap still persists. Thus, there is a vicious cycle: developed countries, being rich, do more research; since they do more research, they become richer, and, on the contrary, developing countries, being poor, do less research and therefore remain poor.

IV

INDIA' PERFORMANCE IN THE DOMAINS OF SCIENCE AND HIGHER EDUCATION

In this context, it is relevant to appraise India's progress towards a knowledge society. Undisputedly, India is moving towards a knowledge society, indicated by the fact that a substantial amount of India's GDP is derived from the knowledge-intensive services such as (a) information technology services, (b) research and development services, (c) architectural, engineering and technical services and (d) communication services (Mani, 2010, p. 11; UNESCO, 2010, p. 324). According to the World Bank, India has emerged as the third largest economy in the world in terms of purchasing power parity (PPP; World Bank, 2016).

Yet, the stark reality is, lately, India has been lagging behind in science and higher education, despite its past achievements, as discussed.

The Domain of Science

In the realm of science, for instance, India made glorious achievements in the past. Sir C. V. Raman (1888–1970) was awarded a Nobel Prize in 1930 in Physics, making him the first Asian to win the prize. India also produced a galaxy of internationally renowned scientists, such as Jagdish Chandra Bose (1858–1937), Prafulla Chandra Ray (1861–1944), Srinivasa Ramanujan (1887–1920), Meghnad Saha (1893–1956), Satyendra Nath Bose (1894–1974), Shanti Swarup Bhatnagar (1894–1955), Homi Bhahbha (1909–1966), Prasanta Chandra Mahalanobis (1893–1972), Vikram Sarabhai (1919–1971) and C. N. R. Rao (1934), to name a few. Some scientists of Indian origin, such as Subrahmanyan Chandrashekhar (1910–1995), Har Gobind Khorana (1922–2011), Amartya Sen (1933), Venkatraman Ramkrishnan (1952), were also successful in winning the Nobel Prize, though only after working in British or US universities. India's achievements in atomic energy, space science, chemistry, pharmacy and information technology are also noteworthy.

Nevertheless, lately, India's performance in science has relatively declined.[8] For instance, India's rank in the Global Innovation Index for 82 countries was 56th in 2008 (UNESCO, 2010, p. 324). India's total contribution in the world's scientific research is only 3.4 per cent, whereas China's contribution is 11 per cent (Adams, Pendelbury, & Stembridge, 2013, p. 11). As indicated in Table 16.5, in many fields of scientific research, India is far behind China—its neighbouring country with which it is competing to be a world power.

Ironically, India and China became independent almost simultaneously in the late 1940s. At that time, India was much ahead of China in scientific achievements. However, during the 1980s, China introduced radical reforms in its economic, scientific and academic policies. Coincidently, around the same time, India started declining in all these fields. For instance, in the 1980s, the GDP of India and China

Table 16.5 *Contribution of India and China to World's Scientific Research in Selected Disciplines, 2013*

Scientific Discipline	India's Contribution (%)	China's Contribution (%)
Chemistry	6.4	20.2
Pharmacology and toxicology	6.1	10.1
Materials science	5.9	24.5
Physics	4.3	13.1
Engineering	4.1	14.8
Biology and biochemistry	3.6	8.8

Source: Adams, Pendleburry & Stembridge (2013, p. 11).

was almost at par, hovering around US$300–400 billion. After reforms, China's GDP jumped to US$9,000 billion in 2011, whereas India's GDP was less than half of China's, that is, US$4,000 billion in the same year (Adams et al., 2013, p. 5). In terms of industrial production, China has now emerged as a manufacturing powerhouse of the world (Krishnan & Arun, 2015). Consequently, economically, China is only next to the USA now, and experts project that its economic power would be equivalent to that of the USA by 2020 if it continues to grow like this (Adams et al., 2013, p. 5).

Domain of Higher Education

Likewise, although India has made strides in higher education after Independence, Indian universities and other institutions, lately, have not fared well (Patel, 2003, 2012). Arguably, failing education system produces a rapidly expanding pool of unemployable graduates. What is worse is that there are no signs of improvement (Shah, 2005). The institutions that are supposed to train competent researchers have mostly become teaching institutions of low quality. Only 1 per cent of students enrolled in institutions of higher education pursue research, and only 0.1 per cent could obtain PhD degree in 2011–2012 (Ansari, 2015).[9] Thus, Indian higher education is not a source of technology for industry. The Parliament's Standing Committee on Human Resource

Table 16.6 *Number of Universities in Top 200 Universities of Asian Countries, Excluding Japan, in World Rankings, 2014*

Sr. No.	Country	Shanghai Ranking (2014)
1	China	06
2	South Korea	01
3	Hong Kong	02
4	Israel	04
5	Taiwan	01
6	Singapore	02
7	India	00

Source: http://www.shanghairanking.com/

Development, in its 248th report submitted on 26 February 2013, noted that Indian universities are too bogged down with routine teaching and administrative work to pay much attention on research (Ansari, 2015). India's performance, even in comparison with some developing Asian countries, is also quite disappointing, as indicated by Table 16.6.

China performs much better as compared to India in research, publication and related academic activities also, as Table 16.7 shows.

Clearly, India's serious weaknesses in scientific research and higher education vis-à-vis other nations, including China, necessitates an examination of factors responsible for India's decline in science and higher education.

Table 16.7 *A Comparison of China and India in Terms of Research, Publication and Related Academic Activities*

Themes of Comparison	China	India
Number of universities in top 200 Universities of the World in 2014–2015*	03	00
Number of researchers** (2009)	More than 1,000,000	Less than 500,000
Number of papers published (2011)**	More than 100,000	Less than 50,000

Themes of Comparison	China	India
Number of the most cited papers (2011)**	1,131 (0.72% of the national output)	235 (0.52% of the national output)
Citation impact (2011)**	More than 0.75	Less than 0.75
Number of patents application filed in 2010**	Nearly 400,000	Less than 1,00,000
GDP in 2013+	$9,240.27 billion (USD)	$1,876.8 billion (USD)
Expenditure on R&D PPP in 2010++	About 15%	3%

Source: * Academic Ranking of World University (ARWU), http://www.
shanghairanking.com,
    ** Adams, Pendlebury and Stembridge (2013).
    + Trading Economics http://www.tradingeconomics.com/india/
gdp,
    ++ https://en.wikipedia.org/wiki/List_of_countries_by_research_
and_development_spending

V

INADEQUATE RESOURCES FOR SCIENCE AND HIGHER EDUCATION IN INDIA

Any activity, to flourish, needs not only funds, but also the adequate sociocultural support. The scarcity of both material and cultural resources for science and higher education in India is evident from the following account.

Inadequate Financial Resources

The allocation of financial resources as a percentage of GDP to the science and higher education indicates the importance given to these areas. In this context, it must be noted that India's economy has been relatively weak, and it allocates unquestionably inadequate financial resources for both fields. For instance, India's GDP (about US$1 trillion as on 2013) is relatively much less as compared to the USA's (about US$17 trillion) and China's (about US$9 trillion) in the same year, according to World Bank figures.[10] India's expenditure in terms of the percentage of its GDP on research and development (0.81 in 2011) is also relatively much less than the USA's (2.79 in 2012) and China's (1.98 in 2012).[11] This is a matter of concern for two reasons. First, research has now become heavily technology intensive. Second, due to the inevitable process of trial and error involved, path-breaking research demands heavy expenditure.

Moreover, India spends much less on higher education. For instance, the public expenditure on higher education in India is very low at 0.6 per cent of GDP, compared to 2.7 per cent in the USA.[12] Consequently, hundreds of thousands of meritorious students prefer foreign universities for higher studies, causing a huge dent on country's foreign exchange reserve, further weakening an already flagging economy.

Allocation of more funds for higher education has been a contentious issue among the policymakers and educationists since Independence. However, the situation has worsened, particularly after the early 1990s, due to the gradual withdrawal of subsidies (Kaur, 2011) and reduction in public funding of higher education (Bora, 2011, p. 8). The government's contribution to higher education in the total planned resources decreased from a high of 1.24 per cent in the Fourth Five-Year Plan (1969–72) to 0.35 per cent in the Eighth Five-Year Plan (1992–97). The spending on higher education, as the percentage of gross national product (GNP), declined from 0.98 per cent in 1980–1981 to 0.35 per cent in 1994–1995. Similarly, higher education's share in the total expenditure on education has fallen from 28.19 per cent in 1990–1991 to 15.7 per cent in 1996–1997 (Tilak, 1995, p. 216). Currently, India spends less than 1 per cent of its GDP on higher education (Goswami, 2015). India also spends much less per student in higher education. For instance, in 2007, India spent US$400 per student, whereas Brazil spent US$3,986, China spent US$2,728, Russia spent US$1,204, the EU21 countries spent US$12,958 and the USA spent US$29,910 in the same year (*Higher Education Spending: India at the Bottom of BRIC,* [*Business Standard,* 26 Feb., 2013]. Therefore, Indian universities find it increasingly difficult to meet even the recurrent expenditure necessary for survival. Funds required for libraries, laboratories, exchange of scholars, research and organizing seminars and conferences have always been in short supply (Shah, 2005). The high teacher–student ratio is the most damaging consequence, perhaps having far-reaching unanticipated effects.

Indian policymakers, however, decided lately to allocate more resources for higher education. For instance, in the Tenth Five-Year plan (2002–2007), the allocation of funds was increased by 76 per cent as compared to the Ninth Five-Year Plan (1997–2002; from ₹24,098 crore to ₹43,825 crore; *Higher Education Spend Stagnates*, 2007). And, in the Eleventh Five-Year Plan (2007–12), ₹84,943 crore were allocated for higher education, which was nine times more than the allocation for the Tenth Five-Year Plan (Singh & Ahmad, 2011, p. 2). However, these additional funds were being used mostly to set up new universities and higher education institutions, ostensibly to increase access to higher education. For instance, in the Eleventh Five-Year Plan, the Government of India decided to set up 15 new central universities, 8 Indian Institutes of Technology, 7 Indian Institutes of Management, 20 National Institutes of Technology, 20 Indian Institutes of Information Technology and 200 polytechnics. However, these newly established institutions are mostly understaffed and extremely deficient in infrastructure, even after more than five years of their establishment, and the existing fund-starved state universities continue to fight for their survival. In the Twelfth Five-Year Plan (2012–17), an ambitious scheme called Rashtriya Uchchatar Siksha Abhiyan (RUSA) was introduced to further strengthen the institutions of higher education with unprecedented amounts of funds and greater participation of the state governments.[13] However, the future of the scheme is in limbo due to the recent abolition of the Planning Commission in 2014.

Similarly, the Technical Education Quality Improvement Programme (TEQIP) was introduced in 2003 as a long-term pro-gramme of about 10–12 years' duration, to be implemented in two or three phases, with the World Bank's assistance. Nevertheless, due to the shortage of academic and non-academic staff and other factors, the scheme has not been able to achieve its target as desired.

Deficiency of Research Culture

However, the financial resources are necessary but not sufficient. Without developing adequate research culture, highly funded universities would be like soulless bodies. Insufficient institution-alization of a scientific culture in Indian academic institutions for some historical reasons is a glaring weak point of Indian scientific research and higher education. The first universities, established in 1857 by the British, were modelled on the University of London, which was mostly a teaching and examining body; the German model of the research university was yet to make an impact in the UK (Howard, 2009, pp. 355–63). As a result, the early Indian universities remained affiliating and examining bodies for a long time. The postgraduate teaching and research departments were set up in the early 20th century (Shah, 2005, pp. 2234–35). It was only after Independence that the functions of universities were reorganized and research was given impetus.

Thus, the research culture in Indian universities is hardly 100 years old. And, before it took firm root in independent India, economic support declined (as mentioned earlier), weakening the already weak research culture (Shah, 2005). Inadequate financial resources not only resulted in poor infrastructural facilities but also in inadequate research grants and acute shortage of teaching and non-teaching staff. Even now, nearly 50 per cent of the faculty positions are vacant in most universities (Chande, 2011, p. 38), resulting in unhealthy teacher–student ratio. Since the late 1980s, most vacant teaching posts have also not been filled up, leave aside adding new positions. Most universities manage to continue the teaching–learning process with ad hoc, temporary or contractual teachers. A latent dysfunction of continuation of this thoughtless policy, for nearly 30–40 years now, is the discontinuity of healthy academic traditions in most of these institutions, causing serious damage to the research culture as it is transmitted from one generation to another. The upcoming generations learn and internalize fundamental cultural values, in any field of society, by emulating seniors, some of whom become their role models. Unfortunately, a large section of the senior academicians in almost all disciplines, some of the outstanding ones, have already retired over a period. Thus, by keeping the academic posts vacant for an abnormally long period in the universities, India has lost almost two to three generations of senior academicians who could have socialized younger generations of students in research culture.

As a result, research has become mostly ritualistic. Instances of extremely poor quality research, often involving plagiarism, are not infrequent. The professional peer review, a widely accepted process in the world, subjecting scholarly works to expert scrutiny, is conspicuous either by its almost non-existence or fragile existence in Indian academia. The related function of 'gatekeeping' in the academic profession, necessary to weed out the incompetent and allow the suitable to enter the profession, performed by competent peers, is also weak. The unconvincing performance of this gatekeeping institution in Indian universities is mostly evident in admissions, examinations and selection processes, often giving primacy to particularistic criteria such as caste, kinship, friendships, communal loyalties and political influence, barring a few elite institutions which unquestionably are the islands of excellence. However, the fact is that the developing countries which have progressed fastest in recent years are the ones that have adopted policies to promote science, technology and innovation (UNESCO, 2010).

Social organizations like universities are not built merely with bricks and mortar. The most important ingredient of the modern university is its research culture, which, as discussed in the following section, is to be cultivated and nurtured with great care.

VI

SCIENTIFIC RESEARCH CULTURE AND ITS TRANSMISSION

Scientific methodology, in brief, is characterized mainly by objectively conducted empirical research and theory building. However, Robert K. Merton, the founder of sociology of science, argued that science is not only about having its independent methodology, but is also a social institution with its own value complex (Merton, [1942] 1968, pp. 604–15; Patel, 1975, pp. 63–71).

Scientific Research Culture

Like any other social institution, values and norms guiding scientific enquiry are commonly accepted by the substantial number of the members of the scientific community and are supported by operative sanctions. Some of the most important norms, discussed further, are considered by Merton as the very ethos of science.

Originality

One of the most important norms of science is originality. Original contributions of scientists are indispensable for the growth of scientific knowledge. Therefore, the institution of science has developed an elaborate and hierarchical system of rewards to encourage scientists to conform to the norm of originality. Since the contributions of scientists are not equally significant, the rewards given for these contributions also vary in importance. For instance, eponymy, the tradition of linking the scientists' names with their valuable contributions, is the highest reward given to them. 'Newton's Law of Gravity', 'Boyle's Law of Gases' and 'Einstein's Theory of Relativity' are some such examples of eponymy. At times, the name of a genius is associated with the age in which he lived, just as the 17th century is also known as 'Newton's Age'. Thus, by eponymy, the scientists become immortal and their names are remembered for all times to come, in almost all parts of the world.

Next in hierarchy are awards such as the Nobel Prize, followed by lesser rewards such as prizes given by scientific organizations, honorary membership of professional associations and honorary degrees awarded by the universities.

On the contrary, research done ritualistically, plagiarism, manu-facturing or distorting evidences or escaping from research to take administrative jobs are all instances of deviant behaviour in science.

Universalism

Another significant value of science is 'universalism', by which a scientist is expected to evaluate the scientific statements or theories proposed by other scientists without regard to their particularistic or ascribed characteristics such as age, sex, race, religion and nationality. The acceptance or rejection of scientific ideas should be based on the universalistic standards of truth and validity established by science. In this sense, the Nazi's rejection of theories or contributions of Jewish scientists was an instance of deviance.

Communism[14]

The value of communism, also known as communalism, emphasizes the collective ownership of scientific findings. The institution of science values the sharing and common possession of intellectual products of scientists. Therefore, free communication of scientific ideas in publications, seminars, symposia, conferences and so on is highly appreciated in the scientific community. On the other hand, the concealment of scientific innovations for military or industrial purposes, retarding the speedy growth of scientific knowledge, is considered a deviation and is abhorred in science.

Disinterestedness

The norm of disinterestedness ensures that scientists evaluate scientific knowledge without regard to any vested interest, personal emotions, likes–dislikes, considerations of benefit or loss, fear or favour and so on while formulating or assessing any scientific opinion, proposition, theory and method. Therefore, unsupported grandiose claims about past scientific achievements of ancient India, for patriotic or emotional reasons, is an aberrant behaviour in science (Top TIFR Scientist Warns of Noisy Fringe, 2015).

Organized Scepticism

Just as faith is valued in religion, scepticism is valued in the institution of science. A scientist is supposed to be a questioning mind, a 'doubting Thomas'. Nothing should be accepted in science at face value, without subjecting it to rigorous and critical scientific scrutiny. Notwithstanding the popularity or sacredness of a theory or a belief in a society, a scientist is expected to test it by the canons of science and accept it only if found true. Scientists look down upon uncritical attitude, which is not in conformity with the scientific ethos.

Merton asserts that in addition to these values, there are some other institutionalized norms of science, such as humility, intellectual honesty, integrity and truthfulness. Undisputedly, all these values are significant from the viewpoint of scientific methodology too, as a scientist interested in making successful predictions cannot afford to ignore these values. A prediction based on inadequate or false or manufactured evidences inevitably fails. However, the scientific community disapproves this kind of behaviour, considering it contrary to the institutionalized values of science. Thus, these values are not only methodologically imperative but are also morally prescribed standards of the social institution of science. Therefore, most of the scientists desiring acceptance by their fellow colleagues conform to these institutionalized norms of science. In other words, the institution of science regulates the behaviour of the scientists by a system of reward and punishment. This mechanism of sanctions creates social pressure on the scientists to follow the institutionalized norms. Moreover, most of the scientists, considering the scientific community as a reference group, seek approval of their behaviour from the group. They are constantly watchful about the evaluation of their own behaviour by their peers and are anxious to be accepted by their colleagues. Thus, these norms also become the internalized source of inspiration guiding their behaviour, apart from being institutionalized prescriptions.

A large number of great scientists, who have imbibed the ethos of science, working together in a university or a research organization, gradually build the research culture of the university or the organization, engendering a creatively stimulating environment. However, this culture needs to be successfully transmitted from one generation of scientists to another for the sake of the continuity of the tradition of scientific research, both in terms of quantity and quality. Is there any mechanism for this? Yes. This is being done by a socialization process whereby the senior members of the community educate the members of the next generation. This process is often latent and less visible, but is an inevitable part of the scientific activity. The observations on the socialization of the Nobel Prize winners by Harriet Zukerman (1977) discussed further, illustrates the point.

Transmission of Research Culture: The Process of Socialisation among the Nobel Laureates

A very important fact noted by Zukerman was that 41 per cent of total 286 scientists who won the Nobel Prize between 1901 and 1977, from all over the world, had either studied or worked under at least one Nobel laureate. Likewise, more than half of the US Nobel Prize winners up till 1972 had a laureate as their mentor. In some instances, ambitious students deliberately chose to work under such mentors, undergoing rigorous and often demanding training, notwithstanding the mentor's idiosyncrasies. On questioning the former apprentices of the masters, Zukerman found that they were hardly interested in learning the subject matter from the latter. A few of them believed that in some areas of their studies, they knew more than their guides. Evidently, they were more interested in learning the method of their mentors as to how they selected a problem, how they tried to crack it or how they pondered different issues.

Clearly, there are no readymade formulas available for becoming a genius. Even the creative genius is often unaware of or unable to explicate the mysterious process. Therefore, their instructions or precepts are less important than the actual performance, the manner in which they conduct the enquiry. By observing the giant, the apprentice gradually acquires some understanding of the intricacies of scientific method, the pattern of scientific thinking, the norms and standards of judging the merits or demerits of an idea or a finding, the right kind of attitudes necessary for great discoveries and all such things that are generally not found in standard textbooks. In short, the intellectual competence and ethos of scientific research required for great breakthroughs can be learnt only after studying or working under the great scientists over an extended period. The mentor becomes the role model for the apprentice. The masters who have kindled a spark of creativity within themselves, after a prolonged and dedicated study (*sadhana*), can alone ignite the spark in their students. In short, excellence breeds excellence.

VII

CONCLUSION

Since modern research-oriented university is the mother of knowledge society, a society in which knowledge industry plays a vital role in enhancing its power and wealth, India will have to build a strong research base in its universities to emerge as a knowledge society. Research universities will also be needed to garner high-quality elites, who are capable of original thinking, to solve rapidly emerging new problems. It will indeed be a stupendous task, due to the recent deterioration in scientific and academic achievements of India. However, it is not impossible. The experience of Germany, the UK, France, the USA and China has shown that it takes two to three generations to transform academic institutions, if determined efforts are made by all the stakeholders. Apart from guaranteeing a consistent flow of substantial financial support, research culture in Indian universities requires to be reinforced at once. Moreover, uninterrupted transmission of that culture as a vibrant tradition needs to be ensured as well.

To instil life breath in the currently unexciting Indian universities, to make them intellectually stimulating and throbbing and to achieve global recognition in the scientific and academic achievements, Indian policymakers will have to (a) study German, American and Chinese models of academic and scientific developments and selectively emulate relevant and useful features, (b) enforce stringent gatekeeping by tightening evaluation, monitoring and reward systems at all levels, including conferring degrees, appointing and promoting academic staff, awarding research grants and research projects, (c) augment the deployment of well-trained and competent faculty, with excellent research record, at all levels, (d) provide them autonomy with accountability and ample resources in terms of money, time and research infrastructure, (e) promote better interaction among them as sustained innovations require intense exchange of ideas among the community of colleagues and (f) enhance international academic exchange and cooperation. Otherwise, India will find it difficult to compete even with China, leave aside reaching the goal of being a world power in the near future, as the knowledge divide will widen. It is relatively easy to provide material resources, but it takes time to recruit and train talented scientists and researchers, to make them independently productive and to reinforce the research culture. Even the established researchers will need sufficient time to innovate and socialize new recruits. Serious damage has already been done by keeping academic posts vacant for unusually long periods. Indian policymakers will have to wake up soon and listen to the adage: 'failing to plan is planning to fail'.

NOTES

1. In 1994, one pound sterling was equivalent to about ₹47. Retrieved 6 May 2015, from http://rbidocs.rbi.org.in/rdocs/Publications/PDFs/56465.pdf. In 2015, the value of pound sterling is around ₹95. Retrieved 5 May 2015 from http://www.exchangerates.org.uk/GBP-INR-exchange-rate-history.html

2. Retrieved 12 March 2015 from http://en.wikipedia.org/wiki/Economic_history_of_Germany

3. German scientists won fourteen Nobel Prizes in science subjects (physics, chemistry, and physiology and medicine) form 1901 (the year in which the first awards were announced) to 1914. Retrieved 10 March 2015 from http://en.wikipedia.org/wiki/List_of_Nobel_laureates_by_country

4. All the three physicists—Johan Barden, Walter Brattain and William Shockley, who invented transistor at Bell Labs and won the Nobel Prize, studied and taught at American universities.

5. Retrieved 15 May 2015 from http://www.intel.in/content/www/in/en/silicon-innovations/ moores-law-technology.html

6. Retrieved 13 March 2015 from http://www.jinfo.org/US_Nobel_Prizes.html and http://www.nobelprize.org/nobel_prizes/physics/laureates/

7. Retrieved 28 April 2015 from http://www.shanghairanking.com/

8. Lamenting the quality of Indian science C. N. R. Rao recently said that India does not have 'a single institution' that can match the best abroad, including that of China (*The Times of India*, 25 March 2015). Retrieved 9 April 2015 from http://timesofindia. indiatimes.com/home/science/Quality-of-science-in-India-lousy-improve-quality-CNR-Rao/articleshow/46689877.cms). However, according to the UNESCO's *World Social Science Report*, Indian social sciences have also lately failed to contribute much (International Social Science Council, 2010, pp. 77–81).

9. A convocation address delivered by Shri M. H. Ansari, the vice-president of India, on 26 March 2015 at the 10th Convocation of the Guru Gobind Singh Indraprastha University, New Delhi.

10. Retrieved 23 March 2015 from http://data.worldbank.org/indicator/NY.GDP.MKTP.CD.

11. Retrieved 23 March 2015 from http://data.worldbank.org/indicator/GB.XPD.RSDV.GD.ZS.

12. Retrieved 13 March 2015 from http://www.newindianexpress.com/columns/Spend-more-on-higher-education/2013/08/02/article1713298.ece.

13. RUSA is a nation-level scheme of the Ministry of Human Resource Development (MHRD) aimed at improving access, equity and quality of higher education in India.

14. Bernard Barber (1952) argues that to avoid ideological connotations, instead of 'communism', 'communalism' would be a better term.

REFERENCES

Adams, J., Pendleburry, D., & Stembridge, B. (2013). Building BRICKS. *ScienceWatch*. Retrieved 8 February 2015, from http://sciencewatch.com/sites/sw/files/sw-article/media/grr-brick.pdf

Ansari, M. H. (2015). Research scorecard of the country: An introspection. *University News, 53*(17), 24–25.

Association of American Universities (2011, January). *University research: Understanding its role*. New York and Washington, DC: Association of American Universities. Retrieved 29 May 2015, from https://www.aau.edu/WorkArea/DownloadAsset.aspx? id=11590.

Barber, B. (1952). *Science and social order*. Glencoe, IL: The Free Press.

Bernheim, C. T., & de Souza, M. C. (2003). *Challenges of the university in the knowledge society, five years after the world conference on higher education* (UNESCO Forum Occasional Paper Series Paper No. 4). Paris: UNESCO. Retrieved 23 March 2015, from http://portal.unesco.org/education/en/file_download.php/697c33597621cdab0b77507d31da8cf8Tunnerman+%28English%29.pdf

Bora, A. (2011). Higher education in India: A few aspects needing attention. *University News, 49*(20), 7–12.

Chande, P. T. (2011). Feats for achieving excellence in higher education. *University News, 49*(33), 36–39.

Clark, W. (2006). *Academic charisma and the origins of the research university*. Chicago, IL and London: The University of Chicago Press.

Cole, J. R. (2012). *The great American university: Its rise to preeminence, its indispensable national role, why it must be protected*. New York: Public Affairs.

de Solla Price, D. J. (1961). *Science since Babylon*. New Heaven: Yale University Press.

———. (1963). *little science, big science*. New York: Columbia University Press.

Doren, C. V. (1991). *A history of knowledge: Past, present and future*. New York: Ballantine Books.

Drucker, P. F. (1969). *The age of discontinuity*. London: Heinemann.

Gillani, B. (n. d). *New challenges*. Retrieved 15 March 2015, from http://edschool.csueastbay. edu/departments/etleads/Chapter1NewChallenges.PDF

Goswami, D. (2015). Financing higher education in India: An analytical discussion. *University News, 53*(06), 8–12.

Grossman, Lev. (2015, July 6–13). What's this all about? Time, 34–35.

Howard, T. A. (2009). *Protestant theology and the making of modern German university*. Oxford: Oxford University Press.

Hussain, S. (2007, February 5). Higher education spending: India at the bottom of BRIC. *Business Standard*. Retrieved 27 March 2015, from http://www.business-standard.com/article/economy-policy/higher-education-spending-india-at-the-bottom-of-bric-107020501062_1.html.

Indian Express (2015, June 25). Top TIFR scientist warns of noisy fringe. *Indian Express* (Vadodara Edition), pp. 1–2.

International Monetary Fund. (2014). *Report for selected country groups and subjects (PPP valuation of country GDP)* Retrieved 7 April 2016, from http://www.imf.org/external/pubs/ft/weo/2015/02/weodata/weorept.aspx?sy=2014&ey=2014&scsm=1&ssd=1&sort=subject&ds=.&br=1&pr1.x=65&pr1.y=8&c=51

International Social Science Council. (2010). *World social science report: Knowledge divides*. Paris: United Nations Educational, Scientific and Cultural Organization. Retrieved 22 May 2015, from http://unesdoc.unesco.org/images/0018/001883/188333e.pdf

Kaur, R. (2011). Financing higher education on India in post economic reform period: The policy perspective. *University News*, *49*(18), 20–24, 30.

Krishnan, A., & Arun, M. G. (2015, May 18). Dancing with the dragon. *India Today*, pp. 23–30.

Larsen, P. O., & Ins, M. v. (2010). The rate of growth in scientific publication and the decline in coverage provided by science citation index. *Scientometrics*, *84*(3), 575–603. Retrieved 13 March 2015, from http://www.ncbi.nlm.nih.gov/pmc/articles/PMC2909426/

Mani, S. (2010). *Has China and India become more innovative since the onset of reforms in the two countries?* (Working Paper No. 430). Thiruvananthapuram: Center for Development Studies. Retrieved 15 March 2015, from www.cds.edu

McClelland, C. E. ([1980]2008). *State, society and university in Germany 1700–1914*. Cambridge: Cambridge University Press.

McLuhan, M. (1962). *The Gutenberg galaxy: The making of typographic man*. Toronto: University of Toronto Press.

———. (1964). *Understanding media: The extensions of man*. Cambridge, MA: MIT Press.

Merton, R. K. ([1942]1968). Science and democratic social structure. In R. K. Merton (Ed.), *Social theory and social structure* (Enlarged Edition, pp. 604–15). New York: The Free Press.

Patel, P. J. (1975). Robert Merton's formulations in sociology of science. *Sociological Bulletin*, *24*(1), 55–75.

———. (2003). Universities in western India: Problems and prospects. *Economic and Political Weekly*, *38*(46), 4841–4845.

———. (2012). Academic underperformance of Indian universities, incompatible academic culture and the societal context. *Social Change*, *42*(1), 9–29.

Seigler, M. G. (2010). *Eric Schmidt: Every 2 days we create as much information as we did up to 2003*. Retrieved 15 June 2015, from http://techcrunch.com/2010/08/04/schmidt-data/

Shah, A. M. (2005). Higher education and research. *Economic and Political Weekly*, *41*(22–23), 2234–2242.

Singh, K. P., & Ahmad, S. (2011). Higher education in India: Major concerns. *University News*, *49*(29), 1–5.

Solow, Robert M. (1957). Technical change and Aggregate production function. *The Review of Economics and Statistics*, *39*(3), 312–320. Retrieved 30 March

2015, from http://faculty.georgetown.edu/mh5/class/econ489/Solow-Growth-Accounting.pdf

The Economic Times (2007, January 6). Higher education spend stagnates. *The Economic Times*. Retrieved 12 June 2015, from http://articles. economictimes.indiatimes.com/ 2007-01-06/news/28411431_1_higher-education-education-sector-assocham.

Tilak, J. B. G. (1995). Privatisation of higher education in India: Capitation fee colleges. In K. B. Powar & S. K. Panda (Eds), *Higher education in India—In search of quality*. New Delhi: Association of Indian Universities, pp. 215–36.

Toffler, A. (1970). *Future shock*. New York: Bantam Books.

UNESCO. (2001). *The state of science and technology in the world: 1996–97*. Montreal: UNESCO Institute for Statistics.

———. (2010). *UNESCO science report, 2010: The current status of science around the world*. Paris: The UNESCO Publishing.

Vedder, R., & Denhart, C. (2014). 22 richest schools in America. Retrieved 18 February 2015, from http://www.forbes.com/sites/ccap/2014/07/30/22-richest-schools-in-america/ #72b595d85e3c

Watson, P. (2010). *The German genius: Europe's third renaissance, the second scientific revolution and the twentieth century*. London: Simon and Schuster.

World Bank. (2000). *Higher education in developing countries: Peril and promise*. Washington, DC: The International Bank for Reconstruction and Development and The World Bank.

———. (2016). Gross domestic product 2014, PPP. Retrieved 7 April 2016, from http://databank.worldbank.org/data/download/GDP_PPP.pdf

Wurman, S. (1989). *Information anxiety*. New York: Doubleday.

Zuckerman, H. (1977). *Scientific elite: Nobel laureates in the United States*. New York: The Free Press and A Division of Macmillan Publishing Co. Inc.

Section IV

Reforming Education

Sectional Introduction

The need for reforming education in India was felt for a long time. During the British period, for example, Annie Besant, President of the Indian National Cogress declared in the Calcutta Conference of the Congress in 1906 that throughout the country a national education should be organized. Gopal Krishna Gokhale introduced a bill in the Legislative Council in 1910 for legislation to provide compulsory primary education to all. The Hartog Committee (1929) suggested measures to reduce wastage in education. The National Planning Committee under the chairmanship of Jawaharlal Nehru pleaded in 1938 for planned development of education. The Sargent Plan (1944) has promised universal primary education within a period of four decades. Independent India has constituted several commissions and committees to reform education. Among many, the Education Commission, the first commission in Independent India that was required to look at the needed reforms in the entire education sector, proposed a large set of sweeping reforms in education. Unfortunately, as Naik (1982) remarked, many of the recommendations made by the Commission were yet to be implemented. Note that many of the recommendations made by the Kothari Commission and earlier committees and commissions did figure in the 1968 National Policy on Education and also in the 1986 Policy. Yet they could not be implemented for various socio-political and structural reasons, but the ideas discussed in the several reports continue to be important issues for policy discourses. For example, as Eswara Reddy describes, the problems and issues relating to university education that were raised by the first Indian Universities Commission 1902, the Sadler (Calcutta University) Commission (1917) and the Radhakrsihnan Commission (1951), to mention a few, are still persistent to date. On university governance, there were several committees, important among them in the recent decades include the Gajendra Gadkar Committee (1971) and the Jha Committee (1977). Eswara Reddy discusses the relevance of the recommendations of these two committees, in addition to the recommendations made by earlier committees and commissions. Some of the subjects raised by several of these committees and commissions have been raised in the Dr Kasturirangan committee on Draft National Education Policy (2019) and the National Education Policy 2020 (MHRD 2020). One of the main problems has been the gap between promise and practice.

A large part of growth in education that took place during the last three decades has been in private sector (Tilak 2009). Today the education market, if not 'education bazaar' (Kirp 2003), has become a common and respectable phrase in discussions on education policies. Looking at the unprecedented growth of the private sector in education that is being experienced in India with the growth of global capitalism, Manish Kumar Shrivastava and Chandan Chowdhary wonder, 'Where are we heading to.' They argue that the main purpose of education is to democratize the minds of students and help them become responsible and sensitive social beings; but the dominant market paradigm subverts and co-opts education for its own benefits, finally in the process turning education and consequently humanity itself into marketable commodities. This will have dangerous implications not only for the education sector, but also for the entire society.

Kishore Singh draws our attention to one major effect of such a growth of private sector in education: aggravating marginalization and exclusion in education; it will have a crippling effect on the principle of equality of opportunity in education, which is a fundamental principle of many nations including India and a principle well established by almost all international human rights conventions. This also puts in jeopardy the principles of social justice and equity, which are key pillars of the modern democratic societies. It has been well recognized for a long time that education is a public good, a unique public good, further producing a large set of public goods (Tilak 2008). Kishore Singh rightly argues that it is the primary responsibility of the state to safeguard the public good nature of education and to foster its humanist mission. Extensively referring to United Nations conventions, and practices in many other countries, Kishore Singh stresses that it is imperative to create a global movement which urges all the governments of the world to take seriously the task of regulating privatization in education, respecting education as a public good, and the principle of social justice.

Finally, at the end of the tunnel, there is some hope. Dr Kasturirangan committee (Government of India 2019) comes out with a set of sweeping reforms in education in its report on Draft National Education Policy 2019, which formed the basis for the government's *National Education Policy 2020* (Government of India 2020). Drawing inspiration from the great ancient Indian centres of learning, the Nalanda and the Takshashila, the Policy intends to build a higher education system that will produce human beings of highest character and values. An important proclamation that the Committee and the Policy make is, education is a public good. As Tilak in the last chapter of this volume and many other scholars on other fora observed, there are many a good intention in the committee report and in the Policy, but there also quite a few serious issues that they have not sufficiently addressed (Tilak, 2020). Even with respect to those many which are in the right direction, implementation of which becomes formidable, the need is to minimize the gap between the policy and practice.

REFERENCES

CABE. (1944). *Report of the Sargent Commission on post-war education development in India* [Sargent Plan]. Central Advisory Board of Education.

Education Commission. (1966). *Education and national development: Report of the Education Commission* [Kothari Commission]. National Council of Educational Research and Training. [Reprint 1972]

Gajendra Gadkar Committee. (1971). *Report of the Committee on Governance of Universities and Colleges* (Chairman: P. B. Gajendra Gadkar). University Grants Commission.

Government of India. (2019). *Draft National Education Policy 2019* (Dr Kasturirangan Committee Report). Ministry of Human Resource Development, Government of India. https://mhrd.gov.in/sites/upload_files/mhrd/files/Draft_NEP_2019_EN_Revised.pdf

Government of India. (2020). *National Education Policy on Education 2020*. https://static.pib.gov.in/WriteReadData/userfiles/NEP_Final_English_0.pdf

Hartog Committee. (1929). *Report of the Auxiliary Committee of the Indian Statutory Commission*. Government of India.

Jha Committee. (1977). *Report of the Review Committee on the University Grants Commission 1974–77* (Chairman: V. S. Jha). Ministry of Education, Government of India.

Kirp, David L. (2003). *Shakespeare, Einstein, and the bottom line: The marketing of higher education* Harvard University Press, Cambridge, MA.

Naik, J. P. (1982). *Education Commission and after*. APH Publishers.

Radhakrishnan Commission. (1951). *Report of the University Education Commission (1949–1951)* (Chairman: Sarvepalli Radhakrishnan). Government of India.

Sadler Commission (Calcutta University Commission). (1919). *Report of the Calcutta University Commission 1919*. Government of Calcutta.

Tilak, J. B G. (2008). Higher education: A public good or a commodity for trade? Commitment to higher education or commitment of higher education to trade [Keynote address delivered in the 2nd Nobel Laureates Meeting in Barcelona 2005]. *Prospects* (UNESCO), *38*(4) (December), 449–466.

Tilak, J. B. G. (2009). Private sector in higher education: A few stylized facts. *Social Change*, *39*(1) (March), 1–28.

Tilak, J. B. G. (2020). A policy with many a right intention. *The Hindu* (3 August). https://www.thehindu.com/opinion/op-ed/a-policy-with-many-a-right-intention/article32254650.ece

Chapter 17

Reforms in Higher Education*
In Retrospect

V. Eswara Reddy

THE IDEAL CONCEPTION OF THE UNIVERSITY

The thought of the university or higher education evokes in us
conflicting and contradictory systems of conception—the ideal and
the real. The ideal concept of the university is that it is a temple of
higher learning. In the spirit of Hindu society, we consider learning as
sacred and symbolize it in the form of goddess Saraswati. Rabindranath
Tagore portrayed the concept of goddess Saraswati in these words:
'The goddess of learning is Saraswati, her seat is in the lotus flower, its
symbolical meaning is that she lives in the centre of life and the heart
of our existence, which opens itself in beauty to the light of life.'[1]
The Indian Education Commission also raves its version of an ideal
university. It (Education Commission 1966, p. 274) states,

> [Universities] are essentially a community of teachers and students,
> where, in some way, all learn from one another or at any rate strive
> to do so. Their principal object is to deepen man's understanding of
> the universe and of himself in body, mind and spirit, to disseminate
> this understanding throughout society and to apply it in the service of
> mankind. They are the dwelling places of ideas and idealism and expect
> high standards of conduct and integrity from all their members.

---

* *Social Change:* December 1985: Vol. 15, No. 4, 3–10.

It was conceived that universities should be rooted in the life of the community and must act as the instruments of development. Rabindranath Tagore expresses this idea: 'The education should be in full touch with our complete life, commercial, intellectual, aesthetic, social and spiritual. It must not only instruct but help to live; not only to think and feel but act and produce.'[2] We are aware that we had a lofty tradition for learning right from the Vedic age. We also had internationally reputed universities in ancient times in Taxila, Nalanda and so on. But in the march of time and in the process of history, we have lost that continuity of tradition for learning and there was considerable period of non-existence of seats of higher learning until we entered into the era of British rule.

Unfortunately, the circumstances and purpose for which the first so-called modern universities were started in India by the British are in no conformity to our ideal concept of university. In a sense, they were not the Indian universities, but they were the British training institutions located in India for the purpose of recruiting the people to serve in their administrations in subordinate positions. Macaulay specifically wrote that the major aim of the British government in locating the universities in India was to train the natives as good English scholars. Endorsing Macaulay's notes, Governor General Lord William Bentinck issued a proclamation which stated:

> HIS LORDSHIP in COUNCIL is of opinion that the great object of the British government ought to be the promotion of European literature and science among the natives of India and that all the funds appropriated for the purpose of education would be best employed on English education alone.[3]

Not only in the purpose but in the structure also they adopted London University model. This was the beginning of deliberately creating a process of alienating education and educated of this country from their native Indian culture and community. This process of alienation is still evident. Even today we are struggling to bring relevance of higher education to the needs of our society.

The other conception of the university which is based on the reality of today's universities in India evokes a feeling of frustration and disappointment. They are no more considered as temples of learning but as devil's workshops. Instead of solving the problems of society, they are becoming problems to the society. Although this is an exaggerated view, a popular one nevertheless.

The three universities started by the British in the year 1857 have multiplied into 20 by the year 1947, that is, the year of Independence. This also means that over a period of 90 years, the three universities multiplied into 20 universities. Since Independence till today, that is, over a period of 38 years, the number has gone up to 140. Both before and after Independence, these universities have been presenting several problems, except that, after Independence, we have recognized more problems. During the pre-Independence period, the problems were essentially identified as those related to the standards, examinations and discipline. After Independence also, the same problems continued in much more acute form and magnitude, and we have recognized the lack of relevance of instruction to needs of the community. With this difference, there is no qualitative change in the state of affairs with the universities. The following resume of the recommendations of the commissions and committees appointed both during the pre-Independence and post-Independence periods will give a comprehensive idea of the nature of problems faced by these universities.

During the British period, the first Indian Universities Commission was appointed in the year 1902 which resulted in the Indian Universities Act passed in the year 1904. The recommendation of this Commission can be summarized in the following words

> The first was the assertion that every university ought to be a teaching university. The second was the principle that no college should be allowed full privileges unless it was thoroughly well installed and equipped. The third was the principle that the teachers must always be intimately associated with the government of the university. The fourth was the contention that the supreme governing body of the university—called in London, as in India—the Senate ought not to be too large. (Sadler Commission 1919, p. 65).

Some of these recommendations were incorporated into the government's resolution of Indian Educational Policy taken in March 1901. Gopalakrishna Gokhale at that time among others was opposed to these recommendations and commented that the Indian universities were among the most completely governmental universities in the world. From the recommendations of this Commission, it is evident that the problems and issues they then dealt with still are persisting to date.

The next important commission was appointed in the year 1917 under the chairmanship of Sir Michael Sadler, the vice chancellor of Leeds University which was known as Calcutta University Commission. This Commission is the result of the dispute between the Calcutta University and the Bengal Government over the financial grant. This Commission's report is responsible for the creation of Boards of Secondary Education and Intermediate Colleges. So far as the university education is concerned, the major recommendations of the Commission are as follows:

1. The desirability of less government control over the university
2. Greater participation by teachers in the control of the university
3. Closer cooperation between the universities and their colleges
4. The appointment of full-time vice chancellor

It is only after the publication of this report that a number of universities were started and reforms were carried out in existing universities.

The next major event so far as education is concerned was the appointment of National Planning Committee under the Chairmanship of Pandit Jawaharlal Nehru in the year 1938 by the Indian National Congress.

This Committee stressed the need for the first time for the planned development of education. The same view was later expressed by the Central Advisory Board of Education in its report submitted in the year 1944 on post-war educational problems. This report known as Sargent Report was the first official report which brought to the notice of the government the need for planned development of education. The other main recommendations, of the report are as follows[4]:

1. The duration of degree courses should be reduced to three years— with one year to intermediate courses without lowering of standards
2. There should be one examination with a twofold purpose serving as a school leaving certificate and an entrance examination to university

3. At least one-third students of the universities should be assisted with the scholarships from the government
4. A grants committee on the lines of University Grants Commission (UGC) of Great Britain be constituted

Thus, it can be seen that this report made very important recommendations most of which were implemented.

With this report, the succession of the commissions and committees in the pre-Independence British came to an end. As we could see from these reports, there was a perceptible change in the approach of the British government starting with the recommendation, aimed at mostly gaining control of the government on the universities and slowly in the later stages, they were a little more concerned with the welfare measures such as the participation of the teachers, in the governance of the universities, scholarships to the students and so on.

In the post-Independence era, the first commission was appointed in the year 1948 known as University Education Commission with Dr S. Radhakrishnan as its Chairman with the charge 'to report on the Indian universities' education and suggest improvements and extensions that may be desirable to suit present and future requirements of the country?'[5] This clearly indicates the realization that the university education should be designed on the basis of the present and future needs of the country, whereas in the pre-Independence era it was to be designed to suit to the needs of the British government. As can be seen in the following paragraphs, the recommendations of the commission mostly reiterated and elaborated on the same problems identified by the previous commissions. They have listed the problems of the universities as follows: 'a marked deterioration of the standards in teaching and examinations and increasing dissatisfaction with the conduct of the university administration and elections to the university authorities'. They recommended that the objectives and methods of work of the universities should be changed for their effective functioning. This Commission also recommended that the first degree course should be of three years duration and the teachers are to be given their due place. Their major stress is on the need for examination reforms. They again recommended for the setting up of the UGC. The Commission further recommended that English as a subject be made a compulsory subject, though accepting the inevitability of giving place to a modern Indian language sooner or later.

In the post-Independence era, no commission of education has received so much of publicity and attention as that of Indian Education Commission, appointed in the year 1964, under the Chairmanship of Dr D. S. Kothari. It received such attention may be because by then UGC came into existence and the Chairman of the UGC was himself the Chairman of the Commission. Further, it may also be because by then the number of universities and colleges had enormously increased and with the result it had become a wider interest for many. In spite of the fact that this Commission was to go into the entire gamut of education at all levels, it made deeper study of the system of higher education and made concrete suggestions. Further, this Commission's report became a basis for a National Policy on Indian Education considered by the Parliament. But it is very sad that some of the crucial recommendations by the commission were not acceptable to the Parliament. This has happened especially with regard to its recommendation favouring selective approach in developing the universities and in the enrolments into the higher education. This is because of the ideological commitment of the party in power. Dr Kothari mentioned the following recommendations, especially in his letter to the Education Minister while submitting the report:

1. Introduction of work experience and social service as integral part of general education at more or less all levels of education
2. Stress on moral education and inculcation of sense of social responsibilities, schools should recognize their responsibility in facilitating the transition of youth from the world of school to the world of work and life
3. Vocationalization of secondary education
4. The strengthening of Centres of Advanced Study and setting up of a small number of major universities which would aim to achieve highest international standards
5. Special emphasis on the training and quality of teachers for schools
6. Education for agriculture and research in agriculture and allied services should be given a high priority in the scheme of the

educational reconstruction. Energetic and imaginative steps are required to draw a reasonable proportion of talent to go in for advanced study and research in agricultural sciences

7. Development of quality of pace setting institutions at all stages and in all sectors.

However, the Commission's main recommendations are given further[6]:

1. The regional languages should be adopted as media of education in higher education. Energetic action be taken to produce books and literature, particularly scientific and technical, in regional languages. English which has been serving as a link language in higher education for academic work and intellectual intercommunication cannot serve as link language for the majority of people. Since Hindi is the official language of the Union and the link language of the people, all measures should be adopted to spread it in the non-Hindi areas.

2. (a) The new educational structure should consist of (i) one to three years of preschool education; (ii) a ten-year period of general education; (iii) a higher secondary stage of two years of general education or one to three years of vocational education; (iv) a higher education stage having three years for the first degree followed by two to three years duration in second degree; (b) pre-university course should be transferred to Boards of Secondary Education.

3. Scales of pay of teachers in colleges and universities is suggested.

4. (a) In order to avoid massive educated unemployment, unplanned and uncontrolled expansion higher education should be restricted. Estimates of manpower needs should be effectively related to the output of the educational system. A system of selective admissions should also be adopted, (b) an objective of giving every graduate an offer of employment along with their degree or diploma should be realized and system of one-year internship now prescribed for medical graduates should be extended to other categories of graduates.

5. (a) Scholarships should be available to at least 25 per cent of the enrolments at the undergraduate stage by 1976 and to 25 per cent of such enrolment by 1986, and (b) scholarships should be available

to at least 25 per cent of the enrolment at the postgraduate stage by 1976 and to 50 per cent of such enrolment by 1986.

6. Regional imbalances regarding educational development should be minimized which should include special assistance to less advanced areas of the country.

7. Steps for reform in the system of examination should be taken immediately and attention should be concentrated to three major areas: (a) reduction of the dominance of external examination; (b) the introduction of reforms which would make them, more valid and realistic measures of educational achievement and (c) the adoption of a good system of internal evaluation. The UGC should set up a Central Examination Reform Unit to work in collaboration with the universities.

8. (a) The most important reform in higher education is the development of some 'major universities' where first-class postgraduate work and research would be possible and whose standards would be comparable to the best institutes in any part of the world. These major universities should have 'critical mass' of students and teachers of outstanding capacity and promise, (b) other universities should be helped, through concentration of resources, to develop excellence in selected departments and ultimately to raise them to the level of centres of advanced studies.

9. Where there is an outstanding college or a small cluster of very good colleges within a large university which has shown the capacity of improving itself markedly, consideration should be given to granting it an 'autonomous' status.

10. Students services should include orientation for new students, health services, residential facilities, guidance and counselling, including vocational placement, student activities and financial and these services should form an integral part of education. A full-time dean of student welfare should be appointed in each university for administration of welfare services.

11. In order to prevent indiscipline among students each agency—students, parents, teachers, state governments and political parties should do their own duties and whole university life should be treated as one and polarization between teachers, students and administration should be avoided.

12. No new university should be started unless the agreement of the UGC is obtained and adequate provision for funds is made.

13. Efforts should be made to organize the courses at undergraduate, postgraduate and PhD levels in all faculties and to develop educational research.

14. Sphere of university autonomy lies in the selection of students, the appointment and promotion of teachers and the determination of courses of study, methods of teaching and selection of areas and problems of research. This should be respected and preserved. Representation of the non-academic element on university bodies should be mainly to present the wider interests of society but not to impose them. The Government of India should request the Supreme Court to frame a suitable policy to help the maintenance of university autonomy.

15. (a) The finance of universities should be placed on a sound footing by organizing it by a suitable system of block grants and simplifying rules and procedures for operating them. Better system would be that the UGC should be enabled to give both development and maintenance grants to state universities; (b) universities should be immune from direct governmental interference and also from direct public accountability.

16. 'Delhi' pattern for selection of the vice chancellor should be adopted. The term of office of the vice chancellor should be five years but the vice chancellor should not be appointed for more than two terms. Age of retirement of the vice chancellor should be 65 years.

17. The machinery for granting of affiliation to colleges and for their periodical inspection should be strengthened.

With this Commission's report, the succession of Commissions in the post-Independence era came to an end. However, later after the submission of the report, two more important committees have been appointed specifically for restricted purposes. The Committee on Governance of Universities and Colleges headed by Gajendragadkar is one of them. The other committee was a Review Committee on the UGC itself headed by Dr V.S. Jha.

Gajendragadkar's Committee on Governance of Universities and Colleges was appointed in the thick of the turmoil in the Indian universities at the time. So naturally its influence is clearly seen in the recommendations of the committee. Its stress on the participatory role of the students and teachers in the governance of the universities and colleges is a pointer in that direction. It emphasized the need for the democratization of the working of the universities, if possible, without resorting to the elections. The committee examined and made recommendations with particular reference to the following (UGC 1971, p. 1):

1. Structure of universities composition of and representations of various university bodies.
2. Relationship of universities with affiliated colleges including conditions of affiliation, constitution of the governing bodies, university representation etc.
3. The question of student participation in statutory bodies of universities/colleges.

The Committee drew its inspiration also from the Education Commission 1964–1966 in terms of the functions of the university and the spirit of reforms.

The Committee was conscious that structure reforms alone cannot improve the quality but at the same time they were conscious that

> an organizational pattern which is not in harmony with the needs of progress can retard the pace of development and that a flexible pattern of organization, which is responsive to the changing needs of society as well as knowledge, can be a powerful factor in accelerating, progress. (UGC 1971, p. 7)

The Committee pleaded for greater participation of students in the affairs of universities and colleges, and for greater provision for scholarships, especially to enable the gifted students to avail the best facilities. Recognizing the large-scale enrolments into the universities, the Committee pleaded for 'radical change in organization and the methods of teaching and examination. It involves the responsibility of introducing the diversified courses and giving difficult options to students' with different aptitudes and different abilities (UGC 1971).

This recommendation implies that unless such diversification in courses is attempted to cater to the needs of people of different abilities and aptitudes, it leads to indiscipline, lack of interest, wastage and so on. The Committee tried to suggest the organizational set up with complete flexibility which is required for creative adjustment to the changing needs and to provide scope for innovation, experimentation and change. They have emphasized the need for autonomy in universities while at the same time recognizing the right of the community to make the universities responsive to the needs of the community. What is important is that the Committee did not believe that autonomy is a 'legal consent' or a 'constitutional concept'. It is, for them, an ethical and academic concept.

So far as the functions of the Academic Council are concerned, the Committee recommended that

> We are therefore contemplating that the Academic Council should deal with general academic issues and should really be the most important academic body. Our anxiety is to save the academic council the trouble and the labour involved in dealing with matters pertaining to all to seven of the faculties though they may not always involve questions of general academic importance. (UGC 1971, p. 22)

Thus, the Committee had to recommend, because it envisaged greater autonomy to faculties and departments in terms of courses, regulations and so on. The Committee concluded by saying that it

> would like to emphasise the fact that in the matters of making the university education purposeful, meaningful and significant for the teachers, students and the general community what ultimately matters is not so much the pattern to which the university and its statutory bodies conform, but the spirit of dedication and the sense of purpose which should guide the activities of those who will function in these statutory bodies. UGC (1971, p. 24)

The Report of the Review Committee on the UGC examined the role played by the UGC, the problems it encountered and the changes it required. The UGC as per the UGC Act 1956 was expected to function as a body for the coordination and determination of standards in the universities. The Committee feels that the UGC could not act effectively because of the restrictions of the 1956 UGC Act itself. This act did not allow the UGC to stop the laissez faire growth in the number of universities and colleges. It merely remained as a passive spectator. This growth we know is mainly responsible for deterioration of standards in higher education, especially in the context of meagre material resources. The Committee stressed the need for bringing higher education into the concurrent list and re-designating the UGC as the University Education Commission. The Committee sought for several powers for the UGC including the appointment of the vice chancellors. The other recommendations of the Committee (UGC 1977) are as follows:

1. A high-level coordinating body with heads of different organizations dealing with higher education and research as well as senior representatives of the ministries of education, health and agriculture and the Planning Commission as its members may be established to deal with the matters of policy regarding the coordination of activities and sharing of resources between areas of teaching and research with a small standing committee.

2. In each state, there should be a coordinating body headed by the chancellor consisting of all vice chancellors, selected college principals, independent academicians and representatives of the stale government as well as of the UGC to effect coordination among higher educational institutions of the state level within the overall national policy.

3. Through proper legislative measure, the UGC should be empowered to have control over the growth of the universities, colleges and enrolments.

4. The UGC should, with the help of academicians, develop remedial courses for students from weaker sections of society to enable them to get admission on a level of equality.

5. A national examination should be organized jointly by the UGC, UPSC and AIU for postgraduates in different subjects and candidates who are declared successful in this examination should be given weightage for selection to the post of lecturers and for research fellowships.

6. Priority attention should be given by the UGC to restructuring the courses, particularly in rural colleges to make them relevant to rural needs.

7. On various items, matching grant should be paid on the same basis to the central as well as state universities by the UGC. However, in the case of colleges, particularly those in remote areas and poorer regions, the matching pattern needs to be further amended to the advantages of the institutions.

8. Centres of excellence, like the centres of advanced study, need to be maintained by the UGC on a regular basis.

9. A suitable organization should be set up as a unit of UGC for the study of various aspects of higher education.

10. The Commission be given power to recommend to government de-recognition of a degree of a university on grounds of lack of standards, as Indian Medical Council is empowered in respect of medical colleges.

11. There should be a system of evaluation of PhD thesis, the examinations, of class teaching, through teams of academicians.

12. A system should also be evolved for assessment of the performance of the teachers on annual basis. There should also be a system of disincentives against the poor performance.

The tenor and spirit of the Review Committee's report is more in the direction and of exercising control over the constituents of the system. However, it begs the same question whether we have the necessary will and commitment to exercise such a control.

The latest of the documents on the development of higher education in India is a policy frame circulated by the UGC in the year 1978. The policy frame also identified the weaknesses of the system and accepted that there are more failures than successes. The only achievement it recognized is the manifold increase in the number of universities, colleges and enrolments. The three major weaknesses identified are as follows:

1. It still continues to be dominated by models and value systems adopted during colonial regime.

2. The system maintains a set of double standards leading to social segregation and perpetuation and strengthening of inegalitarian trends in the society.

3. Even in quantitative terms, it is mainly the upper and middle classes
   that are beneficiaries (UGC 1978, pp. 1–2).

This document further recognized that there is a need for drastic
overhaul. This document, though repeated the reforms that are
suggested by various commissions and committees earlier, emphasized
the adult and extension education. So far as the undergraduate stage
is concerned, it suggested the academic programme consisting of
foundation courses, core courses, some applied studies and involvement
in the programmes of National Social Service. It also pleaded for the
diversification of courses and decentralization of the autonomy to
the university departments and colleges. In order to pull higher
education out of the crisis, it suggested that the government should take
the steps to de-link degrees from jobs, greater responsibility on the part
of teachers and students and nationwide effort to achieve breakthrough
simultaneously on social and educational fronts.

After going through this long journey of 125 years of the existence
of higher education in India, we get a feeling that we are still in the
woods and nothing seems to have changed except that the problems
are felt in a more acute and more magnified manner. V. V. John (1980)
aptly commented that in the long period of 33 years of Independence,
two things have not changed. One is poverty, and the other is
education. He further states that though there can be dispute about
poverty, there is no dispute about education. He quoted the remarks of
the businessman saying that it is only in the business of education that
the customer does not feel cheated. He does not feel cheated because
he does not pay for it.

What is very peculiar to the Indian higher education is that whatever
so called reforms have been introduced have resulted in more problems
and deterioration of whatever the standards it had rather than solving
the problems and improving the standards. The obvious example is
semester system and the grading and internal assessment that go along
with it. Briefly a resume of the reforms attempted in recent times is
mentioned here.

The first major reform attempted in the field of higher education
relates to the introduction of 10+2+3 pattern. It is expected that this
new pattern will revolutionize education in India, though there was

large-scale scepticism and criticism about it in the general public. It is expected that this pattern will strengthen the school and bring in improvement in higher studies on expectations that this will facilitate more mature and better, and it will also facilitate field work and project-oriented studies. Professor Hasan feels that 'the introduction of problem oriented inter-disciplinary courses at the Masters Degree level would also be greatly facilitated with the adoption of 10+2+3 and will provide a society with personnel having a wide spectrum of knowledge and training for its development needs'.[7] This reform called for qualitative changes in the curriculum instruction and organization. The status report brought out by the Association of Indian Universities based on a systematic study clearly proved that many universities have not effected any changes that are consequent on the introduction of this pattern. The university system has failed to receive the students passing out of 10+2 system into +3 stages. Many universities have not even bothered to discuss about it. With the result, we have only readjusted the duration of the courses without introducing changes required in the curriculum, instruction and so on. The public's fears have come true.

The next major reform introduced is the semester system, it is felt that if it is introduced in a systematic manner, this will initiate a process of modernization and improvement in both the teaching and learning processes and will lead to the reforms and flexibility in course content and techniques of evaluation. Out of 126 universities (1979) including agricultural universities, 80 universities have adopted semester or trimester system.[8] Thus, it is introduced on a mass scale. The study made by V. Natarajan of the Association of Indian Universities indicated that, in many universities, the basic principles underlying the design and implementation of semester system have not been understood. The implications with regard to the syllabus, teaching, learning and evaluation are not worked out and if worked out only half-heartedly. It was introduced in great hurry without preparation on the part of the teachers, students and administrators. The internal assessment and the grading system that generally go with the semester system have led to a number of problems. Many universities are now trying to go back to the traditional system.

The concept of autonomous colleges is another innovation the UGC wanted to introduce. In spite of the efforts made since the 1960s, no university came forward except Madras and Madurai. Besides this, the UGC introduced a number of programmes to improve the quality of education some of which are enumerated.

With respect to Centres of Advanced Study in Science and Humanities and special assistance schemes, so far, 14 centres in science, 9 centres in humanities and social sciences are recognized as advance courses. Similarly, under special assistance scheme, 33 departments in sciences, and 21 departments in arts are recognized under the scheme (UGC 1979). But this is a drop in the ocean. Their impact is not yet felt.

Other important programmes are College Science Improvement Programme, College Humanities and Social Science Improvement Programme. Only 1,177 colleges under science, and 146 colleges under humanities and social sciences are covered by this scheme. Again, it may be noted that this is an insignificant number as the total number of colleges is as large as 4,460. UGC has a number of other faculty improvement programmes. But then the coverage is very insignificant.

The enterprise of higher education in India in terms of its size has grown up so much that it has become impossible to introduce improvement programmes on any significant scale. There are about 118 universities, 4,460 colleges, with 30 lakhs of students and about 2 lakhs of teachers. Most of these universities and colleges are not viable. For the successful implementation of reforms, we require two things, namely the resources and the commitment and the spirit of reform and dedication on the part of the teachers, students, administrators and the government as such. We lack both of these.

NOTES

1. Quoted by G.S. Goutam, (1972, p. 3). Goutam, G.S. *Crisis in the Temples of Learning*. S. Chand & Co., New Delhi.
2. G.S. Goutam, p. 4.
3. Quoted by G.S. Goutam, p. 18.
4. Quoted by G.S. Goutam, p. 29.
5. Quoted by G.S. Goutam, p. 30.
6. Quoted from G.S. Goutam, pp. 34–38.
7. Status report series, preparation made by Universities to receive teams of the Association of Indian Universities, Delhi 1979, p. 7–8.

8. Mr. V. Natarajan Monograph on 'Semester system for Universities, Association of Indian Universities' Delhi 1979.

REFERENCES

Education Commission (1966). *The Report of Educational Commission* 1964–66, New Delhi.

Goutam, G.S. *Crisis in the Temples of Learning.* S. Chand & Co., New Delhi.

John, V.V. (1980), Taking Education furiously, *India Express*, 18th November.

Sadler Commission (1917). *The Report of the Calcutta University Commission.* New Delhi.

UGC (1971). *Report of the Committee on Governance of Universities on Colleges*, UGC, New Delhi.

UGC (1977). *Report of the Review Committee on the University Grants Commission*, New Delhi.

UGC (1978). *Development of Higher Education in India A Policy Frame*, UGC, New Delhi.

UGC (1979). *Annual Report*, 1978–79. New Delhi.

Chapter 18

Marketing Education*
Where Are We Heading?

Manish Kumar Shrivastava and
Chandan Chowdhary

I

Introduction

Teachers ought to know everything, old man, everything.... If you only knew the absolute necessity for the Russian countryside of good, clever, educated teachers! In Russia we have simply got to create exceptional conditions for teachers, and that as soon as possible, since we realise that unless the people get an all-round education the state will collapse like a house built from insufficiently baked bricks... [But] They are famished, downtrodden, they live in perpetual fear of losing their livelihood..... For nine or ten months in the year our teachers live the lives of hermits, without a soul to speak to, they grow stupid from loneliness, without books or amusements......All this is disgusting

* *Social Change:* September 2006: Vol. 36, No. 3, 177–94.

The authors are grateful to Ravi Kumar for taking the pains of reading an incoherent first draft and giving suggestions that helped in making the arguments and the strucuture of the chapter more coherent and systematic; Pakaj Pachuri, Senior Editor, NDTV-India, for sharing some unpublished information in his presentation at the Convention on OBC Reservation, held at JNU, organized by JNUSU on May 25, 2006; and also to Divya Cherian for checking the final proofs at very short notice. However, any shortcomings are solely the authors' responsibility.

...a kind of mockery of human beings doing great and terribly
important work.

—Anton Chekhov (Gorky, 1987)

Chekhov shared these concerns about education with Maxim Gorky
who later happened to supervise the translation of world literature for
children with the objective of providing a wider outlook to children
about life and society. He was underlining the role of a teacher and
the material conditions under which he ought to work in order to
provide 'all-round education' to the society. This passage is of greater
significance as we find similar descriptions of working conditions of
teachers in Indian villages as to what Chekhov had described more
than 100 years ago. In order to achieve the literacy 'targets' under
various World Bank and UN-financed programmes, the country's
education system is plagued with underpaid, undereducated para-
teachers (Chandru, 2006). The purpose of this chapter, however, is not
to address the issues relating to the working conditions of teachers but
to examine the present state of education under globalization through
the frames of 'all-round education'. Further, by locating education
in the broader political economy of capital, this chapter outlines some
of the crucial themes relating to pedagogy and education for further
deliberations. The next section elaborates on the idea of 'all-round
education' and the further sections examine the state of education
under globalization.

II

Conceptualizing: What Does 'All-round Education' Mean?

At the very outset, education is about learning and therefore education
must be perceived in the context of the learning process. A man learns
from the world outside him, which consists not only of human beings
but nature and the material products of human labour as well, and it
is also an active participant in it. In other words, human beings learn
from each other in a dialectical process (Friere, 1993). In this process
of learning, the man changes and so does the world. And there lies
the significance of education. Giroux's assertion that 'Education as

a moral and political practice always presupposes a preparation for particular forms of social life, a particular vision of community, and a particular vision of the future' (Giroux, 1998). Giroux assigns education a central position in the social process. Education has this central role to play in the social process because it is an act of a human being and it subjects a human being. To put it differently, education is a mechanism through which human beings produce human beings—human beings as social subject. 'A preparation for particular forms of social life' essentially means that human beings consciously influence the learning of other human beings to mould them in accordance with the 'moral and political' values that they want to build the future society on. Education, therefore, is always 'based on ethics and politics, and even the content of education is politically determined' (Harris, 1979). Or, to put it crudely, education is politics.

Being a political activity, education also becomes an arena of struggle for social transformation. Therefore, when we indulge ourselves in a discourse on education, we need to ascertain what kind of politics are we engaging ourselves with. Is it a 'constructive politics' grounded in the socio-economic realities and engaged in a social transformation agenda aiming at more equitable, just and democratic social relations? Or is it a 'divisive politics' on the basis of manipulations, fabrications and myths either to maintain the status quo of unjust socio-economic relations or to create one in order to maintain the dominance and hegemony of the few? So when we talk about 'all-round education', we must explain what kind of politics we are talking about. In our opinion, 'all-round education' simply means that everybody knows everything; that all kinds of knowledge should be accessible to all. There must not be any exclusion from education at all. In other words, it means an education which eliminates the 'necessity' of some 'expert' to tell us what is right and what is wrong; which enables everybody to decide on their own about what is right and wrong. And, consequently, it is an education, which destroys hierarchies and subjugations, and instead furthers equality, dignity, justice and democracy.

However, in the present neoliberal era, where the logic of the market is being propagated as the ultimate determinant of the future, we find that equality, dignity, justice and democracy are under serious threat. In such a situation, the need for 'all-round education' becomes critical for reclaiming democracy and human dignity because the 'politics of human resistance'—resistance against neoliberalism, is necessary, as Rikowski puts it, first of all within education and training because these are the places where psychologically inherent notions of hierarchy and oppression operate in the most forced, systematic and overt manner (McLaren & Rikowski, 2001). The following two sections discuss how under globalization, education is being transformed and used as a tool of subjugation of human beings for the benefit of the big businesses.

III

Education under Globalization

Education, as a political activity, is essentially concerned with transmission of knowledge, which takes place in an organized form through an institutionalized education system. Therefore, in order to understand the state of education, it is necessary to examine, apart from the content and mode of its transmission, the institutional structure within which the transmission of knowledge takes place. Even a cursory examination of the Indian education system over the last 15 years suggests that the meaning of education has changed from being a public good to a private good. This shift is reflected not only in the content and transmission mode but also in the institutional changes that have taken place over the years. These changes can be understood through an analysis of changes in national policy framework, international economic institutions and in the perception of education in general. The following paragraphs are an attempt towards outlining these changes.

Education Redefined

The decade of the 1990s saw India taking a sharp turn away from the welfare state. With the implementation of the Structural Adjustment Programme and New Economic Policy, as per the IMF–World Bank conditionalities, the state began to withdraw from all social sector services including education thereby leading the way to the commercialization of all services (Tilak, 1996). Ironically, at the same time, the World Bank began funding various literacy programmes to achieve the 'Education For All' targets set by UNESCO at the Jomtien Conference in 1990 (Goldstein, 2004). Today literacy, not education, is the indicator of development. This is understandable as development today means just glowing markets and not strengthening democracy and general well-being of the masses. That's why even the budget speeches of consecutive finance ministers highlight literacy programmes such as Sarva Siksha Abhiyan and Aanganwadi in their remarks on education. This was a shift from universal education to universal literacy as a national policy target. This shift was a result of negotiating between IMF–World Bank conditionalities of reducing public expenditure and giving a free hand to the private sector (neoliberal agenda) and a simultaneous compulsion to fulfil the commitment to the Jomtien declaration on 'Education For All'. The government is thus caught in a 'dichotomous' situation where, on the one hand, it is being 'forced' to commercialize and privatize education, where education becomes available only for those who can buy it while, on the other hand, the Constitution as well as 'commitment' to 'Education For All' programme requires the government to ensure that everybody gets education irrespective of the fact whether they can buy it. It's a pity that in order to come out of this situation, the government chose to compromise with the commitment towards 'Education For All' instead of stopping commercialization and privatization of education. Replacing education with literacy is a dilution of the meaning of education. A literate person cannot be equated with an educated person. It is unfortunate that for the government today the meaning of education is reduced to merely reading and writing, and the values of dignity, justice and democracy are left out.

Trade in Education

The WTO under the General Agreement on Trade in Services (GATS) has made education a tradeable good. This means that now education too can be traded internationally and would be governed according to laws of market and free competition. The Article I of Part I of GATS puts forth four main modes of trade in services (WTO, 1999), which are also applied to trade in educational services. These four modes are called consumption abroad, cross-border supply, commercial presence in the consuming country and presence of natural persons. The consumption abroad mode recognizes the mobility of students for education overseas, that is, students can go to foreign countries for the purpose of getting an education. Under the cross-border supply mode distance learning, any type of testing service, and supply of educational materials through the Internet as well as postal services for crossing the national borders have been acknowledged. Commercial presence enables foreign educational investors to set up educational institutions through direct foreign investment and joint ventures in the host country. The presence of natural persons allows movement of individual educators across the countries for a period, though not well defined in GATS documents but roughly from 6 to 10 years.

The most critical of these four modes are the consumption abroad mode and commercial presence, for they allow the international big education firms to expand their market globally. Various initiatives sponsored by governments, universities and private firms, such as 'education fairs', exemplify the competition over the global education market (Khadria, 2004). Khadria observes that there is nothing new in GATS. All that it contains is mere 'old wine in new bottles'. The only thing that is new is the movement of 'disembodied' human capital but that too is due to changes in information and communication technologies. He is right as far as the modes of trade are concerned but the purpose of education is not the same anymore. Unlike the educational institutes set up by the British during colonial rule in India, the purpose of direct commercial presence today is not to produce clerks for colonial government as per Lord Macaulay's diplomatic move but to produce a global workforce for international business and to earn profit. The purpose of education today is not administrative but economic as clearly mentioned in the background note of the WTO on trade in education. It explicitly states, 'Education enables them [students] to face the challenges of technological change and global commercial integration. Through its capacity to provide skills and enable effective participation in the workforce, education is crucial to economic adjustment' (WTO, 1998: 2). Also, the Most Favoured Nation Clause under the WTO agreement is applicable on trade in education (Part II, Article II of GATS) which essentially means that no country can now set legal and administrative compulsions to direct its education system according to its national requirements. This is certainly not the 'old wine', at least if we consider the post-Independence pre-GATS period.

Changing Perspectives and Selling Education

Along with all the aforementioned changes in the national economic policy and international economic institutions, one very significant aspect that needs to be reflected upon is the changing perception with regard to education among the people. To begin with, as Chekhov significantly underlined the idea and purpose of education, the notion of being educated is associated with a better and holistic understanding of the society and subsequently commanding a great amount of respect in the society. However, in the present socio-economic and political milieu, this notion has undergone a serious change. Being educated now seems to have acquired a new meaning of being able to sell oneself. In the process, 'education' is a tool for the purpose of making oneself better equipped with skills demanded by the labour market. To exemplify, one may note the fact that increasingly youngsters are opting for subjects/courses that would help them in getting a lucrative pay package because the more salary and perks one gets, the more admiration and respect one commands (Khadria, 2004). An increasing demand for such subjects/courses has led to the mushrooming of some accredited and many non-accredited private institutes selling degrees and diplomas. This phenomenon has also changed the perception of education to the limited, market-oriented notion of 'knowledge providers' and 'knowledge consumers'. In the race to attract more students, these institutes follow an extensive campaign strategy, as evident in the national dailies and magazines that are flooded with lucrative advertisements of private educational institutes. At the same time, rating the topmost educational institutes in the country for pursuing higher education in various streams has become almost an annual ritual. For instance, a recent issue of *India Today* (5 June 2006), a weekly national magazine, has come up with its 10th annual survey of best colleges in India in different streams of studies. The survey was conducted by *India Today*–AC Nielsen–ORG–MARG. What this story tells the reader is about the top 10 colleges in India in each field of study—arts, commerce, science, engineering, law and medicine. It also gives the reason as to why the superseded college has got the top position. Apart from this general information, it gives a list of the top five colleges in each stream in selected big cities. As one can easily guess, this issue is full of advertisements of several other private educational institutes.

India Today is not the only magazine that brings out such special stories every year right before the beginning of the academic year. A number of other national magazines too come up with such stories and surveys. They too get as many ads from different educational institutions. All this sounds perfectly normal and desirable to a student who has just come out of the school, to the parents who, no doubt and quite genuinely, wish to see their children moving towards a secure future. But if one tries to locate this annual event of making educational choices and advertising education within the frames of philosophy of education, then this normalcy and desirability is an alarm bell for the future of the society. What this advertising and evaluation or ranking of educational institutes indicates is a perilous tendency of separating education from the existence of human beings, sparing education from its responsibility to inculcate democratic values and ethics of citizenship, making education a commodity and a student a consumer. In other words, it cries out aloud that the education, a crucial public good, is no longer a necessary social entity but a commodity that is available for sale and purchase in the marketplace. It suggests that schools are now an extension of the marketplace and students are primarily consumers. It is not surprising, then, that the educational institutes along with the coaching centres top the list of revenue sources that media gets a huge amount of advertising money from.

It is interesting, in this context, to note that the survey was conducted by a market surveying agency and not by any social science research institute. This invariably implies that the ranking of various colleges must have been defined according to market requirements, that is, what the top colleges provide for the market—a particular kind of workforce to be very precise. Job security arising from being students of a particular college does not necessarily mean that they are responsible social beings, but it guarantees only one fact that the college produces the kind of people that are demanded by the market. This is evident from the advertisements as well. Every institute highlights its links with multi-national companies (MNCs) and industry, its record of placement, significance of its curriculum for the competitive globalized world. In an interview, for instance, Lalage Prabhu, School Director of Pathways World School, said that the International Baccalaureate (IB) Curriculum that the school offers is such that it trains the students in 'international mindedness' so that they do not feel alienated while working in any part of the world (*Times of India*, 2 July 2006). Most of these international or world schools run by big corporations with huge investments who require this kind of 'international mindedness', which allows them the benefits of 'flexible, multi-skilled labour'. Thus, such is the scenario of the so-called 'knowledge economy' today that those who demand a certain kind of 'skill' are the ones who sell it. They sell 'skill' to you at profit and then they appropriate the benefits of your increased productivity, further increasing their profit.

Another aspect of selling education is the loan scheme for students provided by almost all public and private sector banks today (Tilak, 1992). These loan schemes operate on commercial lines like other consumer loans. Students borrow and repay with interest—the only difference between a consumer loan and an educational loan being that in the case of the former, one needs to have a regular stream of income, whereas in the latter case the borrower relies on the expected gain from the education and consequent job. This essentially means that education has a value according to the economic returns it may produce. Only then borrowing for education makes an economic sense, otherwise just for the sake of acquiring knowledge, one would not borrow money and pay interest on it. The economization of social sector evaluation, in short, has been the hallmark of the neoliberal era. Michael Spence's Nobel Prize winning work on 'market signalling' epitomizes this phenomenon. Spence argues that by taking a risk of investing in education, an employment seeker or employee signals the employer that he is superior to those who are not investing (Spence, 1973). Thus, education now is no more evaluated on the basis of its role in building a more just and sensitive society, instead the terms of reference have become increasingly economic.

The philosophy of student loans treats higher education as a highly individualized commodity, as against the well-acknowledged public good nature. Loans are another mechanism to keep the market going. Like other consumer loans, student loans too create demand for commodities by encouraging people to spend their future incomes in advance. Tilak rightly sums up this change in the financial aspect of education by arguing that the introduction of student loans indicates a shift in 'the responsibility of higher education from social domain (state responsibility) to household domain and within households from parents to the children—from present to the future' (Tilak, 2005).

What the previous discussion implies is a twofold phenomenon. First, education is now sold and purchased according to the purchasing power of the student (or parents). In other words, education has become an industry. Second, a good educational institute today means that it serves the industry, not society. Well, remember, industry and society are not synonymous as most of the 'growth' enthusiasts tend to believe. Otherwise, how would one explain the contrast between growing industry and dying people? Thus, what we find today is a breaking up of education–society dialectic and establishing education–industry conformity by redefining the purpose of education. In the next section, we discuss the key institutional changes at the national level that have strengthened the education–industry links in the last 15 years.

IV

Change in Institutional Environment: Cementing Education–Industry Link

Society operates through various institutions. Institutions are understood as norms and compulsions (North, 1990). The state is the most powerful institution that regulates the activities of all the other institutions and structures within a social system. Education being essentially a 'public good' for the betterment of the society in general, and the individual in particular, has been the task of the state and state alone. But the past two changes brought about by the process of privatization, liberalization and globalization. Now, education is no longer an exclusive domain reserved for intervention only by the state but the overarching notion of the market and profit has encouraged an active participation and collaboration of the private players. This phenomenon has been given an added legitimacy by various Supreme Court pronouncements and the proposed changes in the legal framework relating to education.

The conception that higher education generates new knowledge and subsequently a new labour force makes the higher education sector the focal point of interest for the industrial forces. The formation of various committees headed by industrialists (from the Punnaih Committee to the Birla–Ambani Committee during the 1990s) by successive governments at the Centre indicates that the State perceives education as merely a training process to produce the workers for Industry. The Birla–Ambani Report (submitted to the Prime Minister's Council on Trade and Industry in 2000) recommended that the entire higher education sector must be allowed to be privatized and public support from secondary education must be gradually withdrawn. The central argument of the report was that education at all levels must be determined by the market forces (Sadgopal, 2006). This report is a strong indicator towards the fact that the industrial sector is keenly awaiting the full green signal from the government towards making education as a domain of its privilege. Consequently, a gradual strengthening of industry–education links is taking place at a galloping pace thereby automatically creating space for international 'educational shops' to flood the national boundaries. Tilak (2005) has pointed out that a large number of universities have also set up university–industry cells with the support of the UGC (that happens to be the apex monitoring body of higher education in the country). This is being done mainly to promote close links between universities and the industrial sector. Tilak argues that 'though public–private partnership has become a buzzword, many realise that it is not "partnership," but a deal, a business deal to make education and research in higher education institutions, not socially relevant but market relevant.' To further substantiate, it is noteworthy that in a document considered by the committee on Universalisation of Secondary Education; constituted by CABE (Central Advisory Board on Education) in 2005, it was stated that 'now that education has become a commodity, what is wrong in making profit out of it?' This document represented the proceedings of a meeting that the MHRD had with ASSOCHAM on the subject of the role of private 'education providers' in the field of secondary education (Combat Law, 2006).

Decades of the Indian experience depict a different story consistent with a cursory glance at some significant proposed legislations and Supreme Court judgements on issues pertaining to education would clarify how the broader institutional environment is being reconceived not only at the level of higher education but primary education as well. The provisions in Draft Right to Free and Compulsory Education Bill, 2005, such as 'neighbouring school' and providing subsidized infrastructure to private schools (Government of India, 2005) would eventually ensure that the state has no responsibility to provide minimum education to the children of 6–14 age group. Thus, primary education would be an open market for private firms. The various provisions seem to be in conjunction with the recommendations made by the Education Promotion Society for India (EPSI) to the MHRD that suggests that because industries are direct beneficiaries of education, therefore, they should have a higher level of intervention in deciding on education management and curriculum (Combat Law, 2006).

So far as the role of the judiciary is concerned, it is noteworthy that the Supreme Court has passed a number of judgements, which have had a tendency of opening up floodgates of privatization. The classic reference where it all began is the Mohini Jain case (1992) that led to the watershed Unni Krishnan Judgement (1994) in which the Court-ruled 'private educational institutions are absolutely necessary and they must be allowed to continue' and 'they must be allowed to recover the costs by charging higher fees'. In yet another significant Supreme Court judgement, that is, the T. M. A. Pai Foundation Judgement (2002), the Court observed, 'the governmental domination in the educational field must be resisted.' This view of the Supreme Court, as Desai notes, 'was a shocking departure from the earlier view which regarded education as a sovereign function and looked at private intervention only as a supplemental effort'. The Court also made way for extensive capitation fee in this judgement and did away with the concept of free seats and payment seats (Desai, 2006).

This disturbing trend is reflective of the fact that the State too has become a facilitator of the notion of education as one of the many 'consumer goods' and the task of education is 'knowledge production' for the flourishing industrial and corporate sector. Unlike the idea of universities being critical institutions that sometimes preserved and interpreted, and sometimes expanded the history and culture of society functioning independently of the principles of economics, now it is enmeshed in the cycle of producing certain kinds of knowledge. This phenomenon has led to the subsequent hierarchization of knowledge with subjects having a market value gaining a preference over those that do not lead to a profit. On this criterion, the technical and market-oriented subjects (that create engineers, doctors, scientists, economists, commerce graduates, CAs and MBAs) definitely have an edge over other subjects, for example, the rush for these subjects at undergraduate level as evident during the admissions in various colleges of Delhi University in 2006. It shows the differentiation between various knowledge forms, that is, doing away with epistemological significance of education. This is an inevitable consequence of education–industry links as Rikowski rightly notes, 'Intensified efforts of national capitals to reduce education to labour power production and enhancement at the expense of other goals and purposes of education have uncovered the basic instinct within the monster that is capitalist education' (Rikowski, 2002a).

V
Capitalization of Humanity

The previous discussion suggests that humans are increasingly being perceived as workers and consumers only, that is, a subject of capitalist mode of production. As a consequence, men are losing the capacity of being human. In the mainstream development discourse today, educated and trained people are seen as resources. This is, in Rikowski's words, 'capitalization of humanity'. Rikowski (2002b) argues

> capital assumes a number of forms—value, money, commodity, state and other forms. The capitalisation of humanity implies that, as capital, these forms take on real existence within us and within our daily lives as human capital. Furthermore, as this process gathers pace, there is increasingly no 'individual' or 'society' duality, no 'outside' or 'inside'

and no 'beyond' the realm of capital: capital progressively and exponentially becomes all that there is.

Since capital too is a commodity—a commodity that can produce other commodities or can be invested, capitalization of humanity then essentially means commodification of humanity. This commodification has taken place through commodification of the process of producing human beings, that is, education. In this section, we try to outline the commodification of education and consequently of human beings and locate this phenomenon in the broader politico-economic perspective.

Education as a Commodity

A commodity is an object that is exchanged in the market. By the same token, as has been discussed in Section III, education has become a commodity—a market object and, consequently, no longer remains a social good, that is, like all other commodities, it is accessible only to those who have ability to purchase it and only that kind of education would be provided which has sufficient demand for making profit. There would be no state intervention and directives at all. In this section, however, we intend to indicate towards a much larger issue. According to Karl Marx, 'a commodity is, in the first place, an object outside us, a thing that by its properties satisfies human wants of some sort or another' (Marx, 1976). In this context, as has been discussed in Section II of this chapter, education cannot be considered as a commodity in the Marxist sense as it is all about inculcating democratic values and criticality which cannot exist 'outside us'. Democratic values and criticality, however, can be induced in a proper institutional environment, which can be a subject of market activity, market in the sense a place where goods and services are exchanged for goods or services or money. So, as a subject of exchange, education can be a commodity in economic terms but not in the Marxist sense. But as the discussion in Section III clearly shows that education in modern times has been redefined as a marketable good and its only significance lies in making a person saleable in the market, it has become a commodity even in the Marxist sense. And herein lies a reason to worry because it essentially means that education—an institutionalized attempt to shape and sharpen one's intellect and critical faculty—no more influences the consciousness and the ability to change the immediate socio-economic environment. In other words, a man stops being a creator.

Human Beings as Commodities

As has been discussed in the previous sections, the present educational ethos and values of the students and their parents result in opting for that education, content-wise, which is likely to get internationalized in the labour markets. Of late, this tendency has become more than visible in India. Khadria, for example, notes a

> shift in the choice of the 'majors', by students entering the senior secondary schooling (after Class X) and colleges in favour of subjects like commerce and marketable languages, and away from the sciences or social sciences over the last decade. In postgraduate courses too, there has been a definite shift towards the business studies and away from the general university education. (Khadria, 2004)

In Rikowski's words, this is an indication of 'the deepening of capitalist social relations' and along with it we are evolving 'into a new life form: human capital'. He asserts that such 'capitalization of humanity' is inevitable in the development of capitalism where 'humans increasingly become something "other" than human; a new life form, a "new species" human capital' (Rikowski, 2002a, 111).

If we see the political economy of globalization, that is, the ways in which human beings relate to each other through the exchange of the products of their labour power at a global scale through market mediation, then we realize globalization as an attempt of global capital to expand a homogeneous favourable social relation at global level through integrating various national economies. Institutions such as GATS and Trade Related Intellectual Property Rights (TRIPS) are a manifestation of this attempt. A closer analysis of TRIPS, for instance, would reveal that it is another instrument of international capital that institutionalizes the commodification of humanity by facilitating corporate ownership over human beings. TRIPS has been widely debated during the past decade. The focus of the debate has been primarily around its implications for knowledge-based industries such as the pharmaceutical industry and the ownership of knowledge. A patent right essentially means ownership over a product of man's intellect. When we see TRIPS in the context of corporate-financed research (directly in the MNC labs or via public–private partnership) and corporate holding of majority of patents, then it acquires a wider political and ethical meaning. The work of an individual or a team of individual scientists' intellect is owned by an MNCs through patents. Since knowledge is always embedded in a human being and cannot be separated from the existence of the human being, a patent held by MNC means that the person who produced the patented intellectual work is owned by the MNC. With knowledge, the person is also owned by the MNC just like a commodity.

VI

Conclusion

The previous discussion attempts at outlining some of the crucial tendencies relating to education as well as in the institutional environment that are shaping with the rise of global capitalism. In Section II, we have said that the main purpose of education is to democratize the minds of students and help them become responsible and sensitive social beings. Sections III and IV examine the ways in which the dominant market paradigm has subverted and co-opted education for its own benefits. An attempt to understand the political economy of this subversion has been made in Section V where we argue that the intensification of capitalism inevitably leads to such situations where everything, here education and humanity, is turned into a commodity—a distinct and alienated form of capital. This has wider implications for the democratic values and the future of the society. In the end here, we propose to outline these concerns in brief for further deliberation.

Market and Democracy

The previous sections have discussed how schools have become an extension of the market place, thereby reducing students to mere consumers. Within an ever-expanding corporate culture, schools are just another investment opportunity with very high stakes. Such education offers greater monetary returns for those who have access to education and leave others to plunge into the spiral of poverty. In other words, the market makes education exclusionary where a great number of people cannot participate in the social process. Such absence of participation is undemocratic. Such a commodification of education essentially leads to a valueless society. The sheer lack of active engagement with the immediate social environment (all education is targeted to instil 'international mindedness') and lack of a mechanism to inculcate a consciousness that makes humans responsible to other human beings (the sole objective of getting education is to become competitive, superior to others and to achieve individual well-being) can never be conducive to a democratic and sensitive society. As Giroux rightly argues that 'as commercial culture replaces public culture, the language of the market becomes a substitute for the language of democracy...market does not provide guidance on matters of justice and fairness that are at the heart of a democratic civil society (Giroux, 1998). It is common sense that businesses do not like the workers to question or revolt. So they keep them busy and insecure. The drive for higher incomes and luxuries coupled with the worry to repay the loans (today's economy can well be called a credit economy because a major part of total consumption is on credit), of which student loans too is a part, does not allow people to take the 'risk' of engaging themselves with the activities of social transformation. Thus, the logic of the market necessarily undermines participation and therefore democracy.

What May Lie Ahead

Murmann in his study of German leadership in the synthetic dye industry between the 1850s and 1910 provides a fine historical account of why education is an important concern for industry and business for 'economic adjustments' (Murmann, 2003). It also explains how important it is for the businesses to have a favourable institutional environment. The rise of organic chemistry as an important academic discipline in Germany and the abundance of the research in the field of synthetic dyes during that period was a result of change in education policy including setting up new institutes, providing funding and maintaining close links between business and education infrastructure. The current trend of increasing the share of corporate funded research, corporations' intervention in educational institutes' management and changes in the institutional environment at a global level under the auspices of WTO agreements is nothing but a scaling up of the German experience. The increasing emphasis on technical and market-oriented education, setting up of new institutions and diversion of funds towards these areas of study is similar to German experience as well. The role of lobbying that is well documented by Murmann is no secret in the case of WTO negotiations. The logic of phenomenal growth as a justification to education–industry–institution links is very well substantiated by the success of German leadership in the synthetic dye industry.

Murmann's story, however, is not a complete one, as it does not explore the implications of the changed education system, though it was not the objective of their study. But the point here is that today the main discourse about changes in institutions and market–*academia* linkages would happily cite the German 'success' in support of such initiatives without looking at its other possible sociopolitical implications which Murmann does not talk about. We know that Germany experienced the rise of Nazism, an absolutely undesirable sociopolitical phenomenon, in the days after the period of Murmann's analysis. It is well known that the birth of Hitler began in school, supported by students and later the big business in Germany. Can we see a link between education, business and rise of Nazism in Germany? So far, there is no well-documented account exploring any such link (it might be our ignorance as well) but we do know that a huge number of books of art, literature and social sciences were burnt during the Nazi era. How could a well-educated country (Germany had a wonderful history of education facilities and original critical thinking) be fooled by Nazi propositions? Can we seek an explanation in the content and kind of education that was being provided at that time? Our assertion is in the affirmative. When the education system is targeted to produce only technicians, workers, professionals and managers who only know how to take orders, when the education system is devoid of any critical training in social values and ethics, and trains the students to evaluate things only in economic terms then the society becomes uncritical, undemocratic and highly individualistic. And any such society, in the case of economic crisis, may produce fascism (Togliatti, 1976). For instance, the role of education institutes such as Saraswati Shishu Mandirs is more than evident in the rise of Right-wing political forces and communal hatred in India in the last two decades. However, this crucial aspect needs to be examined exhaustively because this nexus between education–business–state has never happened before on such a large scale as under present globalization and, therefore, the perils, even with the minimum possibility, are bound to be disastrous for humanity. And for this very reason, we must explore, analyse and rethink education as a force of social transformation and democratic values.

REFERENCES

Chandru, K. (2006). "Teachers on Sale: Contract-based Teachers are now Gurus", *Combat Law*, 5(1), February-March, pp. 45–49.

Combat Law (2006).*Commodification and Cooption of Language*, 5(1), February-March, pp. 28.

Desai. Mihir (2006). 'Retreat of the Judiciary: Last Frontier Lost?' *Combat Law*, 5(1), February-March, pp. 50–52.

Freire, Paulo (1970) [1993]. *Pedagogy of the Oppressed*, Translated by Myra Bergman Ramos, London: Penguin.

Giroux, Henry (1998). "Education Incorporated?" *Educational Leadership*, 56(2), pp. 12–17.

Giroux, Henry A. (2002). "The Corporate War Against Higher Education", *Workplace*, issue 5(1), available at: http://www.louisville.edu/journal/workplace/issue5pl/giroux.html

Goldstein, Harvey (2004). "Education for All: The Globalisation of Learning Targets", *Comparative Education*, 40(1), pp. 7–14.

Gorky, Maxim (1914) [1987] "Anton Chekhov", in Anton Chekhov, *Collected Works: Volume I - Stories 180–1885,* Translated by Alex Miller & Ivy Litvinov, Moscow: Raduga, pp. 7–22.

Government of India (2005). Draft Right to Free and Compulsory Education Bill.

Harris, Kevin (1979). *Education and Knowledge: The Structured Misrepresentation of Reality,* London: Routledge and Kegan Paul.

India Today (June 5, 2006). *Top Ten Colleges,* pp. 34–57.

Khadria, Binod (2004). "Higher Education Under the WTO Regime of Trade in Services : A Critical Comment", in Kumar, Arun (ed),*Challenges*

Facing Indian Universities: Collection of Papers Based on a Seminar Organised by JNUTA on October 2, 2004 in Jawaharlal Nehru University, JNUTA, New Delhi, pp. 68–72.

Marx, Karl (1976). *Capital Vol. I,* (Translated by Ben FoWkes), Penguin, London.

McLaren, P. & Rikowski, G. (2001). Pedagogy for Revolution against Education for Capital: An E-Dialogue on Education in Capitalism Today, *Cultural Logic: An Electronic Journal of Marxist Theory and Practice,* 4, (1) at: http://eserver.org/clogic/4-1 /mclaren&rikowski html

Murmann, Johann Peter (2003). *Knowledge and Competitive Advantage,* Cambridge: OUP.

North, Douglas C. (1990). *Institutions, Institutional Change and Economic Performance: Political Economy of Institutions and Decisions,* Cambridge: CUP.

Rikowski, Glenn (2002a). "Prelude: Marxist Educational Theory After Postmodernism", in Dave Hill, Peter McLaren, Mike Cole, & Glenn Rikowski (ed), *Marxism Against Postmodernism in Educational Theory,* Oxford: Lexington, pp. 15–32.

Rikowski, Glenn (2002b). "Education, Capital and the Trans Human", in Dave Hill, Peter McLaren, Mike Cole, & Glenn Rikowski (ed), *Marxism Against Postmoderninsm in Educational Theory,* Oxford: Lexington, pp. 111–143.

Sadgopal, Anil (2006). 'Privatisation of Education: An Agenda of the Global Market, *Combat Law,* 5(1), February–March, pp. 22–27'

Spence, Michael (1973). "Job Market Signalling", *The Quarterly Journal of Economics,* 87(3), pp. 355–374

Tilak, Jandhyala B.G. (1992) Student Loans in Financing Higher Education in India, *Higher Education* 23(4), 389–404.

Tilak, Jandhyala B.G. (1996). Higher education under structural adjustment, *Journal of Indian School of Political Economy* 8(2) (April-June), 266–293.

Tilak, Jandhyala B. G. (2005). "Are We Marching Towards Laissez-faireism in Higher Education Development?" *Journal of International Cooperation in Education* 8 (1) (April): 153–165.

Times of India, Delhi Times, (July 2, 2006), *International Curriculum Produces Original Thinkers,* p 1.

Togliatti, Palmiro (1976). *Lectures on Fascism,* New York: International Publishers.

WTO, Council for Trade in Services (September 23, 1998), *Education Services: Background Note by the Secretariat,* S/C/W/49, available at: http://www.esib.org/ commodification/documents/education_wto_backgroundpap.pdf

WTO, Trade in Services Division (October 1999), *An Introduction to the GATS,* available at: http://www.esib.org/commodification/documents/introgatswto.pdf

Chapter 19

Safeguarding Education as Public Good and Regulating Private Providers*

Kishore Singh

INTRODUCTION

Education is a fundamental human right and a core responsibility of governments. However, taking advantage of the limitations of government capacities to cope with such surging demands, private providers of education have been mushrooming, with enterprises and individual proprietors entering this field. Privatization is making inroads in education at all levels.

The phenomenon of education as an attractive business is assuming alarming proportions, with scant control by pubic authorities. Under the spell of neoliberal ideology, states are in fact withdrawing in favour of privatization in education which aggravates marginalization and exclusion in education and creates inequities in society. It negatively affects the right to education both as entitlement and as empowerment. Moreover, it depletes public investment in education as an essential public service. Public policies should critically look into repercussions of privatization in education and put in place a strong regulatory

---

Social Change: June 2015: Vol. 45, No. 2, 308–23.

This chapter is based on the Report (A/69/402, 24 September 2014), presented to the United Nations General Assembly on 27 October 2014 by the United Nations Special Rapporteur on the Right to Education.

framework, with sanctions in all cases of abusive practices by private providers.

PRIVATIZATION IN EDUCATION: AN OVERVIEW

Providing public education is the primary responsibility of states. Education can also be provided by non-state actors including religious institutions,[1] non-governmental organizations, community-based groups,[2] trusts, enterprises and individual proprietors.

International universal education targets in conjunction with economic liberalization policies have led to the push for an increase in private provision as a way to introduce market competition into the education space. One can witness the explosive growth of privatized education, particularly for-profit education. As stated in the concept note for Commonwealth Ministerial Working Group on the Post-2015 Development Framework for Education (2013), the reconfiguration of public services within neoliberal globalization has placed education squarely in the headlamps of the private sector.[3]

A number of scholars have looked critically into the neoliberal model of schooling, entailing 'State withdrawal in favour of privatization' with 'market-anchored conceptions of schooling', and engineering and legitimizing a departure from decades of the welfare state (Zajada, 2006: 4, 6, 9). Civil society organizations have also expressed concern with the profound impact of privatization in education globally as a key emerging issue regarding the realization of the right to education.

Private providers find it lucrative to provide early childhood care and education, which has remained scantly covered by public education system. In most developing countries, the public education system in this respect is rudimentary and private providers find this an open market for catering to the working families and the middle class.

One can witness growth of private providers in the field of basic education, though such education is a core responsibility of governments. Private education is being promoted due to the lack of sufficient public provision of education or underperforming public schools. The emergence of low-fee private schools further undermines public schools.

Private higher education has become the fastest-growing segment worldwide (Altbach & Levy, 2005; Tilak, 2006)—in many countries, private higher education institutions 'represent the clear majority' (Kinser, 2010). Sponsored by a range of entities such as individual proprietors or profit-seeking business interests, such institutions 'involve new international branch campuses and foreign investment and ownership of local institutions'.[4] New nomenclature of the head of private higher institution—'chief executive officer'—denotes their conception analogous to those of enterprises and business.

REPERCUSSIONS OF PRIVATIZATION ON PRINCIPLES AND NORMS UNDERPINNING THE RIGHT TO EDUCATION

A recent study, with an in-depth analysis of issues in private actors in education in the past decade, demonstrates how education itself is being recast as a sector and increasingly opened up to profit making and trade, and to agenda setting by private, commercial interests. Privatization is penetrating into almost all aspects of the education endeavour—from the administrative apparatus to policymaking, and from formal provision in education settings to out-of-school activities, such as private tutoring. This study provides insights into different forms of the private in education, the consequences for individuals and societies, and stakes involved, and shows how the learner is increasingly conceptualized as a consumer, and education a consumer good (Macpherson, Robertson & Walford, 2014).

Another document prepared by the United Nations Educational, Scientific and Cultural Organization (UNESCO) International Institute for Educational Planning, and Organisation Internationale de la Francophonie also highlights similar developments, expressing similar concerns with privatization in education, reducing education to a commodity:

> with diversification in the field of education, the private providers—
> international or local—are more and more numerous. International
> consortiums have specialized in 'selling' education. Number of local
> personalities, (including many teachers, and even educational authori-
> ties) create schools for profit, turning to rather wealthy families with

slogans extolling the quality, or turn toward the disadvantaged public with altruistic slogans, which hide often the profit or political character of their endeavours (...). One can witness above all the emergence of quasi market phenomenon.[5]

Public policies should critically look into repercussions of privatization in education, bearing in mind the principles and norms underpinning the right to education and the state's responsibility under human rights law.

Principle of Non-discrimination

The UNESCO Convention against Discrimination in Education prohibits discrimination in education based, inter alia, upon 'national or social origin', 'economic condition' or 'birth' which has the purpose of nullifying or impairing equality of treatment in education. It provides that 'Discrimination includes any distinction, exclusion, limitation or preference' (Article 1). The United Nations Committee on Economic, Social and Cultural Rights has interpreted Articles 2(2) and 3 (relating to non-discrimination) of the International Covenant on Economic, Social and Cultural Rights in the light of the UNESCO Convention.[6] Discrimination on grounds of 'social origin' and 'property' is prohibited under the Convention on the Rights of the Child.[7] 'Property' as a key element in capacity to pay is an impediment to universal access to education by every child.

Thus, access to private schools, based upon capacity to pay fees, which in many cases can be exorbitant, flies in the face of prohibited grounds of discrimination based notably on 'social origin', 'economic condition', 'birth' or 'property' in international human rights conventions. The increasing privatization of fee-paying, for-profit schools entails discrimination and inequalities in education for disadvantaged children by creating a system that privileges the 'haves' over the 'have-nots', with the risk of developing a two-speed education system.[8]

Principle of Equality of Opportunity in Education

Privatization in education privileges access to education by the privileged. It throws overboard the fundamental principle of equality of opportunity in education, which is common to almost all international human rights treaties.[9] The Resolution on the Right to Education adopted by the Human Rights Council in 2011 urges 'all States to give full effect to the right to education by, inter alia, promoting equality of opportunity in education in accordance with their human rights obligations'.[10]

Privatization is a key factor resulting in unprecedented disparities in access to education. 'The difference between the poor man's school and the rich man's school is becoming starker with each passing year.'[11] Inequalities in opportunities for education will be exacerbated by the growth of unregulated private providers of education, with economic condition, wealth or property becoming the most important criterion to have access to education.

Principle of Social Justice and Equity

Education is instrumental in 'promoting development, social justice and other human rights'.[12] The principle of social justice, which is at the core of global mission of the United Nations to promote development and human dignity, is of perennial importance for bridging the widening gap between rich and poor, and making education an equalizing force and harnessing it for common well-being. This is crucial as the low-fee private schools 'not only constrain social justice in education, privileging access for some over others, but also social justice through education' as their raison d'être is 'monetizing access' to education.[13] This entrenches a neoliberal vision of society at the cost of a humanitarian view of society where human capital is prioritized. It is important to recall the General Assembly resolution: 'Future We Want' which underlines the importance of the 'right to quality education' and expresses resolve of the international community to work for a 'world that is just, equitable and inclusive'.[14] Public debate that can be raised on fundamental justice questions posed by forces of globalization[15] is laudable and deserves to be carried further as being critically important.

Principle of Preserving Education as a Public Good

The privatization has profound adverse impact on education as it purports to 'recast education not as a public or societal good grounded in democratic principles of justice and equal opportunity but as an individual, atomized and personalized private good...'.[16] The importance of preserving social interest in education while promoting the concept of education as public good is of paramount importance (Tilak, 2008). This is invaluable in fostering the humanistic mission of education. This is also crucial for enhancing public investment in education. It provides a conceptual frame for regulating private providers of education so that the social interest in education is not sacrificed for the sake of private profit. The 'State is the custodian of quality education as a public good'[17] and this must become a guiding factor in public policies vis-à-vis private providers. The state is both guarantor and regulator of education. Understanding the multifaceted role of the state in education is a precondition for critically analysing educational institutions and their responsibility for preserving education as a public good.[18]

REGULATING PRIVATE PROVIDERS: STATE RESPONSIBILITY

Legal framework or policy responses are inadequate or non-existent in private higher education where demand-absorbing institutions representing mostly lower-level and lower-quality institutions cater to the surging demands for education, many of these acting much like 'for-profit form' with 'loosened government regulations' or 'in a regulatory vacuum'.[19]

The state is primarily responsible for providing education. Article 13 of the International Covenant, mentioned earlier, clearly regards 'States as having principal responsibility for the direct provision of education in most circumstances; States parties recognize, for example, that the development of a system of schools at all levels shall be actively pursued' (Article 13 (2) (e)).[20] The state also has the obligation to safeguard the right to education in case of its violation. The 'violations of article 13 include the failure to take "deliberate, concrete and targeted" measures towards the progressive realization of secondary, higher and fundamental education'.[21] Regulating private providers is one of the key challenges for public policy.

States must establish and maintain a transparent and effective system which monitors the right to education and regulates private providers. As the countries of the Francophonie have stated, the state is the legitimate authority which enjoys full prerogatives for exercising a regulation covering all levels of education system. The state must notably prescribe rules; define all levels and modalities of certification of students' learning by legitimizing the academic titles and diplomas, control and evaluate the activities of private providers and sanction the private providers who do not respect the rules.[22]

States must accordingly develop national legislation. As an example, one can cite the Education Law (1995) of People's Republic of China which provides that 'Educational activities must conform with the public interest of the State and society' (Article 8) and that 'No organization or individual may operate a school or any other type of educational institution for profit' (Article 25). Ecuador provides another example. Ecuador's Constitution (2008) which ushered in a new model for the state[23] underscores that education shall respond to public interest and will not be subservient to individual or corporate interests (Article 28).

SOME KEY ISSUES REQUIRING SPECIAL ATTENTION

State responsibility vis-à-vis private providers relates to the negative impact of these providers on the right to education, both as entitlement and as empowerment.

Impact of Privatization on Right to Education as Entitlement

Entitlement to education in terms of universal access, especially to basic education, is an essential prerequisite for the exercise of the right to education.

One of the pernicious consequences of private education is that it undermines universal access to education as this is dependent upon high costs for education. This is beyond the reach of the marginalized and the poor who need education most. Often, admission criterion in private institutions is not based on merit or capacity, but the ability to pay, irrespective of merit. This is in contravention of the basic norm laid by the Universal Declaration of Human Rights and by the international human rights conventions. Those who are wealthy can afford to obtain education in spite of their being less meritorious as compared to those from lower economic strata.

Research shows that the scheme of 'vouchers purported to provide economically disadvantaged parents the means to select a private school in fact promotes group differentiation'.[24] It has failed in quality education. The proposition in the Oxfam Briefing Paper[25] that it must be discontinued deserves full support. Courts have also declared in the USA that school voucher funding is unconstitutional, and that public money being used to pay private school tuition should instead be going to public schools.[26]

Provision of basic education free of costs is not only a core obligation of states but also a moral imperative. Social protests against exorbitant fee increases in education, especially in privatized higher education, are well known. Chile became a glaring example of sacrificing social interest in education in favour of privatization in 2011, where protests against such privatization demanding an end to for-profit educational institutions involving high cost for students were violently suppressed by police forces resulting in killing of a student.[27]

Impact of Privatization on Right to Education as Empowerment

Privatization in education also negatively affects the right to education as empowerment in terms of knowledge, values and skills acquired and their quality. The phenomenon of low-fee private schools is projected as an affordable means of getting quality education. However, there is no evidence that 'private schools do anything different to induce more learning than do public schools, (…) many private schools do worse than public schools' (Zajada, 2006: 9, 10). An unregulated free market in higher education may lead to investments in the sector by low-quality providers. There have been instances when fraudulent practices have come to light in which admission rules are relaxed, the evaluation process is distorted and examinations are faked in different ways.[28]

Quality in private schools is also compromised by lack of respect for status of teachers. Many underqualified and underpaid teachers are employed by low-fee private schools, which are run by small and large enterprises. Besides, in some cases, teachers are employed on a temporary basis with no perspective of career. Nor are they provided in-service training for professional development.

Raising Profile of Education as a Core Public Service and as a Social Responsibility

State remains primarily responsible for education on account of international legal obligations and cannot divest itself of such responsibility. This is its core public service function. As the Supreme Court of the United States of America stated in the historic judgement in the Brown v. Board of Education (1954), 'Providing public schools ranks at the very apex of the function of a State' and 'education is perhaps the most important function of State and local governments'.[29] State obligations remain in case of privatization of education.[30] The state cannot abandon its primary responsibility above all for free basic education of quality to the advantage of private providers, who find inadequacies of public education system a fertile ground for making money out of provision of education, reaping uncontrolled profits.

This is a violation of right to education, and an affront to human dignity in a world where more than 1.2 billion people are victims of poverty and where *the richest 1 per cent of the world's* population owns 40 per cent of global assets, whereas the bottom half of the world's population owns just 1 per cent of global wealth. Prioritizing education as an essential public service is imperative to stop society being tipped irrevocably into a world that only caters to the needs of the privileged few.[31] A universal approach to the provision of social services is essential to realizing their full potential as a component of transformative social policy.[32]

Privatization and Public Investment in Education

Privatization is correlated with shrinking public investment. It induces declining spending on public services, entailing decrease in education budget. Public investment in education is all the more important as education—of which both the individual and the society are beneficiaries—is a foundation for human development. As the Oxfam

Briefing Paper, already mentioned, has warned, 'Developing countries are at the greatest risk of rocketing poverty and inequality due to stagnating public spending on public services', including education.[33]

States have responsibility under international human rights law to provide resources for the right to education. Governments must devote maximum public funds to education as a high development priority as a matter of norm.[34] They must also mobilize maximum domestic resources for education on an enduring basis.

Recognition of Studies and Qualification in Private Higher Education Institutions

A large number of private providers operate in various technical areas such as management, marketing, accountancy and communication, and award the diplomas and degrees, devoid of recognition in terms of equivalence or validity. Recognition of studies and qualifications in cross-border higher education is a critical area for regulations. This phenomenon refers to movement of people, projects, programmes and providers across political boundaries including exchange and study programmes, international branch campuses, some form of distant education, joint degree programmes and direct foreign ownership or investment in domestic educational institutions comparable to foreign investment in education.[35]

Online or correspondence providers often operate from locations with no controls at all and offer their own award, free from regulation. Public authorities must find ways of preventing underqualified or fraudulent providers from trading as universities and from issuing worthless qualifications when the providers are based overseas and operating via the Internet.[36]

PRIVATE-PUBLIC PARTNERSHIPS

If private sector has to be made a partner in development with social interest in education, then public policies should foster contribution to education as a priority in terms of corporate social responsibility.[37]

As in developed countries, governments should lay down a legal framework for fostering institutionalized collaboration with enterprises and industry, as this is weak in developing countries. Rich experience available in developed countries, along with the legal framework in particular with respect to the dual system of apprenticeship training in schools and in enterprises based on agreed framework, is most pertinent to the developing world for forging public–private partnership while preserving social responsibility in education.[38]

OVERSIGHT AND REGULATING MECHANISMS: SANCTIONING ABUSIVE PRACTICES BY PRIVATE PROVIDERS

One of the most significant failures of states in face of the privatization of education is the lack of oversight and regulating mechanisms. A potential consequence of the lack of monitoring is that this can create or contribute to a culture that lacks accountability and encourages illegal or exploitative practices. In the absence of a regulatory framework, ill-informed and naive students can be duped by new private universities only in name, established without credentials and recognition.

'The mercantalisation of education and its uncontrolled liberalization, open to all operators for lucrative purposes or objectives is contrary to international commitments by States and national values, and it must be stopped, and sanctioned.'[39] The states have the obligation under human rights law to establish conditions and standards for private education providers and maintain a transparent and effective system to monitor these standards[40] with sanctions in case of abusive practices.

Education is unfortunately becoming a victim of corruption[41] and corruption by private providers remains unscathed due to the lack of financial regulations, lack of scrutiny of their operations and of control mechanisms. As a result, delivery of primary or basic education can be made as a family business by running a school in a private house. Besides, in some cases, teachers in private schools get in hand less than what the proprietors make them declare on paper. Private schools even engage teachers employed by public schools to teach, which is not above board.

By definition, business is profit oriented. Education is all the more attractive as it denotes a certain respectability, which can be projected to disguise business interests, fraudulent practices and corruption. Huge amount of donations demanded by private providers in India as contribution to school development and so on are practices which require strict regulation and sanctions. As a regulator, states must sanction abusive practices by private education establishments. The president of Ecuador closed after investigation and evaluation in 2012, in conformity with constitutional law and Higher Education Act,[42] 14 universities devoid of quality and engaged in education as business.

ROLE OF THE JUDICIARY WITH RESPECT TO THE JUSTICIABILITY OF OPERATIONS BY PRIVATE EDUCATION PROVIDERS

Private providers in education are accountable to the state and to the public for their activities as demonstrated by a large number of court rulings worldwide. The Supreme Court of Nepal issued a verdict demanding that educational authorities devise reform programmes to control private schools—regulating fees, prohibiting the sale of unregistered and overpriced textbooks, and limiting the number of private schools gaining accreditation.[43] In another case, the South African Constitutional Court found that the primary positive obligation with respect to the right to education rests on the state.[44] In a landmark decision, the Supreme Court of India ruled that when the government grants recognition to private educational institutions, it creates an agency to fulfil its obligation to enable the citizens to enjoy the right to education. 'Charging a capitation fee in consideration of admission to educational institutions is a patent denial of a citizen's right to education under the Constitution.'[45]

Existing jurisprudence enables us to better understand obligations which the right to education imposes upon private providers. For example, the Constitutional Court of Colombia ruled in 1997 that excluding pupils on an economic basis only from schools violates their right to education.[46] The court also ruled that because of the fundamental character of the right to education, private schools are bound by specific obligations.[47]

Since education is a social responsibility—involving parents, community, teachers, students and other stakeholders—they can have recourse to complaints procedures and human rights protection mechanisms in cases of violation of the right to education, abusive practices and corruption by private providers. A system which provides the possibility for any entity or individual to initiate legal action in case of abusive practices by private providers as public interest litigation should be encouraged.

CONCLUSIONS AND RECOMMENDATIONS

There is a growing recognition that market-centred approaches to development have exacerbated various forms of inequality. Abusive practices by private providers denote the failure of states to adequately monitor and regulate privatized education. This calls for strengthening human rights mechanisms to effectively address and sanction violations of the right to education by private providers. In this, governments can be inspired by numerous decisions by courts and emerging jurisprudence. It is imperative to create a global movement which urges all the governments of the world to take seriously the task of regulating privatization in education, respecting the principle of social justice.

Primary Responsibility of States for Provision of Education

States remain primarily responsible for providing education on account of their international legal obligations. They should not abandon their primary responsibility, above all, for the provision of free basic quality education, to the advantage of private providers, who find inadequacies of public education a fertile ground for making money out of the provision of education, reaping uncontrolled profits.

Comprehensive Regulatory Framework Governing Private Providers of Education

States should develop a regulatory framework which should govern the privatization of education. Such a framework should be inspired by general principles of social justice and equity as well as by education as a public good, subjecting private providers to full accountability of their operations and to rigorous scrutiny. It should be comprehensive so as to apply to private education providers at all levels from preschool through basic education to higher education, including cross-border higher education and online or correspondence providers. No private higher education institution should be allowed to operate without prior approval and recognition by competent public authorities.

States should put an end to market-driven education reforms providing subsidies to private education. They should not allow and promote low-cost private schools and the provision of school vouchers and so on nor should they allow 'for-profit institutions' in education.

Monitoring and Controlling Private Providers: Transparent and Effective System

States have the obligation under human rights law to establish conditions and standards for private education providers and to maintain a transparent and effective system to monitor these standards with sanctions in case of non-adherence. Such monitoring should also include teaching profession. To that end, states should strengthen human rights control mechanisms to look into the negative impact of privatization, especially to ensure that private providers remain respectful of minimum standards in education and of quality norms, and that they are not allowed to charge exorbitant fees.

Controlling Abusive Practices by Private Providers

Corruption by private providers remains unscathed due to the lack of financial regulations, lack of scrutiny of their operations and of control mechanisms. Nationally designated authorities should undertake a full-scale investigation of fraudulent practices including tax evasions by private providers who reap profits in the name of education. States should ensure that financial operations of all private providers are regularly scrutinized.

Governments should foster the possibility for any entity or individual to initiate legal action in case of abusive practices by private providers as public interest litigation.

Revitalizing and Valourizing Education as an Essential Public Service

Learning from the devastating impact of structural adjustments on education as an essential public service and in face of the prevalent market ideology and privatization in education, countries must recognize the paramount importance of public investment in education as an essential obligation of the state and as a foundation for development. Instead of giving subsidies to private providers, governments should provide the maximum possible resources to public education, with equity-driven initiatives to expand educational opportunities for the marginalized and the poor. A paradigm shift is required so that instead of providing financial support to private providers, states must regulate them. Under no circumstances should a state provide financial support to a private provider of education.

Public-Private Partnership and Mobilizing Investment in Education as a Social Responsibility

States should devise innovative mechanisms for mobilizing national resources for education as part of public–private partnerships. If private sector has to be made a partner in development, then public policies should seek to harness corporate social responsibility to foster contribution to education as a social welfare priority. In all types of partnerships with industry and the private sector, overall responsibility of states remains.

Education is a core public function of the state. It is also a social responsibility, and when states encourage the private sector to be a partner in education development, it should ensure full respect for the public interest. Education is a public good. As a noble cause, it can generate social support and induce public contribution in a philanthropic spirit, if properly encouraged by policies of good governance in the education system.

Making Education System an Equalizing Force

The monitoring function of the state should aim at upholding the fundamental principles of non-discrimination and of equality of opportunity in education. A daunting challenge for public policymakers is to transform education systems into a force for equality. This must be of particular concern to education policy planners to address the impact of privatized education to aggravate inequalities and marginalization in societies.

Preserving Education as a Public Good and Fostering Humanistic Mission of Education

Education benefits both the individual and the society, and it must be preserved as public good so that the social interest is protected against the commercial interests in privatized education. Public authorities should not allow private providers to vitiate the humanistic objectives of education. Humanistic mission of education should be valued and preserved not only by state but also by all key players and stakeholders in education.

Reporting Obligations of Private Providers

It should be obligatory for all private providers to report regularly to designated public authorities on their financial operations including the proceeds of profit and dividends. Such authorities should scrutinize their financial accounts, guided by the principle of human right and of social responsibility in education. Information on operations of private providers in education so scrutinized should be disseminated at large in public interest.

No private school or educational establishment should be allowed to operate unless its credentials and standards are verified by designated public authorities.

Strengthening Human Rights Control Mechanisms

In an endeavour to regulate private providers in education, governments should strengthen existing human rights mechanisms or create special mechanisms, with the mandate to regularly oversee operations of private providers. Such mechanisms should have *suo moto* investigatory power. Governments should implement recommendations made by such mechanisms.

Government should also establish a mechanism to register and process any complaints received with respect to abusive practices by private providers of education and investigate all violations of the right to education.

Fostering Public Interest Litigation

Numerous decisions by courts exist to safeguard the right to education. Public interest litigation centring around breaches of the right to education and abusive practices by private providers must be promoted and supported.

Encouraging and Supporting the Role of Intellectual Community and Civil Society Organizations

The intellectual community and the civil society organizations should be encouraged to expose the negative effects of privatization in education, upholding the principles of social justice and equity. Research, events and expert consultations on the effects of privatization on the exercise and enjoyment of the right to education should be encouraged and supported.

NOTES

1. Liberty of parents and guardians to ensure the religious and moral education of their children in conformity with their own convictions is recognized in international human rights conventions. This should be subject to 'such minimum educational standards as may be laid down or approved by the State' (Article 13(3) of the International Covenant on Economic, Social and Cultural Rights). Such education is primarily not driven by profit or business considerations.

2. A community can construct or establish schools for basic education, assuming social responsibility in education and, in some cases, these are taken over by government later on. The primary purpose is not business through education but to supplement governments efforts. There are also educational establishments for philanthropic purposes, which are again not business driven but promotional of education as a public good.

3. For a scholarly analysis of issues involved, see Commonwealth Ministerial Working Group on the Post-2015 Development Framework for Education: Technical Meeting on Advocacy Strategy Development, London, 18 and 19 September 2013.

4. Ibid., p. 1.

5. 'La régulation du systèmeéducatif: une obligation pour atteindrel'équité et améliorer la qualité', UNESCO International Institute for Educational Planning, Organisation Internationale de la Francophonie, Wallonie Bruxelles, 2014 (p. 7). See also Nambissan (2012).

6. General Comment 13 on the Right to Education (Article 13 of the Covenant), E/C.12/1999/10, 2, December 1999 paras. 31 and 33.

7. The Convention on the Rights of the Child states that 'State Parties shall respect and ensure the rights set forth in the present Convention to each child within their jurisdiction without discrimination of any kind, irrespective of the child's or his or her parents or legal guardian's race, colour, sex, language, political or other opinion, national, ethnic or social origin, property, disability, birth or other status' (Article 2 §1).

8. Report by the Global Initiative for Economic, Social and Cultural Rights: Morocco. http://goo.gl/MTGua8 (last accessed 20 August 2014).

9. Report by the UN Special Rapporteur on the Right to Education: Equality of Opportunity in Education and Normative Action, A/HRC/17/29, 18 April 2011.

10. A/RES/HRC 17/3.

11. Inaugural address by Atal Bihari Vajpayee, former Prime Minister of India at the third meeting of the High-Level Group on Education for All, organised in Delhi in 2003.

12. Global Corruption Report: Education, Routledge, 2013, Foreword by the High Commissioner for Human Rights.

13. Ian Macpherson 'Interrogating the Private-School "Promise" of Low-Fee Private Schools' in Macpherson, Robertson and Walford (2014: 296).

14. A/Resolution 66/288, 27 July 2012.

15. For an insightful analysis, see Macpherson, Robertson and Walford (2014: 9–22).

16. Ian Macpherson 'Interrogating the Private-School "Promise" of Low-Fee Private Schools' op. cit., p. 295.

17. Final Statement, Global Education for All Meeting, Muscat, 12–14 May 2014, UNESCO, Paris.

18. As regards the role of the state in education, see Zajada (2006, Introduction).

19. For a detailed account, see The Global Growth of Private Higher Education: ASHE Higher Education Report, Volume 36, No. 3, 2010 (executive summary).

20. General Comment 13 on the Right to Education (Article 13 of the Covenant), op cit., para. 48.

21. Ibid., para. 59.

22. 'Plaidoyersurl'importance du rôledel'Etatdans la régulation de la qualité et de l'équité de l'éducation', Conférence des Ministres de l'Education des Etats et gouvernements de la francophonie (CONFEMEN), 56e session, Abidjan, Cote d'Ivoire, 12 July 2014

23. A/HRC/WG.6/13/ECU/1, para. 4.

24. Ian Macpherson, 'Interrogating the Private-School "Promise" of Low-Fee Private Schools' in Macpherson, Robertson and (2014: 21).

25. 'Working for the Many: Public Services Fight Inequality', Oxfam Briefing Paper 182, 3 April 2014, available on www.oxfam.org (last accessed 20 August 2014).

26. Ruling by Louisiana Supreme Court, May 2013, http://www.washingtonpost. com/blogs/answer-sheet/wp/2013/05/07/louisiana-supreme-court-rules-school-voucher-funding-unconstitutional/ (last accessed 20 August 2014).

27. Statement by the UN Special Rapporteur on the Right to Education, 11 September 2011.

28. Hallak & Poisson (2007), cited in John Fielden & N. V. Varghese, 'Regulatory Issues', in A New Dynamic: Private Higher Education, World Conference on Higher Education (WCHE), UNESCO, 2009, p. 71.

29. Wisconsin v. Yoder, 406 U.S.205, 92 S. Ct. 1526, 32 L.Ed.2d 15 (1972), as cited in Education Law, Education Series, Chapter 4, 'Students Rights', Law Journal Press, New York, 2002.

30. General Comment 13 on the Right to Education, op. cit. (paras. 46 and 47).

31. 'Working for the Many: Public Services Fight Inequality', Oxfam Briefing Paper 182, 3 April 2014, available on www.oxfam.org

32. Social Inclusion and the Post-2015 Sustainable Development Agenda: UNITAR's Briefing for Delegates: 'Post-2015 Development', Paper prepared by UNRISD, April 2014, p. 5.

33. 'Working for the Many: Public services fight inequality', op. cit.

34. Report by the United Nations Special Rapporteur on the Right to Education on Financing of Basic Education and Legal Framework, (A/66/269), 5 August 2011.

35. The Global Growth of Private Higher Education: (introduction): ASHE Higher Education Report, Volume 36, No. 3, 2010, p. 107.

36. John Fielden & N.V.Varghese, 'Regulatory Issues', in A New Dynamic: Private Higher Education, World Conference on Higher Education (WCHE), UNESCO, 2009, pp. 84–85.

37. It may be recalled that UN General Assembly resolution: 'Future We Want' recognized 'the importance of corporate social responsibility' A/RES. 66/288, 27 July 2012, para. 46.

38. For more details, see A/67/310.

39. 'Plaidoyersurl'importance de rôlesurl'Etatdans la régulation de la qualité et de l'équité de l'éducation', op. cit.

40. See Guiding Principles on Business and Human Rights: Implementing the United Nations 'Protect, Respect and Remedy' Framework, A/HRC/17/31 (2011).

41. *Global Corruption Report: Education*, Routledge, 2013—Preface by Huguette Labelle, Chair, Transparency International.
42. Higher education institutions in Ecuador must be guided by, inter alia, the principles of social responsibility and accountability and established quality standards and accreditation procedures. Higher Education Act.
43. Open Equal Free http://www.openequalfree.org/nepali-private-schools-banned-from-raising-fees/19112.
44. Constitutional Court of South Africa, Governing Body of the Juma Musjid Primary School & Others v Essay N.O. and Others, Case CCT 29/10 (2011), especially para 57.
45. *Miss Mohini Jain vs State of Karnataka And Ors*, AIR 1858, 1992 SCR (3) 658.
46. Sentencia C-560/97, Demanda de inconstitucionalidad contra el artículo 203 (parcial) de la Ley 115 de 1994.
47. Colombian Constitutional Court, Case T-211/95, 12 May 1995.

REFERENCES

Altbach, Philip G., & Levy, Daniel C. (2005). *Private higher education: A global revolution—global perspectives on higher education*. Rotterdam and Taipei: Sense Publishers.

Kinser, Kevin et al. (2010). *The global growth of private higher education. ASHE Higher Education Report* (Vol. 36, No. 3), San Francisco: Jossey-Bass.

Macpherson, Ian, Robertson, Susan, & Walford, Geoffrey. (Eds). (2014). *Education, privatisation and social justice: Cases studies from Africa, South Asia and South East Asia*. Oxford, UK: Symposium Books Limited.

Nambissan, Geetha B. (2012). Private schools for the poor-business as usual? (Special article). *Economic & Political Weekly*, 47(41), 51–58.

Tilak, Jandhyala B.G. (2006). Private higher education: Philanthropy to profits. *In Higher Education in the World: The Financing of Universities*, Global University Network for Innovation, Barcelona and Palgrave Macmillan, pp. 113–125

Tilak, Jandhyala B.G. (2008). Higher education: A public good or a commodity for trade? Commitment *to* higher education *or* commitment *of* higher education to trade, *Prospects* (UNESCO) 38 (4) (December), 449–466

Zajada, J. (Ed.). (2006). *Decentralization and privatisation in education: The role of the state*. Fitzroy, Australia: Springer.

Chapter 20

Promising but Perplexing Solutions[*]
A Critique of the Draft National Education Policy 2019

Jandhyala B. G. Tilak

The first National Policy on Education was formulated in 1968, nearly 18 years after a newly Independent India became a republic and after development planning was launched in the country. Exactly 18 years later came the second National Education Policy in 1986 which was partly modified and adopted in 1992. During the last several years, the need for another policy was increasingly felt, given the significantly changing landscape in all spheres of development in the socio, economic, political, demographic and technological domains, especially in education in India and at the global level. The Government of India initiated measures to develop such a policy with the constitution of a committee of experts headed by T. S. R. Subramanian in 2015: this report was not found acceptable by the government (Government of India, 2015b). Subsequently, another 10-member committee was formed in 2017 under the chairmanship of K. Kasturirangan which submitted its report in June 2019 (Government of India, 2019). It

* *Social Change:* December 2019: Vol. 49, No. 4, 686–712.

This is an edited version of the A. N. Sinha Memorial Lecture delivered at the A. N. Sinha Institute of Social Studies, Patna, on 22 August 2019. Comments and observations on a previous draft received from Dipankar Gupta, Arvind Gupta, M. Anandkrishnan, C. Rammanohar Reddy, J. Veera Raghavan, Surinder Kumar and N. Balakrishnan are gratefully acknowledged. Usual disclaimers apply.

needs to be noted that this report should not be considered as policy *per se,* as is being claimed, but it is essentially a report that can form the basis of framing a National Policy on Education. After all, it is the prerogative of the government to frame any national policy. The final policy document may not necessarily include all proposals made by the committee nor does it need to be confined in principle to the proposals made in the report. Once the final policy is made, strategies, plans and programmes for implementation will have to be prepared in the form of a plan/programme of action, as was done in the case of the 1986 National Policy (Government of India, 1987).

With this understanding, I feel it more appropriate to refer to the document of the Kasturirangan Committee as a draft report rather than a draft policy. This chapter provides a short critical appraisal of the report. Neither exhaustive in scope nor thorough in depth, it comments on some selected issues that have been raised, some are path-breaking and bold, many deserve applause but quite a few require rethinking.

The committee under the chairmanship of K. Kasturirangan prepared the voluminous Draft National Education Policy, though it was not as voluminous as the Report of the Education Commission prepared under the chairmanship of D. S. Kothari in 1966 which was based on extensive research on a variety of issues in education and formed the basis for the formulation of the 1968 policy (Government of India, 1966). The draft was not as critical of the present system as the background report 'Challenge of Education' prepared by the Government of India (1985) in the context of the 1986 National Policy. This is partly because the research base of the present report is rather limited.

The present report opens with a vision for a national education system, drawing on a lot of areas—starting from a human right's perspective on education (*à la* United Nations' Declaration of Human Rights) approach articulated by the Jacques Delors Commission (International Commission on Education for the Twenty-first Century, 1996) to the global Sustainable Development Goals, on the one hand, and from India's rich heritage to the recent education policies and developments especially since 1986, on the other, the committee has proposed a long transformative agenda consisting of a series of major reforms covering the entire education system—from preschool to higher education including higher professional and technical education and research. I wish however that, on the one hand, the 1968 policy and the Kothari Commission Report of 1966 and, on the other, the plethora of development schemes that have been launched during the last three decades, not just the Right to Education (RTE) Act 2009, had also formed some basis of the draft.

The committee recognizes some major challenges that education faces in India and recommends the launch of far-reaching changes at all levels of education—from the pre-primary to higher, including higher general and professional/technical and research. Universal access to high-quality education has been given the highest priority by the committee; it has been recognized as an essential element for building an equitable and vibrant knowledge society. The committee aims at developing an 'integrated yet flexible approach' to education and liberal arts (defined as 'knowledge of many arts') approach in higher education focusing on high-quality research that facilitates the transformation of the education system which in turn will contribute significantly to national development. It aims at evolving an 'India-centred' education system focussing on Indian values and its rich heritage.

In a neoliberal age, dominated by markets in every area, including education in India, one will be pleased to see clear statements and a host of phrases in the report, such as education is a '(basic) public good', 'criticality of public education', 'education must be a not-for-profit activity', 'education and schools are not marketable goods', 'highest priority is accorded to the task of ensuring universal access to an education of high quality and breadth', 'public funding must be committed to and given to public institutions', 'corrupt and substandard "institutions" cannot and must not be allowed to run' and 'thousands of substandard stand-alone teacher education institutions across the country will be shut down'. These expressions however seem to be more in the nature of lofty intentions as no clear definitive strategies have been proposed by the committee to check undesirable tendencies that vitiate these aspects. For instance, in regard to profit-making institutions, quite a few measures suggested by the committee leave plenty of room for private and commercial interests to expand further and further.

With a visionary approach, noble intentions, exhortations, high aspirations, refreshing insights from global and national perspectives, classical and modern ideas, some known and some lesser-known interpretations and assertions and profound thoughts, including some seemingly utopian views and even fancy ideas, the draft provides stimulating reading on what needs to be done for Indian education in the 21st century. But sometimes, the ideas seem to be too far removed from reality and practical application, raising questions and apprehensions on how some of the prescriptions have been made. That said, this draft is an important indispensable discussion document for anyone interested in educational reforms in India (or in other countries).

Among those that prominently figure in the report, one finds a number of commendable positives, and a few important negatives having damaging implications, apart from quite a few controversial ones requiring serious discussions and reconsideration, which are discussed here under the school and higher education sectors separately. In addition, there are a few issues covering the entire system that need attention.

SCHOOL EDUCATION, THE FOUNDATIONAL STAGE

During the process of and after the formulation of the RTE (Right to Education) Act 2009, many academics, policy researchers and civil society members strongly pleaded for extending the act to cover secondary, including higher secondary, education. This approach is based on three perspectives: (a) the Convention on the Rights of the Child, the age of the child being defined up to 18 years, (b) labour market conditions that require a workforce with reasonably good education and skills which can be provided not by mere elementary education but by higher secondary education and (c) the need to look at the entire school education as a continuum. In recent years, the government seems to have been convinced about the need to extend RTE to secondary education and has taken some initiatives, including the launching of the Samagra Shiksha Abhiyan. The committee has also articulated the same goal and promised the extension of RTE to higher secondary education, until the age of 18, by providing universal free and compulsory school education with zero dropout rates. This is the first major welcome recommendation of the committee.

Second, the committee strongly feels the need for extensive curricular reforms and restructuring of pedagogy, so that the focus is on holistic development of children, developing not only digital literacy and other skills required for the 21st century but also critical thinking, moral and ethical reasoning, creativity, scientific temper and human values such as honesty, compassion, spiritual and constitutional values, a democratic outlook, commitment to liberty, justice and fairness, freedom, social responsibility and community service. The suggested reforms include a provision of flexibility and a choice for students to select subjects across music, painting, arts and sciences, humanities, sport, craft, vocational and other subjects, including other curricular and co-curricular areas such as National Social Service, National Cadet Corps, community service and other social engagement activities. Moreover, each subject should be confined to an essential core content.

The committee also suggests reforms in examinations: board examinations to test only core concepts, skills and higher order capacities. It proposes that examinations will be on a range of subjects which students can opt for and also choose the semester when they want to take those examinations. The committee recommends doing away with hard distinctions between the arts and science streams and between academic and vocational streams. It further recommends placing curricular and co-curricular subjects at par, putting them together in one category of curricular subjects.

The whole idea of providing integral education is worth commending. Quite a few academics and committees, for instance, the Yashpal Committee (Government of India, 1993), have suggested a similar restructuring of the school curriculum to reduce rote learning and to develop diverse abilities and skills among children.

The committee also focuses on recognizing ancient India's contribution to knowledge systems including specifically the fields of mathematics, astronomy, philosophy, psychology, yoga, architecture, medicine, as well as governance, polity and society, and recommends inclusion of inspiring lessons from India in the curriculum. Special prominence has been given to Sanskrit and other Indian languages and Indian culture. It also recommends launching an Indian Translation and

Interpretation Mission and the establishment of the Indian Institute of Translation and Interpretation for the translation of books, even though our experience in this regard is not very encouraging.

Fourth, to increase further access to education and also to improve the nutritional status of children, the committee recommends providing breakfast to pre-primary and primary (probably including upper primary/Grade 6 to 8) school students in addition to a midday meal. Most importantly, the issue of inequality has received close attention. The committee refers to various dimensions of inequality, especially identifying under and un-represented groups in education, and proposing measures to make education accessible to them. It argues for the creation of inclusive school environments and an inclusive curriculum.

Fifth, the entire education system, including school education, is presently suffering from a severe shortage of teachers, both in numbers and quality, reflected in the high numbers of vacant positions, untrained teachers, para and contractual teachers. Realizing the critical role that teachers play in the development of education, the committee devotes considerable space in the report to the problem of teacher education. It promises 'full' recruitment of teachers on the basis of merit in all schools and parity among teachers at all levels of school education. The committee also states that no temporary or contractual teachers will be recruited in schools or at the higher education level. So one can expect no more large numbers of vacant teaching posts and untrained teachers in schools. The committee, however, also proposes simultaneously peer instruction and a three-year tenure track system for schoolteachers, both of which require some reconsideration.

Realizing the importance of teacher education, and its pathetic state, the committee proposes sweeping reforms, beginning from the integration of teacher education with higher education, the closure of commercially motivated B.Ed colleges and other teacher education institutions to curricular reforms. Some recommendations are similar to those proposed by the Justice J. S. Verma Commission (Government of India, 2012). The committee also highlights the need for proper career management and extensive continuous professional development programmes for teachers. It further recommends that all stand-alone teacher education/training (B.Ed) colleges should be part of comprehensive higher education institutions.

Sixth, in a multilingual society, like India's, the importance of learning more than one language by students has been recognized by many. The three-language formula originally introduced in 1961 in Indian schools with English, Hindi and the local language is still considered the most suitable method for India. Most CBSE schools follow this formula. I am glad that the committee has also re-emphasized the need to follow this formula. Unfortunately, perhaps in response to political pressure, it quickly backtracked on such a sound proposal without a serious discussion. The committee finally recommended that primary or even elementary education should be in the child's mother tongue, and that students will be exposed to three or more languages which do not have to necessarily include Hindi. I wish the committee also made it clear that the use of the mother tongue as the medium of instruction at elementary/school level should be not only in government schools but also in all, including private schools. It is unfortunate that government primary schools are also introducing English as a medium of instruction. It will be good if additional languages are introduced as subjects only at the secondary level and English as a medium of instruction at the higher secondary level or in higher education. As an aside, it needs to be noted that teaching pupils to just communicate in a language (English and others) is not sufficient. We see the poor quality of graduates who are only taught communicative English or who have completed a course in communications in English. I feel that any language that is imparted should be well taught.

Seventh, the committee favours the adoption of 'school complexes' as a strategy of school development. The proposal of a school complex, originally made by the Kothari Commission, envisages strong networking of schools in a cluster involving a sharing of resources such as teachers and other infrastructure facilities. According to the committee, a complex will be formed around a cluster of around 30 public schools, ranging from the foundational to the secondary stage, all within contiguous geography. It will comprise one secondary school and all neighbourhood public schools. The complex structure will allow a sharing of resources such as playground, libraries, laboratories and sports equipment, and teachers, particularly teachers in arts, painting, music and sports. Social workers, counsellors and teacher communities will be mobilized in a complex for utilization by any school of the complex. This would help particularly small schools which have very small number of students on their rolls (nearly 28 % of primary schools and 14.8 % of upper primary schools had less than 30 students in 2016–2017), inadequate number of (one or two or zero) teachers (nearly 120,000 primary schools are single-teacher schools), and those with inadequate facilities including playgrounds, libraries and laboratories. Such small schools are considered as educationally suboptimal and 'unviable'—economically and managerially—facing threats of closure or merger. These small schools pose 'a systemic challenge for governance and management' (p. 158).

Presently, RTE norms require the provision of minimum facilities to every school, including small schools. But a number of such schools continue to suffer without these infrastructure and other facilities. In several states, such schools are either being closed or merged with nearby schools. Given this situation, a school complex as a strategy needs to be welcomed. However, there is also a danger that the government, central or, more importantly, resource-scarce states/local bodies may use this strategy as a first choice, rather than providing minimum requirements, as per the RTE norms, not only for small, unviable schools but also for medium-sized schools.

Eighth, despite several efforts in the past, vocational education at the school level or even at the higher level has not taken off for many well-known reasons. The committee now wishes all students to receive vocational education in at least one vocation in Grades 9 to 12; also for about 50 per cent of total enrolment in higher education to receive vocational education by 2025. In fact, students will be introduced to practical training in vocational subjects as early as Grade 5. This may induce values like the dignity of labour, if not exactly skills in any vocational subject. The committee also proposes to make Lok Vidya, knowledge developed in India, to be an integral part of the vocational education programme.

Now a couple of minor issues. Universal education requires all children of the relevant age group to be in schools and continue until they complete the given level. So it is not enough to achieve 100 per cent gross enrolment ratio even at secondary level, as suggested by the committee (p. 67) but also to ensure that no child of the given age group is outside the school system, or that the net enrolment ratio reaches

100 per cent. After all, we note that there is a difference between gross enrolment ratio and net (or age-specific) enrolment ratios. Perhaps it is a minor one when the committee overlooked the difference between the two. Second, though it looks minor, not to allow the private schools to use the term 'public' in their nomenclature is an important proposal. I wish a similar ban could be proposed on the use of terms such as 'college' and 'university' by unrecognized institutions of higher education and training, including coaching institutions.

Precarious Recommendations

I now wish to highlight some major recommendations made by the committee that may have an adverse impact on the development of school education.

First, in the context of universal school education, the committee recommends the adoption of multiple ways of learning including open distance learning, open basic education, open school and other ways provided through the National Institute of Open Schooling and State Institute of Open Schooling. In the same context, the committee also recommends adoption of multiple models of schools, including, apart from *gurukulas*, *pathashalas* and *madrasas*, homeschooling, alternative schools, private schools and schools under philanthropic–public partnerships, and multiple boards of assessment—national (central, state and international, including private). The committee feels that these alternatives offer greater educational choices to students.

However, the idea of creating greater educational choices for students and competition among schools (p. 71) may not be a good idea in case of public goods like education. The Western ethic of individual choice and the economic principle of ability to pay do not and should not have a place in case of education. School education, and more particularly elementary education, is considered as a pure public good and even in advanced countries, individual choices are limited. Second, after considerable discussions in the periods preceding and following the 86th Amendment to the Constitution in 2002, finally, in 2009 in the RTE Act 2009, a few parameters were evolved to define what a school is. The RTE has not favoured alternative modes of schooling, non-formal education and open education. According to the RTE, universalization has to be done through a recognized formal school system (I wish it was mentioned as a recognized formal *public* school system). While the RTE has not indicated any direction towards a desirable model like a common school system, alternative ways of learning and the alternative models of schools that the committee recommends not only go against the spirit of the RTE but also would lead us farther away from a common school system.

It has to be noted that various alternative ways of learning and alternative models of schools that exist have resulted in widening inequalities in accessing education between different socio-economic strata of society, and inequalities in the quality of education, both of which further cause inequalities in economic and social spheres. Certainly, universalization of school education might not have been possible in many countries had they depended on alternative models of schools and alternative ways of learning of the kind suggested by the committee. It is necessary to clearly realize that universalization of school education, in its proper spirit, should be attempted only through a formal public school system, which is also the experience of many advanced countries. In fact, a national policy of this kind, with a long-term vision, could have proposed measures towards gradually developing a common school system. A uniform pattern that promises a march towards a common school system should not be viewed as a 'mind-numbing uniformity'.

Second, in the same context, the committee argues for a relaxation of RTE norms regarding inputs in schools. Stating that there has been an overemphasis on inputs, it asks for a limitation of regulation on inputs to ensure the safety of children, access and inclusion, the non-profit nature of schools and minimum standards for learning outcomes. It favours the construction of schools by all parties with greater flexibility. It may be noted that even when strict norms are laid, we find after nearly 10 years, only a fraction of schools satisfying the norms laid down under the act. So any relaxation in the RTE's norms will worsen the situation in terms of the basic infrastructure of schools. After all, a good and attractive learning environment is essential to cure quite a few important persistent ills in school education such as dropouts, no/never enrolment, non-completion and poor levels of learning. Moreover, the legal nature of the RTE provided under the

RTE needs to be respected in any approach we adopt to the provision of schools and their inputs.

Both in school and higher education, it is important to note that while considerations on outcomes are important, according less importance to inputs may be counter productive, as most outcomes that we are expecting critically depend upon inputs.

Third, while the provision of adequate facilities by the state for early childcare accessible to all may be very important, as argued by many, the research evidence is mixed on its desirability and more importantly on making it a part of the free and compulsory education act and making it mandatory for parents to send their three- to five-year-old children to early childcare and education. Some researchers (Belsky, 2011; Melhuish et al., 2015 and other studies) have shown that early childcare education 'disrupts the mother–child attachment relationship, reducing opportunities for interaction, and causing infants to lose confidence in the availability and responsiveness of their parents' (Sroufe, 1988). Unless early childcare is of exceptionally high quality, packed with long hours of child interactions with mothers and childcare at home, it can produce negative effects, according to some research studies. It has been found that the 'more time children spend in various non-maternal care arrangements across the first 4.5 years of life, the more problem behaviour (that is, aggression and disobedience) and conflict with adults' occur (McCartney, 2007). Some research studies have reported 'only modest cognitive and social benefits' from early childcare and education programmes, 'which may be at least partially offset by modest negative effects on social behaviour and health' (Barnett, 2011).

There is also, of course, growing research on the other side too. Given the inconclusive research evidence, it may be better if the RTE covers schooling only from Grade 1 to Grade 12 or 6–18 years of age group with a sufficient public provision for early childcare and development facilities accessible to all children of 3–6 (in fact 0–6) age group by the Ministry of Women and Child Development, though there are quite a few powerful voices which also favour inclusion of early childcare and education in the RTE Act.

Fourth, a major recommendation made by the committee is replacing the 10+2 school system, adopted following the recommendation of the Kothari Commission, by a 'developmentally appropriate curriculum and pedagogical structure for school education' of 15 years, that is 5+3+3+4, for 3- to 18-year-old children. The first five years include three years of early childhood education and two years of early or lower primary education, which together are expected to provide a foundational literacy to all children; then three years of second half of primary schooling, which is considered as a 'preparatory stage' or 'later primary' level; three years of middle, commonly known as upper primary education and four years of secondary (secondary plus higher secondary) education.

The need to alter the structure of the school system so drastically is not sufficiently clear. Also, while we are now planning to upgrade all primary schools into elementary schools of eight years, duration to allow a smooth transition of children into upper primary education and to conform with the RTE Act, the proposed new architecture of school education adds further confusion and even leads to the splitting of the elementary level into three levels and corresponding to three levels of schools, which will have a serious effect on transition rates. Moreover, is it right to get children to formal school at such an early age? According to the committee, education starts at the age of three, while some Scandinavian countries, like Finland, have a school system that starts at the age of seven, with provisions for early childcare but not pre-primary education. The formalization of preschool programmes and regular formal schooling before the age of six may not be desirable. In fact, it may be harmful to the physical, cognitive and healthy development of children.

Another issue that needs considerable rethinking is the recommendation of introducing 3- to 8 year-old children to three languages. The committee has referred to extensive research in neurosciences in this regard. I am not sure whether it is desirable to introduce such young children to three different languages before they even become very familiar with even one. Anecdotal evidence of problems being faced by children with one language at home, sometimes two with their parents having different mother tongues, another language in school and yet another in the neighbourhood is abundant. They are good at none, and make a *kichadi* of the three languages. Hence, introduction of multiple languages at early ages may not necessarily be desirable.

Sixth, educational policies and programmes particularly those which have been introduced during the last three decades have favoured the rapid growth of private schools and private colleges, institutions deemed to be universities and universities. An aggressively expanding private sector has contributed to growth of a variety of problems, especially rampant vulgar commercialization of education and phenomenon of profit-making in education, necessitating often judicial and government interventions, which have no effect. These trends have inculcated among children more market values, selfishness, greed and unhealthy competition, and less human values, ethics and social consciousness. Echoing the feelings of several critics of private education, the committee rightly decries the profit-making nature of education and lays a special focus on universal human values, ethics and morals and Indian values. While these statements need to be welcomed, the committee does not suggest any specific mechanism to check the growth of the commercial, profit-oriented private sector. Instead, it proposes 'rejuvenation, active promotion and support for private philanthropic activity in the education sector' (p. 405); but it has to be noted that (a) under the garb of philanthropy only, profit-seeking private sector has entered this field and grown in size and power, (b) there is no school in India which is *de jure* for profit though *de facto* there are many, (c) philanthropy in general and philanthropy in education in particular have diminished to zero levels in society and (d) philanthropy has dried up in India not necessarily because of state control.

While recommending an increase in public expenditure in education, the committee also recommends the involvement of non-government organizations, private players and philanthropic activities within and outside the framework of corporate social responsibility. It expects voluntarism to make a big difference. It recommends a reliance on these sources even for 'critical needs of existing institutions' (p. 410). It also recommends the establishment of 'a new class of grant-making private institutions' (p. 409) which pool smaller private funds for support new and existing institutions. The committee recommends the government facilitating the establishment of these institutions by using the good offices of large private donors, individual trusts and so on. The experience of the last several decades should make us realize the futility of relying on the private philanthropic sector for supporting any human development area like education on a large scale. Even the Corporate Social Responsibility Act has not yielded much in the case of education. While in principle, one may not disagree with the need to encourage a philanthropic culture, the committee has unreasonably high expectations from such players.

The committee advocates unfettered freedom to private institutions in all areas, including in fixing fee levels; though of course it adds that schools 'shall not increase school fees arbitrarily. Reasonable increases that can stand public scrutiny can be made' (p. 190). But experience shows that the freedom these schools have is terribly misused that it is impossible to effectively regulate fee levels in private institutions at the school or higher levels, whatever be the existing regulating mechanism. In fact, the regulation of private schools has become an uphill task. The committee does not seem to note this or the need for a strong effective mechanism to regulate the functioning of private schools. Instead, it argues for private schools to be placed at par with public schools, and that they should be 'empowered and freed of the regulatory overload' (p. 189). It asks for 'using existing laws diligently' (p. 409) to check the growth of profiteering in education. But as we know, existing laws are highly ineffective.

The committee goes further in case of Clause 12(I)(c) of the RTE Act and states, 'the clause is not quite in tune with the principle of autonomy of institutions' and that this will be reviewed. The clause may have to be reviewed, as it directly and indirectly promotes the growth of private education, encourages the diversion of good students from public to private institutions and provides for public funding of the so-called unaided private institutions (which are even otherwise required to provide admission to weaker sections as these schools are directly and indirectly already subsidized by the state). The RTE may have to be reviewed as it unnecessarily exempts quite a few government and non-government schools from coming under its purview for many other reasons but not for the reason that the committee observes that it is against the principle of autonomy to these private institutions. Canons of a welfare state require the sacrifice of private autonomy and individual freedom for the common good. One would expect the committee to note the need for and argue for tougher mechanisms to effectively regulate the growth and operations of private schools. Instead, it is too soft towards the private sector. It may not be appropriate to treat public and private institutions at par in matters of regulation. The proposal to make regulation 'light but tight' may end up with a 'light and light' regulatory mechanism contributing further to unregulated, unplanned and chaotic growth of private education.

Ninth, the committee recommends, rather it endorses, the government's recent amendment to the RTE on the abolition of the nondetention system in schools and the conducting of examinations at the end of Grades 3, 5 and 8. When the RTE provided for the nondetention of students until Grade 8, it envisaged the development of a system of continuous comprehensive evaluation of the students' performance in all dimensions in place of year-end examinations. Instead of facilitating the development of a continuous comprehensive evaluation mechanism and the preparation of teachers for this approach as a long-term effective strategy, the committee opts for an easy method: an assessment of students' performance through examinations to be conducted thrice in the elementary cycle, in addition to examinations in five–six subjects at the end of each of the eight semesters in Grades 9 to 12. It is doubtful whether the introduction of a semester system at the secondary level is scholastically a sound proposal.

With dwindling student numbers, an under-provision of teachers, both in numbers and quality, and a relatively poor infrastructure, the public school system is in the doldrums. One expects the committee to present measures that will help resurrecting the public school system in a big way. The committee, however, states, 'public institutions will be developed and improved, strongly reaffirming commitment to the national importance of public education' (p. 213). A few measures in this regard were outlined in a report of the Central Advisory Board of Education (CABE) Subcommittee on 'Devising Pathways for Improving Government Schools' (Government of India, 2015a).

For the effective regulation of school education in states, the committee proposes the separation of policymaking from the provision/ operation and regulatory roles and creation of three bodies: Rajya Shiksha Aayog (State Education Commission) for the overall monitoring and policymaking in education in the state; State School Regulatory Authority—an independent state-wide regulatory body as the sole regulator for the entire school sector at the state-level for the regulation of all schools on a very few selected parameters such as safety, security, basic infrastructure, number of teachers, probity and sound processes of governance; and a Directorate of School Education to handle all operations and service provision in the public schooling system. In addition, it is proposed that the State Council of Educational Research and Training (SCERT) will be responsible for all academic matters in the entire school education. The SCERT will also develop a School Quality Assessment and Accreditation Framework which will be used as the accreditation framework by the State School Regulatory Authority for regulation of schools.

There is no basis to limit the regulatory mechanism to a few parameters mentioned earlier. In fact, a comprehensive regulatory mechanism should cover almost every aspect of education. Such a mechanism should also help and promote autonomy in a meaningful way, and prevent the adoption of undesirable methods and unhealthy practices. Self-accreditation of schools, as proposed by the committee, may not necessarily yield reliable results. More importantly, it is not clear whether the separation of roles and responsibilities at the school level will lead to an effective development of a school system or will it create chaos with no proper coordination of several bodies. Absence of coordination and the problems it creates at state level between multiple ministries/agencies dealing with elementary, secondary, higher secondary, vocational, and higher education, and between several boards such as textbook boards and examination boards, are already being noted in many states.

HIGHER EDUCATION AND RESEARCH

In the area of higher education, the committee intended to propose a complete overhaul and re-energization of the entire system. The committee first promises expanding it in such a way that enrolments will form 50 per cent of the eligible age group (18–23) in about a decade-and-a-half or, in other words, we reach a gross enrolment ratio of 50 per cent by 2035 from the current level of about 25 per cent. While the gross enrolment ratio itself will not result in higher economic growth and development, a high enrolment ratio will ensure an abundant supply of skilled and higher educated manpower necessary for a fast and sustained economic growth. The corresponding ratio is much higher in many advanced countries. Thus, the target suggested by the committee is desirable for a medium- to long-term period. But there is no rationale to be too obsessive about the gross enrolment ratio.

Second, with respect to restructuring of universities, the committee makes very drastic changes. It promises to have world-class, multidisciplinary institutions of higher education and a 'nationwide ecosystem of vibrant multidisciplinary universities and colleges' (p. 212). The single-discipline-based universities (particularly 'institutions deemed to be universities' that we find only in India) cannot be regarded as universities *per se* going by the basic definition of a university. This has been stated repeatedly by many experts earlier who have also recommended doing away with such institutions. The Yashpal Committee (Government of India, 1999b) clearly argued for the conversion of all mono-field institutions, including the Indian Institutes of Technology, into multidisciplinary institutions for better knowledge creation and development. The present committee also supports this position and feels the need to break disciplinary boundaries in knowledge development and dissemination. Accordingly, it says that all institutions of higher education will be made into multidisciplinary higher education institutions; professional education, vocational education and all areas of higher education should be an integral part of higher education; and all single-stream institutions, including colleges—presently nearly half the universities a large number of deemed universities and about 35 per cent of the colleges, of which 85 per cent are private, offer only one teaching programme—ought to be phased out. All colleges will then have to be multidisciplinary. This is a welcome recommendation.

Third, noting that we have too many small-sized universities and colleges (for instance, 19% colleges have an enrolment below 100 in 2017–2018 and in only 4% colleges, the enrolment is above 3,000), the committee underlines the need to make every institution enhance its enrolment so that they become pedagogically, economically and managerially viable and corresponding economies of scale can be reaped. It proposes that universities should have a target of on-campus student enrolments between 5,000 to 25,000 or more and colleges 2,000–5,000 or higher, each with residential facilities. Although lower and even upper limits cited earlier are still vastly inadequate and minimum levels should be much higher as targets for a short-term period, this is a welcome recommendation.

The need for every higher education institution to offer undergraduate, postgraduate and research programmes has been repeatedly highlighted by many, including the Yashpal Committee on Rejuvenation of Higher Education (Government of India, 1999b). The present committee too recommends that all higher education institutions, including all Type I and Type II universities should be required to offer liberal education based undergraduate programmes (p. 215), in addition to postgraduate and doctoral research programmes, the latter two together to be known as 'graduate studies' as followed by universities in the West.

Fifth, in an era when technical knowledge and skills carry high premiums in the labour markets, there are only a few who strongly highlight the importance of the arts and humanities in human development and this is being slowly and even widely understood. Given this, it is heartening to note that the committee strongly favours liberal education and recommends the provision of a four-year liberal undergraduate programme with multiple exit options which provide the full range of liberal education with a choice of common core and specializations, including specifically majors and minors. This is similar to or exactly the same proposal that was recently introduced in University of Delhi, and, which was subsequently withdrawn before at least one full cycle of that experiment could be completed. According to the committee, this will be the pattern not only in case of general education but also teacher education (B.Ed degrees) and other areas of professional and technical education, in fact in all higher education. The committee emphasizes that all Bachelor's degree programmes will move towards a four-year degree programme taking a more comprehensive liberal education approach.

Sixth, the committee specially mentions the growth of commercial interests in teacher education: 'Heartbreakingly, the teacher education has been beleaguered with mediocrity as well as rampant corruption due to commercialisation' (p. 283) and argues for a system of checks on the growth of commercial interests in education and even an immediate shutdown of these institutions. But private commercially oriented institutions have mushroomed in their thousands not only in the area of teacher education but also in other general and professional areas, apart from school education. Commercially oriented activities in the entire education system need to be banned.

Seventh, to improve access to higher education, the committee recommends that a National Scholarship Fund be established which will ensure that all students who need financial assistance to pursue higher education in public institutions can get financial support to cover tuition fees, boarding, lodging and other expenditure. It also argues that all private institutions have to fulfil their social obligation and provide scholarships to at least 50 per cent of students, of whom 20 per cent will receive full scholarships.

The special emphasis that the committee lays on research, and support for research is worth appreciating. Focusing on the development of high-quality research, it recommends setting up a National Research Foundation (NRF), through an Act of Parliament with an annual grant of ₹20,000 crore (0.1 % of the GDP), which will be an autonomous body for funding, mentoring and building the capacity for quality research in India in sciences, technology, social sciences and arts and humanities. It will 'aim to seed, grow and facilitate research' in all disciplines through a competitive and peer-review based process, and build research capacity at academic institutions across the country (p. 209). Its funds will be accessible to both public and private institutions. The committee rightly notes that India invests '[an] exceedingly small proportion of [its] GDP' in research and innovation, while many countries invest at least three times higher (p. 266). It also notes that this low level of spending is reflected in the extremely low research–output numbers.

The NRF and its funding is hopefully an addition to existing funding structures and mechanisms. Otherwise, ₹20,000 crore is too small an amount. The current level of spending on research and development in the country, which is very low compared to many other countries, is of the order of about 0.6–0.7 per cent of GDP. Like in many other cases, the committee could have recommended, going beyond the NRF and perhaps also recommending that a reasonable proportion of the GDP for allocation to total research and development in the country as a goal to be achieved in the short and medium terms.

Ninth, on the issue of internationalization of higher education, the committee adopts the same approach that has been recommended by the C. N. R. Rao Committee in its report on the entry of foreign universities into India (Government of India, 2005), to identify and invite only a few from among the top 200 universities in the world to come to India and set up universities or campuses. This significantly is in direct contrast to proposals made in the form of draft bills relating to the entry and regulation of foreign universities prepared in the recent past which facilitate the opening of Indian higher education to outsiders on a licencing pattern to any eligible party, effectively considering the higher education sector as a higher education market. Also contrary to what was suggested recently, the committee has made it clear that such universities will have to follow all the regulatory, governance and content norms applicable to Indian universities. Given all this, the selective approach recommended by the committee is admirable. To ensure this, a legislative framework facilitating such an entry of foreign universities will have to be put in place.

The Question of Feasibility

There are quite a few recommendations and proposals made by the committee about which one might feel sceptical about their feasibility.

While discussing the need for restructuring of India's higher education system, the committee proposes that there will be only three types of higher education institutions in the country, that is, Type I: research universities—that focus on research but will also have high-quality teaching programmes, Type II: universities—that concentrate essentially on teaching, and colleges under Type III: institutions—colleges, whose mandate is also only teaching both in the public and private sectors. This is somewhat similar to, but not exactly the same as, the famous Clark Kerr et al.'s (California State Department of Education, 1960) three-tier structure of universities or the three-tier structure proposed by FICCI (2013). The committee further suggests all Type III institutions, that is, colleges will offer certificate, diploma and degree courses in vocational education and training integrated with the undergraduate education programmes. Perhaps the committee expects that some Type I universities will emerge as world-class universities and secure high global rankings. The committee promises that by 2024, five world-class liberal arts universities will be developed.

There is widespread criticism of the current system that interlinkages between research and teaching are being ignored and that they are getting separated from one another: colleges do not have much research programmes or facilities conducive for research; some good research is being done in central and in a few state universities. But many state universities tend to get confined to only teaching and are pathetic in terms of research output both in quantity and quality, and a good amount of research is being conducted outside university systems. The proposition of the committee tends to strengthen such tendencies further. Teaching will receive low priority in Type I universities and a large number of Type II universities and Type III institutions may ignore research altogether. That research and teaching mutually support each other, is being ignored.

Perhaps the committee realizes that such a clear-cut demarcation of teaching and research roles between the three types of institutions is neither tenable nor desirable. Hence, it proposes that Type II universities 'will focus primarily on high quality teaching across disciplines and programmes, including undergraduate, masters and doctoral, professional, vocational, certificate and diploma programmes, *while also significantly contributing to cutting-edge research*' (p. 214; emphasis added); and all colleges will also carry out cutting-edge research (p. 284). But is it fair to expect the institutions that primarily focus on teaching, also to contribute to cutting-edge research, which is the prerogative of Type I universities? The committee also has the noble intention of building research capacity in all, including in Type III institutions—the colleges!

The committee also proposes to have 150–300 Type I universities, 1,000–2,000 Type II universities and 5,000–10,000 Type III institutions. While it is good to see some quantitative targets, it is not clear how have been these numbers arrived at. Further confusion is added, when other statements are also made with respect to this issue. The committee adds that every district will have all three types of institutions. So if it is every type in every district, in all, we need about 2,175 institutions for the 725 districts we already have. It further proposes that for every population of 5 million, there will be one Type I university; for every 500,000, there will be a one Type II university, and one Type III institution for every 200,000. Going by these norms, simple calculations show that for the country's current level of population, we need to have 230 Type I universities, 2,300 Type II universities and 6,750 Type III institutions. Also imagine that each district such as Thane, North 24 Paraganas, Bengaluru, Pune and Mumbai suburban (the five most populated districts with about 10 million population according to the 2011 Census) will have two Type I universities, 20 Type II universities and about 50 Type III institutions. The committee does not, however, say it will be only one per district. It can be more. In fact, it states that it can be two or three in districts with larger populations (p. 221).

Further confusion arises on the numbers when the committee refers to two missions, named after two most cherished ancient Indian centres of higher learning that stood for excellence and human progress—the Nalanda Mission and the Takshashila Mission:

> Mission Nalanda will ensure that there are at least 100 Type I and 500 Type II HEIs [Higher Education Institutes] functioning vibrantly by 2030 [and] Mission Takshashila will strive to establish at least one high quality HEI in or close to every district of India, with 2 or 3 such HEIs in districts with larger populations. (p. 221)

As an aside, we may note that the committee's intention in naming missions after the two most renowned ancient Indian universities may be that the new institutions would be founded on similar lines, and at least some of them will reach the glorious heights where the ancient universities reached. An admirable expectation!

The committee also foresees that 'in the long term (by 2040) the Indian higher education system will consolidate into a far smaller number of institutions, across the three types of HEIs' (p. 215). This requires closures and mergers on a large scale. While the intentions of the committee may seem laudable, I find it difficult to reconcile these numbers.

Further, one may fear that the now proposed three-type system may lead to discriminatory treatment in terms of resource allocations by the state. More importantly, the differentiation by research and teaching roles of the respective institutions could be seen as reinforcing the prevailing hierarchical system, and the graduates and the teachers from three types/tiers of institutions might be treated differently in the labour market or in society at large, however forward looking are the intentions of the committee in proposing such a typology of institutions. We may need some specific measures to ensure some kind of parity among all.

While these numbers can be taken as indicative, an important question arises: Do we really need more universities? The number of universities is growing rapidly. Presently, we have nearly 1,000 universities, including about 380 private universities. The National Knowledge Commission (NKC, 2006) suggested, with no clear basis however, to have something like 1,500 universities in the country. I feel that there are two issues. If we really plan for large university campuses with 50,000 to 80,000 students, as a few countries like China are planning to do, or even with the smaller size as suggested by the committee, we may not require so many universities. The committee has already noted that a big number of our institutions have very small number of students on rolls.

Second and more importantly, there is a bigger danger of losing the nature of and the contribution of universities, if there are too many, say one in every district or *taluk*. If universities are located in every district, students do not feel the need to go outside the district for higher education. Every university will have students from within the district. Even teachers and administrators are recruited from within the district. As a result, universities become local and localized institutions and even parochial in nature, losing diversity, a necessary feature of a good university. The 'universe' in such universities will be district and the horizons of knowledge will be confined to district boundaries. I feel that this would cause the biggest damage to the very concept of a university. This is already happening with the rapid proliferation of colleges and universities in every nook and corner of the country. University planning need not necessarily adopt the same criteria that school planning is based on, such as demographic parameters (population), geographical units (villages/towns/districts) and physical distance. What we need, as the committee has argued not exactly in a different context, is 'a thoughtful consolidation of existing HEIs into a fewer number of HEIs, considering issues of access, distribution and the quality of existing and future outcomes' (p. 217).

The proposed four-year degree programme has many laudable objectives. Hence, it may be welcomed, but a couple of questions arise: will the provision for multiple exit options result in the production of incomplete graduates? The four-year degree programme is indeed an ambitious idea. It really requires an 'imaginative and flexible curricular structures [that] will enable creative combinations of disciplines for students to study' (p. 207) in such a way that it provides simultaneously: (a) skills for decent employment for those who exit after the first or second year with a diploma/certificate, (b) skills and knowledge good for employment and/or further higher education for those who exit after three years with a degree and (c) skills, knowledge and research capacities suitable for employment, for admission in further higher (master's level) education, and for admission in doctoral research programmes for those who complete four years of the programme. Note that the committee recommends the abolition of the two-year MPhil programme—which presently prepares students for doctoral research—and provides for direct admission into PhD programmes. All this is in addition to developing 'the intellectual, social, ethical, analytical, and aesthetic capacities of all students' (p. 228). This looks like a miracle waiting to happen and, certainly, we do need teachers who can do miracles.

Further, all this, including some of the recent measures of introducing vocational education/training courses at the undergraduate level that involve simultaneous provision of skills and education, reflects a big change in our approach to higher education: for a long time, its goal is knowledge creation and dissemination, now its purpose is being redefined to include skill inculcation. Traditional theories make a sharp distinction between the two—education and training but we tend to gloss over this distinction.

Teacher shortages in higher education are widely recognized. About one-third of teaching positions in central universities and nearly 40 per cent in state universities are presently vacant. Even institutions like the Indian Institute of Technology (IITs) suffer from huge vacancies. The committee also notes this and promises that 'all HEIs will be adequately resourced and staffed with high quality teams of faculty and members in other roles, including leadership roles' (p. 213). In the context of faculty development, and the need for the development of 'energized, engaged and capable faculty', the committee notes the role being played by Human Resource Development Centres in the universities and suggests their integration into the university system. This has been long overdue. Besides calling for the immediate stoppage of contractual appointments and suggesting measures to attract and retain faculty, the committee also suggests a variety of, what I feel are, short-term measures: engaging with other institutions in the vicinity to share faculty, using students, educated members of the community and volunteers as teachers at the school level (under the proposed National Tutors Programme), making use of talent from the private sector; providing teaching assistantships for doctoral students and inviting rolling faculty of eminent and superannuated scientists/professors/experts from industry and inviting overseas researchers. It has to be realized that there is no substitute for a fully qualified and well-trained teacher in education. The committee suggests a desirable student–teacher ratio (not more than 30:1) in higher education (p. 259). But this 'desirable' ratio is the same as in primary schools! Also contrast this with the University Grants Commission (UGC)-stipulated desirable ratio of 1:10 (in postgraduate programmes and also for world-class universities) and 1:25 in undergraduate programmes. The All India Council for Technical Education (AICTE) prescribed it as 1:10. The current ratio in higher education as a whole is 1:24.

Finally, the architecture of the regulatory system. The committee recommends a major restructuring of the regulatory system. Arguing that 'the most basic principle is that the functions of regulation, provision of education, funding, accreditation and standard setting must be performed by independent and empowered bodies' and that 'this is essential to create checks-and balances in the system, minimise conflicts of interest and eliminate the concentration of power' (pp. 322–323), the committee favours setting up not only the Rashtriya Shiksha Aayog (RSA)– National Education Commission, and correspondingly, a Rajya Shiksha Aayog at the state level, but also a National Higher Education Regulatory Authority (NHERA) as the sole regulator for the entire higher education including professional education, Higher Education Grants Council to make grants (the UGC to get transformed into such a council with a responsibility of funding institutions—excluding research and research infrastructure—and individuals and awarding scholarships), Professional Standards Setting Bodies (existing bodies like the AICTE, National Council for Teacher Education [NCTE], Medical Council of India [MCI], Bar Council of India [BCI] and so on to be transformed to align to new roles), and the National Assessment and Accreditation Council (NAAC; the present NAAC to be 'reinvented' and separated from UGC). Diverse and multiple, including private, accreditation institutions/agencies (about 100–150) and methods will be developed at the national and state level for accrediting the institutions. Higher education institutions will be eventually subjected to simple binary accreditation (yes or no) and not to be awarded any grades or ranks. But apprehensions arise: this may contribute to privatization and a thriving business of assessment and accreditation; standards of accreditation may get compromised with the involvement of too many diverse and even private agencies in the process; and a simple binary grading may not serve the purpose well. More importantly, the separation of functions between the independent institutions might lead to the proverbial situation of 'the right hand knowing nothing what the left hand does'.

Thus, the new regulatory system will consist of four different levels of autonomous bodies/sets of institutions, whose functioning will be overseen by the RSA, headed by the prime minister and the union minister of education as vice chairperson. In addition, a General Education Council is to be set up to develop and prescribe 'expected learning outcomes' (also known as 'graduate attributes' that include disciplinary knowledge, and the range of cognitive, social, ethical and emotional capacities and dispositions, which are the outcomes of good education) for higher education programmes, and through National Higher Education Qualifications Framework, it will be concerned with issues such as credit transfers and equivalence. The NHERA will prepare a model act of setting rules and procedures for setting up new institutions of higher education. The RSA will oversee all these and other bodies, including probably the several other professional standard setting bodies.

In response to the recommendation of the NKC and the Yashpal Committee, there has been an effort to set up at the apex level a single regulatory body for the entire higher education system—National

Commission for Higher Education and Research (NCHER) that will encompass all the responsibilities of as many as 16 regulating bodies in higher education. The proposals made by the last two successive governments did not go through. These proposals towards setting up a single body replacing all the bodies in higher education, with different and overlapping roles and responsibilities, were in recognition of the need to promote a holistic and integrated/defragmented approach to higher education. It is not clear whether such a purpose would be served by the new architecture of the regulatory system, consisting of several bodies, proposed by the present committee. Further, the earlier proposal to have a single regulator was also seen as a single window system facilitating easy business in education—in opening new institutions, introducing new programmes, easy entry and exit into/ from the educational market and so on. The last two governments preferred the Yashpal Committee's suggestion of having a NCHER to the NKC's recommendation of setting an Independent Regulatory Authority in Higher Education (similar to the regulatory authority in telecommunications). The present committee prefers setting up an authority—the NHERA.

Marginal Modifications Needed

There are also quite a few major well-intended recommendations that require caution or marginal modifications.

The committee envisages that all institutions of higher education will be multidisciplinary. However, multidisciplinary institutions are defined by the committee as one, which offers 'at least two programmes or majors in the arts and humanities, at least two in science and mathematics and at least one in the social sciences' (p. 212). This seems to be a narrow definition in scope. When the UGC required every new university to have at least four departments, quite a few universities were opened in recent years with four self-financing departments with one or two contractual teachers in each department, making a mockery of the definition of the university. Similarly, the narrow definition of 'multidisciplinary institution' may also get misused by many. Multidisciplinary institutions should offer programmes in a large number of, but not necessarily in all, disciplines.

Recognizing that autonomy of universities is the *sine qua non* for excellence, the committee promises autonomy—full academic and administrative and eventually financial—to the faculty and to institutions: all institutions of higher education to have complete autonomy on curricular, pedagogical and resource-related matters. There will be an independent Board of Governors for every institution. All public and private higher education institutions will have full autonomy in terms of curriculum, pedagogy, recruitment of teachers, teacher education, teacher training, promotion, merit-based career management, mentoring academic leaders, admissions and so on. Institutions will develop institutional development plans and robust faculty development plans. While this seems too attractive to all as proposal, the question may arise: is such a high degree of unlimited autonomy to all institutions desirable and practicable?

The committee seems to be having unflinching faith in technology for the expansion, improvement in quality, for enhancing access of disadvantaged groups to education, for improving teacher education and quality of teachers besides improving overall planning, administration and management of the system. The committee proposes launching a national mission on education through information and communications technology that will provide virtual laboratories and facilitate other interventions. But experience shows that technology tends to help urban schools more and their privileged children and not disadvantaged children located in remote rural areas, thus widening the digital divide. The committee, however, promises that, by 2023, computers/tablets will be provided to every school to cover every student. In higher education, the committee proposes an extensive use of MOOCS in this context. Some caution may need to be exercised on the extensive reliance on technology for an improvement in the quality of education in a big way. Technology has to be seen as a supplement, not as a substitute to teachers. While the use of technology to improve planning and administration can be extensive, its use in classroom has not produced as per available research evidence, unambiguous outcomes. There is a need for the innovative use of technology in education—teaching and research. The committee also proposes setting up a National Educational Technology Forum to evaluate several experiments and pilot studies on the use of technology for the improving quality of education that are being conducted in many places, and advise on their benefits, risks and effectiveness, as well as their potential to scale up in different contexts. The forum, initially to be funded through public resources, is expected to generate its own resources from diverse sources and to be eventually funded by 'neutral technology industry bodies such as National Association of Software and Services Companies (NASSCOM)' (p. 344).

Recognizing problems faced by students with multiple entrance examinations for admission in higher education, the committee recommends a new National Testing Agency (NTA) which will offer a computer-based 'high quality common modular entrance examinations multiple times each year in various subjects' (p. 106), which can be used by universities, instead of conducting their own examinations. While this seems to be a good idea, how far is a uniform common entrance examination for admission into higher education institutions in a highly diverse country desirable? Second, will computer-based entrance examinations (and computer-based evaluation) necessarily be able to test the aptitudes of students necessary for liberal arts oriented diverse higher education? For professional/technical education, this may be appropriate. Above all, such a common test will not necessarily eliminate innumerable coaching institutions, as mainly intended by the committee. The coaching institutions may still continue unabated their business of coaching students to prepare for the examinations to be conducted by the NTA.

The committee also hopes to expand higher education and reach 50 per cent gross enrolment ratio through both conventional and open distance learning methods. While many questions are raised in recent years on distance education programmes, the committee seems to have unequivocally high expectations of the distance education system and its role. All institutions, including Type III colleges, will be allowed, as per the committee to offer open distance learning programmes. Given the attractiveness of the distance education programmes in raising resources, all may jump in offering the same, and, which apart from creating problems on quality and standards, may eventually lead to an oversized system of distance education programme larger than formal higher education. Will this result in contributing to developing a meaningful quality higher education edifice?

The committee further proposes doing away with the MPhil degree programme and admission to research even to the four-year degree graduates. The assumption is that in the fourth year of the degree programme or in the second year of the Master's programme, for those who complete their degree in three years, students will be oriented to research, which might be risky, and the assumption that these graduates will be better prepared for 'cutting-edge research' may need re-examination. Particularly after graduating in a comprehensive multidiscipline/course, a rigorous course of research orientation in a particular area may be helpful for students going for research degree programmes.

The committee also declares that there will be no more unitary universities, no more affiliating universities, no more deemed to be universities and no more affiliating colleges. All colleges will be autonomous colleges, or will become universities or merge with universities and become degree-giving institutions, needing no affiliation with any university. Many ills with the affiliating system were highlighted by scholars and the administrators are aware of these. But how far this is feasible in the next one or two decades to do away with affiliating colleges and make all colleges autonomous colleges, going by some of the bare criteria we have for autonomous colleges, and eventually for them to progress to become equivalent to degree-awarding institutions or universities! Many good colleges are not necessarily willing or are ready to become autonomous colleges. Moreover, the whole phenomenon of autonomous colleges has been confined mostly to private colleges that too in a few states.

While the committee favours extensive professional development opportunities for faculty in higher education, it also proposes that '[f]aculty be appointed to individual institutions and not be transferable across institutions, so that they may feel truly interested in and committed to their institution and community' (p. 257). Presently, most university-level appointments are being made only in this fashion; they are recruited for a specific university and they are non-transferable. This proposal of the committee further adds to my earlier expressed fear that universities might become localized institutions with restricted knowledge horizons. Further, this may be contrasted with the view of some, who argue for the faculty transfer as a mechanism towards the better distribution of talented teachers across the nation. The transferability of IAS cadre officers between several departments across the entire nation is quoted in this content.

REFORMS AT THE SYSTEM LEVEL

While there are several issues that the committee refers to that relate to the entire education system, we may refer to a few such specific proposals.

Now the committee provides for a RSA with the Prime Minister of India as the Chairperson, as a common apex level regulatory mechanism for the entire higher education. The Aayog is the final body, responsible for everything in education—including developing, implementing, evaluating and revising the education policy. It will also review all budget allocations, at the central and state levels and their utilization. Similar earlier efforts such as the creation of NCHER were heavily criticized as centralizing all the powers in a single commission constituted by the central government, eroding the autonomy of institutions and as not recognizing the privileges, roles and responsibilities of state governments in education which is *de jure* a 'concurrent subject'. Lest the Aayog is also subject to such a criticism, proper representation of the states in the Aayog may have to be made. This is more important as the prime minister is proposed to be its chairperson, while in the earlier proposal relating to NCHER, the prime minister was the chairperson of the selection committee to select the chairperson and members of the commission. While the prime minister chairing the RSA may have its own advantages in a political democratic system of our kind, in terms of education receiving high focus and political priority, the dangers of politicization of education need to be avoided.

Second, the database of educational statistics is rather weak. The National Institute of Educational Planning and Administration collects and provides some data on school education through Unified District Information System for Education (UDISE); the Ministry of Human Resource Development (MHRD) conducts All-India Survey on Higher Education; the National Council of Educational Research and Training collects some institutional data through the All India Educational Surveys and also conducts National Achievement Surveys, both on school education, and National Sample Survey Organisation collects household-level data on some important aspects of education. But all put together, still we miss data on quite a few important dimensions. For example, none of the above provides any data on government expenditure on education. The MHRD compiles and gives state-wise data on government expenditure but not in required detail. So it is good that the committee recommends setting of the Central Educational Statistics Division that will be responsible for the collection and compilation of educational statistics. But such a division should be responsible for collecting and building a strong comprehensive database, rather than for analysis of data, as recommended by the committee. In addition, a National Repository on Educational Data is to be set up, as per the recommendation of the committee to maintain all records related to institutions, teachers and students, in digital form.

Third, the committee also sets targets: universal access to early childcare and education by 2025, universal foundation literacy and numeracy in primary education by 2025, total youth and adult literacy by 2030, universal participation in school education by 2030, 50 per cent gross enrolment ratio in higher education by 2035, doubling of public expenditure within 10 years and so on. Quite a few target dates are also mentioned in case of others, more for outcomes and less for provision of inputs and other state actions.

Fourth, on finances. Like the 1968 and 1986 National Policies on Education, the committee also recognizes expenditure on education as an investment in the future of our nation and not merely as expenditure ('financing', however, forms a chapter in Addendum I, along with Addendum II on 'Way Forward' [not in the main text]). The committee recognizes the need to increase the public expenditure on education and recommends 'significant increase in public investment in education' (p. 403). Certainly to implement many of the reforms proposed, a greater financial outlay is needed. Reaffirming the long-pending national commitment of allocating 6 per cent of GDP to education (as resolved in the 1968 National Policy on Education and subsequently reiterated in the 1986 and 1992 policies), the committee feels that this would be possible to achieve 'in the mid-to-long term', given the 'recent decisive actions and encouraging outcomes in this regard' (p. 406). I wish it is re-emphasized by the committee as a short-term (five-year) goal.

There are two important positives on financing education in the committee's approach and recommendations. First, it reaffirms its commitment to '6 per cent of GDP as *public* investment in education' (p. 406). Contrary to some recent efforts to distort this goal to be inclusive of not only public but also all private, including household, expenditure on education and accordingly to conclude that the goal is already achieved, the committee unambiguously refers to this as *public* investment. Second, as the government has more control on government expenditure than on GDP as a whole, it can be welcomed as the committee argues for an increase in public expenditure on education as a proportion of total (centre and states) government expenditure to 20 per cent from the current level that the committee believed to be of 10 per cent, that is to double the level of public expenditure. Certainly, the share of education in total government expenditure is a better norm for the government to plan than the share in GDP.

However, the recommendation to increase government expenditure on education from 10 per cent of the total government expenditure to 20 per cent in a 10-year period is based on a weak database and/or a limited view the committee took. Expenditure on education is incurred by not only the MHRD but also many other ministries/departments. This is true both in the case of union and state governments. Other important ministries include the Ministries of Social Justice and Welfare, Rural Development, Health, Agriculture and so on. The committee seems to have considered only the expenditure on education incurred by the MHRD and observes, broadly and probably drawing from the *Economic Survey* (Government of India, 2018), that the present level constitutes 2.7 per cent of GDP and 10 per cent of the total government expenditure in 2017–2018 (pp. 402, 406). If we consider all the expenditure incurred by all the ministries on education, the total expenditure on education in India forms 4.07 per cent of GDP and 15.6 per cent of all government (centre and states) expenditure in 2015–2016 (budget estimates on revenue account), according to the latest available statistics from the *Analysis of Budgeted Expenditure on Education* (MHRD). Of the total government expenditure, the union government expenditure on education forms 7.7 per cent and in case of states, 22 per cent on average. Since quite a few states are already spending about 20 per cent, it is the union government and other states that have to substantially increase their allocations, as the committee rightly suggests; in fact, we have to set different targets for different states and union government so that the total is raised to the desired level.

Finally, since the average is already 16 per cent, instead of recommending its increase to 20 per cent, going by the spirit behind the recommendation, the recommendation may be read as doubling the share of education in total government expenditure from the present levels and/or increasing the share by 1 per cent every year for the next 10 years. The committee also warns that 'if we don't spend now [on education] then it will not be easy to achieve and sustain such a [10 trillion dollar] large economy' (p. 33). Second, though I welcome specific numbers in terms of allocations of additional resources to different new and existing programmes, it is not clear at all how the numbers are arrived at. It was, of course, mentioned that they are based on 2017–2018 budget estimates. Earlier attempts in this regard (e.g., the Report of the Tapas Majumdar Committee [Government of India, 1999a]) are largely based on projected requirements of the system and desirable unit cost norms by items. It appears that the committee's estimates need further analysis.

Lastly, one need not necessarily expect the committee to cover every aspect of education which is a very vast area. It did, however, cover most critical issues. But one major omission refers to the issue of reservations. The committee does not say a word about it. There is competition among states to raise quota levels in higher education (and employment) to higher and higher proportions, touching or even crossing 70 per cent in many states, much above the ceiling set by the Supreme Court, adversely affecting the principle of equality of opportunity. The caste-based reservations proposed in the Constitution of India in 1951 aimed at the annihilation of caste hierarchy in the country, but actually contributed to its perpetuation. In addition to caste, nowadays, all kinds of reservations, for example, by religion and region, are being introduced. The committee could have taken a considered view on the extent and implications of growing reservations on various aspects of higher education.

Second, the committee has not made it clear as to what happens to some existing structures and institutions, such as the CABE, research funding organizations or the recently created ones such as the Rasthtriya Ucchatar Shiksha Abhiyan and the Higher Education Finance Agency.

Finally, the education sector has been subject to too much and too frequent and unnecessary and undesirable political interventions. The committee opted to remain silent on this issue too, except stating that 'the approach should be to ensure that both political initiatives and administrative systems serve the goal of transforming the education system, and eliminating the power of vested interests, improving the transparency and efficiency of regulation, and investing public resources in areas that build the capital for effecting change' (p. 32).

CONCLUSION

This chapter provides a critique of some selected specific issues raised and recommendations made in the 484-page report on the National Education Policy, submitted by the Dr K. Kasturirangan Committee: some are path-breaking, many deserve applause, some are unacceptable and quite a few require rethinking. Some recommendations are similar to those made by earlier committees such as the NKC, Yashpal Committee and Justice Verma Commission. Some measures have already been introduced. Yet there are many new positives. The report underlines that the system requires a major overhaul, comprehensive reforms need to be attempted and piecemeal/quick-fix solutions will not work. There are equally a good number of negatives: some are damaging to the system, some do not recognize our contemporary and historical experience, and many require serious deliberations. While the approach of the committee is praiseworthy, some assumptions it makes are unrealistic and questionable. Since education is a long-term activity with far-reaching implications for the future of the nation, a long-term vision and not short-term compulsions should guide the formulation of a National Education Policy.

To conclude on a positive note: an important message that resounds from the report is that the education sector urgently requires major reforms, tinkering with the system with piecemeal reforms will not work, and the system cannot wait any longer. The committee also warns that unless the reforms are attempted now, national development goals (including such as emerging as a 5–10 trillion dollar economy or becoming a global superpower) will be at risk.

REFERENCES

Barnett, W. S. (2011). Child care and its impact on children 2–5 years of age. Commenting: McCartney, Peisner-Feinberg, and Ahnert and Lamb. In R. E. Tremblay, M. Boivin, & R. Dev Peters (eds.), Bennett J., topic ed. *Encyclopedia on early childhood development*. Retrieved from http://www.child-encyclopedia.com/child-care-early-childhood-education-and-care/according-experts/child-care-and-its-impact-children-2

Belsky, J. (2001). Developmental risks (still) associated with early child care. *Journal of Child Psychology and Psychiatry and Allied Disciplines, 42*(7), 845–859.

California State Department of Education. (1960). *A master plan for higher education in California 1960–1975*. Sacramento, California: California State Department of Education. Retrieved from http://www.lib.berkeley.edu/uchistory/archives_exhibits/masterplan/MasterPlan1960.pdf

Federation of Indian Chambers of Commerce and Industry (FICCI). (2013). *Higher education in India: Vision 2030* (FICCI Higher Education Summit 2013). New Delhi: Author. Retrieved from http://ficci.in/spdocument/20328/FICCI-EY-Report-2013.pdf

Government of India. (1966). *Education and National Development: Report of the Education Commission 1964–66* (Reprint 1971). (Chairman: Dr D. S. Kothari). New Delhi: NCERT.

———. (1985). *Challenge of education*. New Delhi: Ministry of Education.

———. (1987). *Programme of action*. New Delhi: Ministry of Human Resource Development.

———. (1993). *Learning without burden* (Report of Yashpal Committee). New Delhi: Ministry of Human Resource Development. Retrieved from https://www.academia.edu/4553242/Yash_Pal_committe_report_lwb

———. (1999a). *Report of the group of experts on the financial resource requirements for operationalising the proposed 83rd Constitutional Amendment Bill making the right to free and compulsory education up to 14 years of age a fundamental right* (Tapas Majumdar Committee). New Delhi: Ministry of Human Resource-Development, 1997–1999. Retrieved from http://14.139.60.153/bitstream/123456789/14 36/1/The%20Financial%20Resource%20Requirements%20for%20Operationalising%20The%20Proposed%2083rd%20Constitutional%20Amendament%20bill%20making%20the%20Right%20of%20Free%20and%20Compulosry%20Education%20upto%2014%20Years%20of%20age%20A%20Fundamental%20Right%20D-10057.pdf

———. (1999b). *Renovation and rejuvenation of higher education* (Report of Yashpal Committee on Higher Education). New Delhi: Ministry of Human Resource Development. Retrieved from https://mhrd.gov.in/sites/upload_files/mhrd/files/document-reports/YPC-Report_0.pdf

———. (2005). *Report of the committee on entry of foreign universities in India*. New Delhi. Retrieved from https://prayatna.typepad.com/education/2005/09/cnr_rao_committ.html

————. (2012). *Vision of teacher education in India: Quality and regulatory perspective vision of teacher education in India quality and regulatory perspective—Report of the high-powered commission on teacher education constituted by the Hon'ble Supreme Court of India* (Justice J. S. Verma Commission). New Delhi: Ministry of Human Resource Development. Retrieved from https://mhrd.gov.in/sites/upload_files/mhrd/files/document-reports/JVC%20Vol%201.pdf

————. (2015a). *Devising Pathways for Improving Government Schools* (Report of the CABE-subcommittee). New Delhi: Ministry of Human Resource Development

Government of India. (2015b). *Report of the committee for evolution of the new education policy* (T. S. R. Subramanian Committee). New Delhi: Ministry of Human Resource Development. Retrieved from http://niepa.ac.in/New/download/NEP2016/Report NEP.pdf

————. (2018). *Economic survey 2017–2018*. New Delhi: Ministry of Finance.

————. (2019). *Draft national education policy 2019*. (Dr Kasturirangan Committee Report). New Delhi: Ministry of Human Resource Development, Government of India. Retrieved from https://mhrd.gov.in/sites/upload_files/mhrd/files/Draft_NEP_2019_EN_Revised.pdf

International Commission on Education for the Twenty-first Century. 1996. *Learning: The treasure within: Report to UNESCO of the International Commission on Education for the Twenty-first Century* (Jacques Delors Commission). Paris: UNESCO. Retrieved from https://unesdoc.unesco.org/ark:/48223/pf0000109590

McCartney, K. (2007). Current research on child care effects. In R. E. Tremblay, M. Boivin, & R. Dev Peters (eds.), Bennett J., topic ed. *Encyclopaedia on early childhood development* [online]. Retrieved from http://www.child-encyclopedia.com/child-care-early-childhood-education-and-care/according-experts/current-research-child-care-effects

Melhuish, E., Ereky-Stevens, K., Petrogiannis, K., Ariescu, A., Penderi, E., Rentzou, K., … & Broekhuisen, M. (2015). *A review of research on the effects of early childhood education and care (ECEC) upon child development*. Retrieved from http://ecec-care. org/fileadmin/careproject/Publications/reports/CARE_WP4_D4__1_review_of_effects_of_ecec.pdf; https://www.researchgate.net/publication/309853661_A_review_of_research_on_the_effects_of_Early_Childhood_Education_and_Care_ECEC_upon_child_development_CARE_project_Curriculum_Quality_Analysis_and_Impact_Review_of_European_Early_Childhood_Education_a

National Knowledge Commission (NKC). (2006). *Report to the nation*. New Delhi: Government of India. Retrieved from http://kshec.ac.in/perspectives/NKC%20Report %20to%20the%20Nation%202006.pdf

Sroufe, L. A. (1988). A developmental perspective on daycare. *Early Childhood Research Quarterly*, *3*(3), 283–291.

About the Editors and the Contributors

SERIES EDITOR

Manoranjan Mohanty retired as Director, Developing Countries Research Centre, and Professor of Political Science, University of Delhi, in 2004. A political scientist, China scholar and a peace and human rights activist with special interest in China, India and global transformation, he is Editor of *Social Change* and Distinguished Professor, Council for Social Development, New Delhi. He is Chairperson, Development Research Institute, Bhubaneswar, and Honorary Fellow and former Chairperson of the Institute of Chinese Studies, Delhi. He has taught or researched in many universities including California, Oxford, Copenhagen, Moscow, Lagos and Beijing. He is the author of many publications including *China's Transformation: The Success Story and the Success Trap, Ideology Matters: China from Mao Zedong to Xi Jinping* and edited or co-edited many publications, including, *People's Rights*; *Class, Caste, Gender; India-Social Development Report 2010*; *Exploring Emergent Global Thresholds* and *China at a Turning Point*.

VOLUME EDITOR

Jandhyala B. G. Tilak, formerly Professor and Vice-Chancellor, National University of Educational Planning & Administration, is currently ICSSR National Fellow and Distinguished Professor at Council for Social Development, New Delhi, India. Doctorate from the Delhi School of Economics, Dr Tilak taught, besides in the National University of Educational Planning and Administration, in the University of Delhi, the Indian Institute of Education, and as a Visiting Professor, at Centre for International Cooperation in Education Hiroshima University, Virginia University, and Sri Sathya Sai Institute of Higher Learning. Professor Tilak was also on the research staff of the World Bank, and has been a consultant to many national and international bodies. Author of several books including *Economics of Inequality in Higher Education* (SAGE, 1987), *Education for Development in Asia* (SAGE, 1994), *Higher Education, Public Good and Markets* (Routledge, 2018), *Education and Development* (Academic Foundation 2017), *Dilemmas in Reforming Higher Education in India* (Orient BlackSwan 2018), and *Education and Development in India: Critical Issues in Public Policy* (Palgrave Macmillan, 2018), Professor Tilak edited/co-edited many publications, and also served as the Editor of *Journal of Educational Planning and Administration*. He also served as the President of the Comparative Education Society of India, and is on the Board of Comparative Education Society of Asia. He is the recipient of several honours and awards including Swami Pranavananda Saraswati National Award of the UGC (1999), Dr Malcolm Adiseshiah Award (2003), Inspirational Teacher of the Year Global Education Award (2012) and Devang Mehta Award (2015) for outstanding conurbations to education (2015). Among many other honours, he had the privilege of delivering a keynote address in a meeting of the Noble laureates in Barcelona in 2005.

CONTRIBUTORS

Malcolm S. Adiseshiah is best known as a development economist and educationist. As deputy Director-General UNESCO, he formulated educational programmes for the developing world and as Vice Chancellor of Madras University, he emphasized the role of education, science and culture in the development process. He started the Madras Institute of Development Studies conceived to undertake studies and research on developmental issues on the economy, polity and society with special reference to Tamil Nadu. He served the Tamil Nadu Planning Commission for many years. Closely associated with a number of professional bodies both in India and abroad, he was also a member of the Rajya Sabha, the upper house of the Indian parliament. He was also President, Council for Social Development.

Rajiv Balakrishnan is a writer, an editor, a demographer and a development analyst. As faculty member of the Council for Social Development, New Delhi, he was involved in a range of academic activities. He has edited and authored various books, most of which relate to the area of education. He was Editor, Higher Academic Social Sciences, Orient BlackSwan and on assignment with Indo-Global Social Service Society.

Karuna Chanana, a sociologist, is an independent education professional. She served as Professor in Sociology of Education, Zakir Husain Centre for Educational Studies, School of Social Sciences, Jawaharlal Nehru University, New Delhi, India. A specialist on education of women, she authored several books including *Socialization, Education and Women* and *Transformative Links between Higher and Basic Education*.

Chandan Chowdhary is an IPS officer of 2010 batch, AGMUT cadre. She is currently posted in Arunachal Pradesh. She holds masters and MPhil degrees in political science from Jawaharlal Nehru University, New Delhi.

Vidhya Das, retired civil servant, founder Director of Language and Learning Foundation, is a social activist working through the Agragamayee, a non-profit organization in the areas of policy advocacy, socio-economic and human rights of the tribal people, natural resource management, formal and non-formal education, and skill development involving tribal people. From educating girls to empowering their mothers, Vidhya Das has spent decades defending the rights of scheduled tribes. In the field of tribal education, she has mobilized women to ensure that girls get an opportunity to go to school and also mustered resources for educating tribal children.

Muchkund Dubey, a former Foreign Secretary, Government of India, is currently President of the Council for Social Development and Chairperson of the Asian Development Research Institute, Patna. As an international civil servant, he served at the headquarters of both the United Nations and the UNDP and was the Indian Member on the Executive Board of UNESCO. A former Professor in International Relations, Jawaharlal Nehru University, he also served as Chairperson of the Government of Bihar's Commission on Common School System Commission, and Deputy Chairperson of the Planning Commission of Sikkim. He is also a key coordinator of the RTE Forum.

Rounaq Jahan is a Bangladeshi political scientist, feminist leader and author. Distinguished Fellow, Centre for Policy Dialogue, Dhaka, Bangladesh and Adjunct Professor, International Affairs, School of International and Public Affairs, Columbia University, she was a representative of Bangladesh to the 32nd Session of the United Nations General Assembly in 1977, she founded Women for Women, one of the first feminist research centres in Bangladesh and is director, Research Initiatives, Bangladesh.

D. P. Nayar, an eminent educationist, joined Gandhiji in 1944 and got interested in his experiments about the revolutionary concept of basic education (Nayee Talim). At the time of assassination of Gandhiji, he was in-charge of his work in Bihar, while Gandhiji had to move to Delhi. In 1949, he joined the Ministry of Education and subsequently moved on to the Planning Commission. Professor Nayar has written extensively on problems of Indian Education. His important publications include a monumental research work titled *Towards a National System of Education* (1989) and *Education for Rural Development* (1973).

M. C. Paul, specialist in Adult Education, was Professor, Group of Adult Education, Group of Adult Education School of Social Sciences, Jawaharlal Nehru University, New Delhi. He was previously Director in the same department. Recipient of the '2004 Higher Education and Development (HEAD) Award' and 'Ambassador for Peace', Paul published several books, including *Dowry and Position of Women in India: A Study of Delhi Metropolis* (1986), *Dimensions of Tribal Movements in India: A Case of Udayachal Movement in Assam Valley* (1989) and *Drugs and Substance Abuse Problems: Interdisciplinary Study of Causes, Consequences and Prevention* (edited.) (2005).

Praveen J. Patel is a sociologist, a former Professor of Sociology, M. S. University of Baroda, Vadodara, and former Vice Chancellor, Sardar Patel University, Vallabh Vidyanagar, Gujarat. He is an authority in any discussion and activity of the Indian diaspora.

V. K. R. V. Rao, an Indian economist, educator and institution builder, is synonymous with the high quality of economics education and research in India. He established premier institutions in social science research in India, including notably, the Delhi School of Economics, Institute of Economic Growth and the Institute of Social and Economic Change, Bengaluru. He was also responsible for setting up Indian Council of Social Science Research. In the international arena, he was one of the central forces behind the institution of the United Nation's Development Programme and the International Development Association. He also served as Vice Chancellor, University of Delhi, and as Minister in Union Cabinet, Government of India.

Moonis Raza was an academic administrator, regional planner and geographer. Vice Chancellor of Delhi University, one of the co-founders of the Jawaharlal Nehru University and Director of National Institute of Educational Planning and Administration, Moonis Raza held a large number of positions in departments and commissions associated with the Government of India. He was the creator of and an original signatory to the Talloires Declaration a 10-point action plan devised by the Association of University Leaders for a sustainable future.

V. Eswara Reddy, a sociologist and educationist, was with the State Resource Centre for Adult Education, and also Dean, Faculty of Education, Osmania University. He was also Director of the Project on Assessment of Primary Education in Andhra Pradesh, sponsored by the Council for Social Development and Indian International Centre. He authored several books including *Sociological Aspects of Asian Development, Generative Sources of Disadvantage: The Role of Adult Education, The Out of School Youth, Life Long Learning* and *Sociological Aspects of Development*.

Manish Kumar Shrivastava, MPhil in Economics and PhD in Science Policy from Jawaharlal Nehru University, is Assistant Professor, TERI School of Advanced Studies, Department of Energy and Environment, New Delhi, India. He is an inter-disciplinary researcher by training.

J. P. Singh, a former Professor at the Postgraduate Department of Sociology as well as Pro-Vice-Chancellor of Patna University, Patna, held earlier the post of Reader in Research Methodology at the Tata Institute of Social Sciences, Mumbai, and Director of Higher Education, State Government of Bihar. He holds MA and MPhil degrees in Sociology from Patna University, and Jawaharlal Nehru University, respectively, and PhD in Demography from the Australian National University, Canberra (Australia).

Kishore Singh, formerly the United Nations Special Rapporteur on the Right to Education, has worked at the Division for Human Rights and the Education Sector of UNESCO, and advised a number of international, regional and national entities on aspects of the Right to Education to ensure that it is internationally recognized as a human right.

Ujagar Singh, specialist in Education Sociology, served as Assistant Professor, Department of Economics and Sociology, Punjab Agriculture University, Ludhiana. He also taught in D A V College of Education, Hoshiarpur, Punjab.

Subramanian Swamy is an Indian politician, economist and statistician who currently serves as a nominated Member of Parliament in Rajya Sabha, the upper house of the Indian parliament. Before joining politics, he taught at Harvard University and as a professor of Mathematical Economics at the Indian Institute of Technology, Delhi. He also served United Nations Secretariat, and as member, Planning Commission, and minister in Union cabinet of the Government of India.

Muriel Wasi's career as an educationist flourished long after she had retired from the Ministry of Education. She was a lecturer first at St. Stephens College and thereafter Jesus and Mary College. After an outstanding academic career, she went on to Oxford for further education, becoming a prominent educationist in Independent India and a university teacher. Author of many books, her autobiographical writings and essays address crucial educational theories and practices.

Index

Page 1 Apl 91